Gandhi's Ascetic Activism

Gandhi's Ascetic Activism

Renunciation and Social Action

Veena R. Howard

SUNY
PRESS

Cover image courtesy of Suzanne Geraci

Published by State University of New York Press, Albany

Printed in the United States of America

For information, contact State University of New York Press, Albany, NY
www.sunypress.edu

Production by Ryan Morris
Marketing by Michael Campochiaro

Library of Congress Cataloging-in-Publication Data

Howard, Veena R.
Gandhi's ascetic activism : renunciation and social action / Veena R. Howard.
p. cm.
Includes bibliographical references (p.).
ISBN 978-1-4384-4557-1 (hc : alk. paper)—978-1-4384-4556-4 (pb : alk. paper)
1. Gandhi, Mahatma, 1869–1948—Philosophy. 2. Gandhi, Mahatma, 1869–1948—Religion. 3. Asceticism—Hinduism. 4. Celibacy—Religious aspects—Hinduism. 5. Passive resistance. 6. Nonviolence. I. Title.

DS481.G3H59 2013
294.5′447—dc23 2012011098

10 9 8 7 6 5 4 3 2 1

When established in self-restraint [*brahmacarya*], heroic energy is obtained.

—The *Yoga Sūtra*

For me perfect *brahmacharya* is the attainment of sexlessness, not impotence . . . in which the sexual energy is completely sublimated into spiritual energy. If I had attained that *nirvikara* (passionless) state, I should have but to think a thing and it would happen. I would not have to argue.

—M. K. Gandhi

Persons in power should be very careful how they deal with a man who cares nothing for sensual pleasure, nothing for riches, nothing for comfort or praise or promotion, but is simply determined to do what he believes to be right. He is a dangerous and uncomfortable enemy—because his body, which you can always conquer, gives you so little purchase upon his soul.

—Professor Gilbert Murray, who met Gandhi in 1914

Contents

Notes on Symbols from Indian Language: Vocabulary and Transliteration ix

Preface xi

Acknowledgments xix

Introduction 1

ONE
Challenging the Philosophical Presupposition: Gandhi's Unconventional Synthesis of Asceticism and Activism 21

TWO
Gandhi's Alternative Paradigm: From Traditional Principles to New Political Purposes 37

THREE
The Traditional Roots of Gandhi's *Brahmacarya* 81

FOUR
Gandhi's Unorthodox *Brahmacarya*: Reinterpreting Private Religious Practice for Public Service 123

FIVE
Gandhi's Embodiment of Legendary Heroes and Ascetics: Toward a Coherent Narrative for Nonviolent Activism 163

CONCLUSION
Gandhi's Dynamic Synthesis of Renunciation and Social Action 213

Appendix 1 223

Appendix 2 225

Notes 227

Glossary 265

Bibliography 271

Index 281

Notes on Symbols from Indian Language

Vocabulary and Transliteration

This work includes a large number of textual references from Indian religious and philosophical traditions. It requires the following clarifications:

Sanskrit words consistently appear in their standard form, including *brahmacarya, ahiṃsā, darśan, karma, mokṣa, āśrama,* and *svarāj,* even though Gandhi used their Hindi/Gujarati renderings.

The words derived from Sanskrit words and adopted in Hindi and Gujarati languages—for example, *satyagraha* and *swadeshi*—appear in italicized form. The diacritical marks are omitted because they are not standard Sanskrit words.

Proper names from Sanskrit literature are transliterated.

The radical sign (√) indicates Sanskrit verbal roots.

Preface

This book is a close and comprehensive study of one of Mohandas Gandhi's most controversial practices, *brahmacarya*, through his own words and actions. *Brahmacarya* is generally translated as celibacy, continence, and chastity, but for Gandhi it meant a comprehensive control of the senses and was laden with ethical, religious, and mythical connotations. Gandhi considered sexual control integral to his activist methods of *ahiṃsā* (literally, "nonharming,") and *satyagraha* (meaning "truth-force," "love-force," and "soul-force"). Through renouncing his private pleasures, he sought to extend his love to his fellow human beings. Moreover, for him, *brahmacarya* represented the nexus of inner strength, comprehensive discipline, commitment, and miraculous power; it held the promise that a collective self-control by the masses would shatter oppressive structures of violence. This book makes clear that without his vow of *brahmacarya* and associated austere disciplines, Gandhi would not be the man who awakened the Indian masses—which included people of diverse gender, age, religion, and social strata—for a successful nonviolent campaign against colonial oppression, or the man who continues to inspire millions across the globe. In the nineteenth and twentieth centuries, India was politically ruled by the British Empire. In addition to the problems of colonialism, the country was internally divided on grounds of language, ethnicity, religion, and caste. Despite efforts from revolutionaries and political leaders, India's political movements lacked a broad, coherent strategy and momentum to overthrow the foreign regime. Gandhi realized that Indians became the victims of slavery due to their own internal divisions and complacent attitudes. Furthermore, they had not recognized the power of a collective effort. Through his personal embodiment of a religious figure and use of indigenous symbols for political actions and goals, he made a concerted effort to unify and mobilize Indians to confront the military might of the foreign regime through massive nonviolent resistance. The austere disciplines, intriguingly, helped him shape a creative method to confront injustice and oppression for those lacking physical strength and material power.

This study focuses on three main aspects of *brahmacarya,* which show how this practice was central to Gandhi's nonviolent method requiring a mass mobilization: First, Gandhi's austere practice of *brahmacarya* was an essential prerequisite for public service, and it was multilayered, nuanced, and imbued with ethical, religious, mythical, and cultural meanings, all of which allowed him to engage with social, political, gender, and religious issues. Second, through his embodied renunciation, he acquired the status of *mahātmā* ("great soul"), which became a central factor in mobilizing millions of Indians for action. In the Indian context, spiritual leadership has been and continues to be associated with *brahmacarya.* Furthermore, Gandhi, drawing on the Hindu tradition that ascribes a supernatural value to *brahmacarya,* sought to validate the ascetic power of self-control and to transform it into an active power for nonviolent resistance. Through his personal vow and ethic of austerity, he was able to assert moral power and exemplify self-sacrifice and self-rule. History shows that his embodiment of autonomy and moral power became factors in mobilizing the masses to make sacrifices for India's independence.

Last, through his innovative narrative of *brahmacarya* and performance as an ascetic, Gandhi was able to transform ascetic disciplines and vows of truth, nonviolence, self-sacrifice, simplicity, and poverty into techniques of nonviolent activism, including nonviolent resistance, noncooperation, self-reliance, fearlessness, the willingness to go to jail, and maintaining commitment despite suffering. This book reviews various Indian models, theories, and texts that Gandhi selected and interpreted in order to synthesize an ideology of asceticism and activism in his career as a political leader.

Even though the scholarship on Gandhi is vast, this book takes a unique approach to understanding his life and methods. Through a comprehensive study of Gandhi's own words and cultural and historical context, this book probes the role of Gandhi's ascetic practices, specifically his unconventional *brahmacarya,* in nonviolent activism. Since the beginning of his career as a political activist, Gandhi's revolutionary techniques in the field of social and political conflict resolution have drawn the attention of the international community. Despite scathing appraisals of some of his political ideologies and personal idiosyncrasies, Gandhi's life and methods continue to capture the popular imagination through a variety of media—books, films, plays, and a recent opera. Each year popular and academic volumes are added to the ever-expanding literature on Gandhi's philosophy in a number of areas and disciplines. In recent years, many mass movements across the globe confronting religious, political, and social injustice, environmental and food crises, and economic inequality have generated a renewed interest in Gandhi's life and nonviolent methods, affirming their relevance to contemporary challenges. Curiously, Gandhi's ascetic practices, including his practice of *brahmacarya*, which he considered integral to his methods of social and political activism, continue to cause ambivalence among scholars, students, and activists: they are either ignored or dismissed as peculiar to his personal life, as evidenced in recent popular biographies.

Gandhi's vow and practice of *brahmacarya* evoke a philosophical debate regarding the seemingly paradoxical connections between one's personal sexual life and public political actions. When discussing Gandhi's life, most Gandhi scholars, using various hermeneutical lenses, are conflicted about his decision to take the *brahmacarya* vow at the age of thirty-seven, the apparent tensions this caused even in his family, and, more specifically, his odd public experiments of this private practice for political goals. Undoubtedly, Gandhi's combining of the dichotomous categories of political activism and religious asceticism is puzzling to those living in Western culture. Nevertheless, it is noteworthy that his integration of the two spheres was challenging as well for some of his closest associates and Indian followers of his time, who perceived religious renunciation and political engagement as distinct paths, oriented toward different life goals. Their disagreement, however, arose out of their indigenous philosophical presuppositions, not modern sexual attitudes. Nevertheless, the scholarship that has investigated Gandhi's celibacy generally operates within the cultural assumptions that have developed from the modern sexual ethos.

Thus, it is not surprising that students (some of whom claim to be activists) react to Gandhi's sexual abnegation and adoption of an austere lifestyle for public service either with utter confusion or the impulse to dismiss. During one of the seminars on Gandhi that I cotaught at the University of Oregon, Gandhi's frank autobiographical recollections of his "experiments with truth" intrigued the participants. However, the sections on Gandhi's vow of *brahmacarya*, which exposes his obsessive and antagonistic feelings toward sex, generated a different kind of reaction in the class: a feeling of palpable discomfort, even awe. A wide variety of questions emerged: Why was Gandhi so preoccupied with sexual control? What about love, and, more importantly, what about his wife's feelings and desires? What does a personal sex life have to do with political activism? These inquiries immediately stirred my thoughts, and I realized that these responses are not limited to Western students, but have been part of a worldwide scholarly discourse on Gandhi.

I rifled through my own memories to understand these questions, recalling my experiences with the narrative of Gandhi's life while growing up in India. As a child I listened to stories of Gandhi told by my parents, who were displaced during the partition of India and Pakistan. Almost two decades after settling into their new home, independent India, their memories of India's struggle with the British and the ensuing holocaust were still fresh. In their accounts, Gandhi always emerged as the main character, but they were ambivalent about some of his political decisions. Nevertheless, these bleak stories of suffering during the freedom struggle and the partition were punctuated by their glowing anecdotes about Gandhi's seemingly miraculous *yogic* powers, his spirit of self-sacrifice, and their personal experience of his ability to mobilize and inspire the masses during India's struggle for independence. My mother would often relate to us her own mother's stories in which Gandhi was a saint and a divine incarnation with magical powers. For the *homo religiosus,* he was destined to push British colonial domination out of India through his *satyagraha* (the force of Truth) and *brahmacarya,* whose literal and more complex meaning is "to act in a divine manner." Later, as an adult, my connection with Gandhi became attenuated, limited to yearly national celebrations of his birthday and exposure to his statues and pictures in government offices and street squares.

Student queries, my own reflections, and further curiosity about Gandhi's reasons led me to focus on Gandhi's *brahmacarya* in my dissertation at Lancaster University, U.K. In studying *brahmacarya* through Gandhi's own words, I discovered the centrality of this practice in his nonviolent activism. The present work expands on and modifies my earlier research, drawing on theories related to the role and purpose of mythology, ritual, and embodied performance in mobilizing the masses for social action. It explores Gandhi's discriminating use of classical Indian lore, including epic narratives and his reinterpretation of traditional religious texts, to create a coherent narrative for his unique synthesis of ascetic activism.

Gandhi's *brahmacarya* and his views on sexuality continue to draw attention and cause suspicion among scholars who search for the reasons behind his unusual interest in sexual renunciation and its centrality in his political activism. Yet there exists no comprehensive study that systematically explores Gandhi's own explanations and actions—documented in his thousands of pages of writings—for this nuanced practice, which might help us understand the broader questions of the value of sacrifice, discipline, and ritual and mythical performance in activism.

Undoubtedly, Gandhi himself was aware that his *brahmacarya* was a cause of suspicion among people. Since ancient times the power of love, intimacy, and sex have been canonized in art, literature, and even religion. However, the celebration of these powers has often been balanced by a counterethos that dictates the ephemeral nature of material pleasures. This ethos advocates the power of sexual restraint and the exercise of control over fleshly desires. Most religious traditions prescribe self-control and denial of bodily pleasures for higher spiritual achievements. Within the trajectory of renunciation of physical pleasures, celibacy is a means of loosening the bonds of the body and, thereby, the material world.

However, in the current era, poetic and artistic expressions of sexuality have taken on new license. The everyday barrage of sexual imagery, the overt obsession with sex by youth and contemporary culture, the fixation on sex exhibited by many powerful adult celebrities (in varied fields from politics to sports), Internet pornography, as well as the ever-growing research on the powerful effect of sex on our daily lives, have overpowered the parallel strand of virtuous self-control that until now was common in human societies for much of history. In this contemporary cultural setting, even a discussion of celibacy seems odd.

Celibacy has come to represent an antithesis of life affirmation: it is viewed as denial of the body and emotions; world-rejecting, unhealthy, the solitary pursuit of a few religious men and women, an oddity, and an impossible expectation. Sex, on the other hand, is perceived as an affirmation of all that exists: central to physical, emotional, and social well-being; the foundation of creativity and constructive behavior; the essence of life and the life of love. Unlike Saint Augustine and Swami Vivekananda, who warned their followers against the snares of sex, modern media gurus, including Oprah and Dr. Oz, recount to the masses the benefits of sex and guide them to experience its power. Against this background of an overtly sex-oriented society, on one hand, and the Indian religions' classic bifurcation between this-worldly aspirations and spiritual goals, on the other, Gandhi's celibacy appears on the surface to be a misplaced fixation, particularly as he advocated its practice for nonviolent social and political activism.

Gandhi's celibacy also appears odd due to modern views on female sexuality, which have been profoundly influenced by the sexual revolution of the West. The sexual revolution, which ushered in the belief in the right to sexual satisfaction for women, altered the psychological landscape of sexuality for both men and women. Conventional perceptions of "normal" sexuality shifted from a view of sex as a simple act of physical fulfillment for men, or a necessity for the production of children. It became, instead, an expression of "free love" and equality between both sexes. These new sexual mores, which notably went hand in hand with the women's liberation movement of the latter twentieth century, exist in the subconscious erotic culture of the Western (and now global) mind. But Gandhi lived in an era when this revolution had not yet taken place. From Gandhi's writings, it is apparent that sexuality in his era fit the more stereotypical model. For Gandhi, the constant need for male sexual satisfaction could be viewed as aggressive and violent. It could be seen as an endangerment to women's lives due to the hazards of childbirth; an obstacle to their well-being; and an impediment to their fuller participation in society and emancipation. In this way, Gandhi's *brahmacarya* was a kind of feminism.

Gandhian celibacy can thus be viewed as a sexual counterrevolution, of sorts, arising out of his indigenous views of sexuality. This reformulation of existing traditions included an attempt to pacify men and channel their sexual energies toward nonviolent resistance to injustice, while empowering women and liberating them to engage in a more active and activist lifestyle. No doubt, Gandhi was a complex figure, and his celibacy can be studied using different hermeneutical lenses. But if we are to take Gandhi's methods seriously, it is important to trace the self-representation of his austere practices and his cultural context while weighing his intent. It becomes clear that most of the ascetic principles Gandhi utilized for constructing his method—*svarāj, satyagraha,* and *swadeshi,* for example—carried both ascetic and political values, and they helped create a coherent narrative for moving the hearts of the masses toward action.

Explanation of the Vocabulary

This book includes Sanskrit philosophical terms such as *brahmacarya, nivṛtti* (spiritual freedom requiring renunication), *pravṛtti* (worldly engagement), *yajña* (ritual sacrifice), *sannyāsa* (renunciation), and *tapas* (austerity; self-sacrifice) that are laden with specific meanings and connotations in different Indian traditions and historical periods. Gandhi's use of these words is case specific and requires us to work with his choice of vocabulary. Even though terms such as *religion, celibacy, austerity*, and *asceticism* can be applied cross-culturally, their inherent meanings differ from one culture or tradition to another. We are often reminded that each language contains its specific meanings, which guide the thinking patterns of a specific culture. It is not surprising, then, that Gandhi himself insisted on the use of the term *satyagraha* for his nonviolent method, rather than "passive resistance," and differentiated *brahmacarya* from the commonly understood notion of celibacy. Gandhi's notion of *svarāj* was much more than "home-rule" or political independence; it combined the soteriological goal of self-control with the control of political power. If we are to study Gandhi's own words and narrative, it is important to apply the vocabulary that he himself used. Therefore, when discussing Gandhi's rendering of Sanskrit terms in Hindi versions, I follow the convention of his style, but when speaking about those terms in their root forms in Classical Hindu texts, I use Sanskrit rendering, such as *svarāj* (both "self-rule" and "home-rule") and *svarāj/svarājya* (independent state).

This work also utilizes Western vocabulary such as *myth, austerity*, and *asceticism*—terms that are also charged with multiple meanings and interpreted differently by various scholars. However, for the purpose of this study, both Sanskrit and English words have been used according to Gandhi's own context and writings. In order to communicate his message, Gandhi drew on Sanskrit and vernacular vocabulary as well as the Western terminology in use in his day. For example, even though Gandhi referred to various traditional sources, he used and interpreted terms such as *tapas, yajña*, and *sannyāsa* in a broad general sense of austerity, self-sacrifice, and renunciation. He spontaneously connected such terms with a variety of traditional meanings while at the same time interpreting them anew for his practical philosophy. He was less concerned with the precise traditional interpretations or nuances that surrounded these terms.

In the same vein, Gandhi employed the Western notion of "mythology" to describe, for example, the religious narratives of the *Rāmāyaṇa* and the *Mahābhārata*, which were inspirational for him. Gandhi's use of the word *myth* implies "untrue," but he seems to have distinguished this word from the larger category of mythology. For Gandhi, mythology consisted of sacred stories that represented the "history of the soul." The heroes and sages of mythology were "living realities" to him. Traditionally, *kathā*, the ceremonious public reading of sacred literature, is not concerned with the historicity of its tales, but rather serves as an avenue toward inspiring religious people. Moreover, the words *myth* and *mythology* have been adopted by the Indian scholarly community for describing ancient narratives, legends, and folklores.

Although Gandhi questioned the historicity of religious narratives, he believed, like many other religious celibates (*brahmacārins*), ascetics (*tapasvins*), and laypeople, that the power these heroes derived from the observance of ascetic vows (*vratas*) and from following sacred duty or commitment (*dharma*) was real, and he sought to actuate this power in his personal and political life. While technically the power of *tapas* and *vrata* may be called "mythic," a belief in their actual power continues to this day, as discussed in chapters 3 and 4. Thus, these traditions are still practiced by many who, like Gandhi, seek to actualize the power of *tapas* and *dharma* for achieving various spiritual and material goals. In our present context, the words *myth, mythical,* and *mythic* relate to the characters and accounts of ancient religious narratives (*kathās*). All of these sacred narratives have been termed *myth* by nonindigenous scholars and writers. Moreover, it becomes clear that Gandhi utilized his authority as Mahātmā (a "great soul" or "great being") to treat Indian traditions as sources of inspiration that needed to be reinterpreted and reconfigured for changing contexts. It is hoped that this study enhances the existing literature on Gandhi and also brings new understanding to one of the most controversial aspects of this notable man's life.

Acknowledgments

This work has been supported by many—my colleagues, friends, family members, and students. It will not be possible to name all who helped me in countless ways, but to all of them I extend my heartfelt gratitude. I owe my deepest gratitude to Professor Chakravarthi Ram-Prasad at Lancaster University, UK (Department of Politics, Philosophy and Religion) for his excellent guidance and continued support in this project. Also, my special thanks to Professor James Earl at the University of Oregon (English Department), a good friend and mentor, for patiently editing every draft of this book and providing me with moral and intellectual support throughout this endeavor. I would like to thank Professor T. S. Rukmani, Chair in Hindu Studies at Concordia Univeristy (Department of Religion), Professor Emeritus Nicholas Gier at the University of Idaho (Philosophy Department), and Professor Christopher Key Chapple at Loyola Marymount University, Navin and Pratima Doshi Professor of Indic and Comparative Theology (Department of Theological Studies), and Professor Douglas Allen at the University of Maine (Department of Philosophy) for their encouragement. Many thanks to Professor Deborah Green (Judaic Studies), Professor Mark Unno (Religious Studies), and other colleagues at the University of Oregon and also at Lane Community College for supporting this work in various ways. My special thanks to my friend and colleague Rita D. Sherma, professor and executive director, Confluence Integrative Studies Institute (CISI), School of Philosophy and Religious Studies, Taksha University. I thank my dear friends, Cindy Clague, Sister Kiran, Maria Mapps, Nancy Raymond, and Steven Shurtleff for their support and I am grateful to my brother Charlie Lal for his inspiration through example. Special gratitude to Suzanne Geraci, a local Eugene artist, for generously providing me with her sketch of Gandhi. Suzanne told me that she was truly inspired when she did the drawing, after seeing a wonderful film about his life. "The drawing just seemed to come through me, and I was just the 'channel.' It was truly a work of love." Also, my thanks to Amrit and Rabindra K. D. Kaur Singh (UK) for giving me permission to use Gandhi's images from their book, *Images of Freedom*. I am deeply grateful to the editorial staff at SUNY: Nancy Ellegate, acquisitions editor, for recognizing the need for this volume and her sustained support; Ryan Morris, senior production editor, for patiently assisting me with the editorial process; and Michael Campochiaro, for supporting me through the marketing process. This project would not be possible without the persistent support, patience, and encouragement of my dear friend and husband, Don Howard, and our daughters Mira and Gita. I thank them with my loving heart. Above all, my sincere gratitude to my mother, father, and to my great teacher, Shri Santseviji, examples of ascetic activism, who sadly left their bodies before the completion of this project but continued to guide me through their lifelong teachings and inspiration.

Introduction

> The first thing is to know what true *brahmacharya* is, then to realize its value and lastly to try and cultivate this priceless virtue. I hold that true service of the country demands this observance.
>
> —M. K. Gandhi

Mohandas Gandhi interlinked the ascetic practice of *brahmacarya* and other austere disciplines with his political aspirations. Traditionally, within a secular context and also in India's spiritual traditions, the practice of sexual renunciation for attaining spiritual freedom (*nivṛtti*) and worldly engagement (*pravṛtti*) represent two separate categories. Yet Gandhi, shockingly, made ascetic celibacy central to his success in the political arena and audaciously revealed his sexual views and practices with his literal and metaphorical *nakedness* (which has been a subject of many commentaries on Gandhi's celibacy). Examples of his unconventional celibacy include public announcements of his vow of *brahmacarya*; audacious disclosure of his secret temptations; open association with young female assistants; his advocacy of celibacy for those committed to public service and India's independence movement; and the *experiments* (a term he often used when testing the potency of a certain practice) in his later years, of sleeping naked with young women, without engaging in sexual intercourse, as a part of the practice of *brahmacarya* for his nonviolent activism.

Thus, on the one hand, Gandhi challenged the status quo of his native people, who ordinarily felt "shy" about openly discussing the subject of sexuality; on the other hand, he created a perplexing paradox for native orthodox Hindus, elites, and even scholars, who tended to construe ascetic disciplines and political actions as incongruous.[1] Some of his contemporaries considered his practices nontraditional, but Gandhi trusted the celebrated power of asceticism and sought to experiment with components of austerity for contemporary objectives.

He not only substantiated his celibacy in marriage for this-worldly goals within Indian philosophical thought, but he also corroborated his decision of "sleeping" with women as a self-controlled *mahātmā* within India's mythical traditions. In spite of his unconventional approach to sexuality and celibacy, India's masses deemed him a *mahātmā* and followed his call to sacrifice in a nonviolent movement against the British regime because of this ideology and embodied self-control and self-sacrifice.

The story of Gandhi's life has been told in hundreds of biographies and was brought to life in Richard Attenborough's Oscar-winning 1982 film, *Gandhi*, which made the Indian activist who fought against the British Empire with nonviolent methods a worldwide sensation. Interestingly, it was British actor Ben Kingsley (born Krishna Bhanji and of mixed Indian and British background) who captured the charisma and creative thought of Gandhi as no one had done before, drawing millions of Indians and Westerners alike to fill theaters. The film also generated renewed interest among scholars, as evidenced by the appearance of a diverse and large body of scholarship about Gandhi's life and works that followed the film. But the portrait of Gandhi that was created by Attenborough and sustained by scholarship thereafter is of a universalized, secular figure, dissociated from his Indian context and Indianness, which had mobilized millions. His personal philosophy of renunciation is now fossilized in his honorific title of *mahātmā*. But an examination of Gandhi's biography and, most importantly, his own writings, reveals a very different person than that of popular imagination.

Perhaps the careful remolding and simplification of Gandhi, dissociated from his religious philosophy and his apparently eccentric ascetic practices, is due to a difficulty with his synthesis of the conventionally polarized categories of religion and politics. Many dismiss his ascetic practices as irrelevant to his nonviolent activism, but for Gandhi they were integral to his political strategy. Can we even comprehend Gandhi without understanding his ascetic practices? In order to understand this question, it is important to outline the basic presuppositions of Indian philosophy and religions that were influential in Gandhi's construction of his practical method of ascetic activism.

Philosophical Presuppositions and Gandhi's Unique Interpretation for Activism

Various critiques of Gandhi's ascetic practices arise from assumptions about the polarity of religious and secular spheres, as well as Indian philosophical presuppositions that present binary categories of religious renunciation and worldly engagement. However, a study of Gandhi's writings reveals that, according to Gandhi himself, he built his model of ascetic activism on Indian philosophical assumptions and reinterpreted them for his practical purposes of political activism. A brief discussion of key philosophical and moral ideas that he creatively integrated with specific political and personal goals is essential to the ensuing discussion of Gandhi's *brahmacarya* as the underlying source for his reinterpretation and synthesis of the domains of politics and asceticism.

Asceticism (Tapas) as Technology of Power

Indian philosophical and religious texts are replete with various forms of asceticism (*tapas*), which feature primarily self-discipline, control of desires, and detachment. Asceticism is commonly associated with the ideology of *nivṛtti* in contrast to the path of *pravṛtti*, which will be discussed in the next chapter. Even though asceticism is based on an "otherworldly" orientation and represents withdrawal, the austerities (*tapas*) themselves are described as having potency and miraculous power and traditionally have been utilized to acquire this-worldly material goals.[2] In Indian religious texts and mythology, yogis and ascetics are believed to derive extraordinary powers through austere vows and observances. The religious texts and mythical traditions of India present a wide variety of narratives that illustrate that men and women achieve goals and acquire miraculous powers through their renunciation of the basic desires of sex and food, and by their observation of other *vratas* (religious vows) that also involve restraint. At the dawn of the twentieth century, the religious vocabulary of spiritual strength and asceticism saw a renewal in the public domain in India. This resurgence of asceticism represented the antithesis of the Western forms of material power and, at the same time, provided an alternative to the Western ideologies of hegemony, extreme materialism, and self-indulgence. Gandhi drew on this existing attitude but gave a new meaning to ascetic vows by arguing for the value of *brahmacarya*, fasting, and discipline of the senses as having functional value for those who engaged in pragmatic sociopolitical activism. On the one hand, he emphasized their supernatural power, and, on the other hand, he utilized them as methods for his nonviolent activism. This twentieth-century synthesis based on ancient Indian traditions was uniquely his own.

Mobilizing the Power of Myths

Storytelling in India has long been the medium of communicating everything from moral issues to abstract philosophical thoughts to historical facts. Modern studies in psychology and neurology underline the fact that humans think in narrative structures, but storytelling has always been fundamental to India's religious and historical traditions. The custom of religious storytelling (*kathā*) is rooted in antiquity and is still current today. The success of television renderings of the ancient epics such as the *Mahābhārata* and the *Rāmāyaṇa* confirms India's proclivity for the ancient narratives. In spite of cultural changes due to urbanization and globalization, the tradition of *kathā* thrives not only in villages but in metropolitan areas as well. Through the epics and Purāṇic stories, modern sages (who use modern technology and media) glorify the ideal of *nivṛtti*. Although most household listeners may not be able to practice the ideal, the stories reinforce the status of the renunciate and seek to inspire a rarefied religious sensibility, even among common householders who are unable to engage in renunciation

As the twentieth century opened, the tradition of ancient epics portraying the battle of good versus evil was revived to inspire the masses to fight against the British colonial regime. The ancient myths also explained and communicated what seekers of freedom perceived as the superior moral strengths of India's civilization. According to Gandhi's own accounts, he was deeply influenced and inspired by religious stories and he used them effectively, retelling certain narratives from the epics to encourage the masses to choose the path of nonviolence for confronting injustice. Scholars have deliberated on the "myth" of the *mahātmā* and its effect on Gandhi's nonviolent movement, but have overlooked his own use of Indian "mythology" to substantiate (1) his method of nonviolence and (2) his ideology of asceticism as a personal and political strategy for this goal. Both became important factors in inciting the masses against colonialism.

Brahmacarya as the Expression of Self-Discipline, Sacrifice, Power, and Authority

In the framework of *nivṛtti*, the religious, ritualistic, and world-transcending emphasis of *brahmacarya* has been established by ancient Indian lore and ascetic literature. "In the *nivṛtti* soteriological orientation," Arti Dhand states, "the entire complex of the term *brahmacarya* is evoked: *brahmacarya* is the path that leads to *Brahman* (hence *mokṣa* [spiritual freedom])."[3] It is motivated by the highest goal of self-realization; therefore, by definition, it signifies rejection of mundane values and aspirations, including self-fulfillment, familial responsibilities, social constraints, and, more importantly, political enterprise. Various

Indian critiques of Gandhi arise from this philosophical presupposition, exemplified in the following comment by his contemporary, the politician and philosopher Bal Gangadhar Tilak (1856–1920), who located the life of a *sādhu* (holy man) and that of a politician in two separate spheres: "Politics is a game of worldly people and not of Sadhus." However, Gandhi disagreed with Tilak with "deference" and argued that "it betrays mental laziness to think that world is not for sadhus."[4]

However, Gandhi, who was deeply influenced by the *Bhagavad-Gītā* and Hindu religious narratives, based his practice of celibacy within the political arena on an alternative ideology that integrated ascetic practices with this-worldly aspirations of creating unity among Indians and acquiring freedom from the foreign regime. Theoretically, Gandhi equated his public service, which included his struggle for India's independence, with service to God, and sought, therefore, to utilize the same renunciatory means required when serving God through more conventional religious paths. Gandhi perceived *brahmacarya* not simply as a world-denying observance, but rather as a practice with tangible value for this-worldly goals. He drew on examples from select religious narratives that illustrated the instrumentality of the *brahmacarya* vow for accessing wealth, long life, and various kinds of material and spiritual powers. The *Rāmāyaṇa*'s celebrated characters, Lakṣmaṇa and Indrajīit, according to Gandhi, gained supernormal powers by their vow of celibacy. Gandhi yearned for such a wish-fulfilling state of accomplishment: "If I had attained that *nirvikara* (passionless) state, I should have but to think a thing and it would happen. I would not have to argue."[5] This unusual statement reflects Gandhi's belief in the supernormal power of celibacy, which he sought for realizing his vision of free India (*svarāj*), rather than through the conventional means of a politician.

In his article, "Householder Ascetic and Uses of Self-Discipline," Timothy Lubin analyzes a broad spectrum of ascetic practices utilized by householders. He expounds on the phenomenon of asceticism as a source of power and authority and describes "the ascetic regimen" as a "powerful technology in the hands of a qualified user."[6] From this point of view, Gandhi was seeking to acquire the power and authority to maximize his influence on people for mobilizing a nonviolent movement. But more importantly, he utilized these ascetic practices as a technology in literal terms, transforming them into instruments (for example, discipline in nonviolent resistance to violence, boycott, strikes, fasting, willingness to go to jail, self-reliance, endurance of suffering, defiance, and fearlessness) required for nonviolent confrontation against a foreign regime. Gandhi also viewed *brahmacarya* as a moral imperative in terms of the performance of a ritual sacrifice (*yajña*) for India's independence.

Finally, in the ideology of asceticism, the ascetic—who renounces the pleasures of food and sex—transcends the parameters of society, and gains authority to question the status quo and reinterpret existing norms. Gandhi, by virtue of his self-control, was able to defy the boundaries of caste, gender, and religion to confront structures of violence. His nonviolent strategy was strengthened because of his self-control, because a life of *nivṛtti* (renunciation) is inconsistent with a wish to harm other beings and with any type of ill-will, greed, and wrongful conduct. In his adaptation of *brahmacarya* for modern secular goals, and through his embodiment of an ascetic, Gandhi created a coherent native narrative to communicate his strategy of nonviolence.

Central Questions and Methodology

This study proceeds with three main questions as guidelines: First, aside from Gandhi's personal disposition, what were the main factors that made him gradually situate *brahmacarya*, a private ascetic practice, at the center of his public nonviolent struggle for political freedom? Second, against the backdrop of dichotomous Indian philosophical ideology, how did Gandhi, while using the mechanics and vocabulary from the traditions, present this odd synthesis as logically and philosophically coherent? Third, and most importantly, what were the underlying factors and models from his cultural milieu, philosophy, and myths that Gandhi carefully extrapolated, reinterpreted, and performed to employ *brahmacarya* as the key to his *satyagraha* and as a strategy for mass mobilization?

Over the last four decades numerous scholars who have contributed to the study of Gandhi's life and thought have faced a dilemma: on the one hand, it has been argued that "there is little point in applying rigorous standards of logical *thinking* to Gandhi's programme of *action.*"[7] When using logical standards to assess Gandhi's thought there appears to be at its base a matrix of conflicting ideologies—the religious and the political, the traditional and the modern, the renunciatory and the activist, and the rational and the intuitive—which poses challenges for creating a logical philosophy. On the other hand, Gandhi's voluminous writings create a problem for those who seek to construct a coherent philosophical system out of his life and thought. Joan V. Bondurant states that "it is the unsystematized and often inconsistent jungle of Gandhi's writings that makes it difficult, but tempting to others to formulate a 'Gandhian Philosophy.'" The result is that "in the course of the search for Gandhi's true meaning, one necessarily interprets and abstracts."[8] However, it is important to keep Gandhi's vision in mind. His program was not an intellectual endeavor; it was, rather, a living strategy with a primarily pragmatic purpose (as opposed to a philosophical or merely intellectual one). Gandhi emphasized this focus: "I must not be drawn into a philosophical or religious argument with my friends. I have not the qualifications for teaching my philosophy of life."[9] Throughout his life, Gandhi used philosophical ideas as ways to construct his practical philosophy for addressing the social and political issues of India.

In this analysis, I seek to avoid the temptation to analyze Gandhi's synthesis of asceticism and activism through a specific lens, and instead use his own words as the hermeneutic for understanding his versatile practice of *brahmacarya*. This method does not utilize any particular theoretical prism but instead traces Gandhi's self-representation of *brahmacarya* and its philosophical, ethical, and practical implications in his own writings and performance. The hermeneutic employed here is unconventional in Gandhian studies, in that the focus does not aim at yet another interpretation built on and substantiated by prior scholarly analyses but rather seeks an exposition of *what Gandhi himself said he was doing,* in other words, a close reading of his words. This approach moves deeper toward understanding his aims and methods than the notion that Gandhi was inconsistent in his actions and explanations—something for which he has been frequently criticized

Gandhi admitted the progressive nature of his ideas and asserted that, "in my opinion, there is a consistency running through my seeming inconsistencies, as in nature there is a unity running through seeming diversity."[10] This claim was one of the elements that prompted my use of Gandhi's own words as a method for analyzing his integration of *pravṛtti* and *nivṛtti,* in general, and his *brahmacarya,* in particular. This rather unconventional "inside-out" approach (studying Gandhi on his own terms) may appear naive, but its simplicity allows for a serious study of Gandhi's interpretation of his apparently unconventional ideology. It is hoped that this methodology will supplement other interpretive lenses as well as provide a deeper and more comprehensive understanding of Gandhi's complex and multifaceted *brahmacarya.*

Gandhi's claim to having a "method in [his] inconsistencies" may appear to some as mere defensiveness of his inconsistent statements and actions. Certainly, his response was not satisfying to those who demanded consistency from a *mahātmā* who was known for constantly asserting the value of truth and its power, and it continues to perplex scholars today who seek to formulate a "Gandhian philosophy." However, within the Indian mindset, such inconsistency is not unusual. A. K. Ramanujan, in his seminal essay, "Is There an Indian Way of Thinking?" describes the context-sensitive nature, ethical use, and literary design of Indian thought. He states that "in a culture like India's, the context-sensitive rule is the preferred formulation," as opposed to "context-free." In other words, there is a priority given to contextualization or specification over universalization. Furthermore, he says that Indian texts such as the *Mahābhārata* epic have been discussed "as if they were loose-leaf files, rag-bag encyclopedias." Ramanujan emphasizes the "need to attend to the context-sensitive designs that embed a seeming variety of modes." In these traditional Indian texts, "not unity (in the Aristotelian sense) but coherence seems to be the end."[11] Ramanujan is referring to the dynamic web of ethical meanings in different tales, which apparently may contradict one another, but are coherent in the larger context of the poem due to underlying philosophical presuppositions.

This analogy can be applied to Gandhi's writings and spoken words. Gandhi provided an extensive written and spoken commentary on his ascetic activities. Paradoxically, while Gandhi argued for speech that was laconic in nature (and observed silence once a week), he "spoke" through volumes of writings. In fact, he was one of the most prolific writers and communicators of the twentieth century. An intriguing model of self-representation and self-aware performance, he provided continuous annotation of what he was doing until the day he died.

The methodology of this exposition requires examination of Gandhi's selective use of classical Indian material: his reinterpretation of traditional texts; his use of religious symbols and the vocabulary of *yajña* (sacrifice), *tapas* (austerity), *ahiṃsā* (nonviolence), *sat* (truth), *rāmarājya* (the idealized kingdom of Lord Rāma of the *Rāmāyaṇa*), and so forth; his narration of traditional myths; his explanation of ascetic disciplines as instruments for achieving political goals; his rationale for analogizing political methods as ascetic disciplines; and his embodied performance as an ascetic activist. In order to deliver a comprehensive study of Gandhi's *brahmacarya* as the nexus of his synthesis of asceticism and activism, I have included the discourse of prominent Gandhian scholars relevant to specific topics. For the purpose of creating a fresh perspective on Gandhi's use of ascetic vocabulary and symbolism, as well as on the purposes of his embodied practices, I have also utilized select modern theories regarding such essential concepts as asceticism, myth, ritual, and liminality in order to construct a broader understanding of Gandhi's philosophy. However, this analysis begins and ends with Gandhi's own words.

Gandhi's Paradoxical Ascetic Activism and Popular Imagination

Gandhi himself was paradoxical, a complex combination of an ascetic and an activist. Both of these aspects are visible in his lifestyle, reminiscent of an Indian holy man's, and in his ascetic practices as he applied them to political purposes. As an architect of the politically free India, Gandhi received the honorific title "the Father of the Nation" and, due to his religious disciplines, he was also given the hallowed epithet of "*mahātmā*," meaning a great soul marked with religious qualities. This metaphor of integrity within paradox can be extended to Gandhi's epic life and his works. His writings and speeches spanning the years 1888–1948, including published booklets, speeches, newspaper articles, personal letters, memos, telegraphs, and scribbled notes, have been documented as *The Collected Works of Mahatma Gandhi*, and comprise over one hundred volumes (there is a variation of volume numbers in the printed and digital versions), approximately 50,000 pages—a collection almost ten times larger than the epic of the *Mahābhārata*. The phrase *Yannehāsti, na tadkvacit* ("what is not here is nowhere else") describes the scale of the *Mahābhārata* but can also be applied to Gandhi's voluminous literary output.

It is a repository of a wide variety of material regarding issues that include education, politics, economics, war, sanitation, sex, celibacy, health, culture, social customs, religious practices, interreligious dialogue, asceticism, and extreme worldly engagement. I use Gandhi's own voice, which flows through this large collection, to understand Gandhi's celibacy in terms of its inception, evolution, and efficacy, as well as Gandhi's experimentation with the power of celibacy for personal, social, and political goals.

Gandhi intriguingly parallels his culture's underlying paradoxical ideologies. Whoever goes to India is struck by a wide range of competing and contradictory realities interwoven in its social and religious fabric—threads of severe poverty and lavish affluence; the ubiquitous presence of yogis and ascetics embodying world-negating practices, coexisting with the all-encompassing aphrodisiac moods expressed in the sculpted voluptuaries of Kujaraho temples; serene religious practices of fasting, purity, and rituals, as well as raucous religious discourses, intricate and colorful festivals, and elaborate social protocols. Inundated by these extremes, one attempts to untangle the cultural web by isolating strands that are tightly entangled like the multifarious myths in the *Mahābhārata*. In spite of its complex and paradoxical nature, the underlying unity within India, as within the *Mahābhārata*, emerges in its ideology of pluralistic and paradoxical philosophical thought and practices. These paradoxes are integral to the identity of India.

Like the plurality of India and the myths of the *Mahābhārata*, Gandhi's life, literature, and method represent a dynamic narrative of entangled strings of religious practices, secular aspirations, philosophical ideas, and political goals and strategies. Although Gandhi erected the framework of his philosophy and method on India's philosophical presuppositions, he also embraced Western ideas of social justice, economic and labor equality, and the politically independent democratic state. Furthermore, Gandhi gave a new interpretation to Indian philosophical presuppositions and also to Western political ideologies.

Not surprisingly, this complex mixture creates an impression of an overwhelming and incoherent synthesis of ideas and practices. To create a coherent narrative and a systematic strategy out of Gandhi's philosophy and method of nonviolence, which continue to be relevant for contemporary situations, scholars and activists attempt to isolate these strands by using various hermeneutical approaches. One such approach is separating Gandhi's personal philosophy of asceticism from his nonviolent activism. Historically, scholars and biographers seek to make Gandhi more approachable so that his methods of peace and nonviolence can be universally applied. Their modi operandi make Gandhi's methods more orderly and accessible, as evidenced by the sustained, broad attention they have received by individuals and organizations. However, the value of Gandhi's ascetic renunciation in nonviolent activism, as he himself deemed it, is compromised. One is left to ponder: Is it possible to apply Gandhi's methods without taking his ascetic practices into consideration? Were they merely his "fads," with no functional value in his personal transformation and political struggle?

Gandhi's *Brahmacarya*: Hermeneutical Challenges

Scholars who have analyzed Gandhi's philosophy and politics—as well as his contemporary critics and admirers—have grappled with the purpose of *brahmacarya* in his political enterprise. Gandhi underscored the role of *brahmacarya* in addressing personal, social, and political issues, and deemed it essential for his method of *satyagraha*. "Gandhiji's obsession with continence made him and celibacy interchangeable terms," says Girja Kumar in his comprehensive study, *Brahmacharya: Gandhi and His Women Associates*.[12] Gandhi's apparent "obsession" with celibacy has caused scholars of various disciplines to speculate on the possible reasons for it—including guilt, lack of human love, concern for national health, and a deep spiritual predilection.[13] His approach to *brahmacarya* is often seen as a creation of his own unusual belief, not easily emulated by others. Even within Gandhi's own Hindu religious and philosophical matrix—on which he founded his nonviolent methods—his correlation of celibacy and politics has seemed ideologically inconsistent.

Brahmacarya, an element of *nivṛtti* (renunciation for attaining spiritual freedom), requires extreme restraint and subduing of body, mind, and emotional faculties, whereas engagement in politics (a crude form of *pravṛtti*) exacts an intense involvement of body, mind, and emotions. A prominent scholar, Bhikhu Parekh, opines that "if we ignored the ascetic tradition, Gandhi's theory of sexuality has no support in Hindu thought."[14] The ascetic tradition (*nivṛtti*) to which Parekh refers seeks to transcend physical and emotional involvement for the sake of spiritual freedom, and within that framework, Gandhi's use of *brahmacarya* for success in political goals is odd.

David Cortright, in his work *Gandhi and Beyond: Nonviolence for an Age of Terrorism*, analyzes the difficult question of the relevance of Gandhi's nonviolent method for confronting contemporary terrorism. He extols Gandhi's nonviolent contributions but admits, as other scholars have, the challenge of understanding Gandhi's complicated personal philosophy:

> Every time I tried to approach Gandhi, I found myself intimidated and overwhelmed—not only by the enormity of his accomplishments but also by the austerity and eccentricities of his personality. Gandhi seemed almost inconceivable. How could one so spiritual and detached from the material world achieve so much in altering the course of history? . . . I found Gandhi's asceticism too extreme, his views on sexuality and women bizarre and offensive.[15]

Gandhi's ascetic celibacy and unconventional ways of practicing it generated suspicion in his day as well. Even his closest associates, including Jawaharlal Nehru (1889–1964), were critical of his stance on *brahmacarya*. Winston Churchill's historic comment that caricatured the "half naked" Gandhi as a "onetime Inner Temple lawyer, now [a] seditious fakir" remains a classic snapshot of the confusion surrounding Gandhi's combination of ascetic life and uncanny political ambitions.[16]

In the Western world, Martin Luther King Jr., a leader of the American civil rights movement, followed Gandhi's strategy of nonviolence and passive resistance using his Christian narrative without adhering to religious asceticism as Gandhi did. His example suggests a lack of connection between nonviolent strategy and the need for abstinence in nonviolent activism. King modeled his strategy of civil disobedience and nonviolent activism on Gandhi's and successfully mobilized his people against the evils of segregation and social injustice. Sexual abnegation did not factor into his personal and political activities. On the contrary, King's successful leadership occurred in spite of his transgressions of marital fidelity. Nicholas F. Gier compares the two personalities: "His [King's] commitment to nonviolence was just as consistent as Gandhi's and his sense of justice and courage were equal to any other saint that we know. . . . King's self-control was firm when it came to not seeking prestige and wealth, but it failed regularly with regard to sexual temptation."[17] The example of King seems to suggest that sexual restraint has no bearing on political, nonviolent activism.

For some, this may constitute evidence against Gandhi's conviction about the relationship between public service, nonviolence, and ascetic abstinence. Even though "for Gandhi, the link between celibacy and non-violence was crucial," his celibacy has been "dismissed, in a somewhat embarrassed fashion, as one of his 'fads,'" observes Pat Caplan. Or it has been simply considered "a spiritual project with only derivative political value," as stated by scholars such as Parekh and others.[18] Such opinions undoubtedly arise out of the prevalent binary understanding of the spiritual and political, which Gandhi sought to bridge by spiritualizing politics through his personal austerities. Gandhi was neither surprised nor deterred by public opinion, as evidenced by his numerous discussions with his critics and followers. He understood the reasons for suspicion: most people, of course, find it difficult to conquer the passions. The fact that Gandhi persisted in linking his ideology of celibacy with all kinds of goals—moral, spiritual, social, and political—has puzzled scholars and commentators.[19]

An Overview of the Scholarship: Investigation of Gandhi's Sexuality

Despite extensive curiosity about Gandhi's celibacy, there is only one book-length study on the subject: Kumar's *Brahmacarya: Gandhi and His Women Associates*. Yet Kumar does not focus on the various dimensions of Gandhi's *brahmacarya*; rather he presents painstaking research on Gandhi's close relations with some of his women followers. He explains Gandhi's *brahmacarya* vow by stating that "there are several incidents in the life of Gandhiji that made him hostile to sex," but he does not even mention the reasons that Gandhi himself presents for his vow in his *Autobiography*. He gives a brief description of the unconventional modes of *brahmacarya*, but concentrates on the tensions that Gandhi's celibate practices created in his family and public life. However, the primary focus of the exposition is, as Kumar summarizes, "a faithful record of dialogues that took place for nearly five decades between him [Gandhi] and a bevy of women who encompassed the entire range of *rasas* (human emotions) as depicted in the aesthetic tradition of India."[20] Kumar presents a complex portrait of Gandhi's relations with his close female friends, followers, and relatives—rather than an extended examination of his *brahmacarya*.

Other studies deal with Gandhi's celibacy by applying specific interpretive methods to the context of his life and social and political philosophy. Acclaimed scholars Erik H. Erikson and Sudhir Kakar apply a psychoanalytical methodology to uncover the underlying purpose of the practice of celibacy that Gandhi so overtly related to his sociopolitical activism. Nirmal Kumar Bose, an anthropologist and one of Gandhi's private secretaries, was the first to critically analyze Gandhi's celibate practices and to suggest their psychoanalytical undertones. He recorded them in his memoir *My Days with Gandhi*.[21] Erikson, in his psychological biography *Gandhi's Truth*, carefully analyzes Gandhi's past in order to "inquire into the personal origins of militant nonviolence." Erikson openly identifies his methodology: "I was a psychoanalyst . . . and men of my kind do not merely ask for facts that can be put on the dotted line but really want to discover hidden meanings within the facts and between the lines."[22] Kakar furthers this trend in a compelling chapter, "Gandhi and Women," which is part of a larger "psychological study of the relationship between the sexes in India." Kakar presents a sweeping overview of Gandhi's past, including his childhood and his cultural context, to discover the roots of Gandhi's celibacy (and by extension his odd relations with women). After an analysis of Gandhi's connections with women, Kakar concludes, "Gandhi's relationship with women and the passions they aroused are, then, more complex than what he [Gandhi] reveals in his own impassioned confession." He leaves the reader with a complicated picture of Gandhi as a man who struggled with his emotions.[23] However, the limited scope of the psychoanalytical approach does not lead to a clear understanding of Gandhi's conscious practice of austere disciplines for practical purposes.

Political scientists Susanne Rudolph and Lloyd Rudolph seek to examine Gandhi's sexual restraint in a broader context. Although their acclaimed exposition *Gandhi: The Traditional Roots of His Charisma* has psychoanalytical undertones, they conclude that "Gandhi's charisma had a cultural referent." They argue that Gandhi's "political effectiveness arose in part from the belief of those who observed his career that his self-control did indeed endow him with extraordinary powers." Interestingly, their analysis puts the potency of Gandhi's sexual control (defined by them only in terms of semen retention) and the Freudian theory of sublimation on the same plane: "Asceticism was also thought to bring with it a higher potency, an implication arising out of a theory of sexual hydrostatics reminiscent of Freudian sublimation theory."[24] However, for Gandhi physical control was only an ancillary part of his comprehensive control of the desire for sense objects, and he related it to his ultimate goal of God realization, which he sought through service to his people and which included his project of attaining political freedom for India.

In numerous articles and in his book *Gandhi's Body*, Joseph S. Alter, a sociocultural anthropologist, expounds on the relationship between sexuality, male celibacy, and nationalism in postcolonial India. Alter became tangentially interested in Gandhi in the course of his study of "wrestlers and their preoccupation with sex, food, and self-control." He emphasizes, in the preface of *Gandhi's Body*, that "this book is about the body of a great soul" and underscores "the need for taking embodied experience seriously when engaged in the analysis of history in general and nationalism in particular." Interestingly, in his later chapter, "Gama the Great," Alter compares the daily regimen of the great wrestler Gama with the "heroic magnitude" of Gandhi's self-control and celibacy, arguing that "in order to explicate the hyper-tension of nation building in relation to embodiment and masculinity, it is useful to draw comparison between Gama and another world famous Indian, Mahatma Gandhi, who . . . embodied, nonviolence."[25] Alter's study provides fresh anthropological insights into Gandhi's trajectory of disciplines, but by no means is it a study of Gandhi's nuanced practice of *brahmacarya*, which was apparently antithetical to "masculinity."

Interest in Gandhi's celibacy continues to be explored in the latest studies by historians and biographers. To name the most recent, independent historian Jad Adams—in his cleverly titled, *Gandhi: Naked Ambition*—seeks to elaborate on the deep secret of Gandhi's celibacy and the intention behind his late-life "experiments" of sleeping with naked girls to test his celibacy. After briefly deliberating on Gandhi's "chastity," he passes a verdict on Gandhi's renunciation of sex on the basis of his relationship with his family: "In Gandhi's formulation, it seems less a renunciation of sexual desire than a rejection of wife and family." In his assessment of Gandhi's ideas about diet and sex, which appear to him as "idiosyncratic to the point of mania," Adams neither considers Gandhi's own intentions in his observance of the vow of celibacy, nor does he engage with Gandhi's Indian context.[26]

Joseph Lelyveld's *Great Soul: Mahatma Gandhi and His Struggle with India* created a great sensation among scholars and Gandhi followers, not merely for his fresh material on Gandhi that portrays him as a complex man, but also for his new angle on Gandhi's sexuality, depicted in sensual language. He elaborates on Gandhi's relationship, which he labels as "most intimate, also ambiguous," with his close friend Hermann Kallenbach. Lelyveld's accounts in the chapter "Upper House" leave the reader to grapple with suggestive homoerotic tendencies in this relationship. He also describes Gandhi's later life experiments with his nineteen-year-old grandniece Manu in sensational language. Lelyveld's description in terms of "night cuddles with Manu" and "bedding down next to her on a nightly basis" implies sensuality (Gandhi did not even own a "bed" or have a "bedroom"), which is contrary to the intent of Gandhi's celibacy, and this description is not supported by Manu Gandhi's or other witnesses' accounts. Even though this might not be the intent of the author, such descriptions distract readers from the thesis of the book and leave them with an image of a man who appears to be sexually crazed, deviant, and even dangerous.[27]

In addition to books, we must mention a few articles on this subject. Vinay Lal's "Nakedness, Nonviolence, and Brahmacharya: Gandhi's Celibate Sexuality" focuses on the dynamic play of sexuality and celibacy in Gandhi's life. In his innovative analysis, Lal explores Gandhi's later "experiments," in which "Gandhi took to the practice of taking naked young women to bed with him at night," designating this practice as an "experiment in 'sexual celibacy' or 'celibate sexuality.'" Lal argues that Gandhi's practice points to his "simultaneous reliance on, and defiance of, Indian traditions of sexuality and sexual potency, his advocacy of androgyny, and his articulation of the relationship of nonviolence to sexual conduct." Lal discusses the famous legend of Kṛṣṇa and the gopīs from the *Bhāgavata Purāṇa* (to which Gandhi referred to illustrate his yearning for a complete transcendence of sex-consciousness) and notes that "Gandhi had set for himself the ambition to appear naked before God, which for him was nothing other than Truth."[28]

In his article "Was Gandhi a Tantric?" Gier seeks to explain Gandhi's sleeping alongside young women from the perspective of tantric philosophy. Various tantric practices are highly ritualized and esoteric, and some of them embrace sexual rituals. Gier carefully analyzes Gandhi's spiritual practices from different tantric viewpoints and contrasts them with ten "principal generic features of Hindu Tantricism," concluding that "if we can call Gandhi a Tantric, then it is a very unique" and "nonesoteric practice."[29] Moreover, Gandhi's intent was not to achieve esoteric divine bliss, but to accomplish the practical goal of political freedom and peace by quelling communal violence.

The studies described above seek to understand the underlying causes and meaning of Gandhi's unusual *brahmacarya* practices by using diverse hermeneutical lenses. The majority of the studies focus primarily on how Gandhi's *brahmacarya* relates to his relationship with his wife, other women, and his later "experiments" with women. But they do not focus on how Gandhi perceived his nuanced *brahmacarya* as that which requires soul-force and fosters dynamic possibilities of comprehensive self-control—aspects that Gandhi himself deemed essential to his method. *How* Gandhi sought to apply the methods of ascetic disciplines, which categorically fall into the domain of *nivṛtti,* to social and political issues, which are considered the domain of *pravṛtti,* all the while interpreting political actions (*pravṛtti*) as exercises in renunciation (*nivṛtti*)—remains as puzzling to scholars as it was to some of his closest native followers. "The religion of non-violence [a component of *nivṛtti*] is not meant merely for the *rishis* and saints. It is meant for the common people as well," argued Gandhi in order to assert the application of nonviolence for a larger context.[30] If we are to take Gandhi's methods, principles of ascetic activism, and philosophy of life seriously, then it is essential to explore Gandhi's own words for further understanding. Let *Gandhi* explain what he was doing.

Chapter 1 sets up the classic presupposition in which *pravṛtti* and *nivṛtti* are polarized; this is the backdrop against which Gandhi's synthesis of asceticism and activism is considered paradoxical. I argue that, in spite of the traditional boundaries separating inner disciplines and outer activity, there also exist legendary models (*tapasvins*, kings, priests, and even commoners who use their ascetic disciplines to obtain worldly powers) and modern ones (e.g., Swami Vivekananda, who was both a *brahmacārin* and a religious and social reformer) who reflect the permeability of the boundaries between *nivṛtti* and *pravṛtti*. It is not really so revolutionary that Gandhi used the disciplines of *nivṛtti*; rather, what was unprecedented was the way by which he sought to transform the elements of *nivṛtti—ahiṃsā* (nonviolence), *satya* (truth), *brahmacarya* (celibacy), *aparigraha* (nonpossession), and *tapas* (austerity)—into political "weapons" that could be wielded to achieve goals, including political independence, gender equity, Hindu–Muslim unity, and the eradication of India's oppressive custom of untouchability.

Chapter 2 analyzes Gandhi's impetus to construct a paradigm of synthesis that provided an alternative to the polarized understanding of *nivṛtti* and *pravṛtti*. Gandhi not only reinterpreted ancient myths and texts such as the *Bhagavad-Gītā*, and borrowed ideas from Western sources, but he also redefined Indian religious and philosophical (ontological and ethical) concepts such as *yajña*, *tapas*, and *rāmarājya* to create a coherent narrative for the purpose of inspiring his people so that they could realize both their inner strength and reasons to confront the British regime. The application of traditional vocabulary to modern goals was facilitated by his embodied performance: his practice of *brahmacarya* became central to this synthesis in which binary opposites could coexist.

Chapter 3 provides the traditional context for Gandhi's *brahmacarya*. The complexity of Gandhi's *brahmacarya* becomes clear when we study the broad range of rhetoric regarding the various dimensions of *brahmacarya* he employed to further his agenda. On the one hand, Gandhi located his practice in the Hindu traditions by utilizing the traditional definitions and subtexts of *brahmacarya*. On the other hand, he redefined them for his personal empowerment and political methods. Gandhi claimed to base his practice on these redefinitions, which in turn influenced his personal life and political strategy.

Chapter 4 provides a close look at the historical context of Gandhi's *brahmacarya* vow and argues that, for Gandhi, *brahmacarya* was never a private practice. It was a part of his broad strategy of public service, especially the social and political service to India. Moreover, Gandhi's bold transgressions of the orthodox laws of *brahmacarya* were essential to his strategy. While Gandhi found impetus for his vow and practice of *brahmacarya* in the classical traditions, he simultaneously contravened the orthodox conventions required for a *brahmacārin*. Despite criticism from followers and opponents alike, he defended his practices as essential to and consistent with his method of Truth and nonviolence. For him it represented an indigenous form of spiritual power that was antithetical to the militaristic strength of the colonial regime.

Chapter 5 argues that Gandhi was personally influenced by ancient Indian narratives and that these traditional legends became central to his quest for service and Truth, which required sacrifice (and *brahmacarya* was an essential step in this direction). They also provide an insight into the minds of the common populace of India. These stories present models of well-known figures and ascetics who embody the binary strands of asceticism and activism. Gandhi adopted the vocabulary of such narratives and presented legendary characters as exemplars for substantiating his ascetic activism. Scholars have considered numerous historical, political, and psychological factors that are likely to have played a part in Gandhi's acquiring the stature of a *mahātmā*. However, I explore what role Gandhi's narration of myths and his reenactment of the ascetic archetypes played in developing his strategy of ascetic activism. I recount the legends that influenced Gandhi, his own theories about the myths, and the legends he used to authenticate his strategy.

The Conclusion underscores the relevance of studying Gandhi's own accounts of the various dimensions of his *brahmacarya*, as they evolved over time. Gandhi's vast commentary on what he was doing offers a method for understanding his creative and conscious applications of *brahmacarya* and other related ascetic practices for his vision of a "new" kind of politics. Gandhi's reinterpretation of ancient religious texts, myths, and concepts was undertaken not for scholarly purposes, but rather to create a coherent functional narrative so that Indians could see their rich heritage and indigenous resistance methods, ones sanctioned by their traditions. His embodied performance, research suggests, became instrumental in achieving his political objectives (including freedom from oppression and injustice as well as mass mobilization) and his social objectives (including abolishing the custom of untouchability and improving health, education, social justice, and gender equality). Gandhi's application of the elements of *nivṛtti* for his worldly purposes affirms the "flexible" boundaries of *pravṛtti* and *nivṛtti*. Undoubtedly, a synthesis such as his was bound to create paradoxes, which in turn foster both intellectual tensions and revolutionary possibilities.

This study lays the groundwork for more nuanced contextualized understandings of Gandhi's asceticism in general and of his *brahmacarya* in particular. It suggests an essential connection between renunciation and social action for confronting secular problems. It invites scholars and activists to consider seriously the role of renunciation and self-restraint in nonviolent political philosophy and methodology. It also opens up the possibility of studying myth and symbolism in the way that Gandhi himself employed them, not simply as tools in the hands of a shrewd politician but as a comprehensive indigenous hermeneutic.

CHAPTER 1

Challenging the Philosophical Presupposition

Gandhi's Unconventional Synthesis of Asceticism and Activism

Those who want to become passive resisters for the service of the country have to observe perfect chastity.

—M. K. Gandhi

The Vedic dharma is verily a twofold path, characterized by *nivṛtti* [renunciation] and *pravṛtti* [worldly engagement], designed to promote order in the world.

—Śri Śaṃkarācārya

At the outset we can assume that there are two kinds of men in Hindu India, those that live in the world and those that have renounced it.

—Louis Dumont

Assessing the Philosophical Problem of Gandhi's Synthesis

Many of Gandhi's predecessors and contemporary religious, social, and political leaders and reformers had combined religious ideas with political, religious, and social reforms. However, Gandhi uniquely sought to directly apply and embody the elements of renunciation—ascetic practices of nonviolence, celibacy, nonpossession—to address the social problems of poverty, untouchability, and gender inequity, as well as the political problem of India's slavery under the British regime. Therefore, his ascetic practices have been the subject of analysis by a wide variety of hermeneutic techniques—from political to psychoanalytical, as discussed in the introduction. In spite of these scholarly expositions, there remains ambivalence with regard to the underlying mechanics of Gandhi's widely publicized ascetic practices as he related them to his political activism. Perhaps this ambivalence is due to the fact that Gandhi's integration of ascetic practices with his activist agenda has been analyzed against a backdrop of a historically categorical opposition between religious asceticism and politics.

In the secular postmodern era, as in ancient Indian thought, political activism and asceticism—especially the practice of ascetic celibacy—represent two inherently opposite ideologies. Gandhi never explicitly underscored the dichotomy between the religious path of renunciation (*nivṛtti mārga)* and social and political action (*pravṛtti mārga)*; he addressed it only when asked about it.[1] However, he was often reminded by his critics that these ideologies had traditionally reflected divergent paths. For instance in a 1932 letter to Hanumanprasad Poddar, an author and active participant in India's independence movement, Gandhi described his views on the inseparability of these two paths:

> To tread the truth in itself involves entrance into *pravritti.* Without *pravritti* there is no occasion for treading or not treading the path of truth. The holy *Gita* in its several verses has made it clear that a man cannot exist even for a moment without *pravritti.*[2]

In his life and political methods, Gandhi spontaneously integrated secular objectives with his religious pursuit of liberation (*mokṣa*). He emphasized that "these worldly affairs are not a thing to be looked upon with contempt. It is only through worldly affairs that a vision of the Lord is possible."[3] Gandhi's integration of activism and renunciation is not simply a theoretical puzzle, a problem for the secular critic or activist. This paradox was embedded from its inception in the very ethos of Indian ascetic traditions. Unsurprisingly, many of his religious followers questioned his synthesis.[4] We select the template of asceticism and activism because Gandhi was frequently challenged by his close followers as well as his critics on this topic, and because he so relentlessly negotiated the boundaries of the two.

Gandhi's critics and most scholars find it difficult to establish a logical correspondence between Gandhi's vow of *brahmacarya* and his active engagement in sociopolitical issues. Some of Gandhi's contemporary religious and political thinkers and leaders, such as Tilak and Sri Aurobindo (1872–1950), expressed doubts about his embrace of this twofold ideology. June O'Connor reports that in 1939, in a discussion with his biographer A. B. Purani, "regarding the inherent limitations of Gandhi's tactics, Sri Aurobindo faults Gandhi for 'trying to apply to ordinary life what belongs to spirituality,' suggesting that 'ordinary life' and 'spirituality' are two quite different orders and that consistency between them should not be expected."[5] T. S. Rukmani also describes the paradoxical nature of Gandhi's synthesis, saying that he apparently linked two opposing realms. Gandhi committed himself to a life similar to that of "*saṁnyāsins* and considered the whole world as his family," and desired the religious goal of spiritual liberation. Yet at the same time, she points out, his "energies were solely concentrated on achieving independence for the country and his priority was for winning freedom or *mokṣa* (*svarājya*) for his people from colonial rule."[6]

Unlike traditional yogis, saints, and monks of Hinduism, Jainism, and Buddhism who renounce the mundane reality of social and political spheres, Gandhi was completely engaged in the world, as noted by Gier. Even though Gandhi has been compared to the Buddha, his world-affirming ideology is perceived as contrary to the Buddha's principles. "A critic might say that the most significant difference between the Buddha and Gandhi was that the Buddha was a world-denying ascetic and that Gandhi was not," Gier surmises regarding the sentiments of those who see a difference between Gandhi's and Buddha's ideologies. He quotes a critic who expressed the ideological incoherence between the life of the Buddha and Gandhi: "On the one hand is the tranquil Buddha who walks serenely and calmly across the pages of history," and "on the other hand is the Mahātma, speed and energy in every movement, laughing and sorrowing in his ceaseless endeavour to help mankind with the problems of human life." This is a superficial comparison, as the Buddha was no less a revolutionary. Gandhi himself described the Buddha as an activist deeply involved in social reform. However, as Gier points out, Buddha's methods of social reform and Gandhi's sociopolitical activist strategy were different in nature, and "Gandhi should take sole credit for his own brilliant synthesis of religion and political action."[7] Certainly, Gandhi's casting of the Buddha as an activist was consistent with his own unique interpretations of religious figures and texts. He responded to the renowned scholar and poet, Shri Narasinharao, "When the Buddha with the lamb on his shoulder, went up to the cruel Brahmins who were engaged in an animal-sacrifice, it was in no soft language that he spoke to them; he was, however, all love at heart."[8] Gandhi did not perceive the Buddha to be a passive ascetic, but a man of action compassionately engaged in confronting unjust social and religious customs of his time.

Even though Gandhi was never affiliated with any institutionalized ascetic traditions, his renunciatory practices were reminiscent of traditional ascetics. The ambiguity surrounding Gandhi's integration of ascetic practices with political actions arises from the ideological split between renunciation and worldly engagement within Indian thought. A brief analysis of these polarized ideologies is needed to establish the framework in which Gandhi's political activism as well as his philosophy have been analyzed by scholars. The purpose of the following discussion is not to elucidate subtle differences between various ascetic orders, nor to afford a historical analysis of asceticism; rather it is to establish the generic context of renunciation in which Gandhi propounded the utility of ascetic practices, specifically *brahmacarya*, for the field of political activism. Gandhi's arena of politics included not only striving for political freedom, but also social, economic, and personal reforms. For this purpose he sought to employ methods such as *ahiṃsā*, *satyagraha*, and *asahyoga* (noncooperation) and propounded their organic unity with *brahmacarya*.

Tracing the Roots of the Paradox

Scholars such as Dumont, Greg Bailey, and Johannes Bronkhorst have expounded on India's tradition of the "renouncer" or ascetic as it stands in "opposition" to the tradition of the "householder." Dumont, an anthropologist, speculates about the way in which the Hindu social structure differentiates between the "man-in-the-world" and the "renouncer": "The renouncer leaves the world behind in order to devote himself to his own liberation." He claims that world-negating tendencies permeate Hinduism: "Asceticism, not only as a way of salvation, but as a general orientation, the tendency towards a negation of the world—ultramundaneity—have deeply imbued Hinduism."[9] However, it has been argued by subsequent scholars that "Dumont's structural dichotomy between the renouncer and the man in the world," on the ground level in Hindu society, "was much more complex and much less tidy" than he presents it.[10]

Greg Bailey, in an eminent essay, highlights the distinctive nature of the ideologies of renunciation and worldly engagement.

"The ancient Indians considered the words *pravṛtti* and *nivṛtti* to refer both to a distinctive ideology and the life-style informed by that ideology."[11] He emphasizes the contradictory teleological motivations of these disparate methods. The ultimate goals of these two paradigms thus seem to be in opposition. Renunciation leads to transcendence of the conditional world for the purpose of realization of the absolute reality. Conversely, worldly involvement (family, politics, and social conventions) affirms the conditional reality (as perceived in the Advaita Vedānta) of this empirical world of name and form and relationships, by constantly engaging in it. Bailey claims that the ancient Indians considered these two ideologies "to be alternatives, if not opposite poles."[12]

During her discussion of the historical context of the *Mahābhārata*, Dhand also notes the classic dichotomy between the paths of renunciation and worldly engagement: "*Nivṛtti dharma* is envisioned as the structural opposite of *pravṛtti dharma* . . . and is geared radically toward the achievement of personal spiritual ends." After her thorough analysis of these concepts, she concludes that this is the reason that *nivṛtti dharma* is "frequently used as a synonym for *mokṣadharma*, 'the religion of freedom.'" She also examines the *Mahābhārata's* efforts to reconcile "domestic and ascetic ideals."[13] In particular, *The Bhagavad-Gītā* integrates the ideologies of renunciation (*nivṛtti*) and action (*pravṛtti*) through the concepts of *karma yoga* (the path of action) and *karma sannyāsa* (renunciation in action). The *Gītā*'s (III: 19) command, "do thou ever perform without attachment the work that thou must do," reconciles the dichotomy. The karmic bondage is transcended through nonattachment to the fruits of actions. It is, thus, not surprising that Gandhi often drew on this text for substantiating his synthesis; however, Gandhi's interpretation of the philosophy of *karma sannyāsa* was unconventional, as he literally adopted elements of renunciation including *brahmacarya* in his political activities, which will be discussed later.

As the scholarship demonstrates, the rigid boundaries between these concepts are debatable; the ascetic literature of India and the epic and living traditions of Hindu, Jain, and Buddhist renunciates and laypeople present a more complex picture. Bronkhorst and Bailey describe this norm as prevalent in the ascetic traditions of Hinduism, extending to its heterodox traditions, Jainism and Buddhism. In the social stratification of Hindu society, the *varṇāśrama-dharma*—the codes of conduct (*dharma*) prescribed according to distinct caste (*varṇa*) and stage of life (*āśrama*)—represent stages of movement from *pravṛtti* to *nivṛtti*. A systematized progression within the *āśrama* system leads to the goal of ultimate liberation. Three out of the four *āśramas* are marked by renunciatory celibacy. The *Gṛahasthāśrama* (householder state) permits active engagement in society as well as sex and procreation in marriage. Nevertheless, a life of worldly engagement finds ultimate fulfillment not in extraordinary personal and social achievements but in liberation from worldly bondage.

In the Vedāntic traditions, a life of renunciation is superior (*śreyas*) to a life of mundane involvement: even ceremonial acts, for some, are inferior because of *kārmic* constraints. Śaṃkarācārya argues for the superiority of renunciation in light of the lore of *Upaniṣads*.[14] He cites: "'Beholding the transmigratory life as void of all contents, and desiring to vision the Essence, the celibates, in a mood of supreme detachment, go forth into a life of mendicancy' *Nāradapari. U.* 3. 15."[15] Even in the *Mahābhārata*, Bhīṣma lauds the path of *nivṛtti:* "By acts a living creature is destroyed. . . . Yogins, who see the other side of the ocean of life, never perform acts."[16]

This ideology is also clearly reflected in the heterodox traditions of India. In Jain Dharma, Lord Mahavira propagated a life of extreme renunciation and austerities—including fasting, self-control, and bodily mortification—and declared that all *karmas* (actions) cause bondage. The Buddha himself shunned the world of social relationships and responsibilities to seek a life free from a world ever in flux (*anicca*) and suffering (*dukkha*). Patrick Olivelle notes that the following expression common throughout the Pāli canon reveals the "Buddhist attitude to home life": "The household life is a dusty path full of hindrances, while the ascetic life is like the open sky. It is not easy for a man who lives at home to practice the holy life (*brahmacariya*) in all its fullness, in all its purity, in all its bright perfection."[17] The Buddha also advocates the merit of renunciation: "The thoughtful exert themselves; they do not delight in an abode; like swans who have left their lake they leave their house and home."[18] The Buddha recommends a life of mendicancy to those who are serious seekers of *nirvāṇa* (liberation from the cycle of transmigration and thereby *dukkha*).

In praxis, renunciation requires adherence to a broad trajectory of *vratas* (ascetic vows) such as *ahiṃsa, satya, brahmacarya, asteya* (nonstealing), *aparigraha* (absence of avariciousness), *mauna* (silence), fasting (discipline of food)—all of which pertain to self-control and denial of selfish desires, and lead the way to freedom. Gandhi adhered to most of these practices for the sake of personal discipline and also for the success of his political program. He believed that "it is vain to hope for happiness without undergoing suffering. Thus it is that the life of austerity, the fakir's self-denial and other such practices have everywhere been held in high esteem and their praises sung."[19] *Pravṛtti*, in contrast, is predicated on the desire for offspring, wealth, and status, thus signifying bondage. For the goal of *nivṛtti*—"emancipation from worldly attachments"—*pravṛtti* is a hindrance. The inherent dichotomy of these two ideologies is found not only in the classical Hindu context, but is also a part of the matrix of *Dharma* traditions in general.

Scholars of Indian asceticism, including G. S. Ghurye, M. G. Bhagat, and Bronkhorst, trace the origins of asceticism and illustrate the characteristics of the ascetic traditions of India. Those who tread the path of *nivṛtti* and practice renunciatory disciplines are assigned various nomenclatures (e.g., *sannyāsin, muni, sādhu, tapasvin, śrāvaka, yogin, mahātmā*, and *parivrājaka*) that correspond to specific types of renunciation; however, in English they are generalized under the term *ascetic*. Semantically, the word *ascetic*, from the Greek *askesis* (implying rigorous techniques of exertion), has been commonly adopted to refer to renunciates who choose a life of severe discipline for spiritual and religious purposes. Although at times attempts are made to differentiate "austerity" from "asceticism," they both translate the Sanskrit term *tapas*.[20] *Tapas*, from the root verb *tap*, literally meaning "heat," came to be used in the sense of austerity, bodily mortification, penance, severe meditation, and focused observance, and in this sense it is cognate with the word *asceticism*. In the *Bhagavad-Gītā*, Lord Kṛṣṇa identifies himself with *tapas* (austerity).[21] S. Radhakrishnan defines *tapas*:

> *Tapas* is severe self-discipline undertaken for spiritual ends. It is exercised with reference to the natural desires of the body and the distractions of the outer world. It consists of exercises of an inward kind, prayers offered in the heart, self-analysis and outer acts like fasting, self-mortification, sexual abstinence or voluntary poverty.[22]

Within the Indic traditions that form the context of Gandhi's asceticism there have been many shades and grades of ascetics, but an ascetic is generally identified by disengagement from the social world and by a life of self-denial. Gandhi's writings make it evident that he was unconcerned with the distinctive philological and soteriological underpinnings of the different classifications of ascetics. He often used the words, *ascetic, sadhu, saint, seer, tapasvin, yogin, muni, rishi*, and *fakir* interchangeably to refer to those who pledged a life of self-abnegation, sacrifice, and self-mortification (*tapas*) for a higher purpose.

Some political thinkers argue that because engagement in issues of family, society, and, especially, politics is considered this-worldly and a cause of bondage, politics has received very little attention in Indian traditional systems focused on soteriological philosophical discourses. While tracing the foundations of Indian politics, Richard L. Park speculates:

> Political thought, as such, actually received little attention in Vedic times, perhaps because so little importance was given in the philosophic systems to such mundane and essentially transitory matters as politics and government. Through India's long history, political thought did receive serious attention, but the issues raised and the theories propounded tended to be confined to the realm of maintaining law and order. The kernel of the argument was the best means for equating *artha* (public affairs) with *dharma* (cosmic law).[23]

What Park is referring to is the political thought of India which rests on the principles of *dharma* (the duties assigned according to gender, caste, and stage of life) that ordered society, and which is different from the modern notions of politics based on rights and obligations. Nevertheless, political systems were "varied and complex."[24] Historically, some British thinkers were skeptical about "the possibility of self-government" in India. They questioned Indian people's ability to learn political matters, based on a perception that Indians could not understand the political ethos as imagined by Western models. Rudyard Kipling's remarks are worth noting: "They are 4,000 years old out there, much too old to learn that business."[25] Comments such as these arise out of the Aristotelian framework of politics that determines the political trajectory of the Western experience, that is, the idea of a political organization responsible for developing the conditions for the *telos* of human happiness (*eudaimonia*) in secular terms. Social and political systems based on *dharma* (individual and caste obligation) uphold a *telos* of ultimate happiness in the form of liberation from the cycle of death and rebirth, not conditional happiness.

Such remarks, however, were counterbalanced by other British personnel who documented India's social and political structures in the nineteenth century. Gandhi published some of the writings of prominent Englishmen who, on landing in India, found "a hoary civilization" that not only furnished the country with "political systems" but also with "social and domestic institutions of the most ramified description." They also recorded the orderliness in domestic and public life and upright character of Indians.[26] In fact, historically, Indian political theory took two forms: (1) *dharma* texts, where politics is embedded in the normative stratification of the society as a whole; and (2) descriptive exploration of the organization of power in narratives such as the *Mahābhārata* and the *Rāmāyaṇa*. It follows that if political thought is about power, organizational dynamics, rulership, nations, or other collectives signified by territory and strategic relationships, then classical India certainly possessed systematic politics. It is unique in that politics was not treated as a specific discipline, and was inextricably linked to religious codes of *dharma* that ordered the internal structures of the society.

Nevertheless, this political framework would pose difficulty in governance in nineteenth-century India, because the political scene was religiously diverse. British and other Western contacts brought new awareness to the ideas of religious customs, equality, and justice. Many individuals trained in Persian, Arabic, and British education systems and affected by foreign critiques of the Indian social classification began to question the status quo (caste, gender, and social norms). Not surprisingly, in spite of India's traditional forms of political institutions and indigenous systems of laws (*dharma*), an engagement with Western political ideologies, such as democracy and nationalistic tendencies, stirred many modern political leaders and reformers of nineteenth- and twentieth-century India and gave rise to many reform movements.

While these leaders were influenced by modern Western paradigms of politics and social ideologies, they maintained a high regard for their native religious models. Thus, they sought to link religious reform with political involvement, and individual spiritual liberation with political freedom. Consequently, a politicized version of Hinduism emerged that combined secular elements with religious values. Gandhi's ideology of an independent state (*svarājya*) and his vision of free India were deeply influenced by his predecessors and contemporary thinkers who laid this groundwork. However, Gandhi succeeded in communicating a synthesis of religious values and political ideals through his own personal actions and embodiment. Robert D. Baird's edited volume, *Religion in Modern India*, is a valuable resource providing a comprehensive account of many religious movements and thinkers. These thinkers helped create a constructive vision for India. Consequently, after independence, the Indian "secular state" was defined not as "a Godless State" but one in which no one religion would be privileged.[27]

Gandhi's Blurring of the Boundaries of *Pravṛtti* and *Nivṛtti*

Gandhi's unconventional applications of ascetic practices, which included *ahiṃsā* and *brahmacarya*, brought him into conflict with contemporary Hindu nationalists and orthodox Hindus who were distressed by his use of ascetic methods in politics. Within the Indian cultural milieu, characterized by these two distinct and opposing ideologies of religious pursuit and political aspirations, it becomes apparent that Gandhi's renunciatory practices and active political engagement do not quite fit either of the traditional paradigms. J. T. F. Jordens alleges: "In a tradition where the distinction between the 'renouncer' and the involved 'man-in-the-world' was a basic one, he [Gandhi] strove to be both."[28] However, though Jordens claims that Gandhi strove to be both the renouncer and the man-in-the-world—which makes sense in the traditional ideological context—it cannot be confirmed by Gandhi's own words.

In his introduction to the commentary of the *Gītā*, Gandhi announces that he was not a renouncer, in the sense of a man of *nivṛtti*—withdrawing from the conventional path of action—for the purpose of spiritual pursuit. Alter comments, "Gandhi is very clear in pointing out that renunciation is worthless unless it manifests itself in selfless service and social reform."[29] For Gandhi, a *sādhu* (holy man) is defined by actively participating in solving "political problems." He was disheartened by a general apathy in Indian *sādhus* toward India's social and political issues. In a speech at a public meeting he warned: "As long as sadhus do not lend a hand in solving these problems they cannot have the virtues of a sadhu."[30] At the same time, for his goal of service, Gandhi never aimed to be a "man in the world"; rather he embodied renunciation in every aspect of life. Even though Gandhi was never initiated into any renunciate tradition, he resembled an ascetic more than a householder. In his renunciation, Gandhi sought to acquire internal capacities that would enable him to awaken his people to reject foreign rule.

Was Gandhi's synthesis of ascetic disciplines with worldly political methods and goals a novel idea? Was it philosophically coherent? In spite of the apparent contradiction, the synthesis of asceticism and activism can be located in the ancient philosophical and religious systems of India. According to Indian religious lore, *tapas* is commonly considered one of the spiritual disciplines; however, unlike "asceticism" (in the commonly used sense of the word), it is not always observed for the purpose of "spiritual ends," but also for the sake of "various motives where the ends are not purely material but also not moral."[31] Hindu myths depict examples of kings and demons, like Rāvaṇa in the *Rāmāyaṇa* epic, who gain powers through austerities and use them unscrupulously toward practical ends. J. A. B. van Buitenen elaborates on the notion of *tapas* in the *Mahābhārata*, which he translates as austerities, asceticism, and mortification, and states that "the term comes to describe any specific act of self-deprivation aimed at an increase in spiritual power." He elaborates: "The power thus acquired makes the ascetics a kind of new Gods on earth, rivaling and surpassing the Gods, and divinely unpredictable."[32] Many ancient stories illustrate a rivalry between the material strength of the king and the sage's power of austerities, and they often culminate with victory of spiritual strength over material. Gandhi often told the stories of two legendary sages, Viśvāmitra and Vasiṣṭha. These sages are archetypes of such tension. Viśvāmitra was a king, but after witnessing the supernatural power of asceticism of the sage Vasiṣṭha surpassing the might of his entire army, he seeks to acquire the "superior power" through *tapas*.[33] He turns to extreme austerities: "The fire of concentration seemed to burn and reduce all creation to ashes. The gods appealed to Brahma to stop Viswamitra's austerities."[34] Viśvāmitra performs intense *tapas* to overcome *krodha* (anger), and he finally achieves the highest status of a sage. Gandhi considered these legends "allegorical," but believed in the literal potency of *tapas*, power that he sought to acquire in his personal life through his *brahmacarya*, fasting, and other vows. He publicly transformed these austerities into the methods of nonviolent resistance for confronting the military might of the Empire.[35]

The *Bhagavad-Gītā* describes the different forms of *tapas*, observed for the purpose of securing both spiritual and material goals or as simply a practice of "self-torture."[36] Gandhi made a clear distinction between these various forms of *tapas* (*brahmacarya*, nonviolence, and control in speech, for example) and sought to utilize their acclaimed power as an instrument for acquiring specific worldly objectives. Simultaneously, he adopted the vocabulary of *tapas* for the techniques of nonviolent resistance that required self-suffering.

Furthermore, Rukmani's historical analysis traces various phases of religious and philosophical development in India during which the boundaries of dichotomous ideologies were not rigid. For example, according to Rukmani, the prominent Advaita Vedānta philosopher Śaṅkara "expanded the functions of a *saṁnyāsin* to include what is known as *lokasaṁgraha*, i.e. action done selflessly for the welfare of the world." She illustrates that Śaṅkara traveled throughout India with the mission of "the spiritual upliftment of the people at large" and led the way to the ideal of combining the goals of self-liberation and welfare of the people. In the nineteenth and twentieth centuries, this ideal was "enriched at the hands of reformers like Vivekananda, Dayananda Saraswati et al."[37] Bailey, in his treatment of *pravṛtti* and *nivṛtti* as distinct ideologies, and Dumont, in his discussion of the householder and renouncer, seem to overlook the permeable boundaries between *pravṛtti* and *nivṛtti*.

At the dawn of the nineteenth century, an integration of *pravṛtti* and *nivṛtti* began to be more clearly expressed. Many reformers sought to synthesize the realms of religious and social activism and renunciation. Many of these were *sannyāsins* who were deeply engaged with social and political issues. Reformers of this period who combined religious sentiments with social reforms include Raja Ram Mohan Roy (1772–1833)—who devoted himself to rejuvenating Indian culture by reforming politics, education, and social customs—and Swami Ram Tirtha (1873–1906) who propagated a progressive spirituality. Gandhi often referred to these reformers as well as to his contemporaries—such as Shyamji Krishnavarma (1857–1930), Tilak, and G. K. Gokhale (1866–1915).[38] Gandhi was also in contact with Hindu nationalist leaders including Vinayak Damodar Savarkar (1883–1966), who had utilized religious platforms and the rhetoric of celibacy for the purpose of building a Hindu nation and awakening the Indian people to their ancient heritage.

Gandhi claimed that he was not a pioneer in integrating the goal of religious freedom with the ideal of welfare of the world and never claimed to have invented the methods of nonviolent resistance (*satyagraha*) and noncooperation (*asahyoga*) for the ideal of *svarāj*. Although he was unique in popularizing them in the field of political activism, Gandhi admitted that these methods had been introduced by his predecessors.[39] Gokhale had talked of "spiritualizing politics."[40] The objection of philosophical incoherence between the yogic traditions and Gandhi's "this-worldly asceticism" had, therefore, already been addressed to some extent by Indian reformers; Gandhi's synthesis was merely an extension of the earlier formulations. However, Gandhi was unique in constructing his own theories and was also ruthlessly selective and original in interpreting and enacting traditional texts and practices to substantiate his program.

This discussion leads us to the fundamental issue of Gandhi's modus operandi in which, unlike his predecessors or contemporaries, he explicitly advocated ascetic practices, especially *brahmacarya*, as necessary components of his methods to address social and political problems. In other words, it was not entirely unique that Gandhi's philosophy combined the elements of asceticism and activism, because the flexible parameters of both were traditional, as shown by Rukmani and others. Rather, what was unprecedented was that he sought to transform the elements of renunciation into political "weapons" that could be wielded to achieve the social and political goals of self-rule, improved gender relations, self-reliance, elimination of untouchability, and Hindu–Muslim unity. Moreover, Gandhi broadened the scope of those disciplines from their individual-oriented applications for personal liberation to a communal endeavor for the issues at large.

Gandhi's Use of the "Technology" of *Nivṛtti* for the *Telos* of *Pravṛtti*

Nevertheless, the confusion that scholars point to is visible in Gandhi's own words on this subject of *pravṛtti* and *nivṛtti*. It is peculiar that Gandhi, in spite of his title of *mahātmā*, was not a *sādhu* or a *sannyāsin* in the strict, traditional sense of the words. In a 1924 discussion with workers, he declared: "I am not a saint; I am a politician." But he was also not a typical politician. Gandhi explained in an interview, "I have plunged into politics simply in search of Truth." On some occasions while speaking on the subject of his transgression of caste customs, Gandhi would also say that he was a "fakir" and "sannyasi" who was "not bound by social customs."[41] The apparent contradictions, and Gandhi's wavering between the roles of *sādhu* and politician, have caused some scholars and even his contemporary critics to cast him as a "shrewd fellow," and "cunning."[42]

On one hand, Gandhi configured his political actions as religious rituals of *yajña* and *tapas*, and, on the other hand, he prescribed ascetic practices as political methods. This paradox is reflected in Gandhi's choice of words. For example: *ahiṃsā* is "the mightiest weapon" and *satyagraha* is "an all-sided sword."[43] This binary set of propositions, by definition and in practice, is oxymoronic—the prior requires withdrawal, and the latter mandates intense action. Moreover, the practice of *brahmacarya*, which Gandhi deemed compulsory for the purpose of public service, directly relates only to a renunciate. As social anthropologist Peter Phillimore comments, within India's traditions it is not easy to conceive of the practice of celibacy as "divorced from striving for a religious goal."[44] The vow of celibacy generally relates to religious aims. This is usually accurate when the religious ends are differentiated from secular objectives, but Gandhi combined his religious goal with political aspirations as a tactic.

According to Gandhi's own writings, his ascetic methods did not represent the contrived effort of either a *sādhu* or a politician; rather they organically emerged out of his predisposition toward renunciation and service as well as his insight into the superiority of moral power over physical strength and nonviolence over violence. Gandhi realized that he could not command sufficient physical strength to confront the British regime. Instead, he sought in asceticism a defiant force that was an alternative to material and physical strength. His attitude toward extreme self-denial brought him criticism. He answered a correspondent who accused him of having been "an oversexed individual given to excessive indulgence," whose libidinous tendencies seems to have created in him "a sort of disgust towards the sexual act":

> It is wrong to call me an ascetic. The ideals that regulate my life are presented for acceptance by mankind in general. I have arrived at them by gradual evolution. Every step was thought out, well considered, and taken with the greatest deliberation. Both my continence and non-violence were derived from personal experience and became necessary in response to the calls of public duty.[45]

Gandhi was not concerned about securing the title of an "ascetic." Apparently, the underlying difference between Gandhi and an ascetic who chooses austere disciplines for spiritual achievement is that Gandhi prescribed these practices required for a *brahmacārin* as useful tools for nonviolent activism for acquiring the goal of political independence, which he defined as self-rule. Symbolically, the British regime represented the force of unrighteousness, and overcoming it for him required the righteous means sanctified by the religious myths and traditions.

For him, the disciplines of nonviolence and continence had their roots in antiquity, and he discovered their functional value. He claimed himself to be a "practical" visionary, who saw the sum value of any religious observance in terms of its application to the secular and this-worldly. Gandhi intellectually synthesized the goals of *nivṛtti* and *pravṛtti* by saying, "I am endeavouring to see God through service of humanity, for I know that God is neither in heaven, nor down below, but in every one."[46] Thus, each act of confronting injustice and oppression of his people also constituted his *sādhana* (practice, performance, also means of effecting) for God realization.

Indeed, Gandhi was aware of the deep-seated classic bifurcation of the ideologies of *pravṛtti* and *nivṛtti* within his culture. He often faced tough criticism and even dismissal of his ideas as being "impractical." He once stated in a letter to a young man that it would be "cowardice" to "dismiss" his ideas "by saying that I have renounced the world, that I have turned a sadhu, that my ideas are good but impracticable." Gandhi insisted that he was a "practical man."[47] Although his synthesis to some extent carried on a trend begun by his immediate political predecessors as well as some of his contemporaries, Gandhi's political aspirations for Western ideals of democracy, gender and caste equity, and political freedom were original. The means of *ahiṃsā, satya, brahmacarya,* fasting, and poverty became tangible tools for political ends.

Gandhi selectively chose vocabulary and analogies to make his synthesis plausible. For example, he transposed the mundane goal of political independence into the ideal of *svarājya,* which he construed not simply as "self-rule" but as *rāmarājya* (the mythical kingdom of Lord Rāma) and *dharmarājya* (kingdom of righteousness). In a 1921 meeting, he called on *sādhus* to act as volunteers and participate in the social and political reform to reclaim *rāmarājya* with "divine weapons like *yama-niyamas* [restraints and observances traditionally undertaken for spiritual evolution]." He suggested to them that "with just a little practice, you can make these weapons effective." He not only redefined the ideal of a *sannyāsin* and *sādhu,* but also the disciplines of withdrawal.[48] *The yama-niyamas* are traditionally placid disciplines, but their practice requires immense willpower and is believed to yield supernatural powers. Speaking at a meeting of *sādhus,* Gandhi ascertained that if he could practice truth, nonviolence, and *brahmacarya* to perfection, he "would be in possession today of all the supernatural powers they speak of . . . the world would be at my feet and no one would ever want to laugh me out or treat me with contempt."[49]

Whenever Gandhi spoke of the power of ascetic practices, he also recounted their utility for personal discipline and public "purification," for the practice of self-restraint as well as for *svarājya.* He pitted the power of asceticism against armed power. The struggle for *svarājya* by nonviolent methods necessitated that Gandhi and his followers endure physical and emotional hardships such as imprisonment, flogging, and insult. Gandhi's call for the comprehensive practice of ascetic restraint on the part of Indians may have also been directed at Indians working for the regime who were physically involved in intimidating their countrymen.[50] Gandhi also found that the austere life of jail was comparable to the regimen voluntarily observed by a *brahmacārin*: "My first experience of jail life was in 1908. I saw that some of the regulations that the prisoners had to observe were such as should be voluntarily observed by a *brahmachari,* that is, one desiring to practice self-restraint." He concluded that "when they [disciplines] are self-imposed, they have decidedly salutary effect."[51] Gandhi recognized the practical implication of ascetic disciplines and began emphasizing for his *satyagraha* movement its symbolic value in inspiring the masses for social action.

Gandhi's approach may have been religious in nature, but it was political in strategizing the struggle for independence. For example, he interpreted methods of *satyagraha, ahiṃsā, asahyoga* (noncooperation), and *swadeshi* (home-grown goods or self-reliance) as ascetic and ritualistic practices, but directed them toward acquiring sociopolitical goals. Even though Gandhi sought to create a functional plan by combining two apparently different ideologies, he needed to construct a coherent narrative to communicate his strategy and mobilize the masses, conditioned as they were by the tradition of polarized ideologies. Gandhi never claimed to be a scholar, but for his practical purposes he selectively chose texts and models and interpreted them to construct ontological, ethical, mythical, and political theories. Gandhi drew on selected philosophical texts and paradigms within the traditional lore to support his synthesis of these two ideologies, which for him represented complementary rather than contradictory principles. He sought to create a plausible narrative, which utilized the vocabulary and models of the religious traditions of India, yet ideologically defied the norm.

CHAPTER 2

Gandhi's Alternative Paradigm

From Traditional Principles to New Political Purposes

> Never mind what the orthodox people who claim to have studied the scriptures may have to say; they do not represent the masses nor do they represent the real interpretation of the scriptures as I hold it.
>
> —M. K. Gandhi

> Even though Gandhi was married, he vowed to follow a celibate life like the *saṁnyāsins* and considered the whole world as his family.
>
> —T. S. Rukmani

Within the traditions of India, as discussed in the preceding chapter, the components of *nivṛtti*—including *yama-niyamas* and the notion of *tapas*—are aimed at personal liberation (*mokṣa* or *nirvāṇa*). Nevertheless, within the ancient religious narratives and even in the modern Indian context these disciplines have been practiced not only by ascetics but even by laypeople in order to achieve material and worldly objectives (the domain of *pravṛtti*)—including the goals of social improvement and the welfare of the people.

Gandhi's voluminous writings are a repository of myths, folklore, and philosophy that are closely integrated with his personal aspirations and political ideals. In their respective analyses of aspects of Gandhi's life, including his personal and political philosophy, a number of studies have examined his traditional religious context, usually in relation to "fairly standard" Hindu concepts. Some scholars, in their attempt to understand Gandhi's practices, have drawn more unusual comparisons. For example, as discussed earlier, Alter draws a unique comparison between Gandhi's bodily disciplines and the regimen of *pahalwans* (Indian wrestlers).[1] Stanley Wolpert, as another example, correlates the Hindu notion of *tapas* with the Christian notion of *passion* ("the suffering of pain"), as in Gandhi's "passionate resolve to suffer."[2] The Rudolphs and other scholars using psychoanalysis draw comparisons between the Freudian theory of sublimation and Gandhi's conviction in the potency of self-restraint. For Gandhi, the disciplines were also laden with practical, moral, and spiritual meanings.[3]

These varied interpretations have enriched our understanding of Gandhi's nuanced personal and political philosophy in relation to indigenous paradigms. However, many of the foundational elements—Indian and Western—on which Gandhi erected the edifice of his integrated philosophy have been dealt with in isolation and within narrow theoretical frameworks. A reexamination of Gandhi's words within his own historical context supplies a deeper understanding of his usage of ascetic elements in his political methods. In order to create a plausible and functional strategy, Gandhi gave new meaning to religious texts and to the components of renunciation, such as ethical precepts of restraints and observances. He not only established his own version of "philosophy," but he also redefined ascetic disciplines of *sat* and *ahiṃsā* as essential to political goals. Moreover, he located his political principles in prevailing textual, religious, and philosophical prototypes—including the inherent power of truth (Act of Truth), the ideal kingdom of Lord Rāma, ritual sacrifice, and *tapas* (austerity).

Gandhi as "Solely a Path Philosopher"

In order to understand Gandhi's synthesis of *pravṛtti* and *nivṛtti*, it is necessary to begin with an inquiry into the way he used the terms *philosophy* and *philosopher*. The renowned Indian philosopher S. Radhakrishnan emphasized that "philosophy has its roots in man's practical needs."[4] Gandhi defined philosophy not in terms of the analysis of abstract metaphysical, moral, and epistemological questions about reality, the universe, and man; rather, he delineated the function of philosophy only in the context of its application. "Philosophy to be worth anything," wrote Gandhi, "has got to be applied in one's own life."[5] Gandhi's life and works reveal that his philosophy did not pertain to the realm of abstraction; rather its domain was the field of action. In analyzing Gandhi's moral and political thought, Raghavan Iyer notes that "Gandhi was not a philosopher in the sense in which the word is understood today in the West" and asserts that he "was not concerned with epistemological or logical enquiries." Gandhi "was not even a moral philosopher in the strict sense; he was not concerned with the nature of moral appraisals or with the logical status of imperatives, principles and concepts."[6] Gandhi was not bereft of an analytical aptitude: rather it was through reasoning and practical experimentation that he developed his approach to personal and political philosophy. To describe this investigation into truth and morality, Gandhi used the term *prayoga,* which literally means "application," and is generally translated as "experiment." Julius Lipner appropriately suggests, "Gandhi was *par excellence* a thinking activist." "In fact," Lipner emphasizes that Gandhi "claimed to have neither the interest nor the talent for philosophy proper."[7] Gandhi perceived theoretical ideas as inseparable from their practical applications and was hesitant to designate his ideas as "philosophy":

> Well, all my philosophy, if it may be called by that pretentious name, is contained in what I have said. You will not call it Gandhism; there is no ism about it. . . . All that I have written is but a description of whatever I have done.[8]

Pondering abstract philosophical ideas, Gandhi claimed, did not suit him. In fact, when a friend of Gandhi once suggested that he write a treatise on "the science of ahimsa," Gandhi replied, "I am not built for academic writings. Action is my domain . . . All my action is actuated by the spirit of service."[9] Gandhi's journalistic and other writings were part of his domain of action.

Gandhi's experimentation with integrating renunciation and activism and his search for freedom (*mokṣa*) presupposes his understanding of *freedom* as the "ultimate value"—as recognized in Indian philosophical systems. For the attainment of freedom, Indian texts and philosophies recommend undertaking a discipline leading to renunciation, as noted by Karl H. Potter.[10] In a discussion of renunciation as the path to freedom, Potter categorizes philosophers primarily into two camps: "path philosophers" (who advocate a specific path to liberation) and "speculative philosophers" (who speculate about freedom's meaning and methods to achieve it). Potter explains that some philosophers, such as Śaṃkarācārya, Rāmānuja, and Gautama Buddha, are path philosophers as well as speculative philosophers. But according to Potter, "Mahatma Gandhi might be considered solely a path philosopher." Emphasizing the variety in the approach of the

Indian path philosophers, he argues that they "by no means agreed about the theory of paths," but simultaneously notes the common ground they share, that is, "the importance of renunciation and non-attachment [*vairāgya* or *virakti*—literally 'without passion'] to the fruits of actions as the core of renunciation."[11] Within this philosophical milieu, it is evident that Gandhi focused on the practical applications of philosophical ideas, striving for freedom through the path of action. Gandhi himself defined the philosophic mind as having a twofold attitude—detachment and "sympathetic understanding": "A philosophic mind has always meant for me a detached mind and liberalism, a sympathetic understanding of men and things."[12] In this definition, Gandhi combines both intellectual detachment and compassionate attitude toward other beings.

Although Gandhi rejected the formal abstractions of philosophical discourse, he presented his actions as integral to his philosophical goal of spiritual freedom (*mokṣa*), which he described as his "greatest endeavour." He defined both action and *mokṣa* for his purpose: "*Moksha* means elimination of all action, that is, elimination of ego. But that elimination is possible only by burning away the desire for reward. Action is connected with the body and it will go on. We must be its witness."[13] He proclaimed: "All my activities are for *moksha*," and admitted that for him "even the effort for attaining swaraj is part of the effort for *moksha*."[14] In seeking to establish a unity between action and freedom, Gandhi cognitively integrated his immediate goal of *svarāj* with his ultimate goal of *mokṣa* and proceeded to utilize compatible means to achieve it, emphasizing that "Truth, non-violence and the keen observance of *brahmacharya*, etc. are a means to attain *moksha*."[15] These renunciative disciplines were the very techniques that he sought to transform into political means in his fight for *svarāj*.

Most scholars of Indian philosophy have elucidated the philosophy of the *Bhagavad-Gītā*, emphasizing the ontological, ethical, epistemological, and spiritual arguments of this text. Gandhi's commentary on the *Bhagavad-Gītā* is a speech of exhortation that illustrates the value of action for spiritual attainment: "For one who aspires to master *yoga*, the only means is work. If a person lets himself be beaten for a long time on the anvil of work, some day he may be shaped into a *yogi*."[16] Gandhi's effort to unify spiritual life with action in this world, which included actions in the field of politics and social reform, is perceived to be very different than that of the ancient yogis.

Anthony Parel surmises that Gandhi saw "the spiritual life" as "inseparable from action in the world, from the active life in the fields of politics, economics, and social reform. In this respect his spirituality differed radically from the spirituality of the yogis and ascetics of the past and the present."[17] In his assessment, however, Parel is looking at those traditional paradigms that mark the boundaries between action and renunciation. Gandhi himself saw his ideology of active engagement and renunciation from a different angle and judged it to be on par with that of the ancient ascetics. "Do you know that the *rishis* of old were poets, philosophers, cooks, scavengers all rolled into one?"[18] Through such statements, Gandhi sought to provide a dynamically engaged image of ancient sages, who usually are portrayed as reclusive and disengaged from daily activities.

Gandhi was not concerned with establishing the logical compatibility of his concepts; rather he aimed to develop a living strategy in which renunciation and activism, spiritual liberation (*mokṣa*), and political freedom (*svarāj*) were understood to be compatible, rather than antithetical. Accordingly, he integrated ancient concepts with modern aims so that the Indian masses would understand the religious nature of the political enterprise. Gandhi's practice of renouncing sensual gratifications on the path of *karma* was not a unique undertaking. Renunciation is appraised as the supreme ideal in Indian philosophical traditions and literature. The classic Indian poet Kālidāsa aptly describes the supreme ideal of life as "owning the whole world while disowning oneself."[19] Gandhi's originality was that he practiced renunciation as a part of his comprehensive strategy for sociopolitical endeavors. To assess Gandhi's synthesis it is essential to understand the traditional foundation that made this odd mixture both coherent and discernible.

Gandhi's Theoretical Framework: Reinterpretation of the *Bhagavad-Gītā* and the Ancient Narratives

Many Gandhian scholars refer to the *Bhagavad-Gītā* as a philosophical blueprint for Gandhi's ascetic activism. Gandhi's writings reveal that he read the *Bhagavad-Gītā* for the first time in England (1888–89) and was instantly impressed by its teaching of renunciation in action. In a discussion of Gandhi's effort to find "an alternative route," "the otherworldly, esoteric approach to moksha," Parel asserts that "the *Gita* was the single most important influence on his life."[20] Gandhi himself claimed that he derived his political, ethical, and renunciative ideas from the *Bhagavad-Gītā*. He recorded in his *Autobiography*: "The book struck me as one of priceless worth. The impression has ever since been growing on me with the result that I regard it today as the book *par excellence* for the knowledge of Truth." He called it "an infallible guide of conduct" that he continually consulted for spiritual and political guidance.[21]

Like many of India's renowned religious leaders and reformers—from Tilak to Acharya Vinoba Bhave—Gandhi proclaimed the *Bhagavad-Gītā* to be the epitome of Hindu thought. The number of commentaries written by great philosophers and religious leaders confirm this opinion. Most commentators on the *Bhagavad-Gītā* concur that the text integrates distinct strands of Indian philosophy and attempts to resolve the dichotomy between the path of action and renunciation. As a text advocating inaction (*nivṛtti*) in action (*pravṛtti*), the *Gītā* sets up a cognitive resolution of the problem through *karma yoga*—performing actions without attachment (*anāsakti*)—wherein these two polarized ideologies can achieve unison.[22] A prominent modern scholar of *yoga* philosophy, Georg Feuerstein considers Gandhi as a "superb example of a *karma-yogi* and action" and posits that "the fulcrum of Karma-Yoga is our ability to transcend all karmic necessity *in our consciousness*."[23] According to common consensus, the *Bhagavad-Gītā* suggests that *kārmic* transcendence even includes escaping the consequence of committing violence, the most reprehensible form of action.

On the surface, the *Gītā*, in which Lord Kṛṣṇa encourages the warrior Arjuna to fight against his cousins, teachers, and elders, is not overtly pacifistic and does not seem to correlate with Gandhi's ideas of nonviolent activism. Gandhi was often reminded by his "Hindu friends" that in the *Gītā*, "Sri Krishna has encouraged Arjuna to slay his relations," and also that "there is warrant in that work for violence and that there is no satyagraha in it."[24] Given the exegetical traditions of the *Gītā*, it is easy to understand the vexation of Gandhi's friends. Although Gandhi never claimed to be a scholar of the *śāstras* (religious texts), he was acquainted with the acclaimed interpretations of the *Bhagavad-Gītā*—including those of Śaṃkarācārya, Aurobindo, and Tilak. Gandhi acknowledged that he read these commentaries, and also that he drew ideas from them, but without complete satisfaction: "Shankara is dear to me, and so are Ramanuja, Madhav, Vallabha and others—I have relished delicacies from all, but have not been able to satisfy my hunger through what I got from any of them."[25] Gandhi's desire for nourishment through such commentaries was directly connected to his reason for studying religious texts: to satisfy the needs of suffering people, not merely to speculate on the ideas.

These commentaries on the *Gītā* neither deal directly with the choice between violent or pacifistic solutions for political problems, nor do they connect politics to asceticism. Gandhi compared these traditional scholarly expositions to delicacies that can be enjoyed only by the elite. His own garnering of ascetic elements from the *Gītā* for the purpose of nonviolent political activism took a different direction than that of his predecessors.

For example, prominent commentators such as Śaṃkarācārya (eighth century), a proponent of Advaita Vedānta (nondualist philosophy); Rāmānuja (1017–1137), the renowned philosopher of Viśiṣṭadvaitā (qualified nondualist philosophy); and Madhavācārya (1238–1317), a representative of Dvaita Vedānta (dualist philosophy) found justification in the *Bhagavad-Gītā* for their philosophical stances. Arvind Sharma notes that "the *Gītā* has been used either as a base or as a supporting column by commentators to raise the superstructure of their own philosophies."[26] Nevertheless, these commentators did not treat Arjuna's dilemma as a specific issue for guiding ethical conduct.[27]

The exegetical tradition of the *Bhagavad-Gītā* was revived during the nationalist movement in India and was used to incite people to fight against colonial rule. Because of the historical context, the *Gītā*'s call to participate in the *dharma yuddha* (ethical struggle) took on a new resonance. At the turn of the twentieth century, when the nationalist movement for freedom was in full swing, there was a surge of literature on the *Gītā* written by revolutionists and nationalist elites—such as Bankim Chandra Chatterji (1838–1894), Tilak, and Aurobindo—who focused on the text in order to justify the freedom-fighting movement.[28] These politically oriented commentaries intertwined nationalist politics with the spiritual teachings of the *Gītā*, and they all concurred with the call to "action" as the preferred path, rather than the ideal of withdrawal from worldly duties. This trend was utterly innovative in comparison with traditional exegetical conventions. Thus Gandhi himself was not entirely original in this regard.

Tilak and Aurobindo, who each took an active part in the battle for India's independence, presented very sound philosophical arguments that authenticate the way of action for politics—a way that does not exclude violence when necessary. Tilak, a prominent thinker and political figure, wrote an extensive two-volume pedagogic commentary, *Srimad Bhagavadgītā-Rahasya or Karma-Yoga-Śastrā*. In his analysis, Tilak reasoned that since the *Gītā* begins with Arjuna's hesitancy to act and ends with his readiness to fight, the war context and Kṛṣṇa's advice to engage in the fight can be interpreted literally. He notes that when the warrior Arjuna "wanted to back out of the fight, fearing that it would entail the death of Bhīṣma and the others,—though it was his duty to fight—Śrī Kṛṣṇa made him take up the fight of his own accord." Thus, Tilak emphasized the intent of the *Gītā* is to "induce" Arjuna to fight as "the Blessed Lord has, in various places, said: 'Do you, therefore, fight!'" He concluded that the *Gītā* teaches engagement in action with a renunciative frame of mind—rather than physical renunciation of the world.[29]

Another nationalist leader and philosopher who was a contemporary of Gandhi, Sri Aurobindo, saw the slaughter of battle as a necessity for Arjuna because it entailed his individual duty (*svadharma*). "His [Arjuna's] virtue and his duty lie in battle not in abstention from battle; it is not slaughter, but non-slaying which would here be the sin."[30] Aurobindo was inspired by the *Gītā's* gospel of *niṣkāma karma* (desire-less action), but he understood "Sri Kṛṣṇa's admonition of Arjuna literally." In 1908, Aurobindo was arrested in a case implicating him in a bomb conspiracy. A few days before his arrest he questioned the pacifistic attitude in confronting opponents invoking the *Gītā*:

> A certain class of minds shrink from aggressiveness as if it were a sin. Their temperament forbids them to feel the delight of battle and they look on what they cannot understand as something monstrous and sinful. "Heal hate by love, drive out injustice by justice, slay sin by righteousness" is their cry. Love is a sacred name, but it is easier to speak of love than to love. . . . The *Gītā* is the best answer to those who shrink from battle as a sin and aggression as a lowering of morality.[31]

In another essay on the *Gītā*, Aurobindo considered it impossible to destroy evil without "the destruction of much that lives by the evil." During the independence movement in India, he saw the impossibility of following the principle of *ahiṃsā parmo dharma* (nonviolence is the highest law):

> It is impossible, at least as men and things are, to advance, to grow, to fulfill and still to observe really and utterly the principle of harmlessness which is yet placed before us as the highest and best law of conduct.[32]

Aurobindo was skeptical of Gandhi's unequivocal trust in nonviolence for confronting the unjust empire, and he later renounced the political sphere altogether and chose a life of seclusion as a yogi.

Historically, Gandhi's interest in the *Gītā* was prompted in 1889, in England, when two "Theosophists invited him to read with them the *Gita* in Sir Edwin Arnold's translation," and then in 1903 (ten years after his arrival in South Africa), he was once again inspired by Theosophists "to consider his own Hindu tradition." As a result, Gandhi began reading the *Gītā* regularly. After returning to India, Gandhi began to incorporate the message of the *Gītā* into his Satyagraha struggle. Jordens notes the historical beginnings: "He had called a hartal [strike] on Sunday, May 11 [1919], and had suggested that people should observe a fast and read the *Gita*." However, Gandhi's call to read this text for a nonviolent confrontation "led some Hindus to question the appropriateness of that work on such occasion, since they felt it promoted violence."[33] Gandhi became cognizant of the fact that the context of the *Gītā* had motivated many political revolutionaries to participate in social and political actions, including aggressive, militant activism. This became the impetus to convey his own understanding of the core message of the *Gītā* to his fellow Indians.

Gandhi joined the band in formally interpreting the *Gītā* and produced his interpretation (1926), which was published under the title of *Anāsakti Yoga* (yoga of freedom from attachment). Gandhi had already prescribed the disciplines of restraint and detachment for his Satyagraha movement, but with his daily talks on the *Gītā*, which he delivered to his followers as a *kathakar* (religious storyteller), he crystallized his thinking in order to answer his Hindu critics. Ultimately, Gandhi wrote more on this text than on any other subject.[34] Gandhi's interpretation will be addressed later. That he identified the *Gītā* as a treatise of *anāsakti* (nonattachment) provides a clue to the focus of his commentary. He understood *anāsakti* to be central to the *Gītā* and defined it thus: "*Anasakti* certainly means freedom from attachment to anything concerning oneself and one's relations, but also such deep attachment . . . to Truth, to God."[35] Nonattachment was not simply to disconnect from worldly attachments, but a means to connect to Truth. For Gandhi, the pursuit of Truth demanded confronting the untruth (injustice and oppression) of the foreign regime.

Gandhi, who made a commitment "to see God through service of humanity," found it necessary to obtain freedom from attachment to all things personal. For this reason, he considered it essential to observe the vows of *brahmacarya, ahiṃsā,* and *aparigraha*. He selected specific episodes from the epic literature and other religious myths and texts to support his view. For example, he emphasized the importance of nineteen verses in the second chapter of the *Bhagavad-Gītā*. Jordens notes the peculiarity of this focus: "In his favourite text he selected the second chapter, and even more narrowly, the last nineteen verses of that chapter, as its central message."[36] These verses give a description of *sthitaprajña* (a man with perfect control, i.e., an *anāsakta*), which was Gandhi's ideal: "There is a sort of contentment in self-denial," and commanded, "let everyone practise self-denial and be a *Sthitaprajna*." In this section, the *Gītā* explains the comportment of *sthitaprajña*, and "self-denial" for all was not an obvious instruction; rather it was Gandhi's distinctive reading of this section of the text. When asked whether the central teaching of the *Gītā* was selflessness or nonviolence, Gandhi replied, "He who would be *anasakta* (selfless) has necessarily to practise non-violence in order to attain the state of selflessness."[37]

Unconcerned with philosophical consistencies, Gandhi interpreted war symbolically, making it consistent with his practice of ascetic disciplines and advocacy of the nonviolent method. Gandhi interpreted the war context of the *Gītā* as allegorical, representing the "perpetual duel" between good and evil "in the hearts of mankind."[38] Unlike Tilak's and Aurobindo's interpretations, Gandhi's analysis of the *Bhagavad-Gītā* has been evaluated, by some, as "something uncritical" and "on the verge of the sophomoric." Perhaps it is sophomoric for those who are looking for sound philosophical arguments. But for Gandhi it supplied the glossary with which to express his conviction as well as the performance and narration of his strategy: "Just as I turned to the English dictionary for the meanings of English words that I did not understand, I turned to this dictionary of conduct for a ready solution of all my troubles and trials."[39] He utilized the vocabulary and the authority of the *Gītā* in bringing *nivṛtti* into *pravṛtti*. Paradoxically, he espoused the lesson of *karma sannyāsa* (renunciation in action) by literally combining action and renunciation. To support his method of nonviolence, however, he disregarded the explicit message of Kṛṣṇa to fight the war by interpreting it as a literary device.

It is difficult for scholars and believers to see the *Gītā* as the "impetus" for Gandhi's political activity. Kees W. Bolle reflects on the familiar question, "how does Gandhi's political activity, his social action, indeed, how does action in general find its impetus for Gandhi in the text? The answer we must give, I believe, is: 'not very well.'" Gandhi's unconventional interpretation of the *Gītā* renders it a treatise advocating nonviolence. Bolle outlines Gandhi's paradoxical position stating that "he preached nonviolent resistance, while in the text of the *Gita* Krishna repeatedly calls Arjuna to action—and that action is war."[40] This analysis is somewhat myopic, on a par with reading the New Testament of the Bible as a manual for resistance to the Roman

Empire. In fact, Gandhi viewed the *Bhagavad-Gītā* as a text with universal ethical purport in which the war was merely the historical context for Kṛṣṇa's call to action.[41]

In his unconventional rendering of the purport of the *Gītā*, Gandhi seems to be influenced by the New Testament and Edwin Arnold's *The Light of Asia*, subtitled *The Great Renunciation* (1879), a book presenting the life, character, and philosophy of the Buddha. Gandhi recalls in his *Autobiography*:

> [T]he Sermon on the Mount . . . went straight to my heart. I compared it with the Gita. The verses, 'But I say unto you, that ye resist not evil: but whosoever shall smite thee on thy right cheek, turn to him the other also. And if any man take away thy coat let him have thy cloke too,' delighted me beyond measure. . . . My young mind tried to unify the teachings of the *Gita*, *The Light of Asia* and the Sermon on the Mount.[42]

It is also important to remember Western influences in shaping Gandhi's moral thought. In his formative years in London, Gandhi's contact with various thinkers and texts inspired him to think about the questions of vegetarianism, sexual morality, and above all "to value his own heritage." Gandhi's contact with "Ethical Societies" in South Africa seems to have inspired him to put emphasis on ethics as the fundamental and shared principle of all religions.[43] Throughout his life, Gandhi established morality as the touchstone of religion. Furthermore, in his early years in South Africa, Gandhi came across the writings of Leo Tolstoy and became influenced by his life and teachings. In *Indian Opinion*, Gandhi published an article ratifying Tolstoy's philosophy of renunciation, poverty, service, and denunciation of war. Gandhi summarizes the core of Tolstoy's teaching: "Real courage and humanity consist in not returning a kick for a kick."[44] Eulogizing the great author after his death in the *Indian Opinion* (November 26, 1910), Gandhi compared him to a "*maharishi*" who believed that "all religions held soul-force to be superior to brute force and taught that evil should be requited with good, not evil."[45] In his commentary on the *Bhagavad-Gītā*, Gandhi echoes these influences:

> When Tilak . . . was alive, he cited this verse in the course of a discussion about violence and nonviolence. I argued that we should bear with a person who might have slapped us. In reply, he cited this verse [IV.11] to prove that the Gita

> upheld the principle of "tit for tat." That is, we should act towards a person as he acts towards us. I cling to the reply which I gave to him then. . . .
>
> One cannot do evil to others and expect good for oneself. Man has no right to return two slaps for one.[46]

In reaction to this interpretation, Gandhi was harshly criticized by his fellow revolutionaries. In *Young India*, Gandhi published an entire letter from a critic, who accused him of having a philosophy that more resembled that of Tolstoy and the Buddha than that of Indian culture and traditions. To this correspondent Gandhi replies: "I do not believe that 'my philosophy' is an indifferent mixture of Tolstoy and Buddha . . . [although] I owe much to Tolstoy and much to Buddha." He further asserts that "'my philosophy' represents the true meaning of the teaching of the *Gita*."[47] Gandhi's conviction in his interpretation was not based on the mythical context of the text, but rather on the core teaching of equanimity (V: 18): "The men of self-realization look with an equal eye on a Brahmin possessed of learning and humility, a cow, and elephant, a dog and even a dog-eater."[48] For Gandhi, his teaching does not leave room for violence toward an enemy.

Gandhi's interpretation of the *Gītā*, examined within the Indian exegetical tradition, is not scholastic, nor does it advocate a logical philosophical point of view. In the *Gītā*, Arjuna, who implements the teaching of Kṛṣṇa, is neither a nonviolent activist nor an ascetic. Indeed, in the *Mahābhārata*, Arjuna performs ascetic practices to acquire celestial weapons for the battle. How does Gandhi derive his idea of nonviolent activism and ascetic practices for politics from this epitome of traditional Hindu thought? In her acclaimed book *Gandhi's Religious Thought*, Margaret Chatterjee shows the progressive nature of Gandhi's philosophy, which had its roots in Hindu scriptures and folk traditions but also "reaches forward to times which are yet to come." She also analyzes the impact of thinkers such as Tolstoy and posits that Gandhi "interprets the *Gītā* in an idiosyncratic fashion, seeing the message of non-violence in it, a message which belongs more properly to Buddhism and Jainism."[49] However, the renunciate traditions among these religions do not support political engagement of any type; the virtue of nonviolence, in Jainism, requires withdrawal from active life. But Gandhi embodied renunciation in the midst of political activity and sought to convey the underlying core of the teaching, which he crystallized as "detachment." The *Gītā* (IV: 20) states: "He who has renounced attachment to the fruit of action, who is ever content and free from all dependence—he, though immersed in action, yet acts not."[50] Thus, he attempted to make his message of nonviolent resistance, not only by simply renouncing attachments to outcome but also by shedding all forms of dependence on outward means, congruent with the *Gītā*'s philosophy of *karma sannyāsa* (renunciation in action).

While Gandhi may have interpreted the *Gītā* outside of the conventional boundaries of the Indian tradition, he nevertheless thought of his exposition as being congruent with the ever-evolving nature of traditional standards, which had always included radical reinterpretation of existing norms. For Gandhi this interpretation was essential for his conceptual framework of ascetic activism and it functioned on multiple levels: (1) it served to authenticate his combination of activism with renunciation; (2) it provided the vocabulary for his struggle against the colonial regime; (3) it substantiated the strategy of *ahiṃsā* and *satyagraha,* which entailed renunciation of attachments to the body and to family relationships; (4) it afforded a hermeneutic for an alternative interpretation of religious texts and myths so as to create a coherent narrative for his nonviolent struggle; (5) its concepts provided a platform from which to embody and advocate vows such as *brahmacarya* and *ahiṃsā*; (6) and it allowed him to attach new meanings to religious concepts of *sannyāsa, yajña, mokṣa, dharma, ahiṃsā,* and *yama-niyamas*—in the way that the *Gītā* itself has given a new meaning to *karma, sannyāsa, yajña,* and so on.

Gandhi used the same perspective from which he had interpreted the *Gītā* to interpret other Indian literature, especially selected myths, in order to communicate his strategy of ascetic activism. To support his philosophy he selectively chose references from the *Upaniṣads,* the *Purāṇas,* the *Mahābhārata,* and the *Rāmāyaṇa,* as well as from Jain and Buddhist literature. He adopted renunciative concepts that carry inherent spiritual power—illustrated in the myths of India—for his method, his vocabulary, and his embodiment of an ascetic activist. This is especially visible in Gandhi's concept of *satyagraha,* which for him was "*tapasya* [austerity] in its purest form."[51] An analysis of Gandhi's *satyagraha* as it relates to the metaphysical and mythical ideas of the power of Truth is essential in order to understand how he created a strategy that substantiated his method and mobilized the masses.

The "Power of Truth" and the Political Strategy of *Satyagraha*

Numerous scholars, such as Jordens, maintain that the "idea of passive resistance to evil came to Gandhi from a variety of sources."[52]

In his outstanding book, *Gandhi and the Nonconformists,* James D. Hunt examines the possible influence of the "passive resistance campaign then underway in Britain against the Education Act of 1902" on Gandhi's *satyagraha* movement in South Africa against "discriminatory restrictions." Hunt shows the significance of this movement in Gandhi's campaign, stating that "it was an important model for Gandhi" during the inception of his method of passive resistance (although Gandhi does not mention this in his *Autobiography*).[53] The earlier sources, acknowledged by Gandhi himself, include the writings of Tolstoy and the *Gītā,* the Sermon on the Mount, and Shamal Bhatt's poem "For a Bowl of Water." The obvious reason for Gandhi's omission of the origins of the method of Satyagraha from the *Autobiography* is that he refers the reader to his earlier writings in South Africa.[54] More importantly, Gandhi had moved away from the notion of "passive resistance" to establish the distinctiveness of his method of Satyagraha.

In a 1917 article, Gandhi differentiated the idea of "passive resistance" from *satyagraha* by citing a more recent model, the Suffragette Movement in England:

> 'Passive Resistance' conveyed the idea of the Suffragette Movement in England. Burning of houses by these women was called 'passive resistance' so also their fasting in prison. All such acts might very well be 'passive resistance' but they were not 'satyagraha.'

Gandhi wanted to disassociate his method from passive resistance because that phrase suggested passivity and was also imbued with conflicting contextual meanings. He replaced the term *passive resistance* with *satyagraha,* which, rather than implying inertness or passivity, represented a "strong weapon." Gandhi said that neither "passive resistance" nor its Hindi rendering *"nishkriya pratirodha,"* very accurately described "the force denoted by the term." He later said that "Satyagraha is not physical force . . . Satyagraha is pure soul-force. Truth is the very substance of the soul."[55] He also called it "Loveforce" because it seeks to transform the opponent through love.

In India, Gandhi also sought to mold his movement according to indigenous religious models and the vocabulary known to the people of India. Not surprisingly, some scholars, such as Bondurant, Heinrich Zimmer, Iyer, and Parekh, have also explored the roots of Gandhi's *satyagraha* within the Indian traditions. Their analyses present ethical, epistemological, and metaphysical connotations of the "*sat*" of *satyagraha.* Bondurant posits that "the *satya* of satyagraha is understood in the ethical sense."[56] Iyer comprehensively reviews Eastern and Western philosophical concepts of truth and submits: "The Rigvedic and Platonic notion of the ever-existent Absolute Truth was essential to Gandhi for the purpose of endowing truth . . . [with] the highest moral value and the highest human end."[57] Gandhi himself described the "etymological meaning of the word *satya*" in this way: "It is derived from the root '*sat*,' which means to exist eternally. That which exists eternally is *satya*, Truth, it can be nothing else." In the same discussion of Truth, Gandhi said that he preferred *sat* as the name of God, not because "I was . . . led to the conclusion that Truth is God by considering that God is formless and so is Truth. But I saw that Truth is the only perfect description of God." He wrote in his first "Thought of the Day": "Hence verily Truth is God," and, through this characterization, he embraced a more universal notion of God (Reality), which eventually helped him relate to the people of different religious traditions and even to atheists.[58]

Satya is also considered "at times as entirely equivalent to *dharma*."[59] Gandhi perceived the inherent unity between metaphysical truth and the cosmological principle of *dharma* (which he usually equated with morality) when he said that "morality is the basis of things, and that truth is the substance of all morality."[60] *Sat* (Truth) in Gandhi's *satyagraha* does not merely mean empirical truth. Gandhi explains his notion of Truth as, "Not truth simply as we ordinarily understand it, that as far as possible we ought not to resort to a lie . . . But here Truth, as it is conceived, means that we have to rule our life by this law of Truth at any cost."[61] In this notion of *satyagraha*, a term combining the two principles of renunciation and activism, namely, *sat* (Truth, Being, and Reality, connoting stillness) and *āgraha* (persuasion, hold, force, signifying action), Gandhi sought to make the law of truth an active principle of personal and public strategy. In this creative combination of the two words *satya* and *āgraha* (derived from a response to his public call for an alternative term for passive resistance), he combined aspects of *nivṛtti* with *pravṛtti* for social and political goals. In this way, he embraced the metaphysical and moral meanings of *Sat*: *Sat* as *Brahman* (Ultimate Reality), *sat* as virtue, and *sat* as one's own moral duty (*svadharma*). Although Gandhi's *satyagraha* was a political strategy—which Parekh describes as "an ingenious combination of reason, morality and politics"—for Gandhi it also meant mobilizing the "miraculous power" of truth celebrated in Indian religious narratives and traditions.[62] In 1942, during a long interview with Gandhi (which lasted for several days), biographer Louis Fisher asked him, "How do you account for your influence over so many people?" Gandhi replied: "I think my influence is due to the fact that I pursue the truth."[63] Gandhi was referring to the miraculous power of truth that enables whoever possesses it to perform miracles. In a 1921 article, "What Is Truth?" Gandhi writes:

> And when the sun of truth blazes in all its glory in a person's heart, he will not remain hidden. He will not, then, need to use speech and to explain. Or, rather, every word uttered by him will be charged with such power, such life, that it will produce an immediate effect on the people.[64]

Gandhi affirmed the ancient belief that the magical power of truth can be manifested in the hearts of humans who cling (*āgraha*) to their truth, namely, to their moral duty. Iyer states: "[Gandhi] held to the Indian belief that a man who has lived in accord with the law of his true nature . . . can cause anything to happen by the simple act of calling to witness the power of Truth or God." This belief also entails that such a person endowed with the power of truth "becomes a living channel of cosmic power, the power of Eternal Truth, the highest expression of his inmost soul."[65] The concept of activating the power of the truth or the moral force (*satyagraha*), in order to perform his duty to fight against social injustice might appear to be Gandhi's unique conception—particularly in the context of modern-day politics—but this belief in the power of truth is ancient. Gandhi admitted that his belief in the superiority of "the power of truth" or "soul-force" was not his "invention." He pointed out that "it is a doctrine enunciated in our Vedas and Shastras. When soul-force awakens, it becomes irresistible and conquers the world."[66]

Gandhi was referring to the power of truth and moral virtue, which has been explicated by Indologists such as Eugene Watson Burlingame, Zimmer, and W. Norman Brown. This notion is expressed by the words *saccakiriyā* or *satyakriyā* (Act of Truth; oath) found in the parables, fables, and anecdotes of ancient Sanskrit and Pālī literature.[67] This motif was initially described by the prominent American philologist Burlingame as "a piece of magic."[68] Zimmer and Brown demonstrate that common to these narratives is the view that the power of truth manifests itself when individuals perform their duty (*dharma*) to perfection and with an adherence to moral quality. Both scholars mention Gandhi as a modern example of someone who relied on the truth-force to fulfill his duty of confronting social injustice observing the moral quality of absolute *ahiṃsā*.

Brief citations from the above scholars' expositions further illuminate the concepts underlying Gandhi's *satyagraha*. Zimmer defines truth as "that radiance of being which shines through the man or woman enacting perfectly the part of dharma."[69] In his seminal article "Duty as Truth in Ancient India," Brown also notes: "There existed in ancient India a belief that Truth has a power which a person with the right qualifications can invoke to accomplish wonders or miracles." By citing legends from Buddhist and Hindu texts, he notes that the Act of Truth is "based upon some quality or attainment of the user of the Act."[70] This quality is usually an observance of a specific moral virtue and varies according to the nature of the agent who performs the *satyakriyā*. The observance of moral virtues such as nonviolence, truth, celibacy, or charity necessitates the willingness to renounce all for the sake of the virtue.

In their respective articles, Burlingame and Brown both show how performance of an Act of Truth, as narrated in the ancient legends is made possible by individuals when they religiously adhere to their *dharma*. Brown explicates:

> One who can rightly be called "true," meaning "fulfilling his duty perfectly," has the power to perform "miracles." Such, as I understand the Vedic belief and the belief in later times, is the sanction for the Act of Truth. When a person fulfills his duty perfectly, he gains this power.[71]

Traditionally, an Act of Truth is applied in individual situations, wherein an agent performs *satyakriyā* for a specific purpose. Burlingame and Brown provide examples from the Buddha's "birth tales," Buddhist legends (such as the story of the prostitute Bindumati in the kingdom of emperor Aśoka), as well as the stories of King Śibi (Śivi), and Damyantī from the *Mahābhārata*. King Śivi possessed the virtue of generosity; the princess Damayantī practiced pure chastity; the prostitute Bindumati acquired power by serving all men alike, whether of high or low position. Brown concludes that, according to the legends, "it seems clear that in every case the Act of Truth is effective because it is based on the rare phenomenon of personal duty completely fulfilled."[72] The fulfillment of duty is enabled through an absolute commitment to a single virtue or vow.

Zimmer also sees fulfilling one's role in life as equivalent to performing an Act of Truth: "[T]he one who has enacted his own dharma without a single fault throughout the whole of his life can work magic by the simple act of calling that fact to witness."[73] Brown maintains that this ancient belief is found in the myths, "that Truth—of the right sort—has such power still persists in an attenuated form in India." He asserts that "in modern India, Gandhi had something partly similar in mind when he taught that the highest goal of human behavior is

Satyāgraha, a Sanskrit term meaning literally 'Steadfast adherence to Truth.'"[74] He sees a recurrence of the mythical motif of *satyakriyā* in Gandhi's commitment to the duty of serving India by observing the method of absolute nonviolence. In his writing and speeches Gandhi often remarked "that in everything that he did, he was prompted by his love for truth and dharma."[75]

Gandhi's *dharma* and love for truth manifested themselves in his avowal to confront social injustice in the form of inequity and unjust foreign rule. Gandhi's declaration to take up his duty occurred in South Africa (1893), where on a dark night he was pushed out of a train by a white man because he was "colored" and had no right to travel in the first-class compartment. During that night Gandhi made a solemn commitment, he recalled many years after, to confront social injustice related to color prejudice: "I began to think about my duty . . . I should try, if possible, to root out the disease and suffer hardships in the process."[76] This incident became the cornerstone of his duty (*dharma*) to public service (which eventually resulted in the Satyagraha movement to secure political freedom) and led him to sacrifice all for this goal—his lucrative profession, dedication to his personal family life, and physical gratification.

Thematically, Gandhi's declaration of *satyagraha*, for which he observed the vow of *ahiṃsā* (nonviolence, which for him necessitated observance of the ascetic disciplines) certainly had undertones of the moral power reminiscent in an Act of Truth (*satyakriyā*). The epic literature, according to Gandhi, is replete with examples of those who followed the path of truth and worked wonders. For instance, in the *Mahābhārata*, Bhīṣma, to fulfill his duty toward his father, takes the *brahmacarya* vow and acquires marvelous powers. Gandhi often quoted the legend of Sāvitrī in the *Mahābhārata* that illustrates the procuring of boons through the performance of one's own *dharma*: Princess Sāvitrī liberates her husband from the jaws of *Yama* (Death) by following the *dharma* of a virtuous wife. Gandhi's recounting of his favorite mythical characters displaying the miraculous power of Truth is addressed in more detail in chapter 5.

Gandhi drew on ancient legends that illustrate the power of commitment to truth. In his daily discourse and numerous publications, as he developed his Satyagraha movement, he cited such myths in order to illustrate the power of Truth and its demands for sacrifice:

> And in order to satisfy the definition [Truth, which is not simply factual], I have drawn upon the celebrated illustration of the life of Prahlad. For the sake of Truth, he dared

> to oppose his own father, and he defended himself, not by retaliation by paying his father back in his own coin, but in defence of Truth, as he knew it, he was prepared to die without caring to return the blows that he had received from his father . . . with a smile on his lips, he underwent the innumerable tortures to which he was subjected, with the result that at last, Truth rose triumphant, not that Prahlad suffered the tortures because he knew that some day or other in his very life-time he would be able to demonstrate the infallibility of the law of Truth. That fact was there; but if he had died in the midst of torture, he would still have adhered to Truth. That is the Truth that I would like us to follow.[77]

Gandhi believed that "working under this law [moral force] of our being, it is possible for a single individual to defy the whole might of an unjust empire."[78] Brown sees Gandhi as a modern example of someone performing a Truth Act:

> It [The Act of Truth] was also Gandhi's way. He seems to have considered that whatever end he felt was a just one constituted truth. The practice of ahiṃsā "Nonviolence" was in his view such an end; in fact, in the whole realm of ethics it was apparently for him the cardinal principle; unfailing observance of it would bring victory over injustice. Hence, he inaugurated a campaign of Satyāgraha, "strict adherence to Truth," which had as its most important doctrine the unswerving practice of Nonviolence.[79]

Gandhi's writings and actions reveal that for him nonviolence required a comprehensive control of the senses. His conviction in the power of Truth mirrors the above examples from the ancient legends. However, his performance of the Act of Truth—if we can call it such—appears to differ in several notable ways from traditional applications of *satyakriyā*. First, Gandhi extended the *satyakriyā* from individual performance to a community affair—mass participation—by testing its power in the political arena. His objective was not personal; rather, it was for a larger concern, that of acquiring social justice and political freedom. Second, Gandhi believed in the *śāstra's* (scripture's) declaration that even one self-controlled person is able to accomplish difficult tasks; however, he knew that *satyagraha* against an empire mandated adherence to Truth by a great number of people, not merely a single individual.

> Satyagraha is an immutable law. We are now applying it to a new field. Till now, its application has been confined to the individual family relationships. We have enlarged the scope of its application and have also moved from the individual to the mass. I have realized from numerous experiments that its extension in both respects is possible.[80]

Third, the Act of Truth as described in the ancient narratives is powerful, yet a rarity, applied by a few virtuous individuals for specific purposes, as Brown suggests. In the Vedic literature it appears to be often monopolized by "the authoritative ritual specialist, in particular the Brahmin."[81] In his exemplification of *satyagraha*, Gandhi sought collective performance of Truth—not by some specialist sages or Brahmins or virtuous individuals—but by the marginalized masses. Gandhi acknowledged that the thousands who took part in the famous Salt Satyagraha were "average" men and women: "They were erring, sinning mortals" who were participating with him in the movement of Truth-force against an unjust law.[82]

Fourth, Gandhi universalized the Act of Truth by citing examples of individuals from traditions other than his own—Daniel, Socrates, Jesus Christ, Latimer, Imams Hasan, and Hoosein—who demonstrated their dedication to Truth. These legendary figures illustrate the power of firmness in Truth and the readiness to sacrifice all for duty.

A fifth difference between the traditional application of an Act of Truth and Gandhi's application of the Truth-force is evident in his mechanism of *satyagraha*. Brown insists that the success of a *satyakriyā* depended solely on the personal veracity and will of the performer and this "success 'is not dependent in any degree upon the favor or grace or will of any deity.' "[83] Gandhi, however, although firm in his own will power, emphasized that he relied upon God's aid for the success of his Truth-force. "I am a conscientious follower of Truth, and I have hope and faith that God will give me the strength to pass Truth's ultimate test."[84] Even though Gandhi defined God in an abstract term as Truth, he trusted in the power of prayer and the Divine will.

Last, the goal of Gandhi's application of Truth-force was not the magical power of supernatural achievement, but rather the miracle of making the millions of ordinary Indians firm in their search for *svarājya*, rendering the empire ungovernable and thereby forging a change in British minds and hearts. He believed that a collective effort in following Truth could provide *svarājya* to India:

> Truth shines with its own light and is its own proof. In these evil times, it is difficult to follow truth in such perfection

> but I know it is not impossible. If a large number from among us strive to follow it even in some measure, we can win swaraj. We can also win it if a few of us pursue it with utmost consciousness.[85]

Gandhi realized that the method of *satyagraha* for the freedom of the masses required a massive effort by many, a miracle of a different sort. Its goal was to engender inner empowerment of Indians and, at the same time, to create a feeling of powerlessness among the British authorities.

Thus, Gandhi's version of *satyakriyā,* with its unconventional objective of securing political freedom, required a nontraditional approach—collective involvement in the performance of the Act of Truth. This in turn needed a constructive strategy that could unite different factions within India. Gandhi asked: "But how is one to realize this Truth which may be likened to the philosopher's stone or the cow of plenty?" He reached the conclusion: "[T]he quest of Truth involves *tapas*—self-suffering, sometimes even unto death. There can be no place in it for even a trace of self-interest."[86] Gandhi knew that the idea of self-suffering for higher goals is present in some form in all religions and was therefore something to which people of different faiths would be able to relate. In his writing one can see Gandhi beginning to realize that austerity—willingness to sacrifice all for one's duty—is the core of Truth-force:

> [H]e alone is a satyagrahi who gives up everything for the sake of truth—forgoes wealth and property, allows his land to be auctioned, parts from his relatives, from his parents, his children, his wife, and sacrifices dear life itself. He who thus loses for the sake of truth shall gain.[87]

Gandhi's *satyagraha,* based on the moral quality of absolute *ahiṃsā,* is predicated on a life of *tapas*—austerity and voluntary suffering. Gandhi's combination of ascetic practices for *satyagraha* is metaphysically consistent with the law of the Truth Act, but at the same time it has a practical side, as it prepares the nonviolent resister for self-sacrifice.

Activating the Power of *Sat* through *Ahiṃsā*

Gandhi saw a direct connection between *ahiṃsā* and *satya.* He announced in his *Autobiography*: "[A] perfect vision of Truth can only follow a complete realization of Ahimsa."[88] *Ahiṃsā,* for Gandhi, was a comprehensive principle and involved the observance of *brahmacarya* and other renunciatory practices. It was the touchstone of Truth—the highest *dharma*—manifesting itself in compassion and goodwill. Moreover, *ahiṃsā* was not merely abstaining from violence; nor was it a political tool. It was comprised of supernatural potency. Gandhi proclaimed the miraculous power of *ahiṃsā*:

> Anyone who has completely shed hatred and ill will, who has succeeded in making his life a perfect embodiment of Truth, can command everything in life. He does not have to ask that anything be done. He has only to wish and the wish will be fulfilled.[89]

Gandhi made the notion of *sat* the metaphysical basis for his *satyagraha,* and construed the ethical principle of *ahiṃsā* as the fulcrum for his power of Truth. However, they were, in his opinion "obverse and reverse of the same coin."[90]

Gandhi's distinguished contemporaries such as Lala Lajpat Rai (a reformer and political leader) and Aurobindo were skeptical about elevating *ahiṃsā* to such a high status. Dennis Dalton, comparing Gandhi with Aurobindo, notes that Aurobindo "saw nonviolence as less powerful than violence."[91] Lala Lajpat Rai believed that "the elevation of the doctrine of *ahimsa* to the highest position contributed to the downfall of India." However, Gandhi's *ahiṃsā* was the nexus of his Truth-force. Gandhi provided an anatomical metaphor asserting the deep connection between *sat* and *ahiṃsā:* "Ahimsa and Truth are as my two lungs. I cannot live without them."[92] On the relationship between Gandhi's *satyagraha* and *ahiṃsā,* Dalton says: "Satyagraha could be activated only through strict adherence to *ahimsa* because the real energy of the former came from the latter."[93] For the purpose of understanding *ahiṃsā* as the activating agent of *satyagraha,* it behooves us to consider how Gandhi defined *ahiṃsā*—a component of *nivṛtti*—for his activist strategy.

Bondurant gives a brief historical analysis of *ahiṃsā* within the Indian religious teachings: "This aphorism [*ahiṃsā parmo dharmah*] is known in every village in India, as are stories from Hindu, or Buddhist, or Jain classics illustrating the spirit and duty of non-violence."[94] *Ahiṃsā,* etymologically, with the negative prefix "a," is the negation of the word *hiṃsā,* meaning "to kill" or "to injure"; hence it is translated as "not harming" or "non-injury."[95] *Ahiṃsā* is the highest principle of *dharma,* the ethical code of conduct and is the comprehensive principle of noninjury in thought, action, and speech. Zimmer elaborates on the singular value of *ahiṃsā* in the *dharma* ethics: "*Ahiṁsā*, 'non-violence, non-killing,' is the first principle in the dharma of the saint and sage—the first step to the self-mastery by which the great yogīs lift themselves out of the range of normal human action. They attain through it to such a state of power that when and if the saint steps again into the world, he is literally a superman."[96] However, Gandhi related both *sat* and *ahiṃsā* as instruments of "self-mastery," bringing them both within the reach of the common masses in the struggle for the political freedom of India. "'Satya,' in truth, is my God. I can only search Him through non-violence and in no other way[,] and the freedom of my country as of the world is surely included in the search for truth."[97]

Gandhi utilized a mythical vocabulary lauding the virtue of *ahiṃsā*. However, his approach to *ahiṃsā* as a political weapon differed from traditional praxis on four grounds: (1) stipulation for those who practice *ahiṃsā* to not merely do works of compassion or goodwill but to confront acts of violence; (2) the integration of a militaristic approach into *ahiṃsā*; (3) an expansion of the scope of *ahiṃsā* by directly relating it to other *yamas* (restraints or required disciplines of self-control); and (4) the evocation of *siddhi* (supernatural power) associated with observance of *ahiṃsā* for his nonviolent movement.

The common understanding of *ahiṃsā* in the ascetic traditions of India equates it with indifference and passivity—abstaining from actions that involve conflict. Parekh elaborates: "For Hindus and Jains, *ahiṃsā* was born out of either indifference to or passive goodwill towards the world, and even the latter was not the same as compassion."[98] Gandhi was born and raised in Gujarat, a state with most of the world's population of Jains. A central tenet of Jain belief is the doctrine of nonviolence. Gandhi had many conversations with Jain *munis* (renunciates) who avoided actions that potentially harm or do violence to creatures. Gandhi proclaimed the impossibility of following absolute *ahiṃsā* while living and stressed that "even the forest-dweller cannot be entirely free from violence in spite of his limitless compassion. With every breath he commits a certain amount of violence. The body itself is a house of slaughter."[99] Even though he was influenced by Jainism's principle of *ahiṃsā*, he did not agree with the Jain version of extreme nonviolence toward minute creatures. He expanded the definition of *ahiṃsā* arguing that "passion and malice are nothing but violence. Non-violence does not merely consist in sparing the lives of bed-bugs or flies. That indeed is non-violence in its lowest form." Furthermore, Gandhi deviated from the normative tradition and redefined *ahiṃsā* as an activist strategy in the sociopolitical sphere. He reverses the conventional religious wisdom that suggests the observance of nonviolence by minimizing activities and declares, "Ahimsa without action is an impossibility."[100] The virtue of *ahiṃsā* has to be performed in the arena of life in order for it to be effective. Just as he sought to give new meaning to the power of Truth, he transformed the concept of *ahiṃsā* from being an element of passive withdrawal from action to an element of active engagement in confronting violence. Gandhi made a novel connection between the practice of *ahiṃsā* and participatory resistance to violence: "No man could be actively nonviolent," he pronounced in 1940, "and not rise against social injustice no matter where it occurred."[101] This proclamation commanded an active participation in public life, not renunciation.

Not only did Gandhi seek to transform *ahiṃsā* into an activist instrument, he translated *ahiṃsā*—a restrictive vow—into a virtue with the positive connotations of love and compassion. Is this unique? Indian traditions also advocate practicing the virtues of *maitri* (compassion and friendliness) and *abhayadānam* (giving protections to living beings), and cultivating an absence of ill-feelings toward living beings. In his discussion of Gandhi's theory of nonviolence, Parekh surveys the multifarious understanding of the virtues of *maitri* and *ahiṃsā* in Hinduism. He notes that the "Hindu religious tradition enjoins on man the duty of universal *maitri* or friendliness and goodwill."[102] Gandhi unequivocally related compassion and forgiveness to the practice of *ahiṃsā* and also conveyed its inherent miraculous power. He selectively chose references from ancient teachings: "Our civilization tells us with daring certainty that a proper and perfect cultivation of the quality of ahimsa which, in its active form means purest love and pity, brings the whole world to our feet."[103] In imputing supernatural value to this virtue, Gandhi cited religious lore:

> Our *shastras* seem to teach that a man who really practises ahimsa in its fullness has the world at his feet, he so affects his surroundings that even the snakes and other venomous reptiles do him no harm. This is said to have been the experience of St. Francis of Assisi.[104]

Which "*shastras*" was Gandhi referring to? Gandhi often referred to the *Yoga Sūtra of Patañjali*, which describes the ten moral disciplines for self-control (including truthfulness, nonviolence, and celibacy) and classifies them as *yamas* and *niyamas*.[105] In the texts of both heterodox and orthodox traditions, these disciplines, in some form, are deemed necessary for those who tread the path to *mokṣa* (liberation). Parel states that in Patañjali "non-violence was considered as the personal virtue of the yogi. Its ultimate aim was to encourage him to withdraw from society and polity into the solitude of spiritual life."[106] However, Gandhi sought to make this virtue a public strategy by drawing on the inherent power ascribed to nonviolence by Patañjali himself. Through his innovative rendering, he envisaged an instrument for social action that would serve both social and political ends: cultivation of empathy for fellow beings oppressed under discriminatory systems and a collective confrontation of the British regime.

Gandhi concurred in the importance of these vows for the discipline of mind and body and held that those "who have gone through the preliminary discipline" are "eligible for yogic practices."[107] But Gandhi also noted that the *Yoga Sūtra* imputes a supernatural achievement to each of the restraints. With regard to the practice of *ahiṃsā*, the *Yoga Sūtra* (II: 35) says: "In the presence of one firmly established in non-violence, all hostilities [*vaira*] cease." Various commentators of the *Yoga Sūtra* cite examples from ancient Hindu myths describing how "even wild animals forget their nature of causing pain in the presence of one established in *ahimsa*."[108] Ancient literature provides examples in which animals with hostile relationships, such as snake and mongoose, or cat and mouse, leave their antagonistic nature in the presence of a *yogin* "who is grounded in the abstinence from injury."[109] It seems that through his advocacy of a collective performance of *ahiṃsā*, Gandhi was seeking to engender the absence of hostility among various factions in India—Hindus and Muslims, higher caste and untouchables, British authorities and Indians—and that he felt a sense of failure when violence erupted.

Despite his setbacks, Gandhi continued to believe in the exalted power of *ahiṃsā* to transform the heart as well as the surrounding environment. In his *Autobiography*, Gandhi recorded a childhood incident in which he handed a letter confessing his stealing to his stern father. After reading the letter, "pearl-drops trickled down his [father's] cheeks." Gandhi interpreted this response, which was without any feelings of anger, as one of "pure *ahimsa*." He concluded: "When such *Ahimsa* becomes all-embracing, it transforms everything it touches. There is no limit to its power."[110] Using the same principle, Gandhi, by calling for a mass performance of nonviolent resistance, sought to awaken the British conscience to the realization of the injustices of their governance.[111] Dinanath Gopal Tendulkar writes in his biography of Gandhi: "Gandhi's ambition was nothing less than the conversion of the British through non-violence, so as to make them see the wrong they have done in India."[112]

Gandhi not only redefined *ahiṃsā* as *pravṛtti* for the sociopolitical sphere; he also related his form of *ahiṃsā* back to the traditional disciplines of *nivṛtti, yama,* and *niyamas.* He transferred the value of practicing all restraints (*yama-niyamas*) to his method of *ahiṃsā* in his pursuit of *svarājya.* He saw *ahiṃsā* as being intimately connected to all the disciplines of *nivṛtti*:

> If we wish to strive for non-violence we should follow the *yamas* and *niyamas*. This advice of our forefathers is absolutely correct. I am not placing anything new before you. I shall show what strength underlies our forefathers' advice. I have derived this from their own books. We cannot observe ahimsa without fulfilling the vows.[113]

What is also unique in Gandhi's rendering is that he considered *yamas* to be interconnected disciplines rather than separate restraints: "Truth includes non-violence, *brahmacharya,* non-stealing and other rules. It is only for convenience that the five *yamas* have been mentioned separately."[114] In combining these disciplines he not only sought to create a comprehensive moral program—which included cultivating fearlessness (*abhaya*) and self-reliance (*swadeshi*)—for the success of his Satyagraha movement, but he also sought to build up collective spiritual power. It is apparent from Gandhi's writings and his *āśrama* vows (which were based on these religious disciplines) that transgression of any one of these disciplines—from sense-control to nonpossession—was a cause of violence in some form, mental or material. Gandhi connected *ahiṃsā* to self-control in general. The means of self-control would lead an observant to autonomy and freedom. Even though Gandhi was striving for the political freedom of India, he constructed his model of self-rule (*svarāj*) on the basis of this moral strategy.

Svarājya and *Rāmarājya*: Integrating the Political Independent State with Kingdom of Rāma

Gandhi used the vernacular forms of the Sanskrit terms *pūrṇa svarājya* (complete independence or self-rule) and *rāmarājya* (the Kingdom of Rāma) to define his notion of an independent political state. Some scholars consider these to be idealistic concepts: "There was a strong streak of idealism running underneath Gandhi's attempts to create the actual, historic state in modern India," says Parel.[115] Gandhi's notion of *swaraj*—a combination of the two words, *swa* (one's own; a derivative of *sva*) and *raj* (derived from *rāj*, rule or kingdom)—is generally translated as "self-rule" or "an independent state." This word *svarājya* appears in the Vedic literature and connotes being "self-resplendent." In the *Ṛg Veda, svarājya* also means "independent dominion or sovereignty."[116]

The idiomatic use of *svarāj* was not Gandhi's invention. Dalton provides a comprehensive review of the scriptural roots and historical accounts of the origins of Gandhi's ideal of *svarāj*, which comprise both "political and spiritual" meanings and were used by his predecessors, the "philosophers of freedom." These connotations of *svarāj* "came from India's ancient traditions into the twentieth century to inspire the independence movement with a philosophy of freedom." Tilak and Dadabhai Naoroji (1825–1917) used the term to describe "political autonomy." Indian theorists later augmented the term "to forge a synthesis of two meanings of freedom, political ('external') and spiritual ('internal') liberation."[117] Aurobindo and Bipin Chandra Pal (1858–1932), who were critics of Gandhi's nonviolent methods, "insisted that swaraj was too sacred a word to be translated as the Western notion of political liberty." Pal defined it as "the conscious identification of the individual with the universal." Dalton underscores Aurobindo's sentiment: "An ideal of 'true *Swaraj* for India' must derive from the Vedantic concept of 'self-liberation.' " Although the foundations of Gandhi's *svarāj* lay elsewhere, "it was Gandhi who translated the theory of swaraj into political reality," asserts Dalton.[118]

The present discussion focuses on the practical side of Gandhi's comprehensive and mythicized goal of *svarājya*, which was central to his synthesis of asceticism and activism. Gandhi's goal of public service, which included fighting for India's independence using nonviolent methods, seems to have spurred him to rearrange the established notion of *svarājya*. In order to distinguish his concept of *svarāj* from that of others, Gandhi reinterpreted the term: "The word *Swaraj* is a sacred word, a Vedic word, meaning self-rule and self-restraint, and not freedom from all restraint which 'independence' often means."[119] To explain his interpretation, Gandhi embellished his version of *swaraj* by attaching the adjective "*purna*" (derivative of the Sanskrit word *pūrṇa*, meaning complete) to *svarāj* and by envisaging his ideal as the kingdom of Lord Rāma—*rāmarājya*—celebrated in the epic *Rāmāyaṇa*. Devout Hindus believe that in *rāmarājya* the subjects were disciplined and the ruler embodied self-control, and there was perfect harmony and no sorrow. This reading of Lord Rāma's kingdom provided Gandhi the terminology with which to communicate his strategy, which, according to him, required "disciplined rule from within," resulting in inner joy and contentment.[120]

Celebrated ascetic practices of absolute self-control are believed to lead to exalted rewards, not simply to the mundane. Likewise, in theory, Gandhi's political method of *satyagraha*, comprised as it was of *yama-niyamas*, would not merely lead to political freedom, because that could be sought and attained through other strategies. Gandhi equated individual autonomy, which is derived through self-restraint, with "the truest swaraj": "Government over self is the truest swaraj. It is synonymous with *moksha* or salvation." He saw it as an antecedent to his notion of political self-rule. He proclaimed: "Swaraj of a people means the sum total of the swaraj (self-rule) of individuals."[121] Gandhi's predecessors also used the term *svarāj* for their political objectives and apparently meant only an indigenous expression for political freedom. Unlike Gandhi, they did not call for vows of restrictive ascetic practices to develop self-rule in the terms of self-control of the senses.

In order to communicate that his ideal exceeded "political freedom," Gandhi invoked the image of the kingdom of Rāma or "*dharmarajya*" (kingdom of truth and righteousness) and presented the possibility of realizing it on this earth. Peter van der Veer points out that "when Mahatma Gandhi wanted to communicate his political ideal of *ramrajya*, the ideal social order of lord Rama in Aydodhya, he turned to the language of Tulsi Das." He also notes that "Gandhi continually quoted the *Ramcaritmanas*, with which most literate Hindus would be familiar, in order to bolster his political views." Gandhi's analogizing of his vision of the Indian political state as the kingdom of Rāma was evocative of moral governance but at the same time it appeared to some as exclusive to Hinduism. Van der Veer posits that even though Gandhi gave an "inclusivist" rendering of *Rāmarājya*, "it was a sort of appeal that totally ignored and alienated the 'Muslim other' in India."[122] Historically, this theme has been picked up by many other scholars who criticize Gandhi for presenting ideals couched solely in the Hindu tradition. However, Gandhi interpreted the struggle of Rāma (to destroy the demon Rāvaṇa symbolically) to inspire his fellow Indians—who understood the significance of this popular legend of high moral values—to eradicate the evil tendencies in their hearts. Ironically, the same motif of Lord Rāma's fight against the demon had been used by some radical Hindu groups in a literal way for confronting foreign forces. Gandhi was familiar with such misinterpretations of the use of legends and in an inclusive approach rejected the Hindu import of the idiom in a 1947 speech: "Let no one commit the mistake of thinking . . . that *Rama-rajya* means a rule of the Hindus. My Rama is another name for Khuda [another name of

God in Islam] or God. I want *Khudai raj,* which is the same thing as the Kingdom of God on earth."[123] Gandhi fashioned his vision of an ideal political state on the basis of the life of moral restraint:

> Now for Ram Rajya. It can be religiously translated as Kingdom of God on Earth; politically translated, it is perfect democracy in which, inequalities based on possession and non-possession, colour, race or creed or sex vanish; in it, land and State belong to the people, justice is prompt, perfect and cheap and, therefore, there is freedom of worship, speech and the Press—all this because of the reign of the self-imposed law of moral restraint.
>
> Such a State must be based on truth and non-violence.[124]

On the one hand, Gandhi envisioned the kingdom of Rāma as the rule of righteousness in the form of a perfect democracy; on the other hand, he proclaimed it as an inner state of freedom to which a life of restraint automatically leads. He believed in the necessity of inner transformation for attaining such a political state. "If," Gandhi insisted in a 1927 speech, "we wait for the Kingdom to come as something coming from outside, we shall be sadly mistaken."[125] For Gandhi, *rāmarāj* was, instead, a symbolic ideal based on principles of self-restraint and self-sacrifice, "where there would be 'rights alike of prince and pauper,' 'sovereignty of the people based on pure moral authority,' 'rule over self,' [and] 'the kingdom of Righteousness on earth.'"[126] Gandhi used this mythical concept of *rāmarāj* to communicate his vision for the independent Indian state.

In his notions of *rāmarājya* and *pūrṇa svarāj,* Gandhi sought to fuse the personal disciplines of restraint that yield "soul-force" and righteousness, with the economic, social and political uprightness exemplified in the scriptural accounts of *ramarājya*. For Gandhi, the ideal state would be a direct result of the means of truth, nonviolence, and observance of moral restraint that he sought to utilize. Gandhi explained that in his "philosophy of life" "means and end are convertible terms." Gene Sharp observes, "In Gandhi's view the end which is actually achieved grows out of means which are used in the effort to achieve the intended goal."[127]

Thus, in Gandhi's reasoning, methods of self-control and inner freedom would lead to a political state equivalent to *rāmarājya.* Even though Lord Rāma's struggle with the demon king was not nonviolent, Gandhi stressed to his people that "when we pledged ourselves to achieve *purna swaraj* we also took the vow that whatever we do in furtherance of the goal would be in consonance with truth and non-violence." Gandhi's proposition required a life of renunciation. He defined his notion of *rāmarājya* accordingly: "*Ramraj* means renunciation all along the line. It means discipline imposed by the people on themselves."[128] He focused on the moral framework and the nobility of sacrifice in Rāma's legend, making it congruent with his own method of soul-force and his vision for the people of India.

Some scholars, and even some of his contemporaries, classified Gandhi's prospect of acquiring *pūrṇa svarājya* through soul-force as "utopian." Gandhi himself quoted a student who accused him of preaching "the gospel of soul-force to all and sundry" and questioned whether there was "any chance of [his] utopian advice being seriously taken." Gandhi said that he was not discouraged by such statements and insisted on the power of solidarity and soul-force. Just as he believed that collective participation in the movement of Truth could yield a miraculous change of heart in the opponent, he held a similar conviction that a shared participation in "goodness" would bring the "Kingdom of God" on this earth. "To a person who is good, the whole world becomes good. If millions did that, the Kingdom of God would be realized on earth."[129] He was constant in emphasizing the role of the individual in such a state.

At the same time, Gandhi was realistically aware of the limitations of his people in following the methods of self-control. He acknowledged the impossibility of realizing the perfect state of *svarāj* based on the principles of truth and nonviolence in his present historical context. But he emphasized that "if Euclid's point, though incapable of being drawn by human agency, has an imperishable value, my picture has its own for mankind to live. Let India live for this true picture, though never realizable in its completeness." It seems that even a fractional realization of this state was acceptable to Gandhi because "the establishment of such a *rajya* would not only mean welfare of the whole of the Indian people but of the whole world." In his 1947 speech, he was envisaging the ramifications of this social and political model in the community at large.[130]

Gandhi used mythical terminology as a way to stir the religious imagination of the masses—especially that of women—and to incite participation in the Satyagraha movement. He intentionally utilized different terms for *svarāj* when addressing men and women. In 1925, during a speech at a women's conference, Gandhi said: "To women I talk about *Ramarajya. Ramarajya* is more than swarajya."[131] Was this variation due to women's proclivity for the ancient narratives? Historically, the oral tradition of reciting the *Rāmacaritamānasa* is most widespread in rural areas and vernacular versions of the story have been available to literate and illiterate alike. F. S. Growse calls it "the best and most trustworthy guide to the popular living faith of its people."[132] (The national penchant for this epic, especially among women, was evinced by the popularity of a televised version in the 1980s.) While establishing *rāmarāj* was the perceived goal of Gandhi's nonviolent strategy, the ideal of *rāmarāj* was also necessary for the coherence of his narrative. Communicating through the myth seems to have also been strategic on his part. For example, in bringing women into the *svarāj* movement, Gandhi invoked the widely known model of Lord Rāma's wife Sītā. The popular newspaper *Amrita Bazar Patrika* reports Gandhi's speech at a women's meeting in which Gandhi invoked the role of Sītā in creating *rāmarāj*:

> [B]y swaraj he meant dharma raj or Ram raj. Without dharma and morality there could be no swaraj for India. For Ram raj, he wanted to have Sitaji. It was for Sitaji that we could worship Ramachandra. If Sita did not take birth, there would have been no existence of Ramachandra. Mahatmaji prayed that his sisters be like Sita. Sita kept heart as well as body pure.[133]

Gandhi inspired women to emulate the iconic Sītā—a symbol of purity, truth, and sacrifice—so that India could realize *rāmarājya*. In his innovative interpretation Gandhi cast the image of Sītā as a strong woman who was responsible for making Rāma into a venerable being. Gandhi insisted that "dharma has always been preserved through women" and often asked women to follow in the footsteps of Sītā and Damayanti by being charitable and adopting *swadeshi* and simplicity. He implored women to emulate Sita's character, even though Sita is generally characterized as lacking independence, and take an active part in the public life, and he prophesied that "as long as the women of India do not take part in public life, there can be no salvation for the country."[134]

In *Sita's Story*, Jacqueline Suthern Hirst shows that even today various versions of this story enjoy a widespread popularity in India. The character of Sītā has also been a popular subject of academic discourse, especially among female scholars and students. Through the complexity of Sītā's story, Hirst seeks to address issues that Indian women are facing today. On the one hand, Sītā is considered to be an "ideal of womanhood," representing the values of "purity, faithfulness, self-denial and gentleness." On the other hand, her extreme self-denial and self-sacrifice causes ambivalence in many modern women who perceive the idealization of Sītā's role as an aspect of an "overarching ideology of male superiority and female dispensability."[135]

On many occasions Gandhi appeared to have vacillated between traditional patriarchal views of women and his progressive vision of *svarājya*, in which women played equal roles. Once he was asked by a correspondent to defend a figure like Rāma, who "made Sita go through the ordeal of fire and yet later abandoned her." In response, Gandhi recounted the grief Rāma experienced after he "wronged" his wife. Although Gandhi did not endorse Rāma's behavior, he stopped short of criticizing Rāma—beyond saying that "men are impulsive"—and went on to praise "the patience of women" and their "forbearance" as "a mark of strength."[136] However, by using indigenous female characters, familiar to rural women, as embodiments of strength and fearlessness, Gandhi sought to make women realize the value of their native heritage, to empower them to become equal participants in free India.[137]

Given that *satyagraha* entailed self-suffering and inner strength, Gandhi also sought to engender such "feminine" virtues in men, and recounted the cultural models of virtues to communicate the power of sacrifice, purity, and forbearance for both men and women. In a study of Gandhi's success in mobilizing women to take an active role for India's independence, Anup Taneja points out that Gandhi has been criticized for relegating women to "a somewhat inferior position in the male dominated patriarchal society." But he stresses that "it would be fair to say that in extolling these feminine virtues Gandhi had not excluded men."[138]

Gandhi's methods of self-suffering and sacrifice, as well as the constructive programs for self-autonomy such as *swadeshi* (self-reliance and homegrown), spinning, and bodily labor in which women could equally participate, were consistent with his ideal of *svarāj*. In order to communicate his message to the masses and incite them to act, he used the analogous symbols of *yajña* (sacrifice) and *tapas* (austerity). He maintained that "the *yajna* of the swaraj movement requires the services of virtuous, fearless, simple, brave, honest and resolute men and women."[139] For this immediate goal of political freedom, Gandhi adopted this vocabulary to portray his political actions as religious observances and his nonviolent activist strategies as *tapas*.

Redefining *Yajña* and *Tapas*: Sanctifying Mundane Actions

Historians and scholars comment on the innovative manner in which Gandhi united various elements of Hinduism and utilized its symbols. Dalton notes that "Gandhi drew from Hinduism the core ideas that gave his thought continuity and coherence, yet he repeatedly reexamined that tradition for purposes of social reform."[140] Gandhi carefully selected texts and concepts and made them relevant by giving them fresh meanings for his purpose and time. As Parekh observes, "Gandhi gave an inward or spiritual orientation to the central categories of Hinduism, and his reinterpretation of them was no less radical."[141] However, it must be noted that Gandhi's reinterpretation of the notions of *sat, ahiṃsā, yajña,* and *tapas* was not "an inward spiritual orientation" alone; rather he sought to transform these elements into concrete political actions. Gandhi's reinterpretation may seem radical if one is seeking ideological consistency with ancient norms, but it can be viewed as broad and practical from the perspective of his intent to secure *svarāj* for India. Our present aim is to analyze how Gandhi reinvented and embodied ancient ritualistic and ascetic practices in order to render them accessible for mass participation in the Independence movement, which he termed as *svarāj-yajña* (the ritual sacrifice for freedom).

The metaphysical notion of *sat* constituted the conceptual nexus for Gandhi's *satyagraha;* the ancient Hindu practices of *yajña* and *tapas* provided the connective tissue for his *pravṛtti,* that is, the political and disciplinary activities required in his fight for *svarāj.* Although Gandhi eschewed traditional ritualistic performance of *yajña* in his *āśrama* routine, he symbolically transferred the value of *yajña* to all actions performed for the "good of others." Gandhi did not do away with the commonly understood notion of the *yajña* that was limited to ritual performance by "purchasing a few faggots of wood and then burning them with ghee [clarified butter] to the accompaniment of certain hymns." Instead, he broadened the definition of *yajña* in terms of "selfless work." [142] In his commentary on the *Gītā,* (III. 9), he states: "We accept a broad definition of *yajna. Yajna* means any activity for the good of others . . . The word *yajna* comes from the root *yaj,* which means 'to worship,' and we please God by worshipping Him through physical labor." Gandhi was aware that his meaning might appear too unorthodox; he therefore justified his definition by saying that "there is no harm in enlarging the meaning of the word *yajña,* even if the new meaning we attach to the term was never in Vyasa's mind."[143]

Gandhi's extensive use of the notion of *yajña,* and his application of the term to various sociopolitical activities, demonstrates that he was cognizant of the archaic connotations of this practice, which included animal sacrifice, as well as the modified definition—interior mystical expressions of sacrifice in the *Upaniṣads* and later yogic literature. He was also aware of the enduring presence of *yajña* in Indian society. *Yajña*, meaning "worship," "devotion," "prayer," "offering," "oblation," and "sacrifice," is the most ancient ritual of Hinduism that continues in modern day. During his conversations, Gandhi conveyed his view that *yajña* is not only a purifying but also a potent force for achieving spiritual and material goals. Traditionally, *yajña* signifies communal ritualistic participation for a higher good. It represents a prototype of sacrificing for the sake of acquiring greater personal and shared benefits in the community. The Vedic sacrificial ritual "is always performed for the Sacrificer's benefit, both here and hereafter."[144] In early Vedic tradition, the sacrifice is performed to achieve "objects of ordinary desire—children, cattle, etc., or to get one's enemy out of the way."[145] The gods, appeased by the sacrificial offerings, reward the worshipers "with success in war," elaborates A. L. Basham, "progeny, increase of cattle, and long life, on a *quid pro quo* basis."[146] The performance of the sacrifice is always transactional, to use a modern term. W. Brown expounds:

> It is a duty of men to perform the sacrifice and thus give the gods something they want, enjoy, and profit from. In return it is the duty of the gods to respond to the sacrificer's prayers for favors by granting those favors, which most often are for victory over enemies, wealth, and numerous offspring.[147]

Gandhi's method required sacrifice and he drew on the *yajña* technology of acquiring awards through acts of sacrifice. He considered *yajña* to be "a beautiful and highly suggestive word," which "can be interpreted to mean worship, sacrifice or service for others. Gandhi applied it to a wide variety of actions, which established, for him, the value of sacrifice. "The man who does no *yajna* can win nothing in this world," asserted Gandhi.[148] By describing the pursuit for *svarāj* as a *yajña*—"*swarajyajna*"—Gandhi not only sought to spiritualize his this-worldly goal of political independence, he also created a platform on which he could perform as oblation all actions directed toward his goal.

Gandhi precisely defined *yajña* as "work done in the spirit of *yajna*, done without egotism for our higher good and for the service of the others."[149] Like his predecessors and many of his contemporary religious reformers (including Swami Dayananda and Vivekananda), he considered the practice of *yajña* from the perspective of universal welfare. His portrayal of actions as *yajña* was also not completely original; his predecessors had used a similar vocabulary. For example, in his commentary on the *Gītā*, Tilak defines actions as *yajña*.[150] Authors such as Tilak justified their reinterpretation of classical terms such as *yajña* on the basis of the *Gītā* itself, which gave new meanings to many ancient ideas. Similarly, Gandhi provided reasons for his reinterpretation and emphasized that "like man, the meaning of great writings suffers evolution," and ". . . we notice that the meaning of important words has changed or expanded." According to Gandhi, the *Gītā* presented a license to further reinterpret the ideas for his time. He claimed that "the author of the *Gita*, by extending the meanings of words, has taught us to imitate him."[151]

However, in his spirit of imitation, Gandhi exceeded his predecessors in reinterpreting the concept of *yajña*. First, he applied the term to a very broad spectrum of sociopolitical activities, fluently characterizing such diverse actions as spinning, sacrificing jewelry, renouncing the use of foreign cloth, manual labor, cleaning latrines, sharing wealth with others, striving and conquering desire, and noncooperation all as *yajña*. Second, he called for a "mass *yajna*" that unconventionally included men and women as well as people of all castes and classes. "The more the people do *yajna* for self-purification, the better. A mass *yajna* has an altogether miraculous effect," proclaimed Gandhi. For instance, in 1945, Gandhi organized a twenty-four-hour spinning *yajña* on the anniversary of his wife Kasturba's death. Third, unlike other Indian religious reformers, Gandhi sought to broaden this Hindu-specific ceremonial practice to people of diverse faiths: "The term *yajna* can be interpreted in a number of ways but there is only one meaning acceptable to men of all faiths, and that is, to be ready even to lay down one's life for true welfare."[152] For Gandhi, the ultimate sacrifice was that of one's own self, and he extolled the names of those of different traditions who made sacrifices for the sake of truth, including Pārvati, Hariścandra, Socrates, Daniel, Jesus, and Imams Hasan and Hoosein. During his discourses on the power of sacrifice, Gandhi often clumped together these and other names of religious martyrs and various gods and kings from varied traditions in order to illustrate the universality of sacrifice and to communicate his message to people from different backgrounds.

In seeking to transform *nivṛtti* into an activist instrument for his Satyagraha movement, Gandhi also defined *yajña* in terms of the conquest of desires: "To strive and conquer desire is also a form of *yajna*," pronounced Gandhi in his commentary on the *Gītā*.[153] Gandhi symbolized political activities as *yajña* and at the same time ritualized self-suffering as *yajña*—rendering it synonymous to another Hindu religious idea, that of *tapasya* (physical and mental austerities). While ideologically *yajña* (ritual performances) might be differentiated from *tapasya*, in Gandhi's mind they were intimately connected, for he believed that the power of ritual was activated in proportion to the faith, purity, and austerity of the ritual performer. In response to a 1926 letter that described the transformation of the lives of the villagers after the spinning wheel was introduced to them, Gandhi wrote:

> If the sacred *mantra* and similar verbal symbols have immense power in them, it is because we have absolute faith in their power and do *tapascharya* in order that our faith may bear fruit. In the same way, if we try to spread the use of the spinning-wheel with the faith that we shall thereby serve the poor and purify both society and ourselves, and if we do *tapascharya*, even lay down our lives, in order that our faith may be rewarded, it certainly will be rewarded.[154]

Gandhi's consistent analogizing of the ancient sacred practices of *yajña* and *tapascarya* for mundane social and political actions can appear to be contrived associations. Parekh notes Gandhi's unique position, saying that for Gandhi "*Yajna* consisted not in conducting formal *karmakānda* and rites but in seeing the entire life as one continuous offering at the altar of mankind."[155] Nevertheless, Gandhi thought of himself as "imitating" ancient texts that attest to a gradual transformation of archaic forms of *karmakānda* (ceremonial acts such as *yajña*) into contemplative methods. Gandhi was aware that initially, in the Vedic period, *yajña* entailed invocation of *mantras* while pouring material offerings into the fire. During the later development of the *Upaniṣads*, new and revolutionary approaches were applied to *yajña* rituals. The complex and precise performance of the rituals (which had at times included animal and human sacrifices) metamorphosed into *japayajña* (sacrifice by means of prayer) and *jñāna-yajña* (sacrifice by means of knowledge).[156]

In the classical Hindu literature, the performance of duty (*dharma*, integrity in a person's commitment to his or her specific duty) also became a "sacrificial act" when performed with great diligence because the sacrificer was willing to sacrifice all for the fulfillment of Truth. According to Brown, "Life then becomes a sacrificial act, a rite (*kriyā*), and as such, when perfectly executed, it can accomplish any wish, compelling even the gods, as we are taught in the Vedas and Brāhmaṇas is possible through the sacrifice when performed with exactitude."[157] The transubstantiation of ascetic practices (*tapas*) into inner sacrifice became prevalent in the Upaniṣadic and the yogic texts.

Mircea Eliade, a historian of religion (who himself had met Gandhi in India), portrays the phenomenon of self-restraint and mental practices as "ritual interiorization" in his account of the historical development of *yoga*. Ascetic practices become equivalent to *yajña*:

> For *tapas*, too, is a "sacrifice." If, in Vedic sacrifice, the gods are offered *soma*, melted butter, and the sacred fire, in the practice of asceticism they are offered an "inner sacrifice," in which physiological functions take the place of libations and ritual objects.[158]

Gandhi defined both *yajña* and *tapas* in terms of the actions and disciplines of purification, self-suffering, and penance required for *satyagraha*. He called for a daily mass "spinning *yajna*" for the purpose of obtaining an independent state. Some of his close associates worried about this emphasis on spinning and *khadi* (hand-spun cloth). For example, even though Rabindranath Tagore (1861–1941) supported the "revival of India's handicrafts," he was unable to understand the "greater symbolism of the spinning wheel."[159] They thought that it "would be unwise to lose sight of the fact that it was the machine age, and reverting to the old methods of production would impede the country's development." The spinning wheel for Gandhi, however, among many other benefits, created "the bond of brotherhood that united all Indians; *khadi* became the uniform of the national movement," states biographer Yogesh Chadha.[160] Gandhi was seeking to induce the spirit of sacrifice and declared that if "all people live in a spirit of *yajna*, the problems of life would disappear." In order to substantiate his narrative, Gandhi quoted verses from the *Ṛg Veda* (X: 130, 1) to illustrate that spinning and weaving were regarded as sacrifice.[161] Gandhi understood *yajña* and *tapas* to be equally purifying and potent means for achieving spiritual and material goals. He saw himself as following the call of the *Bhagavad-Gītā* (XVIII: 5), which explicitly commands: "Action for sacrifice [*yajña*], charity [*dāna*] and austerity [*tapas*] may not be abandoned. It must needs be performed. Sacrifice, charity and austerity are the purifiers of the wise."[162] Furthermore, Gandhi sought to include the common masses—from all social strata—in his version of *yajña* and *tapas*, practices traditionally available only to those from higher echelons or deeply spiritual people.

Gandhi also maintained that *yajña*, *dāna*, and *tapas* were prescribed by the *śāstras* as essential purifying actions for sustaining personal and social order and evolution. In the spirit of the Vedic *yajña*, Gandhi called for sacrifice—not the sacrificial performance of religious ritual but the sacrifice of foreign clothes, food, and selfish desires; the sacrifice of cooperation with unjust laws; and ultimately the sacrifice of one's own life. The desired outcome of the *yajña* included this-worldly political independence, not the attainment of miraculous powers or heavenly gifts. *The Bombay Chronicle* in 1918 published a speech by Gandhi in which he said that "in South Africa, when thousands went to jail, I never appealed. There can be no appeal when we wish to go to jail by way of *tapascharya*."[163] Thus he sanctified his political actions of civil disobedience and resistance.

The above statements notwithstanding, Gandhi's motives should not be seen as divorced from the goal of personal spiritual liberation, for he also connected *yajña, dāna,* and *tapas* to the redemption of the oppressed, redefining these religious concepts as instruments of *satyagraha* for service of the country:

> *Yajna, dāna, tapas,* are obligatory duties, but that does not mean that the manner of performing them in this age should be the same as in ancient times. *Yajna, dāna,* etc., are permanent principles. The social practices and the concrete forms through which they are put into practice may change from age to age and country to country. The right gift which a seeker of *moksha* in this country and this age may make is to dedicate his all, body, intellect and possession, to the service of the country. And, likewise, the right *tapas* for this country and this age consists in burning with agony at the suffering of countless untouchables and others who are starving for want of food or because of famines. Anyone who performs these three important duties certainly becomes purified and he may even have a vision of God's cosmic form which Arjuna had.[164]

Gandhi presented acts of service that required sacrifice and self-suffering as a means to see the Divine, the ultimate goal of Hinduism making his entire endeavor spiritual in essence, although it was practical in nature.

Seeking coherence, Gandhi borrowed from the traditional meanings of *yajña* for his struggle for *svarāj*. He did not hesitate to analogize even the notion of war sacrifice found in the ancient myths. B. Sullivan writes: "The war between the gods and demons is a frequent topic of Vedic literature; indeed, from the *Vedas* on, it has been the central myth of Indian civilization."[165] War as sacrifice for the sake of sustaining *dharma* is an ancient notion that became fully developed in the *Mahābhārata*, a text Gandhi called a repository of wisdom. The tension between gods and demons expresses the conflict between *dharma* and *adharma*. Gandhi proclaimed that his duty for sustaining *dharma* was to fight against social injustice and the British Empire. He identified the "Imperial Government" as "Satanic," thus construing his fight as a dharmic battle reminiscent of an age-old clash between demonic and divine forces.[166]

Gandhi audaciously used the symbol of offering oneself on the battlefield (*ātmayajña*) for sacrificing oneself in his nonviolent war—a battle of "*swaraj yajña*": "A gentleman asked me: 'Can our activities be described as war?' I had no hesitation in replying: 'Our struggle has all the attributes of a war.' "[167] Gandhi allegorized nonviolent confrontation as *yajña* and echoed the traditional rendering of sacrifice, which traditionally represents a performance of "an exhaustive series of symbolic acts," explicated in great detail by Ananda Coomaraswamy.[168] Gandhi demanded self-sacrifice from his *satyagrahis*: "[T]he satyagrahi starts a *yajna* on behalf of the whole country and offers himself as an oblation." In his authoritative voice, he invites his followers to offer the highest of all gifts—the self:

> I am asking my countrymen in India to follow no other gospel than the gospel of self-sacrifice which precedes every battle. Whether you belong to the school of violence or non-violence, you will still have to go through the fire of sacrifice and of discipline. May God grant you, may God grant our leaders the wisdom, the courage and the true knowledge to lead the nation to its cherished goal! May God grant the people of India the right path, the true vision and the ability and the courage to follow this path, difficult and yet easy, of sacrifice.[169]

Gandhi's call to unite in sacrifice and his invocation of the transformative power of rituals and ritual symbols became a factor in his campaign.

Using the symbols of *yajña* and *tapas*, Gandhi sought to arouse rarefied religious experience in the masses. Radhakrishnan speculates on the role of religious symbols in the human imagination: "The different symbols, however remote from reality, wake up and nourish a rich religious experience."[170] For the success of his political strategy, Gandhi stimulated people's religious imagination by invoking traditional vocabulary, which demanded sacrifice, as well as by embodying sacrifice through his personal ascetic practices. The tangible effect of this framework on India's people will be discussed later in this book.

Gandhi's Ritual Performance and Creation of *Communitas*

Even though Gandhi did not approve of the performance of Hindu rituals in his *āśrama* communities, he predicated his use of ritualistic symbols on traditional lore. As we saw earlier he quoted references to spinning and weaving in the *Ṛg Veda* in order to substantiate his spinning-*yajña* and make it relevant to the context of his day. The *Ṛg Veda* calls on common accord in the shared performance of rituals.[171] Even though *yajña* is inherently a community affair, its ritual performance is mainly conducted by qualified male Brahmins (priests). Gandhi expanded the performance of *yajña* to people of all castes and classes, giving it universal application. He noted that his symbolic representation of sociopolitical actions as *yajña* and *tapas*, as well as his observances of purifying disciplines such as fasting, poverty, and *brahmacarya*, had encouraged some of his enthusiastic followers to engage in ceremonial veneration of the *charkha* (spinning wheel) and the ritual worship of the *Gītā*. Perhaps Gandhi's fervent veneration of the *Gītā* as *Mātā* (mother) inspired his followers to deify the text. Gandhi stated that he was not in favor of people performing rituals but confessed that because ritual worship was so widespread, he tolerated its performance and did not oppose it publicly.

Indian people's penchant for ritual worship is evident in their historical reverence for Gandhi. While he acknowledged that worship of his "image . . . has become most widespread," Gandhi claimed that "since such worship of human beings runs in the blood of Hindus, I have remained indifferent to them."[172] It is evident, however, that if Gandhi remained "indifferent" toward his status as a figure of worship, he creatively utilized that religious sentiment for making his ideas accessible to the common people in their familiar idiom.

Gandhi's ritualization of social and political actions emerged organically from his combination of the components of *pravṛtti* and *nivṛtti*, nevertheless ritual performance did become one of the factors in the mobilization of the masses. There is ample literature that explores the religious, symbolic, healing, and communicative significance of rituals. For example, scholars who study ritual phenomena in the building of community suggest that ritual taps into the imagery and emotions of a social group, generating *communitas* (intense community spirit and cohesive bond), to use Victor Turner's terminology. Ladelle McWhorter construes ritual in Foucauldian terms as "a technology of power" that has been employed by "kings and clerics in controlling the masses."[173] However, Gandhi's ritual performance was not used simply as discipline to control the masses. Unlike "kings and clerics," Gandhi aimed to stir and free the masses. Moreover, Gandhi *ritualized* every aspect of his life, which became a testament of his commitment to the cause; it was his personal performance of ritual that was to be imitated.

A comprehensive theorization of Gandhi's ritual performance and its effect on the mass mobilization of Indians is beyond the scope of this book. Nevertheless, the ritualistic symbolism and performance of his political activities, such as public fasts and the Salt March in particular, was a dynamic that communicated his strategy and inspired thousands of men and women to join the Independence movement. Gandhi's Salt March (a move to protest the unjust tax on salt) was laden with the ritualistic symbols of "sacred pilgrimage," which will be discussed later. This "battle-field of satyagraha" became a defining moment for the Indian nationalist movement. He designated the ultimate destination in religious terms as "the temple of the goddess of swaraj." To launch the march, Gandhi called for the sacrifice by millions, not merely a few: "in this struggle for swaraj millions should offer themselves for sacrifice and win such swaraj as will benefit the vast masses of the country."[174]

In his call to sacrifice, Gandhi combined several traditional metaphors designed to arouse people's emotions. Dalton eloquently captures the effect Gandhi's tactics had on the masses: "On the fact and legend of the march, on the wings of Gandhi's creative imagination, the Indian nationalist movement soared, elevated by the symbolic forces, sustained by dramatic impact."[175] The common bond of defying the unjust law transcended the differences of caste, gender, and color, and united thousands in the shared purpose of obtaining *svarāj*. T. C. Kline III underlines the claim that rituals that involve the community can have socially transformative effects: "Ritual transforms and channels our originally unshaped desires into more complex and ultimately satisfying forms of expression."[176] Concrete social and political actions assumed new meaning and inspired the religious imagination when they were encased in Gandhi's language of the sacred—prayer, fasting, and performance of *yajña* and *tapas* for obtaining *rāmarājya*.

The miraculous power of the performance of *yajña*, as well as the spiritual power of ascetic "ritual interiorization," played functional roles in creating *communitas*. As the leader of the Satyagraha movement, to what extent was Gandhi's embodiment of an ascetic lifestyle—with its sacrifice, penance, austerity, and especially its *brahmacarya*—a crucial ingredient in mobilizing the masses? Anthropologist Turner analyzes the relationship between ritual and emotion in the context of political movements.[177] Interestingly, Dr. Martin Luther King Jr., who was deeply influenced by Gandhi, ritualized his Civil Rights Movement using his Christian vocabulary of the power of love (*agape*), instead of the power of *Sat* (Truth), for inspiring the masses for action.

Theoretical attempts have been made by scholars to understand the factors in Gandhi's leadership that united his followers. For instance, Dalton cites James Burns who, in his study of leadership, places Gandhi in the category of a "transforming leader" who "taps the needs and raises the aspirations and helps shape the values—and hence mobilizes the potential—of followers." According to him, "transforming leadership ultimately becomes *moral* in that it raises the level of human conduct and ethical aspiration of both leader and led, and thus it has a transforming effect on both. Perhaps the best modern example is Gandhi."[178] Gandhi exemplified the qualities of a leader who was endowed with the fully functioning qualities of thinking and reasoning. But for Gandhi the capacity for leadership was itself derived *from* an observance of morality. His highest sense of morality was represented by his vow of *brahmacarya,* which comprised the very foundation of leadership in his movement. Gandhi proclaimed that "Religious satyagraha . . . best succeeds under the leadership of a true man of God who will compel reverence and love even of the opponent by the purity of his life, the utter selflessness of his mission and the breadth of his outlook," and he believed that the leader of such a movement must preferably be a "*brahmachari*."[179] Thus, Gandhi epitomized and called for a much higher ideal of leadership than that offered by scholars such as Burns.

Undoubtedly, the various factors examined by scholars and historians—political, social, religious, and psychological—contributed to Gandhi's success as a leader in mobilizing the masses. However, it would be a substantial oversight to ignore his utilization of the components of *nivṛtti* and his reliance on traditional Indian models of penance and soul-force for his effectiveness as a leader. Specifically, with his paradoxical vow of *brahmacarya* in marriage and his advocacy of it for his political movement, which included untouchables and women, Gandhi represented what Turner calls a "liminal" persona. Turner defines liminality—in the context of ritual process and performance—as a "betwixt-and-between" or peripheral condition that is "attributed with magico-religious properties."[180] Turner's theory in the context of Gandhi's paradoxical "threshold" role will be dealt with later. Here I am simply noting that Gandhi, in his ascetic practices and performances, was able to step outside of established social structures—not to transcend the world, but rather to further his commitment to public service and specific political objectives.

Thus, Gandhi was neither an ascetic nor a politician (in the conventional definition). He stood between the two roles—freely utilizing religious symbols, ritualizing his personal and political life, politicizing his ascetic practices, and sanctifying his private and public life with a halo of higher purpose. Gandhi stood on a threshold, an ascetic politician transcending a defined circumference, and he was able to trample limiting hierarchical social norms of behavior—male and female, lower caste and higher caste. While stepping beyond clearly defined cultural boundaries may cause confusion, it also opens the possibility of creating cross-cultural and religious *communitas*. As a liminal figure Gandhi was able to create universal *communitas*—a community open to people of all classes, castes, genders, and religions.

Self-control, which is generally associated with isolation, paradoxically, became essential for Gandhi to create a disciplined community of activists. The Rudolphs locate the roots of Gandhi's charisma in his self-control: "He assumed that his capacity to compel the environment depended upon the degree of his self-perfection, the degree to which he purged himself of lust, self-interest, and anger, and he prepared himself by self-imposed discipline."[181] Evidently, Gandhi strove to embody self-control not just to manage social and political events through inner discipline; that was only part of his reasoning. Self-control also defined Gandhi's method of *satyagraha*, which inherently carried metaphysical significance and was imbued socially with symbolic value. Gandhi sought to embody purity and selflessness in his life, and *brahmacarya* was essential in his embodiment of the disciplines of self-restraint. Gandhi's bodily control in the form of *brahmacarya* awakened the religious imagination of the thousands who joined him, as evidenced by public response. Anthropologist Mary Douglas interprets "the body as a vehicle for social symbolism."[182] In her monumental study, Elizabeth Abbott also suggests that the practice of celibacy has a utilitarian purpose, freeing the mind to pursue a specific goal, and it is ubiquitous in various cultures, religions, and professions in some form. Gandhi trusted in *brahmacarya*'s traditionally ascribed spiritual and miraculous power, and he yearned to materialize it for practical objectives.[183]

Gandhi considered the practice of *brahmacarya* indispensable for the fulfillment of his duty of public service and leadership. He sought to bridge the gap between *pravṛtti*—both in the sense of ceremonial *yajña* and sociopolitical activities—and *nivṛtti*, austere disciplines and the methods of *satyagraha*. Even though Gandhi's vow of *brahmacarya* was initially taken for practical purposes, it became essential for this integration of renunciation and social action. His political strategy demanded the high level of sacrifice and purity exemplified by his vow of *brahmacarya*, a broad form of self-control. Gandhi's paradigm for the synthesis of *pravṛtti* and *nivṛtti* became an alternative to treating these two ideologies as binary; it does not rest solely on any particular philosophical ideology or text, but rather on his enactment and interpretation of ancient principles and myths for his purpose. Interrelated strands of philosophical, ethical, and mythical ideas are effectively integrated in Gandhi's embodied practice of *brahmacarya*. This practice becomes the nexus of his communal ritual performance and defining the ascetic disciplines as activist methods. How was Gandhi able to assign politically functional value to a practice that had traditionally been understood as a practice for religious autonomy and isolation? Analysis of the various elements of *brahmacarya* practice, which Gandhi extrapolated, is necessary to understand his application of it to his Satyagraha movement.

CHAPTER 3

The Traditional Roots of Gandhi's *Brahmacarya*

> The word in Sanskrit corresponding to celibacy is *brahmacharya* and the latter means much more than celibacy. *Brahmacharya* means perfect control over all the senses and organs. For a perfect *brahmachari* nothing is impossible.
>
> —M. K. Gandhi

> Brahmacharya means the absence of a frame of mind in which women are seen as objects of enjoyment.
>
> —*Śri Rāmānuja Gītā Bhāṣya*

Gandhi's *brahmacarya* may appear to be a world-denying practice and a misplaced virtue in the political arena; nevertheless, Gandhi understood it to be essential to his nonviolent activism and also advocated its practice by others, especially by those who were committed to the service of humanity. Given that Gandhi himself asserted the essential role of his *brahmacarya* vow and tested its efficacy in his personal and public goals, numerous biographers delve into his ideal of sexual renunciation in some depth. Judith M. Brown reasons: "Because Gandhi's attitude to sex is so at variance with contemporary understanding of the essential and creative role of sexuality in human growth and life, this aspect of his religious development has generated much theorizing and speculation, and not a little criticism for its apparent harshness."[1] Indeed, Gandhi understood *brahmacarya*, not sexuality, to be filled with creative possibilities, which he sought to experiment with for achieving personal and political freedom. It is not surprising that in their analyses, authors consider specific, inherently religious and social elements of *brahmacarya*, such as the psychosomatic power of semen control, the social value of self-control, and the health benefits of the disciplines of self-restraint. These exegeses demonstrate the versatile and complex nature of Gandhi's *brahmacarya* and have enhanced our understanding of him as a man and as a political figure. However, if we are to fully understand Gandhi's synthesis of *pravṛtti* and *nivṛtti* we need a comprehensive survey of the traditional understanding of ascetic *brahmacarya* he drew on.

A close study of Gandhi's own words reveals that his *brahmacarya* was imbued with a fourfold purpose: first, it demonstrated his personal commitment to self-discipline and self-sacrifice for public service; second, it represented the observance of self-control mandated by *satyagraha*; third, it reflected his belief that its traditionally acclaimed instrumentality in attaining spiritual freedom could be applied to achieving political freedom; and fourth, it underscored his conviction that the magical powers accrued by *brahmacarya* could mobilize the masses and materialize social and political goals. For the purpose of this study, it is essential to weave together the historical, personal, and philosophical turning points of Gandhi's life, the references from classical Indian texts and oral traditions that he extrapolated, and his own interpretations of the material for his nonviolent strategy for collective social action.

Suspicion Regarding Gandhi's Practice of *Brahmacarya* in the Political Arena

The relevance of Gandhi's private preoccupation with, public display of, and reinterpretation of *brahmacarya* in the political arena was questioned by some of his native contemporaries, who were apprehensive about the compulsory application of this renunciative practice to his activism. In the *Harijan* (1936), Gandhi printed an extract from a long letter by a young man whose attitude, according to Gandhi, represented many youths' grievance:

> You want everyone to become moral in order to change the world. I do not exactly know what you mean by morality—whether you confine it to matters sexual, or whether it covers the whole field of human conduct. I suspect the former, because I do not see you pointing out to your capitalist and landlord friends the great injustice and harm they are doing by making huge profits at the expense of labourers and tenants, while you are never tired of castigating young men and women for their moral lapses in

> sexual matters and upholding before them the virtues of celibacy. You claim to know the mind of Indian youth. I do not claim to represent anybody, but as a solitary young man I beg to challenge your claim. . . . It is all a conflict between the old and the new ideas, resulting usually in the defect and misery of youth. I humbly request you to be kind and compassionate to the youth and not to judge them by your puritanic standards of morality. After all, I think every act, when it is performed with mutal [*sic*] consent and mutual love, is moral whether it is performed within marriage or without.[2]

This type of distrustful interpretation of Gandhi's views on ascetic celibacy and sexuality, so audaciously conveyed by this young man (but also, intriguingly, published by Gandhi), was not confined to this individual; it was voiced by many others, including his followers, who were wary of mixing politics with the asceticism of *sādhus*. These not only included Gandhi's followers but religious and political leaders as well, such as Tilak. Nehru, a close follower of Gandhi who became the first Prime Minister of independent India, was also skeptical of the relevance of Gandhi's ideology of sexual restraint for the common men and women of this world. He writes in his *Autobiography*: "Sexual restraint is certainly desirable, but I doubt if Gandhiji's doctrine is likely to result in this to any wide-spread extent. It is too extreme, and most people decide that it is beyond their capacity and go their usual ways." Nehru was appalled that Gandhi did not believe in "the natural sex attraction between man and woman."[3] Moreover, within the traditional context of India, as discussed earlier, sexual renunciation is for hermits or ascetics—those who have chosen to renounce ties with the world for religious or spiritual purposes.

The virtue of political leaders is not usually thought of in terms of their renunciation and it certainly has not traditionally included *brahmacarya*. Therefore, for some of Gandhi's associates, his *brahmacarya* seem to resemble a "puritanic form of self-discipline," that of "mediaeval Christian ascetics" or "Jain recluses."[4] Other scholars draw parallels between Gandhi's views of sexuality and Victorian ideas of celibacy. However, Gandhi's writings indicate that his ideal of sexual renunciation is, in fact, couched in the vocabulary, myths, ethos, and symbols of Indian traditions. It was much more complex and multifaceted than the rigidly moralizing views of Jain ascetics who seek complete isolation or the repression of sexual acts, ideals that also characterized Victorian morality.[5]

Gandhi deliberately differentiated between celibacy as mere abstention from sexual acts and *brahmacarya*—the control of all the senses in mind, word, and deed. During his discourses and correspondence, he often referred to the various religious connotations of restraint. Even though scholars have selectively referred to the resonance of *brahmacarya* with Gandhi's cultural context, they tend to analyze his sexual practices first and only then seek to determine how they fit within the traditional design of *brahmacarya*. Their interpretive techniques simply do not allow the full investigation of the traditional connotations of Gandhi's asceticism. I propose to invert the interpretive process: begin with an analysis of Gandhi's own use of the traditional meanings and nuances of *brahmacarya* as he related them to his personal and political purposes; *then* highlight the elements that lead to an understanding of his alternative paradigm, which incorporates *brahmacarya* and other ascetic practices into nonviolent activism. What does *brahmacarya* mean? Are celibacy and *brahmacarya*, in historical fact, synonymous? What are the traditional elements of *brahmacarya* that Gandhi extrapolated from the classical texts to construct his philosophy? What factors inspired Gandhi to transform this ascetic practice, which mandates detachment from worldly concerns, into a subversive alternative method for confronting social and political challenges? Before probing these issues it is essential to briefly examine Gandhi's cultural background and his own account of his study of those religious texts and traditions that played an integral role in his formulation of various definitions of *brahmacarya*.

"The Mind on Fire"—Testing Ancient Principles in the Modern Context

Gandhi was raised in a religious Hindu family and was exposed to Jain communities and their ideologies of nonviolence and asceticism. The state of Gujarat, where Gandhi was born and grew up, has a large Jain population, and his mother had a close affiliation with Jains. Gandhi recalls, "Jainism was strong in Gujarat, and its influence was felt everywhere and on all occasions."[6] Gandhi's mother was a devout woman and he attributes his initial proclivity for austerity to her. Bose, an associate of Gandhi, wrote: "I do believe that his [Gandhi's] ideas—which he derived from his mother—and also the austerity which he saw in his mother was very much reflected in his own character."[7] However, the way Gandhi systematically intertwined his political and public actions with celibacy, fasting, and poverty, is unique. Inclinations toward deep austerity among *gṛhasthas* (householders) are not often seen in Hindu society or even in Jain communities. Both Hindu codes of conduct and Jain *vratas* (disciplines) do not require an ascetic lifestyle for householders; they clearly give consent to fulfilling family obligations and enjoyments. In these traditions, the vow of *brahmacarya* is taken only by monks and *sādhus* who have renounced worldly relations in order to seek autonomy or by laypeople for short periods for specific religious purposes.

Given this absence of paradigms of lifelong austerity for householders in Gandhi's cultural context, what could have induced him to choose an ascetic path for his political goals? According to Gandhi's own accounts, even though he was raised in a religious household, he did not have deep knowledge of India's religious texts. Gandhi confesses: "For home reading I had an intense dislike. . . . During my student days in England too, the same habit persisted of not reading outside the books for examinations."[8] However, realizing his lack of a broad knowledge, Gandhi became interested in reading a variety of texts on different subjects. Gandhi never claimed to be a scholar of religion or philosophy, yet in his writings and lectures, he often referenced various texts and oral traditions to validate his experiments in ascetic practices, including *brahmacarya*.

Gandhi also did not claim to have a guru, someone who typically guides his followers in religious matters. In his *Autobiography*, Gandhi does speak of Raychandbhai, a businessman and "a real seeker after Truth," for whom he had great respect due to his moral earnestness. Raychandbhai or Rajchandra was a poet and he practiced religion in the midst of a very active business life. Raychandbhai became a source of great inspiration for Gandhi. "In my moments of spiritual crisis, therefore, he was my refuge," recalls Gandhi in his *Autobiography*. "And yet in spite of this regard for him I could not enthrone him in my heart as my Guru." Perhaps Gandhi was hesitant to commit himself because he believed in "ceaseless striving" and in experimenting with different ways for acquiring truth, not to be confined to one particular teacher or path.[9] By not choosing any specific spiritual guide he did not associate himself with any *sampradāya* (religious sect), and was able to openly draw wisdom from different traditions. With traditional yet open views toward spirituality, he consequently attracted followers of various sects within Hinduism and other traditions.

Against this background, then, how did Gandhi, a lawyer and politician (both worldly occupations), become familiar with and fond of the traditions of renunciation? During his stay in England

(1888–91), when faced with the Western elite, Gandhi soon realized his ignorance of India's texts and traditions. Due to his upbringing in a religious family, he was exposed to oral traditions and religious tales but, ironically, his European friends seemed to have a much better understanding of the philosophical and religious literature of India than he did.

> I felt I ought to read for the sake of gaining general knowledge. . . . The year 1893 I devoted to religious striving. The reading was therefore wholly religious. After 1894 all the time for sustained reading I got was in the jails of South Africa. I had developed not only a taste for reading but for completing my knowledge of Sanskrit and studying Tamil, Hindi and Urdu.[10]

Gandhi became an avid reader of religious and philosophical literature and continued his study during his incarceration periods. Was it this study of literature that awakened Gandhi to the value of *brahmacarya* and led him to experiment with its power?

Gandhi's conviction that the transgression of *brahmacarya* was a root cause for all evils prompts Jordens to state that Gandhi launched a "hysterical indictment to all sexual activity." In search of the sources for Gandhi's ideas, Jordens traces "the conception of the finite treasure of generative fluid as a source of spiritual power" to "the classical Hindu heritage." Jordens looks to Gandhi's autobiographical records and concludes that he discovered these ideas in 1903, after his return from South Africa, "when he read and studied the *Yoga Sutra*, and two commentaries on it by M. N. Dvivedi and Vivekananda."[11] Gandhi says that the ideas of self-control had been percolating in his mind long before 1903. In fact, his inclination toward *brahmacarya* seems to begin in the year 1893, when he committed himself to the serious study of religious literature.

In a 1936 letter to a young man (quoted earlier) who accused him of having excessively indulged his sexual appetites, Gandhi wrote: "I awoke to the folly of indulgence for the sake of it even when I was twenty-three years old, and decided upon total *brahmacharya* in 1899, i.e., I was thirty years old." Hence, the beginnings of Gandhi's experimentation with religious asceticism can be closely linked to his spiritual quest and study of religious texts, which, he claimed, opened a new passage for him to personal and political freedom. In "Jail Experiences" (1922–24), Gandhi catalogs a long list of books that he had read.[12] These religious and nonreligious books, which include the Hindu epics, must have set Gandhi's inquisitive mind on fire and provided insight into Eastern and Western cultures, as well as cemented his conviction in the acclaimed power of renunciation. Evidently, he also acquired the vocabulary and models that he utilized to communicate his strategy.

Due to his sustained study, experimentation, and personal experiences, Gandhi continued to discover various nuances to the practice of *brahmacarya*, as evidenced in his writings and speeches—subtleties that correspond to the references found in the religious texts and oral traditions of India. However, Gandhi seems to have consciously chosen specific models of *sannyāsa* and *brahmacārin dharma* (laws of celibate renunciation) and rejected others—namely, those having to do with *gṛhastha dharma* (prescribed laws and duties for householders) and *rāja dharma* (political laws). "He rarely referred to the erotic tradition and its creative expressions in art, literature, and sculpture," notes Parekh, ascribing to Gandhi a "narrower view of spirituality than his predecessors."[13] Gandhi, however, was seeking to utilize renunciatory disciplines in creating a comprehensive nonviolent political strategy, as well as in constructing a cohesive narrative that supported his method of *satyagraha*. This becomes clear if we look at examples from some of the texts that Gandhi read (with available translations) and the oral traditions to which he was exposed.

Brahmacarya Defined

According to Gandhi, religious literature presented him with an alternative to material methods for attaining power and freedom. Instead of using physical powers, these methods utilize inner force, obtained through a life of renunciation, of which celibacy is the utmost expression. Gandhi later realized that *brahmacarya* was a way of acquiring the self-control and inner strength required for the battle of *satyagraha*. He admitted that the vow required constant vigilance and likened it to the difficult task of "walking on the sword's edge."[14] Gandhi asserted that *brahmacarya* and other disciplines provided preparatory means for him to initiate his Satyagraha movement. "For the battle of satyagraha one only needs to prepare oneself. We have to have strict self-control."[15]

For Gandhi, *brahmacarya* was not merely sexual abstinence, but comprehensive self-restraint—control of all the senses. Gandhi defined *brahmacarya* as follows:

> Let us remember the root meaning of '*brahmacharya*'[.] '*Charya*' means course of conduct; '*brahmacharya*,' conduct

> adapted to the search of Brahman, i.e., Truth. From this etymological meaning arises the special meaning, viz., control of all the senses. We must entirely forget the incomplete definition which restricts itself to the sexual aspect only.[16]

Brahmacarya, etymologically meaning divine conduct, is much more comprehensive than sexual control. It represents "self-control" of the highest type, as it includes the control of all senses and leads the way to *mokṣa* (liberation).[17] Even though Gandhi at times rendered *brahmacarya* as chastity or continence simply due to a lack of a direct equivalent in English, he understood it to be a transcending of all types of sensual pleasures. *Brahmacarya* is a comprehensive principle of intense mental and spiritual discipline used to control the ever-active senses and thereby attain liberation (*mokṣa*). Although *brahmacarya* implies much more than mere sexual restraint, celibacy is so crucial to its practice that the terms eventually became synonymous. Because sexual temptations are intrinsic to bodily existence and are particularly difficult to overcome, celibacy is a physical representation of striving toward a passionless state leading to the realization of *Brahman*. Gandhi was aware that *brahmacarya* has always been an indispensable component of the pursuit of spiritual freedom within the Indian traditions. It is a prerequisite for Vedic learning, the definition of *sannyāsa*, the essence of virtues, and the zenith of restraint.

Hence, although many scholars of Gandhi interpret his *brahmacarya* as negation of sex, Gandhi defined *brahmacarya* not in the commonly translated sense of celibacy, but in the literal sense of the root of the word, "leading to Brahman" or "divine conduct": "What is *brahmacharya*? It is the way of life which leads us to Brahman [God]."[18] Gandhi was fond of the *Rāmāyaṇa* and the *Mahābhārata*, which emphasized the value of purity of speech, body, and mind for the realization of *Brahman*. The epics accord *brahmacarya* the highest status among all other virtues: "What is called Brahmacharya is considered as the means of attaining to Brahma. That is the foremost of all religions [*dharmas*]. It is by the practice of that religion [*dharma*] that one acquires the highest end."[19] For Gandhi the "highest end" was inextricably connected to his goal of *svarājya* (political freedom) and the service of society, as noted in his *Autobiography*.

The idea behind the emphasis on celibacy is "common to all Indian religions, being that to remain celibate is to be unpolluted by sex and to control sexual energy which, usually understood as the retention of semen, can be sublimated for a religious purpose," explains Gavin Flood.[20] But, by definition *brahmacarya* is not merely sexual abstinence, which people take up for various reasons—ritualistic, medical, social, and political. Rather, it implies renouncing the desire for mundane pleasures so that one may pursue religious goals. Phillimore notices the underlying religious motives of this practice: "Sexual abstinence, whether of short or long duration, either inside or outside marriage, is for Hindus generally motivated by religious ideals, expressed through individual transcendence of worldly desires and obligations in pursuit of salvation."[21] However, even though the *brahmacarya* vow primarily is motivated by soteriological objectives, this view is one-dimensional, focusing on the most obvious; traditionally the vow has been observed by men and women for different purposes—from health benefits to obtaining material goals.

Gandhi was not a classic *brahmacārin*, solely intent on the realization of *Brahman*; nor was he a traditional renunciate (*sannyāsin*) who gives up this world for ultimate liberation. "Ordinary sexual existence," Geoffrey Ashe argues, "seemed to him [Gandhi] 'insipid and animal like.' *Brahmacarya*, meaning self-control, could be a step toward a higher humanity."[22] Gandhi emphasized that "life without self-control has no meaning. Without self-control no real service is possible." As explored in the previous chapter, Gandhi perceived an integral relationship between the two ideals: the political objective of self-rule, in the sense of collective independence from foreign rule, was an extension of the personal goal of self-rule, in the sense of individual freedom from being enslaved to the "passions." "The first step to swaraj lies in the individual. . . . If we are ever torn by conflict from within, if we are ever going astray, and if instead of ruling our passions we allow them to rule us, swaraj can have no meaning for us."[23] Gandhi's vision of free India was unconventional: it aimed to bring freedom within and without, and self-control was a prerequisite to this end. Gandhi's practice of *brahmacarya* was not just a spiritual search for *Brahman* but was interconnected with all aspects of physical life, including politics, social service, physical fitness, and emotional health.

This integration of disparate concepts may seem unprecedented. Parekh, in his critical analysis of Gandhi's celibacy, does not find precedence for Gandhi's "theory of sexuality" elsewhere in Hindu thought *except* in the "relatively minor strand within the Hindu cultural tradition."[24] Parekh's conclusions refer to the binary ideologies of ascetic and householder—which are traditionally perceived to be in opposition (we earlier discussed the theories explored by Bailey and Dumont in this regard). The renouncer is often defined by abnegation of worldly concerns and desires, of which *brahmacarya* is an utmost expression. However, this view overlooks the various meanings and applications of *brahmacarya* as a technology of power within the Indian classical traditions and Indian narratives. Gandhi was innovative in his theory and practice of *brahmacarya*, but he functioned within the Indian religious framework. The following section focuses on how Gandhi utilized the full vocabulary of *brahmacarya* and its traditional subtexts—*brahmacarya* as *sat*, as a definition of studentship and sacrifice, as the nexus of *nivṛtti*, as *tapas*, and as a source of psychosomatic and supernatural power—for empowering his strategy of ascetic activism. The analysis of these subtexts shows how Gandhi utilized them, not as a contrived approach, but rather in intuitive, strategic ways—not only in spiritual and mundane contexts but also in his narration and performance of ascetic activism.

Brahmacarya as *Sat* (Truth)

Gandhi explored the various meanings of *sat* and differentiated between "limited truths" and "one absolute Truth which is total and self-embracing." According to him, the "indescribable truth" is God: "He, therefore, who understands truth, follows nothing but truth in thought, speech and action, comes to know God and gains the seer's vision of the past, the present and the future. He attains *moksha* though still encased in the physical frame."[25] Gandhi not only explained the ontological meaning of Truth, he also referred to the miraculous power of following truth as one's own *dharma*, as has been analyzed in chapter 2 in the context of his construct of *satyagraha*.

In the present context we explore how Gandhi established an intrinsic relationship between the practice of *brahmacarya* (a way to *Brahman*) and the pursuit of *sat*, which he made the core of the method of *satyagraha*. He made the practice of *brahmacarya* central to his *satyagraha* movement on the basis of his definition of *satya*, which he claimed to derive from traditional sources: "Truth includes non-violence, *brahmacarya*, non-stealing and other rules. . . . That a man who has known truth can be lecherous is as inconceivable as that darkness may exist despite the sun shining."[26] In this vein, according to Gandhi, a *satyagrahi* must be a *brahmacārin*.

During his imprisonment in the Yeravada Central Jail (1922–24), Gandhi interrupted the account of his daily reading to categorize "Truth" and "Untruth" in two columns in his "Jail Diary" (1922). He enumerated the substances that he considered to be Truth (*sat*) in one row and the items that he regarded as Untruth (*asat*) in the other. For example:

Truth is	**Untruth is**
gold	brass
light	darkness
diamond	a pebble
celibacy	adultery
Brahman	A soul in delusion
virility	impotence
valor	cowardice
deliverance	bondage
restraint	self-indulgence
Truth is one	Untruth has many forms
love	hatred

The total list contains about twenty-five entries. In analyzing this record it is worth noting that Gandhi placed "celibacy," "*Brahman*," "virility," and "love" into the same column, implying his view of the pure nature of these elements. But he juxtaposed celibacy with adultery, not with *kāma* (sexual desire) as such. Was Gandhi suggesting that a sexual relationship in any form—including in marriage—is *asat*, "untruth" and "adulterous"? If to Gandhi Truth meant commitment to One (*Brahman*), then to juxtapose adultery with celibacy was logical. He certainly advocated celibacy even in marriage and considered sexual desire in any form as "lust." "The perfect marriage is founded on *brahmacharya*," he declared.[27] He disregarded the conventional Hindu view that celebrates physical love in marriage. Judith Brown explains that Gandhi "argued that *brahmacharya* was not just for a few specially chosen souls, but for all truth-seekers. Even within marriage there should be abstinence from physical relations except on the few occasions when a couple specifically wanted a child." His critics and scholars have speculated on the reasons for his extreme position on sexuality and the challenges in its practice, noting he apparently "wrestled with guilt, anger, depression and lust."[28] Simultaneously, many could not but notice Gandhi's uncanny self-control and calm amid personal and political firestorms, a subject to be discussed in chapter 5.

In any case, the classification of these categories in this manner illustrates Gandhi's strong conviction of the role of *brahmacarya* in the pursuit of Truth. Gandhi's reasoning is apparent in his commitment to Truth, *brahmacarya,* and the method of Truth-force: if there is an essential relationship between Truth and celibacy, then one also exists between his method of *satyagraha* and his vow of celibacy. *Satyagraha*, by definition, denotes firmness in Truth and renunciation of passions. In a 1914 letter Gandhi reflected: "The more I reflect, the more insistently I feel the importance of truth and *brahmacharya.* The latter, together with all other rules of morality, is comprehended in Truth. . . . *brahmacharya* is important enough to share the place of honour with truth. It is my unshakable faith that these two can conquer any obstacle whatever."[29] Evidently, in these formative years of *satyagraha* in South Africa, Gandhi was considering the wider value of these disciplines and virtues for overcoming personal and social difficulties.

Gandhi considered *brahmacarya* (a bodily expression of *ahiṃsā*) essential in activating the illustrious power of Truth against what he considered to be the forces of *asat*—injustice and oppression. In this way, *satyagraha* parallels the phenomenon of *satyakriyā* (Act of Truth), as discussed in the previous chapter. Indologists (such as Burlingame, Zimmer, and W. Brown) expound on the "Holy Power" of Truth obtained through being steadfast in *dharma* and adhering to virtues. Zimmer notes: "The sage is both worshipped and feared because of the miraculous soul-force that he radiates into the world."[30] Gandhi, who made the force (literally, *āgraha*) of *sat* the underlying principle of his ascetic activism, was consistent with traditional lore about the miraculous power of Truth—which could only be accessed by a *brahmacārin*, a student of Vedic knowledge, or a sage who observes strict austerities.

Without the practice of *brahmacarya*, the realization of the absolute power of Truth is impossible, so declare the ancient texts. Indulgence in sexual acts defines birth and bondage, while *brahmacarya* signifies cessation of bondage and thus freedom from the cycle of death and rebirth. Ramchandra Gandhi succinctly compares the functions of sexuality and *brahmacarya*: "Sexuality is a search for the most hidden sensation of the human body, brahmacarya is a search for the insentient heart of consciousness."[31] In the pursuit of Truth and freedom, diverse *yogas* of Hinduism and various teachings of both Buddhism and Jainism utilize the practice of *brahmacarya*, among other restraints. In the *Gītā*, Gandhi's infallible guide, Lord Krṛṣṇa praises the virtue of restraint.[32] According to Gandhi, the practice of *brahmacarya*—noncooperation with the passions (which represent *asat*)—was essential to activating the power of Truth for attaining personal and political freedom.

Brahmacarya as the Stage of the Student

Gandhi trusted in the celebrated power of *brahmacarya* for creating a nation based on moral laws and for its instrumentality in the method of truth (*satyagraha*). For the success of his Satyagraha movement, he was aware of the need for the mass participation of students, who represented the future of independent India. The method of *satyagraha* mandated self-restraint yet, according to Gandhi, students educated in the modern Western system had "fallen from the ideal." During his numerous visits to colleges, Gandhi called on students to devote themselves to the service of the Motherland rather than seek a "lucrative career."[33] The ancient ideal of the student stage of life defined by observance of celibacy (*brahmacaryāśrama*) provided the standard by which Gandhi authenticated the relationship between moral discipline, service, selflessness, and education. In a didactic 1925 speech to students at Samaldas College, he specifically invited the students to return to the ancient ideal of *brahmacaryāśrama*:

> According to Hinduism, the student is a *brahmachari*, and *brahmacharyashrama is* the student-state. Celibacy is a narrow interpretation of *brahmacharya*. . . .
>
> Though there is nothing left of the ashramas today which we may hold up to the present generation as something to learn from and copy, we may still hark back to the ideals that inspired the original ashramas. . . .
>
> We are thinking, knowing beings and we must in this period distinguish truth from untruth, sweet from bitter language, clean from unclean things and so on.[34]

In this address Gandhi was referring to the Vedic system of the *varṇāśrama-dharma*, which includes a requisite stage of studentship known as *brahmacaryāśrama*, during which *brahmacarya* is central to a pupil's imbibing of sacred knowledge. Within the Vedic and mythical lore, *brahmacaryāśrama* is a temporary stage of abstinence, which students of Vedic knowledge adopt while living in their brahmin teacher's *āśrama* (hermitage). Chastity and restraint are so fundamental to this stage of life that a student has come to be identified as a *brahmacārin*: "The *brahmacārin by definition* is one who observes chastity, and this for *twelve years or more*. *Brahmacarya* presupposes sexual maturity but prohibits sexual activity," explains Walter Kaelber in his discussion of the state of studentship in Hinduism.[35]

Notwithstanding the fact that *brahmacaryāśrama* had never been accessible to students of all classes, castes, and genders, Gandhi looked to revive a hybrid form of *brahmacaryāśrama* that would be available to all students of secular education. He asked students to observe the vow of *brahmacarya* traditionally observed only by students of Vedic learning. At the same time, he called on them to actively participate in the Indian independence movement. Gandhi reminded students that it was their "religious duty" to follow in the footsteps of ancient sages and practice *brahmacarya*. Such rhetoric is another example that illustrates his combining of this-worldly goals and traditional moral codes for higher castes.

The *brahmacaryāśrama* forms the foundation of the character and conduct of the *brahmacārin* for the following three stages of life—*gṛhastha, vānaprastha,* and *sannyāsa*—in the *varṇāśrama* system.[36] A *brahmacārin* (student of Vedic knowledge) seeks to purify himself from the passions because they inhibit the flow of knowledge from the teacher. His life of *brahmacarya* itself becomes a sacrament—a *yajña*.[37] Because some students continue the stage of *brahmacarya* for their entire lifetime, the term *brahmacārin* is also used to refer to a sage or monk. "The [lives] of a *brahmachari* and a sannyasi are regarded as spiritually similar," reminded Gandhi during a speech to students.[38] Most people familiar with Indian culture are aware that *brahmacarya* is traditionally regarded as critical not only for the study of Vedic texts, but also for obtaining self-realization—the ultimate goal of human life. The *Muṇḍaka Upaniṣad* (3.1.5) mentions *brahmacarya* among other disciplines required for self-realization.[39]

Gandhi once called attention to the story of Indra and Virocana (of the *Chāndogya Upaniṣad*), which illustrates the necessity of *brahmacarya* in sustaining a "genuine thirst for knowledge."[40] In Vedic teachings, *devas* (gods) and *dānavas* (demons) both had to observe *brahmacarya* during their apprenticeship to Prajāpati in order to acquire higher knowledge. The *Chāndogya Upaniṣad* narrates how Virocana, among demons, and Indra, among gods, both observed *brahmacarya* for 32 years before approaching Prajāpati to learn the nature of the real Self. Virocana was satisfied with Prajāpati's first explanation—the self as the bodily self. But Indra continued his search for even higher knowledge of the Self and kept his vow of *brahmacarya* for 101 long years.[41]

Gandhi made it clear that celibacy, however, is only a part of the trajectory of physical and mental restraints—he expanded the definition of a *brahmacārin.* A *brahmacārin,* according to Gandhi, was a restrained and compassionate human being. He wrote in 1921: "One who is a *brahmachari,* [is one] who has conquered sleep and eats little, one who is free from vices and is truthful, one who speaks little, who suffers because he thinks of others' sufferings."[42] He also echoed the *Manu Smṛti,* which enumerates a list of observances for a *brahmacārin* and mandates that the student must control "all his organs, in order to increase his spiritual merit."[43] Mental and physical disciplines make a student's mind free and able to absorb subtle knowledge. Zimmer speculates on the value of celibacy in acquiring knowledge:

> The pupil, eager to receive, under the magic spell of the spiritual teacher, the whole charge, the total transference, of the divine knowledge and magic craft of his vocation, seeks to be nothing but a sacred vessel into which that precious essence flows. . . . Strict chastity (*brahmacarya*) is enjoined. . . . This is the period when the mere natural man, the human animal, is to be absolutely sacrificed, and the life of man in the spirit, the supernormal wisdom-power of the "twice-born," to be made effective in the flesh.[44]

The freedom from passions through the vow of *brahmacarya* serves as the gateway for entering into the citadel of wisdom. Gandhi—who was looking not only for political freedom for India but also for a comprehensive reform of the social, economic, and political spheres—utilized the model of *brahmacaryāśrama* to communicate his ideal to students. By summoning them to observe the life of a *brahmacārin*, he sought to instill the power of Truth-force in their minds.

Gandhi's call to revert back to *brahmacaryāśrama* seems contrary to the contemporary trend of acquiring Western education in which he himself had participated. Historically, before and during Gandhi's life, the orientation of education, even for the higher castes, had gradually shifted away from the traditional model of the *brahmacaryāśrama* to secular universities and colleges. By the 1850s, many of the students who acquired a Western education "belonged to the highest caste." British officials sought to provide "superior education" by establishing universities modeled after the Western system in cities such as Calcutta, Bombay, and Madras. Lord Canning, in emphasizing the need for Western education, "hoped the time was near when the nobility and upper classes of India would think that their children had not had the dues of their rank, unless they passed through the course of the university."[45]

Many young men were sent to study in Westernized Indian universities and even some to the hostels of Cambridge and Oxford. These young men were indoctrinated into Western thinking instead of traditional Indian wisdom. A famous dozen of Gandhi's contemporary religious and nationalist leaders and social reformers, including Rabindranath Tagore, Veer Savarkar, Sri Aurobindo, and Nehru, were educated in England.[46] The trend grew despite "intense opposition from orthodox Hindus and the social ostracism the returning traveler risked for having violated the rules of his caste."[47] Gandhi was also a part of this paradigm shift. He recalls in his *Autobiography* that a learned Brahmin and family friend, whom he called Joshiji, initiated the discussion of sending Gandhi to England for his education. Joshiji emphasized the value of Western education for the future of modern India because "the times are changed" and he strongly advised that Mohandas study in England if he wanted to secure a bright future.[48]

However, in spite of his brother's approval and promise to secure funding, Gandhi, like many other orthodox Hindus, faced resistance from his mother. His mother had been told that young men "got lost" in England and even took to eating meat and drinking liquor. Gandhi assured his mother and, in the presence of Becharji Swami, took the solemn vows of abstaining from touching women, meat, and wine. Gandhi recalls: "He [Becharji Swami] administered the oath and I vowed not to touch wine, woman, and meat. This done, my mother gave her permission." Notwithstanding this promise, his caste members were "agitated" over his going abroad. Many upper-caste Hindus ascribed to the rules that dictated purity and pollution. Traveling overseas ("crossing the waters") would result in the loss of one's caste. But Gandhi was not deterred by their objections, as he had already secured the permission of his mother and blessings of his brother.[49] This was Gandhi's induction into observance of religious vows, which he would later develop into a tool for discipline for the *satyagrahis* to make them firm in commitment.

In 1888, leaving behind his wife and young child, Gandhi sailed to England to receive his training as a barrister. There he was exposed to Western ideologies, such as civil disobedience, passive resistance, and social justice. Inexperienced in the Western lifestyle, Gandhi experimented with new modes of living but never felt comfortable with them. Ironically, it was during his stay in England that Gandhi became acquainted with his native texts, mythology, and culture; nevertheless, he eventually became opposed to the idea of students studying abroad. He emphasized: "That experience is the richest and contributes most to growth which springs from the soil."[50] Was it simply reactionary on Gandhi's part to seek a return to archaic ways? Deliberating on the complexity of Gandhi's message, Nehru wrote: "As for Gandhiji himself, he was a very difficult person to understand, sometimes his language was almost incomprehensible to an average modern."[51] It is interesting, however, that Gandhi's religious language and his garb of a peasant was oriented toward average people, perhaps not to those who were swept up by the tide of modernity. Moreover, Gandhi's own accounts reveal that his experiences in

England and South Africa had made him aware of the inadequacies of Western-style education, focusing on material growth, not spiritual development. He explained his views on this subject in his manifesto, *The Hind Swaraj* (1909).

Gandhi's nonviolent program required self-restraint, and his idea for a free India was a state based on moral values, so he used vocabulary and concepts that would inspire his people to this goal. He was aware that the value of traditional ideas in the modern context would not easily be grasped, either by students who were exposed to Western education or those traditionalists who endorsed the child-marriage tradition based in Hindu law books. Gandhi was also wary of the fermenting secular tendencies and the magnetism of sexual literature in student circles. In his 1929 "Weekly Letter" for *Young India*, Pyarelal records Gandhi's speech at a students' meeting in Hyderabad. The students had presented an address in Sindhi language to Gandhi, confessing their "failings." In his response Gandhi, expressed concern over the "poisonous literature from the West that was inundating the country and sought under the respectable and attractive garb of science to seduce them from the path of purity and self-restraint." He emphasized that "the path of self-indulgence and moral indiscipline was the surest way to perdition."[52]

In his struggle for independence Gandhi advocated Western ideas such as democracy, gender equality, and dignity of labor; however, he always appeared to be cognizant of the inadequacies of modern Western ways when compared to the principles and traditions of India. During his conversations with students, Gandhi often advocated changing the course of India's destiny, not through the embrace of secular Western education but instead by reverting to native systems and ideals, including the practice of *brahmacarya*. Gandhi's vision of independent India was a mixture of the traditional ideology of *dharma* rules and Western principles of democracy and equal rights.

Gandhi's turning back to the traditional values was not a novel enterprise. His predecessors and contemporaries, including Tilak, Bankim Chandra Chatterjee, Keshub Chandra Sen, Swami Dayananda, and Mahatma Munshiram, also asserted traditional values in their efforts to reform Hinduism and reinvigorate the masses. Gandhi spoke of Mahatma Munshiram (1856–1926) who "wanted his boys to be saturated with Vedic teaching" and "he wanted them to be and remain *brahmacharis* during their training." In contrast, Gandhi sought to reach out to students in a unique way. Unlike others, he did not insist only on Vedic learning but aimed to utilize the principles of discipline and self-control set forth for students of Vedic learning in his modern goals. He traveled to various schools and colleges to impart his message, underscoring the connection between individual and national freedom. He redefined *brahmacaryāśrama* and broadened the scope of *brahmacarya* by advocating the observance of *brahmacarya* for all students, not just for those of higher caste. He also called on female students to practice *brahmacarya*, which traditionally has been defined in terms of male celibacy. In 1927, during his speech to Mysore students, Gandhi invited them to "think of the ideal of *brahmacharya*, ponder over it in your wisdom and act upon it with conviction" for both individual and national freedom.[53] In 1929 he went so far as to advocate the practice even for married students:

> An ideal hostel will be a *brahmacharya* ashram, i.e., a colony of students living the life of *brahmacharis*. The word 'student' is of recent origin—a modern word. The old word for a student—*brahmachari*—is richer in meaning and connotes the ideal of student life more truly. *Brahmacharya* or spiritual discipline—control of the senses, purity of body and mind, and devotion to studies with a view to attaining the Ultimate Reality—is absolutely necessary during the period of study. In the rather topsyturvy conditions obtaining today, I would like married students also, if admitted into the hostel, to observe *brahmacharya* until the completion of their studies. This means, among other things, that during this period they should live away from their wives.[54]

In the modern secular world Gandhi's ideal of *brahmacarya* for all students appeared to be unrealistic, and some students expressed "perplexity" about his emphasis on the control of passions for national service.[55] Through his rhetoric of sacrifice, Gandhi sought to galvanize many young men and women to sacrifice for the nonviolent movement. Historically, students participated in picketing, strikes, and his movement of nonviolent resistance. The vow of *brahmacarya* demands the ultimate sacrifice, the sacrifice of sense-gratification, which is precisely the same sacrifice required for *satyagraha*. Gandhi argued: "The conquest of lust is the highest endeavour of a man or woman's existence. Without overcoming lust man cannot hope to rule over self. And without rule over self there can be no Swaraj or Ramaraj."[56] By invoking a symbiotic relationship between the ancient ideal of the *brahmacaryāśrama* and modern secular education—and between self-rule and self-control—Gandhi sought to sanctify education and at the same time inspire students to observe self-discipline, which he deemed essential for good citizenship, sociopolitical activism, and public service.

Brahmacarya as the Axis of *Nivṛtti*: A Way to Liberation from *Kāma* (Desire)

The practice of *brahmacarya* within the Indian religious context directly relates to a life of religious renunciation and *nivṛtti*: "To be celibate," Phillimore explains, "is a corollary of ascetic ideals, and it is hard to imagine celibacy and chastity entirely divorced from striving for a religious goal."[57] This is a common understanding in Indian traditions, where rarely is there found a secular modality of celibacy, except the prescribed chastity for widow women and unmarried girls. Just as the word *brahmacarya* has become identified with the student stage of life, similarly, a life of asceticism for seeking liberation has become associated with *brahmacarya*. "A man who observes *brahmacharya* is a sannyasi by nature," proclaimed Gandhi.[58] This notion is expressed in the *Chāndogya Upaniṣad* (8.5.2) when it identifies *brahmacarya* with silent asceticism.[59]

The renouncer seeks to transcend the net of bondage engendered by the passions by observing the vow of *brahmacarya*. The multitude of Eastern and Western religious writings that Gandhi studied warns against the bewitching passions and advocates seeking to transcend them. Gandhi was specifically influenced by the *Upaniṣads*, the *Bhagavad-Gītā*, Jain asceticism, the Buddha's legend of renunciation, and Hindu myths. In the religious lore, sexual temptations are represented by the figures of Kāma. Another name for Kāma is Māra—Death. Māra torments souls by a continuous cycle of life that ends in the ultimate suffering, death. The Buddha realized *nirvāṇa* after conquering the delusion of Māra, also known as the Tempter. Gandhi reiterated the concern, found in religious and philosophical texts, that the captivating power of the passions is an obstacle on the way to freedom. Zimmer underscores this central concern of Indian philosophy in the terms of freedom from the snares of desire:

> [T]he whole concern of the major portion of Indian philosophy is the way to . . . release (*mokṣa*) from the world-bounding, binding power of the divine being "who does not let go," the cosmic magician, Namuci. And throughout the traditional literature on the subject, the first step of this goal of goals is described as the refusal of Kāma's bait.[60]

Indian religious thought collectively agrees with the axiom that renunciation of the passions leads the way to isolation from worldly entanglement and finally to a state of liberation. The other non-Vedic traditions of India that informed Gandhi's ethos, in spite of their rejection of Vedic prescriptions, are also in concert in upholding the value of *brahmacarya* for the path of liberation. Both Gautama Buddha and Lord Mahavira, the great leader of Jainism, chose lives of *brahmacarya* to escape the wheel of *saṃsāra* (the cycle of death and rebirth).[61] The wheel of *saṃsāra* is propelled by sexual life. Sexual life is binding due to its concomitant attachment to spouse and progeny. In his article "Brahmacarya," Ramchandra Gandhi speculates about the Buddha's views on the attachment inherent in a sexual life:

> [The Buddha's] pursuit of individual brahmacarya would appear to have been inspired by disgust with unillumined sexual life which is procreative, actually or incipiently, in abject ignorance of the meaning and destiny of human life. When news is brought to him of the birth of his son, he says, naming the offspring of his pre-illumination life, that Rāhula, i.e. 'a fetter,' is born.[62]

Perhaps these undercurrents of Indian ethos motivated Gandhi to take the *brahmacarya* vow. Gandhi, like the Buddha, found children to be a hindrance in his goal of service. Gandhi confessed his belief that "procreation and consequent care of children were inconsistent with public service."[63] Due to this spirit of renunciation, even his contemporaries compared Gandhi to the Buddha.

The Jain tradition, with which Gandhi was acquainted from childhood, accords with Hindu and Buddhist teachings about the passions binding the soul to matter. To attain *kaivalya* ("isolation") it is essential to isolate the soul from the bondage of *karma*, which a life of attachment only perpetuates. In one Jain legend, the Lord Parśva (the twenty-third Tīrthāṇkara) contemplates:

> The desire for pleasure is only heightened by enjoyment, as the virulence of fire by the addition of fuel. Pleasures at the moment are undoubtedly pleasurable, but their consequences are bad; for to satisfy the cravings of the senses, one is forced to range in the realms of pain, paying no heed to moral injunctions and indulging in the worst vices. Hence the soul is compelled to migrate from birth to birth.[64]

The practice of *brahmacarya* is essential as a prerequisite to treading the path of liberation—not only among Jain virtues but also among the *panca śila* (five precepts) of Buddhism and among the five *yamas* of the *yoga* tradition. The teachings of Sikhism also consider *kama* to be one of the cardinal vices that inhibit the way to divine realization.[65] During his discourses, Gandhi often referred to the anthropomorphized figure of Kāma as an inner enemy who hinders the path to personal freedom and public service. In an article, "Sex Education," Gandhi declared sexual desire as the root of all sensual desires:

> All great religions have rightly regarded *Kama* as the arch-enemy of man, anger or hatred coming only in the second place. According to the *Gita*, the latter is an offspring of the former . . . The *Gita* of course uses the word *kama* in its wider sense of desire.[66]

Most of Gandhi's followers came from these traditions and understood the references, evidenced by accolades bestowed on him by the people from a wide variety of religions and backgrounds. Moreover, Gandhi often couched this ideology in universal terms. Not surprisingly, many people from traditions different from his (Islam and Christianity, for example) found resonance with Gandhi's message of overcoming sensual desires for moral progress, bolstering their support of Gandhi. In a 1925 letter, a correspondent asked Gandhi, "Is there Satan in Hinduism?" In his response Gandhi suggested that "we shall continue to talk of passions as if they were persons. Do they not torment us as much as evil persons?"[67]

For Gandhi, the practice of *brahmacarya* provided a fence, as it were, to stop the intrusion of Kāma. In his commentary on the *Gītā* (III: 37), Gandhi warns his followers against the evil nature of Kāma: "This *kama* harms, like an enemy, even a man of spiritual knowledge."[68] In a famous Hindu legend, Kāma even torments the great yogi, Lord Śiva. Kāma represents bondage to this world; victory over Kāma symbolizes liberation.

It is not surprising that Gandhi included in his *āśrama* hymnal a song that warns of the power of Cupid. "Cupid is hunting down the helpless people who will not give up greed and lust and who have lost the true path in the midst of self-gratification."[69] Kāma—the personification of sexual love—by its nature deludes (*moha*) and renders self-forgetful those who come into its grasp. *Brahmacarya* and other restraints purify the passions that inhibit self-awareness. Gandhi was aware, through personal experience, of the riveting power of Kāma as described through Indian literature.[70] In the chapter of his *Autobiography* called "My Father's Death and My Double Shame," Gandhi narrated how Kāma had blinded (*viṣyāndha*) him at the time of his father's death and how he left his father's bedside to satisfy his sexual desire. This caused Gandhi feelings of pain, shame, and remorse that haunted him throughout his life:

> It is a blot I have never been able to efface or forget . . . although my devotion to my parents knew no bounds and I would have given up anything for it, yet it was weighed and found unpardonably wanting because my mind was at the same moment in the grip of lust. . . . It took me long to get free from the shackles of lust, and I had to pass through many ordeals before I could overcome it.[71]

At the time of his father's death (1885) Gandhi was married, but was only sixteen years old. Many speculate that this incident was a cause of his proclivity for ascetic celibacy, which he sealed by formal vow in 1906. Kakar says: "Gandhi talks of his life-long feeling of remorse that blind lust had deprived him of the chance of rendering some last service to his father thus missing the patriarch's 'blessing' which was instead received by the uncle."[72] Additionally, perhaps, one of the main reasons behind Gandhi's regret was that he failed in his duty as a son, who traditionally offers the final rites to his parents (as prescribed in the *Dharma* literature). Traditionally, a son plays an important role in taking care of ancestors and his rites make the way for them to heavenly worlds. Other scholars (Bose, Erikson, and the Rudolphs) who also utilize a psychoanalytic approach relate Gandhi's sexual indulgence at the time of his father's death with his later obsessive attitude toward celibacy. For example, Gandhi's secretary Bose maintains that " 'repression of the sexual instinct,' [was] prompted by a self-imposed penance for 'having proved untrue to his father during the last moments of his life.' "[73] Gandhi's own stated reasons for his vow of celibacy will be explored in the next chapter.

Ramchandra Gandhi explains: "Brahmacarya is rooted in self-consciousness, [and] sexual love in self-forgetfulness."[74] Gandhi narrated many stories from the *Mahābhārata*, the *Rāmāyaṇa*, and the *Purāṇas* that bear witness to the alluring power of lust—which overpowers even gods such as Śiva and acclaimed ascetics such as Viśvāmitra and Bhārdwāja. In these traditional tales, by the mere sight of beautiful maidens, the protagonists become consumed by the flame of love, and the extreme powers they had acquired by burning their passions are dissipated. This volume's last chapter, on myths, expands more fully on Gandhi's deployment of these tales.

During the process of developing his strategy for confronting injustice, Gandhi, who was steeped in the cultural mindset of India's ancient traditions and already committed to service, could well have reflected back to this event and reasoned: if the service of his father demanded a passion-free state of mind, the service of humanity must then necessitate complete renunciation of passions (*viṣayas*) and sexual relations. Gandhi confesses: "I learnt in the school of experience that *brahmacharya* was a *sine qua non* for a life devoted to service."[75] Gandhi's personal experiences and study of religious texts during the formative years of his life confirmed his conviction that a correlation exists between renunciation and service. As has been detailed in the first chapter, he made *nivṛtti* the foundation of *satyagraha* and facilitated it by his personal *brahmacarya.* Gandhi used *nivṛtti* not in the commonly used sense of withdrawal but as an activist tool—in which the practices of renunciation not only empower the individual but become instrumental in resistance. He argued:

> No worker who has not overcome lust can hope to render any genuine service to the cause of Harijans, communal unity, khadi, cow-protection or village reconstruction. Great causes like these cannot be served by intellectual equipment alone, they call for spiritual effort or soul-force.[76]

What kind of political freedom was Gandhi imagining by mandating celibacy for worldly men and women? Are only those who practice *brahmacarya* fit to render social service? What lay behind Gandhi's persistent repudiation of sexual desire? These questions can be, and have been, addressed from different viewpoints, such as the psychoanalytical, anthropological, and religious. However, from Gandhi's own point of view, it appears that he adopted the path of *nivṛtti* in order to achieve both personal and political freedom. From that perspective, denying fulfillment of the carnal desires for sex and food was vital. In his comparison of Tolstoy and Gandhi, who both "denied that erotic love was a value," Martin B. Green notes that "asceticism is the root of all life for them, including political life." Green quotes Gandhi: "I saw that nations, like individuals, could only be made through the agony of the Cross and in no other way."[77] The pangs of suffering and spirit of sacrifice are required in any revolution—violent or nonviolent. The only difference between a violent and nonviolent revolution, according to Gandhi, was that the former used methods that inflict suffering on the other, but the latter used techniques that required self-suffering. When religious value is ascribed to the methods of resistance, the participants feel energized, perceiving the greater value of their actions.

As we discussed earlier, Gandhi equated *rāmarājya* with *svarājya*. According to Gandhi, *brahmacarya*—in the sense of a comprehensive principle of restraint—was an infallible method to secure both. Gandhi used religious symbolism to differentiate between the reigns of Kāma and Rāma: "The reign of *kama* is different in its effect from the reign of Rama. . . . Like Kumbhakarna *kama* is ever waiting, open-mouthed, for its prey."[78] Kumbhakarṇa, a demon in the *Rāmāyaṇa*, has an insatiable hunger. Lord Rāma has to conquer the demon Kumbhakarṇa—a representation of voracious desires—to establish *rāmarājya* (the Kingdom of Truth). Of course, one must remember that Rāma's assault against the demonic forces of Rāvaṇa is motivated by his deep love for his wife, Sītā, who had been abducted by Rāvaṇa. Facts such as these appear to contradict Gandhi's autodidactic lessons from the classical texts.

However, Gandhi was not seeking logical connections by narrating such myths but rather was employing a didactic strategy to impart the message that inner empowerment could be acquired through the practice of renunciation. To confront the forces of foreign rule, oppression, and injustice—which he considered evil—as well as to attain freedom with the weapon of *satyagraha*, it was, according to him, necessary to conquer the passions via renunciation. Gandhi often reinterpreted episodes of the *Rāmāyaṇa* and other religious literature from an allegorical viewpoint: his *Rāmāyaṇa* is a tale about the power of chastity, Sītā's resistance to Rāvaṇa, and the detachment of Rāma—themes which will be dealt with in the chapter on Gandhi's myths.[79]

Was it realistic for Gandhi to apply the model of *sannyāsins* to *satyagrahis* seeking political freedom? Nehru thought Gandhi to have gone to an "extreme."[80] Gandhi could not have been so naive about the captivating power of sensual desire as to believe that a universal demand for the observance of celibacy would be embraced by significant numbers of people. However, the metaphor most easily accessible to the Indian mind was that of the *sannyāsin*—the symbol of renunciation, compassion, and power at the same time—a symbol that was made popular by his contemporary social and religious reformers. Gandhi adopted this metaphor to communicate his message of self-autonomy and, thus, freedom.

Brahmacarya as *Tapas*: A Method for the Purification and Destruction of Evil

One of the prominent religious concepts that Gandhi commonly referred to in explaining his private practice of *brahmacarya* and its effectiveness was *tapas*. *Tapas* (or *tapasya*) encompasses the intrinsic energy associated with self-abnegation and it purifies the performer. As mentioned earlier, *tapas*, literally derived from the Sanskrit root √*tap*, connotes "burning," "consuming," or "heat."[81] The word *tapas* has its origins in the ancient Vedic ritual of fire sacrifice, *yajña*. Agni, the god of *yajña*, is the embodiment of heat. "Agni, as the fire, destroys or consumes through *tapas* [heat]."[82] In the *Upaniṣads* and the *Yoga* literature, this concept becomes homologous to physical and mental austerities, which produce inner heat, and the term *tapas* "is used to designate ascetic effort in general."[83] *Tapas* is also associated with the conscious infliction of physical suffering on one's self. Gandhi clarifies his view of *tapasya*:

> Self-torture is only so called. The right word is self-purification. The flesh must be subdued. The flesh has gained such mastery over us that it has to be dislodged. We are born slaves of the flesh. Freedom from that bondage is mastery over the flesh, the self. All *tapasya* is self-torture.[84]

The Vedic students' life of *brahmacarya*, defined by chastity, and the ascetic life, symbolized by the utmost renunciation of sensory attachment, are both regarded as forms of *tapas*. Eliade, speaking about the unique feature of *brahmacarya* in the yogic traditions, remarks that "sexual abstinence (*brahmacarya*) is not only refraining from sexual acts but 'burning' carnal temptation itself."[85] Refraining from sexual acts is a restraint that requires discipline, but it is the burning of the craving itself that yields magical potency. Passivity in sexual relations does not produce the "magical heat"; rather, the creative heat is produced by burning the "carnal temptation" and "exertion." Gandhi, utilizing the traditional connotations of *brahmacarya*, makes a similar distinction:

> Now mere abstention from sexual intercourse cannot be termed *brahmacharya*. So long as the desire for intercourse is there, one *cannot* be said to have attained *brahmacharya*. Only he who has burnt away the sexual desire in its entirety may be said to have attained control over his sexual organs.[86]

However, the peculiarity of Gandhi's observance of *brahmacarya* was that he sought to eliminate all desire for temptation—not by isolating himself from women (as *yogins* have done), but rather by associating closely with women and confronting the temptations directly. (This topic will be discussed in the next chapter.) Therefore, Gandhi was not merely observing celibacy in his vow of *brahmacarya.* Rather, by means of the constant exertion of sustaining the vow, he claimed to engender "fire" within himself—the fire which creates, purifies, and consumes. Gandhi documented his endeavors in "burning" the sexual desire and generating the heat that could destroy the "enemy" that was the British Empire—just as his ancestors had destroyed the *Rākṣasas* (demons):

> I enjoy the privilege of having many English friends, but I am a determined enemy of the English rule as conducted at present and if the power—*tapasya*—of one man could destroy it, I would certainly destroy it, if it could not be mended.[87]

Gandhi is seemingly referring to the intrinsic power of *tapas* as recognized in the religious texts of India. In the ascetic literature, *tapas* (voluntarily suffering in the form of bodily mortifications and mental disciplines) is undertaken for inner purification; nevertheless, those who practice austerities are aware of the inherent powers of the restraints. The ascetic purifies the inner self and acquires powers, not by ritual sacrifice (performance of *yajña*) but by the sacrifice of the desires themselves. Burning up latent impressions and karmic afflictions requires that the ascetic observe the extreme discipline of *brahmacarya* and other *vratas* (vows). In his discussion of Gandhi's idea of *tapasya,* Iyer explains:

> *Tapas* means that which burns up impurities, purificatory action, austerities, penance. The original meaning of the word denotes warmth or heat. Man becomes enslaved by his contact with the sensory world, falls into ignorance and involuntary suffering. . . . In the attainment of *moksha* he requires *tapas*, ceaseless self-restraint, an acceptance of suffering, the dispelling of his delusions by a clear vision of his real nature and his essential identity with all other beings.[88]

This exposition corresponds to Gandhi's intent for *mokṣa,* which he defined in terms of serving his fellow beings. Traditionally, the heat of *tapas* is regarded as creative and purificatory. In 1920, Gandhi wrote in an article that "*tapasya* is the basis of all creation."[89] For example, at the cosmogonic level, in the *Ṛg Veda, tapas* is regarded as the creative force and its powers are "creative on both the cosmic and spiritual planes."[90]

In the ancient religious texts, the power of austerity is often called on to conquer evil forces. Gandhi sought to destroy the evils of his society—such as untouchability—as well as the British regime, which he characterized as "satanic" and "*Ravanarajya*" (the kingdom of demon Rāvaṇa)—with the nonsatanic means of nonviolence and truth. During a speech in 1920, Gandhi emphasized that "to punish the Satan they should not employ Satanic means. . . . Just as light disperses darkness they could disperse falsehood by truth and evil forces by soul-force."[91] However, unlike the tradition in which demons are destroyed by gods, Gandhi differentiated between the British regime and British people. "British system is Satanic. But, in spite of British system being Satanic, I love the British like my brothers," asserted Gandhi, keeping with his conviction to identify with all beings.[92]

In the *Ṛg Veda*, the destroying power of Agni is invoked to obliterate enemies and evil doers. The *Ṛg Veda* suggests that the sacrificer himself, who has been purified by intense austerities, may generate sufficient destructive heat to eliminate his enemies.[93] Utilizing such fierce force to destroy opponents is a recurring motif throughout India's religious literature. The confrontation with the enemy was by no means nonviolent; and neither was there any consideration of a compassionate treatment of the enemy by the *tapasvin*. Historically, in ancient Indian thought, the high status of the warrior class is a testimony to the necessity of war and conquest in the state polity. Even though the advent of Buddhism and Jainism created awareness of the doctrine of nonviolence, "war was generally accepted as a normal activity of the state," notes Basham. Moreover, nonviolence was a personal virtue and "was never at this time taken to forbid war or capital punishment. It was only in modern times that Mahātmā Gāndhī reinterpreted it in this sense."[94] Gandhi's motive was not a violent overthrow of the British regime but rather transformation of their attitude toward Indians. For this he sought to utilize "no other method" than that of *tapasya*, which, according to him, "was practised in ancient India" and "is found nowhere else."[95] It is not surprising, however, that many revolutionaries cited the ancient lore in defense of militancy, but Gandhi interpreted the tradition more broadly to substantiate his nonviolent method.

According to Gandhi, his personal *tapasya* meant developing complete control over passions and it was represented by his absolute observance of *brahmacarya.* His life was a ceaseless effort to realize self-control. In 1927, he lamented that he was not able to achieve this goal:

> Despite the prevailing climate I have not lost hope regarding the practice of *brahmacharya,* etc. There will rise from our midst a true aspirant who will clear the prevailing atmosphere. . . . My own *tapascharya* is hopelessly imperfect. I have been observing external, physical *brahmacharya* for nearly 30 years. I have, however, not freed myself from passion; I am trying to. I think complete control of all the five sense-organs is essential for the observance of perfect *brahmacharya.*[96]

Gandhi's accounts reveal that he fluently applied the terms *tapascarya, yajña,* purification, and penance to his austere vows of *brahmacarya, asvādavrata* (control of palate), *ahiṃsā,* etc. Gandhi often observed periods of fasting and silence, claiming that fasting was a "mighty force," and likened spiritual fasting to "*tapas.*" He asserted that "all *tapas* invariably exerts a purifying influence on those on whose behalf it is undertaken."[97] In ascetic exertion, *tapas* carries in itself all the original potency of the praxis of *yajña.* At the ritual level, *yajña* is the essence of Vedic culture—it sustains the relationship of humans with the gods for maintaining order and procuring prosperity. Fire is the mediator in the communion between the gods and the sacrificer, who scrupulously follows the minute details of the sacrificial ritual. The inner heat produced by such restraint and exertion in austerities came to be known as *tapas,* and it afforded the sacrificers the same miraculous energy of purification, creation, and destruction for which the *yajña* itself was conducted. The original sacrificial meaning of *tapas*—the heat generated by *yajña* and the sacrificer—thus became analogous to asceticism and "self-imposed austerity." Therefore, the ascetics are known as *tapasvins.* Kaelber makes the connection:

> The meaning of *tapas* as ascetic effort may be clearly seen in its repeated correlation with the root *śram,* "to toil," to "weary one's self," "to exert one's self." . . . [S]elf-imposed "suffering" and pain, generates an inner heat. This inner heat is also referred to as *tapas.*[98]

Gandhi underlined the importance of vows: "A vow means unflinching determination, and helps us against temptations. Determination is worth nothing if it bends before discomfort."[99] Gandhi personally experienced his mother's resolve. She would "take the hardest vows and keep them without flinching," wrote Gandhi in the first chapter of his *Autobiography.*[100] Observance of austere vows is a common theme in the Vedic and Hindu classical literature, as well in the heterodox traditions of India. For instance, the *Brāhmaṇas* emphasize that the sacrificer has to observe a *vrata,* denoting the "ascetic regimen (e.g., the *vrata* of an *iṣti* rite, the soma *dīkṣā,* the observances of a student of Veda) intended to purify and empower the performer, giving him a quasi-divine capacity," asserts Lubin. A *vrata* "becomes the most generic term in Brahmanism for rules or regimens in which a fixed rule of behavior, involving restrictions as well as prescribed actions, is thought to produce specified results for whoever performs it." Lubin summarizes that in the *Atharva Veda* and the *Brāhmaṇa* texts the observance of rules requires "exertion (*śrama*) and fervid dedication to fasting and celibacy (i.e., *tapas*)."[101] Charles Rockwell Lanman notes that "the oldest forms of asceticism were doubtless fasting and continence, and the prime motive was doubtless the hope of some kind of reward." The evils and temptations of "gluttony and lechery" are known to all, and curbing these appetites requires firmness of will.[102] The ascetic regimen purifies the performer and creates the "magical heat" necessary for inviting divine favors, including the destruction of evil forces.

In his discussion of Gandhi's fasts, Jordens notes that "fasting has a certain inherent power," but he only intimates the traditional meaning of *tapas* without elaborating on the general understanding within India's traditions that fasting is a component of *tapas*. The following discussion of the traditional relationship between austerity and power helps us understand the underlying meaning of Gandhi's narrative and his methods of ascetic activism. Gandhi himself stressed: "The function of my fast is to purify, to release our energies by overcoming our inertia and mental sluggishness. . . . My fast isolates the forces of evil; the moment they are isolated they die."[103] Gandhi's reliance on vows for the purpose of self-purification and self-discipline—such as fasting, celibacy, and silence—mirrors the references from the ancient literature. However, Gandhi was unique in his application of these vows: he sought to extend the range of sacred vows beyond the realm of an individual's private observance for personal purification to the entire community's commitment to religious vows for the purification of India's political and social ills. His public fasting for the sociopolitical issues of communal harmony and eradication of untouchability, and his advocacy of vows of *brahmacarya*, truth, nonviolence, poverty, and control of palate for his movement of Satyagraha, are unique in application.

For his method of *satyagraha* (which requires self-suffering), Gandhi seemed to be invoking the "agony" that accompanies an inner battle with sensory desires, as facing this inner battle would in turn prepare *satyagrahis* to confront outer struggles. Wolpert, in *Gandhi's Passion*, makes the connection between *tapas* and the Passion (the suffering of Christ). He deliberates on the instrumentality of Gandhi's *tapas*:

> He [Gandhi] turned himself into a cauldron of pain so brilliantly illuminating as to endow him with an aura of goodness and light, magnetizing millions to enter prison without flinching when he called, and to die for him, if ever he asked.[104]

Wolpert is correct in assessing the mobilizing power of suffering. However, his psychological account of suffering is not on a par with Gandhi's idea of voluntarily suffering. To Gandhi, *tapas* never represented a "cauldron of pain" but rather a vessel of joy: "No sacrifice is worth the name unless it is a joy," wrote Gandhi in the *Young India.*[105] *Tapas*, according to Gandhi, was not conceived for the purpose of cultivating pain. He referenced the passage in the *Gītā* (XVII: 19) that describes the *tapas* that is taken up for "torturing oneself as *tāmasic* (arising out of delusion) and undesirable." However, Gandhi seems to contradict himself, for, as we saw earlier, he also referred to *tapasya* as "self-torture." Gandhi's definition of *tapasya* meant joyful suffering, in which pain is a torture of the flesh. The one who practices *tapas* must rise above the feeling of pain.

Gandhi likened his political and social service to the performance of *yajña*, and presented his actions of resisting injustice and evil rules as "Acts of Truth" confronting the falsehood of slavery and oppression. "To the orthodox Hindus I need net [*sic*] point out the sovereign efficacy of *tapasya*. And satyagraha is nothing but *tapasya* for Truth."[106] Gandhi quoted examples from religious literature to illustrate the creative, purifying, and destructive powers of *tapas*: "Through *tapas* the world exists, through it Bhavani won Shambhu, Savitri brought back Satyavan to life, Lakshmana defeated Indrajit and Rama defeated Ravana."[107] To move the latent powers of his native people who considered themselves inadequately equipped to confront the powerful British regime, Gandhi reminded them of the "divine weapon" of *tapascarya* that their ancestors used to fight their battles: "There is no parallel in the world for the *tapascharya* that this country has voluntarily gone through. India has little use for steel weapons; it has fought with divine weapons; it can still do so."[108] *Brahmacarya* energy symbolizes concentrated mental energy achieved through nonattachment and single-minded focus. Gandhi trusted the power of austerities in attaining *svarāj*. In 1921, on his Silence Day, Gandhi wrote in a letter to Mahadev Desai:

> I know, of course, if I can completely follow non-violence, truth and *brahmacharya* in action, speech and thought, then we should certainly get swaraj this year; we may also get it if someone else from among us can do these things, or if the *tapas* of all of us taken together proves sufficient for the purpose. In the first instance, however, I hate not given [*sic*] up this hope in regard to myself.[109]

This reflection evinces that Gandhi was serious in his endeavor to mobilize the power of *tapas*. India achieved freedom more than twenty-five years after this letter. Gandhi incessantly sought to perfect his and his followers' *tapas*. His writings show that in his personal life he used even unconventional methods in his practice of *brahmacarya* in order to materialize its power.

The practicality of obtaining self-rule through the power of *tapas* in this modern age was questionable to some. Many of Gandhi's critics were concerned about the primarily Hindu expressions of his ideology for rousing the masses. His "modernist" critics, who equated all religion with "irrationalism and obscurantism," also "resented Gandhi's saintly idiom."[110] Some latter-day historians argue that Gandhi may actually have "contributed to the communal polarization." Gandhi's vows, and his advocacy that others also adopt them, were the subject of considerable opposition. Iyer notes that "Gandhi's attitude toward vows was challenged by two of his closest admirers, C. F. Andrews and J. C. Kumarappa," who perceived them as hindrances to new growth and as a possible cause of mental laziness and conflict.[111] Even Gandhi's family, especially his eldest son, resented his father's austere lifestyle. But the common masses, mesmerized by his image of ascetic power and nostalgia for India's legendary eras (as evidenced by the emergence of Gandhi's stature as a *mahātmā*), responded to Gandhi's call. A detailed analysis of this response is presented in the chapter on Gandhi's myths.

Intent on experimenting with the celebrated power of austerities, Gandhi sought to test the potency of *tapas* in all contexts—personal, social, and political. On the one hand, through his own practices of renunciation, Gandhi was committing himself literally to the power of *tapas*; on the other hand, through evoking the imagery of *tapasvins*, he was metaphorically reinventing the magic of *tapas* as means of mass mobilization. The motivating force that lay behind both was his belief in the pragmatic instrumentality of *tapas* as a political method and the faith that, if he could somehow manipulate its spiritual power, he would succeed in his goals.

Brahmacarya and Psychosomatic Power

Alter provides a snapshot of modern literature describing the relationship between physical and mental power and celibacy. He quotes Swami Shivananda (1984): "The more a person conserves his semen, the greater will be his stature and vitality. His energy, ardor, intellect, competence, capacity for work, wisdom, success and godliness will begin to manifest themselves."[112] Thus, within the tradition of the renouncers, as told in the traditional myths, *brahmacarya* not only epitomizes *tapas* and ascetic practices that confer or produce "magical" heat or energy and supernatural potency, it is also said to yield tangible *physical* powers—including enhanced stamina, clarity of mind, fearlessness, and profound concentration. These themes resonated with nineteenth- and twentieth-century Indian religious revivalists. To Gandhi as well, *brahmacarya* was not only an essential requisite for *nivṛtti* and symbolic of the ultimate "sacrifice," it was also a *vrata* that afforded substantive physical and mental prowess to the *brahmacārin*. Undeniably, Gandhi himself exhibited great capacity for self-control, equanimity, fearlessness, concentration, and exceptional physical stamina. Jeffery Paine says: "Gandhi was rarely sick, rarely moody, and he displayed tremendous powers of concentration."[113] This of course could be attributed to his genetic disposition, psychological self-cultivation, skillful adaptation, and the like; nevertheless, it would be difficult to separate his discourse on *brahmacarya*—infused as it was with the mythical and religious—from the mental and physical abilities he personally demonstrated. According to Gandhi, *brahmacarya* harnesses the life force—the source that creates living beings—which in turn revitalizes the mental and physical faculties. Gandhi emphasized that "the physical, mental and moral strength of one who has been able to observe unbroken *brahmacharya* must be seen to be believed; it cannot be described."[114]

Gandhi often referred to Patañjali's *Yoga Sūtras* to support his argument for observance of the five *yamas*. *The Yoga Sūtra* (II: 38) glorifies the power of *brahmacarya* for acquiring heroic strength (*vīrya*). A commentary by Vyāsa on this *Sūtra* became a testimony for those who associated "unimpeded" physical and mental energy with *brahmacarya*:

> Unimpeded power includes unobstructed knowledge, action and power like the power of minification or reducing oneself to a small particle. Incontinence deprives the nerves etc. of vital powers. Practice of continence prevents loss of vitality and increases Vīrya or energy . . . thereby gradually leading to accumulation of unhindered powers. And having attained knowledge, he is able to instil [*sic*] it in his disciples. The words of wisdom of an incontinent person do not go deep into the mind of a disciple.[115]

Since Gandhi trusted the truths of this tradition, through his vow he was seeking to instill his message of nonviolence and Truth in his followers' minds. Although *brahmacarya* is only one of the *yamas* (restraints) required in the disciplines of yoga, its practice has been thought to convey immense psychic and physical powers. Accruing mental and physical powers is known as *ojas*. *Tapas*, especially the intense discipline of *brahmacarya*, affects the psychosomatic tendencies of an individual by generating radiance (*tejas* and *jyotis*) as well as vitality (*ojas*), the principle of vital strength. Feuerstein elaborates:

> *Ojas* is generated especially through the practice of chastity, as a result of the sublimation of sexual energy. It is held to be so potent that the ascetic can influence and change his or her destiny and the destiny of others.[116]

The relationship between *brahmacarya* and vitality is intrinsic to the therapeutic, religious, and philosophical thought of India. In the Āyurveda the potency of the life force—*ojas*—is acclaimed for physical and mental well-being. According to the *Carak Saṁhitā*, the life force consists in physiological fluid, *ojas:* "It is the *ojas* which keeps all living beings refreshed. There can be no life without *ojas*. It marks the beginning of the formation of the embryo. . . . Loss of *ojas* amounts to loss of life itself." *Ojas* is also understood as "vitality" or "immunity."[117]

Historically, many religious and political leaders of the nineteenth and twentieth centuries sought to apply "seminal energy" to invigorate the ailing social and political life of India. For the purpose of infusing youth with vigor for social and spiritual evolution, Swami Vivekananda propounded celibacy on the grounds of its psychophysical potency:

> The Yogis claim that of all the energies that are in the human body the highest is what they call "Ojas." . . . The Yogis say that that part of human energy which is expressed as sex energy, in sexual thought, when checked and controlled, easily becomes changed into Ojas . . . chastity has always been considered the highest virtue. A man feels that if he is unchaste, spirituality goes away, he loses mental vigour and moral stamina.[118]

Perhaps the above understanding was the reason that Gandhi was deeply disturbed when he had a nocturnal emission on the night of January 18, 1936. In a 1936 letter, he lamented to one of his female associates: "If my *brahmacharya* had been completely free from discharges, I would have been able to place before the world very much more than I have succeeded in doing." Gandhi perceived *brahmacarya* as an essential source of energy for a *satyagrahi*: "Without *brahmacharya* the satyagrahi will have no luster, no inner strength to stand unarmed against the whole world." The *satyagrahis* who were able to confront their own passions would also have the strength to remain fearless when faced with difficult situations. Notably, Gandhi rarely used the word *tejas* in his vast writings and only then in the context of the "purity of character" of women such as of Sītā and Draupadi, not in terms of male seminal power. He states, "If the womanhood of India attained her complete *tejas*, the foreigner would not be here."[119] However, Gandhi often used the terms such as *luster* and *inner strength* denoting the power of purity and truth.

Ancient thinkers incorporated religious, ritualistic, mental, and physical reasons to advocate *brahmacarya* for retaining the seed that has power to create another life. If the seed is controlled, its creative energy could be applied to any task—for example, the study of Vedic knowledge, concentration in *yajña*, and incessant toiling on the path to liberation. Radhakrishnan elaborates on the psychosomatic reasons for practicing *brahmacarya*:

> When the seed is wasted in sex excesses, the body becomes weak and crippled, the face lined, the eyes dull, hearing impaired and the brain inactive. If *brahmacarya* is practised, the physical body remains youthful and beautiful, the brain keen and alert, the whole physical expression becomes the image and likeness of the Divine.[120]

Gandhi not only offered a comprehensive definition of *brahmacarya* as control of all sense organs, he also stated the necessity of conserving generative fluid for physical strength. He echoed the refrain of the traditional Indian belief systems: "He who has conserved his generative fluid is known as *viryavan*, a man of strength."[121]

In his *Autobiography*, Gandhi confronts his own physical and mental frailties and openly admits his childhood fears, his self-effacing nature, and his lack of physical strength. He recalls an amusing episode that occurred while he was a student living in England:

> My cowardice was on a par with my reserve. . . . My landlady's daughter took me one day to the lovely hills round Ventnor. I was no slow walker, but my companion walked even faster, dragging me after her and chattering away all the while. . . . She was flying like a bird whilst I was wondering when I should get back home. We thus reached the top of a hill. . . . In spite of her high-heeled boots this sprightly young lady of twenty-five darted down the hill like an arrow. I was shamefacedly struggling to get down. . . . I somehow managed to scramble to the bottom. She loudly laughed 'bravo' and shamed me all the more.[122]

In his later writings, Gandhi often connected infirmity and weak health with lack of sexual control, and health and vitality with *brahmacarya*. Gandhi even imputed his lack of physical stamina to his early marriage, which might have depleted him of physical strength. And he also correlated *brahmacarya* with psychophysical health:

> The sexual glands are all the time secreting the semen. This secretion should be utilized for enhancing one's mental, physical and spiritual energy. He who would learn to utilize it thus will find that he requires very little food to keep his body in a fit condition. And yet he will be as capable as any of undertaking physical labour. Mental exertion will not tire him easily nor will he show the ordinary signs of old age. Just as a ripe fruit or an old leaf falls off naturally, so will such a *brahmachari* when his time comes pass away with all his faculties intact.[123]

Was Gandhi referring to his own experience with the enhanced prowess—mental, physical, and spiritual energy—that he believed he acquired through *brahmacarya*? Perhaps his unflinching trust in *brahmacarya* made him consider that it was "too serious to be treated with 'moderation.' "[124]

Gandhi himself certainly ascribed his physical stamina, mental clarity, and social charisma to his *brahmacarya* practice, but was it only limited to the somatic aspect, namely, retention of sexual fluid? Gandhi often spoke in terms of male sexuality but he also described the importance of *brahmacarya* for women. Meena Khandelwal sees sexual fluids as metaphors and argues that "although female celibacy was abhorrent to classical orthodoxy, many contemporary Hindu religious leaders have advocated celibacy for men and women." She further states: "If the hydraulic model of semen retention were the only model available, then one might expect the practice of celibacy to have little relevance for women." It would therefore be a mistake to infer that Gandhi was linking physical strength strictly to the retention of semen. In Khandelwal's view, Gandhi advocated celibacy for both men and women "as a matter of emotional self-control and conservation of one's energies (energy to accomplish tasks rather than energy used for magical powers)."[125] Even though Gandhi defined *brahmcarya* broadly and also extended its practice to women, there is evidence, nonetheless, that Gandhi vacillated between the literal and metaphorical meaning of sexual restraint; he sought to achieve conservation of both types of energies and he varies his vocabulary according to the time and the context.

An analysis of Gandhi's views on sexuality reveals that he often contradicted himself; on the one hand, he was obsessive about "retention of semen" for physical strength, and, on the other hand, he conceded that physical and mental stamina could be achieved without *brahmacarya*. Perhaps Western models of strength made him forfeit his absolute claim for the power of celibacy.

> The Westerners do not practise *brahmacharya*, yet they are not weak physically or mentally. Their untiring industry and spirit of adventure are worthy of imitation. It can be said of Gurkha, Pathan, Sikh, Dogra and British soldiers—all of whom have fine physique—that none of them are *brahmacharis*. Thes [*sic*] will outdo the students of our gymnasia in physical exercise. We can cite many such examples, to prove that physical strength, a certain kind of mental strength, ceaseless diligence and adventure—all the four of these can be attained without practicing *brahmacharya*.[126]

Gandhi's views on sexuality remain a center of debate: journalist Arthur Moore confronted Gandhi on his seventieth birthday about his views on sexuality. He underscored, in an essay presented to Gandhi, "Mr. Gandhi's attitude to sex is more completely opposed to modern psychology and medicine than one could have imagined it possible for any man to be."[127] Moore was referring to the modern Western studies that attribute creativity and physical and mental health to sex; Gandhi also was intent on creative energy and physical and mental health but through sexual control. His idea of self-control was also related to his pursuit of moral-force and spiritual aspirations.

Gandhi often stated that his concept of *brahmacarya* did not symbolize "merely mechanical celibacy, but it means complete control over all the organs and senses enabling one to attain perfect freedom from all passion."[128] It is clear that he was referring to his comprehensive commitment to that total mental and physical discipline that yields inner strength and facilitates fearlessness in sacrificing all for the sake of Truth. Thus, his concept of *brahmacarya* appears to have not only been a narrative for his bodily commitment to politics but also simply one element of a larger discipline. In his writings, lectures, and daily life, Gandhi drew from the magical, seminal, psychophysical descriptions of *brahmacarya* in the texts and myths of Indian traditions to motivate himself and to mobilize the masses. His method of confronting social injustice by nonviolent means required self-sacrifice, an austere lifestyle, fearlessness, and the willingness to die. Gandhi utilized the symbols and vocabulary of the ancient ethos of India to awaken a mass of people slumbering in slavery. His vow and practice of *brahmacarya* substantiated his alternative paradigm—ascetic activism—in challenging the prevailing social and political ills.

Gandhi invoked the power of restraint to generate life in the abeyant soul of India: "India is today nothing but a dead mass movable at the will of another. Let her become alive by self-purification, i.e., self-restraint and self-denial, and she will be a boon to herself and mankind."[129] Kakar analyzes Gandhi's celibacy under the lens of psychoanalysis and asserts a connection between his celibacy and the birth of the "weapon of nonviolence":

> For Gandhi, celibacy was not only the sine qua non for *moksha*, but also the mainspring of the political activities. It is from the repudiation, the ashes of sexual desire, that the weapon of nonviolence which he used so effectively in his political struggle against the racial oppression of the South African white rulers and later against the British empire, was phoenix-like born.[130]

The burnt offerings of *yajña* cause the gods to shower bounties on the sacrificer; destroying *kāma* in the fire of intense discipline gives rise to lustrous powers. In the same way, out of the "ashes" of selfish desires, *dharmarājya*—the Kingdom of Truth—would be born. This was Gandhi's conviction. A *brahmacārin*, a *brahmin*, or a *yogin* becomes a medium to accrue celestial force, which purifies as it destroys. Operating within the milieu of this tradition, Gandhi moved with the determination that the destruction of evil in any form—*kāma, rākṣasa,* bodily ills, the evils of untouchability, or foreign rule—requires the same paradigm of sacrifice. "Those who are engaged in forwarding the movement of non-co-operation, hope to produce a moral effect by a process of self-denial, self-sacrifice and self-purification," believed Gandhi.[131] Self-sacrifice—manifested in the stern vow and the practice of *brahmacarya*—results in purity and power, both personal and collective:

> When we offer up our bones to burn like wood, pouring out our blood like ghee in order that they may burn, and sacrifice our flesh to the flames, that alone will be true *yagna,* and by such sacrifice will the earth be sustained. Without such *yagna,* such sacrifice of self, it cannot be sustained.[132]

Gandhi, on the one hand, uses the religious language of symbols for his political strategy and, on the other hand, transmutes metaphors into a literal reading as evidenced by his practice of *brahmacarya.* Gandhi perceived and presented his political movement as a "movement of purification" and performed personal sacrifice in the form of *brahmacarya* for serving the cause of his country. This correlation between two dissimilar properties seems anomalous. However, models of assimilating and reinterpreting ancient traditions exist within the traditional norm.[133] For his political movement, which Gandhi perceived and presented as a "religious movement of purification," *brahmacarya* was the nexus—with its various traditional connotations.

To activate the power of the Truth-force, Gandhi depicted the myths on the canvas of his own body, embracing all of the underlying potencies of *brahmacarya*: creative, purificatory, destructive, and psychosomatic. When Gandhi, as a *brahmacārin,* transferred the symbolism of *yajña, tapas,* and *ojas* to his social and political actions—elimination of the curse of untouchability, confrontation of the evils of the British Empire, noncooperation, and passive resistance—the Indian mind recognized him as the paragon of the ancient ideal of a *tapasvin,* evidenced by the success of his movement. Abbott sees the instrumentality of Gandhi's *brahmacarya* in mass mobilization: "Gandhi's brahmacharya was not the personal eccentricity or curiosity it might have been in another man. He and his countrymen saw it as an essential and appropriate instrument to ready himself for a crusade."[134] Indeed, the Indian mind recognized the spiritual power of *brahmacarya*, and Gandhi's followers must have understood its instrumentality not merely in terms of pragmatic significance but rather in terms of the spiritual power of a traditionally celebrated sage.

Brahmacarya and *Siddhis*

Parekh notes Gandhi's belief in the miraculous power of *brahmacarya*: "Gandhi was convinced that a few score *brahmachāris* like him would be capable of transforming the face of India."[135] In his discourses, Gandhi often referred to characters from traditional tales and myths who displayed the immense authority attained by the practice of *brahmacarya* and other austerities. *Brahmacarya*—in traditional Hindu thought—is imbued with magical potency. Due to the intense discipline it demands, the observance of *brahmacarya*, even for short periods, brings miraculous power to the ascetic. In the *Mahābhārata*, Grandsire Bhīṣma declares: "He who practises it [*Brahmacarya*] duly attains to Brahma; he who practices it half and half, attains to the status of gods; while he who practices it indifferently, is born among Brahmanas [Brahmins] and possessed of learning attains to eminence."[136]

Gandhi believed in *brahmacarya*'s power. However, he was also aware that *brahmacarya*, when defined as "perfect control over all the sense organs," was impossible to realize while living in the world of daily activity. Nevertheless, he sought to come closer to the acclaimed ideal state. He asserted: "So may a perfect *brahmachari* exist only in imagination. But if we did not keep him constantly before our mind's eye, we should be like a rudderless ship. The nearer the approach to the imaginary state, the greater the perfection."[137]

In his experimentation with *brahmacarya* Gandhi seemed to be testing its power in achieving social and political goals. The potency of *brahmacarya* permeates Hindu discourse of the colonial era as illustrated in Alter's ethnographic studies of a wrestler's regimen. Expositions by other scholars such as Jordens and Parekh also underscore that the potency of celibacy was a focus of religious and nationalist discourse of cultural movements such as the Arya Samaj and the Ramakrishna Mission, which sought to revive ancient Vedic teachings. Religious and cultural revivalists cited ancient texts that describe *brahmacarya* not simply as a necessary restraint for realizing liberation but also as an instrument for achieving all kinds of this-worldly desires—from physical vitality to prosperity. For instance, the *Atharva Veda* (XI. 5. 17–19) speaks of the wish-fulfilling nature of *brahmacarya*.[138]

Even though Gandhi asserted the value of *brahmacarya* for his spiritual pursuits, he admitted that his striving for celibacy was aimed at worldly goals when he said, "my purpose is to plead for *brahmacharya* as a temporary necessity in the present stage of national evolution."[139] In the context of analyzing Gandhi's *brahmacarya*, Paine notes that even though Gandhi did not perform "miracles," he, rather, performed "things not lacking in wonder": "Not all the magi and maharishis of Indian legends—those who ascended ropes into the ether and healed by psychic touch . . . could match what Gandhi accomplished in fact." He goes on to recount Gandhi's accomplishments in maintaining peace during the Bengal riots. But Gandhi also differed from legendary characters in that he sought collective observance of *brahmacarya* for the purpose of generating collective power and self-autonomy among the populace, which he hoped to transfer to the larger context of political liberation. Paine observes that while Plato supposed "a small band of lovers might defeat all the armies in the world. Conversely, Gandhi appeared to believe that a few dozen *brahmacharyis* . . . if pure enough, could arouse India from centuries of defeat and stagnation."[140] This might explain why, to launch his historic Salt March (1930), Gandhi chose only those *satyagrahis* who had been practicing *brahmacarya* in addition to other prescribed ascetic practices.

Gandhi was deeply fond of India's epic literature and often referred to the myths of ascetics in the *Rāmāyaṇa* and the *Mahābhārata*. Yet he approached acquiring the inherent power of *brahmacarya* in a manner distinctly different from that of the ancient ascetics and contrary to the practice of *brahmacarya* in the religious literature of Hinduism. In the myths, a *brahmacārin* scrupulously seeks to avoid all contact with women lest he deviate from his vow. Gandhi, while observing the formidable vow, mingled freely with his female associates. Lal sees Gandhi as defying the "narrow" standard for a *brahmacārin*. Gandhi claimed: "He [the *brahmachari*] has to be as free from excitement in case of contact with the fairest damsel on earth, as in contact with a dead body."[141] Gandhi was setting a difficult ideal, and his tests of celibacy through constant experimentation with his female associates cost him his friends and impeccable reputation. This subject will be taken up in the next chapter.[142]

Gandhi was pursuing the celebrated power of austerity by his practice of *brahmacarya*. In the ancient Indian tales, gods tremble in fear of the power of the ascetic. In trepidation about losing his kingdom to such sages, Indra—the king of gods—sends celestial maidens to disrupt the vows of the ascetics. Johann Jakob Meyer reflects:

> As an irresistible power dwells in perfect asceticism, and heaven and earth are no more than clay in the hands of such a holy one, so even the gods in heaven tremble before him, and Indra, who fears to be dethroned by the mighty one, is well known to send at such times one of the unspeakably lovely fays of heaven, one of the hetaera-like Apsarases, down to the dangerous one.[143]

In one famous legend, Indra sends the Apsarā Menakā to interrupt Viśvāmitra's intense asceticism. On observing Menakā's celestial beauty, Viśvāmitra falls victim to love (*kāmvaśa*) and lies with her. The power of lust shatters the strict vows of the sage. Under the spell of Kāma, Viśvāmitra begets a daughter, Śakuntalā, and his power to usurp the control of the kingdom of Indra is wasted away. Interestingly, this story is the birth story of the King Bharata. (See appendix I.)

By harnessing the fire of passion with the superior fire of *tapas*, ascetics accumulate supernormal powers. The attainment of powers is not limited to male ascetics—women are also known to acquire magical potency as a result of the observance of *brahmacarya*.[144] Gandhi gave various reasons—from birth control to cultivating absolute nonviolence and compassion—for his commitment to and propagation of the practice of *brahmacarya*. However, his discourses on celibacy often led to the topic of the inherent power of celibacy. "He believed in the literal truth of the law that chastity is power," argues Robert Payne.[145]

Gandhi's abstinence may resemble the puritanical celibacy conceptualized in the West, but his vocabulary and symbolism of *brahmacarya* were indeed traditional to classical India. His *brahmacarya* was deeply rooted in his conviction in the power of renunciation that is glorified in Indian traditions. However, his unconventional applications sharply diverged from the customary modes of practice. His unique methods of integrating religious ascetic practices with political objectives, and his eccentric ways of practicing these, inspired many people, and also caused perplexity in others. Gandhi's pragmatic and creative application of ancient paradigms prompts Gier to construe Gandhi as a constructive postmodernist. Gier quotes Parekh to note a common trend in Hindus' view of the traditions: "For [Gandhi] as for Hindus in general the past was a source of inspiration and self-confidence, never a model or blueprint for the present."[146] For Gandhi, the traditional "models" were a foundation to construct his edifice of ascetic activism to address India's political and social problems. A closer study of his creative reconstruction of the components of *brahmacarya* is required in order to comprehend how Gandhi reinterpreted and redefined ancient principles for his modern goal of inspiring Indian people to seek social and political justice.

CHAPTER 4

Gandhi's Unorthodox *Brahmacarya*

Reinterpreting Private Religious Practice for Public Service

My *brahmacharya* knew nothing of the orthodox laws governing its observance. I framed my own rules as occasion necessitated.

—M. K. Gandhi

One who has taken that [*brahmacarya*] vow should not speak with women.

—*The Mahābhārata*

Gandhi, who abhorred sex, was yet the most consummate player at the game of sexuality.

—Vinay Lal

Gandhi upheld the traditional connotations of *brahmacarya* to advocate for the self-restraint and moral strength mandated by his nonviolent methods, yet in his personal application and public proclamation of *brahmacarya*'s value in addressing sociopolitical problems, Gandhi deviated sharply from its orthopraxis. In his sexual frankness and public experiments with sexuality he also transgressed the orthodox conventions required of a *brahmacārin* ascetic. He ultimately did this to communicate the essence of renunciation to a broader audience who were from rural areas or traditional in their thinking.

Some of Gandhi's close associates voiced dissent regarding his obsessive stance on celibacy. Nehru disagreed with Gandhi's insistence on sexual abstention for men and women and reasoned that "for an ascetic that is natural, but it seems far-fetched to apply it to men and women of the world who accept life and try to make the most of it."[1] Biographer Ashe observes the difference between the orthodox ascetic's and Gandhi's *brahmacarya* practices by calling attention to Gandhi's unconventional practices of having close friendships with women: "Orthodox *brahmacharya* was a practice for ascetics who could live as hermits away from women. But Gandhi made women his allies and co-workers." He also cites Gandhi's odd way of including women in his close circles and receiving personal services from them, which included massages. He encouraged this openness in his communes in which "ashramites of opposite sexes nursed each other in illness without restraint."[2]

Scholars and critics debate Gandhi's unrelenting public assertion of the value of celibacy in politics, which included his idiosyncratic experiments with his female associates to test his control of the senses. In a 1947 letter, Gandhi gives his own definition of the practice of *brahmacarya* to his close woman associate Amrit Kaur:

> One who never has any lustful intention . . . who is capable of lying naked with naked women, however beautiful they may be, without being in any manner whatsoever sexually excited. Such a person should be incapable of lying, incapable of intending or doing harm to a single man or woman in the world, is free from anger and malice and detached in the sense of the *Bhagavadgita*.[3]

Gandhi's unorthodox suppositions about and experiments with *brahmacarya* (including "the use of young women as subjects") were a source of contention, especially in the last crucial moments of India's independence movement. Gier makes a point of mentioning Gandhi's odd proposal "that 'lying naked with a naked member of the opposite sex is the ultimate test for not doing violence to another.' "[4] Although Gandhi tried to quell the controversy by locating the rationale for his actions in the mythical traditions, many commentators such as Pyarelal, Erikson, and Kumar document that orthodox Hindu contemporaries and some of Gandhi's closest associates directly opposed him for doing *adharma* (amoral action) and even abandoned him after finding out about his nontraditional "experiments."[5]

Sixty years after Gandhi's death, scholars continue to discuss the underlying reasons behind his passion for *brahmacarya* and possible reasons for his aberrant practices—neither of which fully reflected Indian traditional models nor mirrored the puritanical Western precedents of his era. On the one hand, Gandhi summoned the acclaimed supernatural power of *brahmacarya* as described in the ancient religious literature; on the other hand, he resisted being confined by traditional barriers and parameters, transgressing conventional rules in order to utilize *brahmacarya* for the purposes of nonviolent activism and social reform.

Ancient texts and sages systematically laid out regimens of dietary regulations, social and physical prohibitions, and other observances for those attempting to subdue deep-seated human passions. Gandhi himself referred to such rules for a *brahmacārin*—the so called "nine-fold wall of protection" laid down in the *Śāstras*:

> Thus he may not live among women, animals and eunuchs, he may not teach a woman alone or even in a group, he may not sit on the same mat with a woman, he may not look at any part of a woman's body, he may not take milk, curds, ghee or any fatty substance nor indulge in baths and oil massage.[6]

However, Gandhi lived among women and did not hesitate to take personal services from them, or even solicit advice in private matters, including inner struggles with sexual thoughts. Gandhi's own accounts reveal that he formulated his ascetic rules according to the context at hand rather than abide by conventional ones. Therefore, two main questions are the focus of this chapter: First, how and why did Gandhi, who unequivocally drew on the traditional symbols and terminology of *brahmacarya* in promoting his ascetic activism, circumvent such rules in practice—especially the conventions of seclusion, gender bias, and rigid segregation of men and women? Second, how was he able to selectively choose some and reject other standards of *brahmacarya* and still justify his practice by citing Indian texts and traditions? Moreover, while Gandhi utilized the traditional vocabulary of the ascetic vow, he initially took the vow for reasons quite different than those motivating a traditional *brahmacārin*. A careful review of the historical context that led to Gandhi's vow of *brahmacarya* is crucial to understanding the nonconformist nature of his practice.

The Etiology of Gandhi's *Brahmacarya*

In his *Autobiography*, Gandhi reflects that "the more or less successful practice of self-control had been going on since 1901," but he deliberately took the lifelong vow of *brahmacarya* during the long marches of the Zulu Rebellion in South Africa in 1906.[7] Jordens argues that Gandhi's decision to commit himself to celibacy seems to have been a practical one: renunciation of sex was necessary "if he wanted to continue and to expand his life of public service."[8] Gandhi himself emphasized his conviction that the pleasures of family life and procreation were not consistent with his goal of public service. Aside from psychological and political factors that may also have contributed to his vow, Gandhi's reflections on his service during the Zulu Rebellion clarify his underlying reasons for taking the solemn decision. His reasons were apparently fourfold.

First, during the Zulu rebellion, Gandhi realized that the service of humanity required risking all—including health and even life—and necessitated a "less demanding intimate family life," as well as not having more children.[9] Gandhi had formed an Indian Ambulance Corps assigned with the task of "nursing of the wounded Zulus." The ambulance corps was exposed to ghastly hygienic conditions and health hazards while treating injured Zulus whose "wounds were festering" because "the white people were not willing nurses for the wounded Zulus."[10] Gandhi and his ambulance corps dedicated themselves to care for unattended Zulus:

> We had to cleanse the wounds of several Zulus which had not been attended to for as many as five or six days and were therefore stinking horribly. . . . The work for which we had enlisted was fairly heavy, for sometimes during the month we had to perform a march of as many as forty miles a day.[11]

These extreme conditions made Gandhi susceptible to disease and death. As a father and a husband, he found family responsibilities inconsistent with his full dedication to public service of volunteering: "I should not have been able to throw myself into the fray, had my wife been expecting a baby."[12]

The direct experience of the horror of war and suffering sent Gandhi into "deep thought." He seemed to be looking for a way to obtain freedom from the responsibility of having more children so that he could serve humanity. If this was the only reason, however, why did Gandhi not resort to other birth control options? According to his own accounts, although he had read about contraceptives while in England, he preferred the method of "self-control" suggested by Mr. Hills, president of the Vegetarian Society. Gandhi recalls pondering "over *brahmacharya* and its implications" during his service in the

Zulu Rebellion.[13] The vow of *brahmacarya* undertaken by ascetics is not simply a method for birth control; it is a method of withdrawal and isolation (*nivṛtti*) from family relations and attachments, which coincided with Gandhi's developing theory of dedication to public service. As mentioned earlier, Gandhi from his early childhood was familiar with various forms of self-control as well as with the inherent power of *brahmacarya* and other religious vows. Eventually Gandhi chose the vow of *brahmacarya* rather than adopt other birth control methods available to him, but he redefined this discipline, making it consistent in terms of service to, not isolation from, public life. Nonetheless, many scholars look for ulterior motives and other psychological factors because Gandhi's approach appears to contain a negative attitude toward sex.

Second, after witnessing the interaction between the Zulus and the British in South Africa, Gandhi realized that "strength does not come from physical capacity. It comes from an indomitable will." He recalls in his writings that an average Zulu was much stronger than an average Englishman. However, their physical strength was impotent without inner strength because in spite of their "Herculean bodies" they were helpless in front of an English boy: "The average Zulu is any way more than a match for an average Englishman in bodily capacity. But he flees from an English boy."[14] When British soldiers would shoot men, women, and children sleeping in their beds, there was no resistance from the Zulus despite their immense bodily strength. Gandhi surmised in the *Young India*:

> Bravery is not a quality of the body[,] it is of the soul. I have seen cowards encased in tough muscles, and rare courage in the frailest body. I have seen big bulky and muscular Zulus cowering before an English lad and turning tail if they saw a loaded revolver pointed at them.[15]

Gandhi concluded that strength of spirit is required to confront and resist evil and violence, and that strength is obtained not through physical means, but through self-sacrifice and moral force. He recognized that his premise of the superiority of the soul-force was different from that of the popular modern conventions. "My reading of our civilization is that we are expected to believe in soul-force or moral force as the final arbiter and this is satyagraha," Gandhi was later to argue. He insisted that the English respond to "courage and suffering" and Indians must develop "indomitable courage and a faculty for unlimited suffering" in order to confront brute force.[16]

Gandhi seemed to be testing his will through his vow of *brahmacarya,* because the renunciatory practice, especially in the midst of family and social life, demanded resolute will. Many years later Gandhi admitted that "for me the observance of even bodily *brahmacharya* has been full of difficulties." He confessed in his *Autobiography* that although he had been striving for self-control since 1901, "up to this time [1906] I had not met with success [in observance of *brahmacarya*] because the will had been lacking."[17] Gandhi may not have fully understood the "mystic power" of *brahmacarya* at that time, as Jordens suggests, but it would be naive to assume that he was unaware of its vital role in acquiring the inner strength evidenced in the traditional lore. Apparently, Jordens is using the term *mystic* to connote *brahmacarya*'s essential role in self-realization, but Gandhi was seeking to acquire a tangible moral power that could be utilized in his political enterprise.[18]

Third, Gandhi took his vow in order to personally practice nonviolence in all forms—from concrete to subtle—so as to alleviate the suffering of others. Witnessing the suffering of the Zulus had a vicarious effect on Gandhi that must have reminded him of the dark night when he himself was pushed out of a train because he was "colored." Gandhi admitted that the "Zulu 'rebellion' was full of new experiences" and that the "Boer war had not brought home to me the horrors of war with anything like the vividness that the 'rebellion' did."[19] He was so galvanized by witnessing the torture and inhumane treatment inflicted by one human on another in South Africa, especially in the Zulu conflict, that "he saw himself as the spokesman and champion of the poor and the oppressed everywhere," speculates Parekh.[20] This meant resistance to all forms of violence—physical as well as emotional. Ramchandra Gandhi writes: "A brahmacāri is also he who cheerfully renounces sexuality as a gesture of equalisation towards victims of unmerited suffering, sexuality being the commonly stated and believed reason for living."[21] Was the impetus for Gandhi's vow to renounce the private pleasures of life in part "a gesture of equalisation" in the face of pervasive suffering? To prepare himself for serving humanity, Gandhi sought to transform his private life through renunciation of all sensory gratification. This decision is peculiar for a public servant.

Fourth, Gandhi equated serving suffering masses with serving God, which traditionally requires a state of detachment. After deliberating on his fierce campaign and subsequent triumph against the unfair taxation of Indians, Gandhi reflects in his *Autobiography*: "I had made the religion of service my own, as I felt that God could be realized only through service." It cannot be certain if Gandhi had developed the synthesis of public service and self-realization at that early age, or if he was actually reflecting back on the incident with his mature understanding as an ascetic activist. It is apparent that his philosophy gradually evolved. He admits that his contacts with his Christian friends in South Africa and the guidance of Raychand Bhai as well as his reading of various religious texts (including the *Upaniṣads* and the Life of the Buddha) stimulated his "self-introspection." It can be surmised that these influences led him to believe that public service required sacrifice of selfish desires. Later, he puts forth his conviction: "In a word, I could not live both after the flesh and the spirit."[22]

Gandhi quoted the *Gītā's* axiom *"sarvabhutamabhutatma"* (whose self has become the self of all beings), and during his public talks on the *Gītā* he explained that "man's real nature is to serve others and to work for self-purification." According to Gandhi, this spiritual goal was an underlying reason that he decided to give up the life of flesh for public service. He concluded that the vow of service and the pursuit of God are incompatible with the desire for enjoyments. Gandhi carried this message to both men and women equally. During his public meetings, he had been asking women to forgo their jewelry to help the poor. In 1927, on his Silence Day, Gandhi wrote a letter to *āśrama* women asking them to cultivate a sense of connection with their fellow beings: "Do we not sing *atmavatsarvabhuteshu*? We should regard all as ourselves . . . on finding someone else suffer would ourselves suffer and seek a remedy for the suffering."[23] Traditionally, only a yogi or ascetic is sanctioned to exercise such authority to give homiletic advice to women. It is evident that Gandhi's direct encounters with suffering and inequity countenanced by the establishment made him averse to private pleasures. He later outlined the dichotomy between service and sensual pleasures:

> Every servant has to practise *brahmacharya;* how can anyone who has taken the vow of service enjoy the pleasures of sense? It is necessary for one to practise self-control even to render the limited service to one's parents; it cannot be rendered if anyone yields to his passions as I did. Similarly, how can anyone who would serve the Ashram, serve men and women, boys and girls, how can he afford to gratify his sensual desires? And serving the Ashram is such a small matter; it is like a drop in the ocean. Hence anyone who would serve the world should flee his desires.[24]

Unlike other public servants who balance public and private life, Gandhi sought to sacrifice his private pleasures and also those of his close relations in order to completely dedicate himself to serve his people. Taking the vow of *brahmacarya* marked the beginning of his career as an ascetic-politician, providing him a framework for the endeavor. Parel, in his discussion of Gandhi's celibacy and sexuality, suggests that "it was celibacy that facilitated the transition from family to nation to humanity."[25] Although Gandhi was pledging himself to a life of celibacy for seemingly practical reasons, he soon realized its potency, which he had earlier thought to be an "extravagant praise of *brahmacharya* in our religious books."[26] Gandhi directly related his taking of the vow to the inception of his strategy of *satyagraha*. Although *brahmacarya* occupied a central place in that strategy, in his struggle to sustain the formidable vow Gandhi was also led to experiment with dietary measures and to observe other physical and mental restraints drawn from traditional ascetic disciplines.

The practice of *brahmacarya* certainly meant more to Gandhi than simply renunciation of sex for having no more children. Ashe argues that Gandhi's "motive, at the stage of taking the vow, was still not religious but moral and psychological."[27] However, the idea of the vow had been percolating in his mind as a result of his reading of religious texts and many conversations with Raychand Bhai, whom he met right after returning from England. Gandhi was also cognizant of the socioreligious connotations of *brahmacarya* and his decision was almost certainly rooted in its religious value. As mentioned earlier, among his seminal readings in 1903 was the *Yoga Sūtra* and its commentaries, including that of the prominent Vedāntist monk Vivekananda who extolled the value of *brahmacarya*.

Gandhi's predecessors laid the groundwork for the synthesis of religious ideals with political aspirations, but their ideals were not able to capture the religious imagination of the masses as Gandhi's paradigm did. Within the nationalist movement of India's independence, many of Gandhi's contemporaries also followed the course laid down by their forerunners, but their success in inciting the masses was limited. During the nineteenth century, various leaders of religious reform movements incorporated religious concepts and technical vocabulary to reinvigorate their countrymen who "had fallen prey to waves of foreign rule because they had become passive, effete and devoid of energy as a result of their sensuous and self-indulgent lifestyle."[28] Vivekananda specifically emphasized the power of celibacy and used symbols that combined patriotism with religion, yet he "failed politically," Kakar argues. He quotes Pamela Daniels who reflects on Vivekananda's efforts to synthesize ancient principles and politics: "Religious and political ideas briefly and powerfully combined under the banner of militant nationalism, but the alliance was not sustained. The politicians went their way, and the mystics theirs."[29] Gandhi himself had a great respect for Vivekananda, who in his short life of forty years beseeched his fellow Indians to recognize oppressive social and religious customs as well as their glorious heritage.

Gandhi extrapolated select connotations of the traditional practice of *brahmacarya* to communicate his strategy; at the same time, he approached *brahmacarya* not as a private virtue but as a public practice essential to the *satyagraha* movement. According to him, the transformation of ascetic practices into tools for activism required open public discourse, reinterpretation of the orthopraxis of *brahmacarya*, and experimentation designed to validate its acclaimed power.

Brahmacarya is a bodily expression of the renunciation of desires as well as the defiance of instinctive needs and social norms. Specifically, the practice of *brahmacarya* indicates sacrifice of the highest type and provides the renunciate with unsurpassable religious authority. In their study of cross-cultural perspectives on celibacy, Elisa J. Sobo and Sandra Bell discuss deliberate abstinence as a means of conveying social distinction: "Self-conscious abstinence from elementary human behaviors such as sleeping, eating, or having sex can contribute to the creation of a certain status or socially intelligible identity."[30] The embodiment of physical restraints has played an important role in creating a socially acclaimed status for the renouncer in India's traditions. Evidently, it was Gandhi's practice of *brahmacarya* and his ascetic life that enabled him to embody the liminal persona of a *sādhu-politician* and that caused others to confer on him the title of *mahātmā*—a status that made it possible for him to transcend family bonds and social constraints and devote himself to public service.

It is essential to explore the unorthodox ways that Gandhi approached *brahmacarya*. Gandhi not only redefined the ancient ideal of *sannyāsa* (the Hindu ideal of renunciation), he created *āśrama* communities that schooled and housed his followers for the purpose of training them as nonviolent activists. These *āśramas* allowed him to embody the persona of an ascetic and, at the same time, impart methods that combined components of *nivṛtti* and *pravṛtti*. In spite of a continuous barrage of criticism, Gandhi made the private ascetic virtue of *brahmacarya* a part of the public discourse—not only for individual liberation but also for the freedom of his people.

Ascetic Liminality and Gandhi's Political Strategy

Nehru asserted that Gandhi's "attitude is that of the ascetic who has turned his back to the world and its ways, who denies life and considers it evil."[31] This assessment draws on the classic ideology of an ascetic—one who chooses the path of *nivṛtti*—as described in the ascetic traditions of India. Even though Gandhi was utterly engaged in the world, due to his ascetic celibacy he was still classified as one who denies life. Not only Gandhi's close Hindu followers but even modern scholars perceive Gandhi's ascetic disciplines as idiosyncratic due to the dichotomy between the goals of a traditional ascetic and those of a worldly person. For example, Dumont describes Hindu social structure as making a clear distinction between the householder and the renouncer. The homeless state of the renouncer represents detachment and symbolizes interruption of the flow of *saṃsāra bandhana* (the fetters of the world). The idea of "stepping outside" the world is a metaphorical refusal to follow the flow—implying that a renunciate transcends the world, not physically but socially.

Within the ascetic norm, a renouncer is primarily identified by celibacy, customarily symbolized by the ascetic loincloth. Generally speaking, "for a person seeking liberation, overcoming desire and attachment is the major goal, for which ascetic celibacy is the only path."[32] Gandhi was aware of the classic bifurcation of the ideologies of *pravṛtti* and *nivṛtti* but sought to integrate them. He adopted the traditional ideal of the renouncer (as well as the garb) and stated that those who observe *brahmacarya* are *sannyāsins*. Then he placed the *sannyāsin* squarely in the political arena: "In this age, only political *sannyasis* can fulfill and adorn the ideal of *sannyasa*, others will more likely than not disgrace *sannayasi's* saffron garb. No Indian who aspires to follow the way of true religion can afford to remain aloof from politics."[33] For him, participation in politics meant public service in its true sense, not acquiring power. Instead of denying life as "evil" (as Nehru put it) with his practices of sexual restraint, Gandhi embraced this-worldly aims. He undertook ascetic vows to engage with the world. Jonathan Schell finds it novel that Gandhi practiced the vows of asceticism not to free himself from action but precisely for action. He writes:

> Vows of poverty and celibacy were, of course, no novelty. . . . In the religious traditions of both East and West, holy vows have usually been accompanied by a withdrawal from the world and especially from politics. Gandhi pro-

> ceeded in exactly the opposite direction. He took his ascetic vows in order to free himself for action.[34]

Moreover, Gandhi's vows did not merely provide him with freedom for action, but, in fact, became actions of nonviolent resistance. Within India, other religious revivalists had considered celibacy essential to leadership, and the value of this practice expands beyond India. Abbott, in her extensive study (which includes Gandhi as an example), observes celibacy as a "staggering panorama of reality, involving humanity everywhere and always." She gives accounts of men and women throughout the ages, "driven by individual missions—art, literature, science—who opted for celibacy to forestall relationships that would consume the time and energy they longed to direct to their work."[35] What is unusual about Gandhi's celibacy and ascetic practices, enough so that they have attracted unprecedented attention, is that he advocated their use equally for spiritual and sociopolitical goals.

On the one hand, Gandhi's sexual restraint, with its inherent mythic and psychosomatic power, was defined by the traditional underlying connotations of *brahmacarya.* In congruence with the religious literature, Gandhi related *brahmacarya* to additional restraints including control of appetite, taste, and speech. "Control of the palate is the first essential in the observance of the vow," declared Gandhi.[36] Religious texts of the Hindu tradition identify *brahmacarya* with various types of austerity—including *mauna* (silence) and *anāśakāyana* (fasting as penance). He repeatedly emphasized the value of fasting in controlling the sexual organs and committed himself to weekly silence vows.[37] On the other hand, Gandhi defied ascetic conventions by actively engaging in politics, discoursing openly about sexuality, disclosing his private emotions, and involving himself in close associations with women.

Gandhi's personal struggle to conquer the passions and his public discourse on the utility of self-restraint in personal, social, and political affairs gave him the status of a *sādhu,* one who steps outside the world of social relationships and constraints. At the same time, as a politician and public servant, Gandhi remained committed to worldly pursuits. He often received letters from correspondents who "noticed inconsistency" between his "'idealization' of sannyasa and his struggle for swaraj," asking "how he reconciled the one with the other." In his response Gandhi emphasized: "I do not for one moment grant that a sanyasin need be a recluse caring not for the world. A sanyasin is one who cares not for himself but cares all his time for others . . . [he] must care for swaraj, not for his own sake (he has it), but for the sake of others. He has no worldly ambition for himself." Gandhi argued that "a sannyasin, having attained swaraj in his own person, is the fittest to show us the way. A sannyasin is in the world, but he is not of the world."[38] Through such statements Gandhi sought to bridge the gap between renunciation and action.

Even though Gandhi's proclamation that *sannyāsins* must engage in politics appears contrary to the *status quo*, which defines *sannyāsa* as worldly renunciation, the ideal of the *sannyāsin* becoming involved in social reform (as we saw earlier) is not unique. In her ethnographic study of *sādhus*, Kirin Narayan observes that "[s]*ādhus* are ideally celibate. They do not work for wages but are rather dependent on alms and donations. They do not identify with ties of blood or caste." This renunciation of "ties of blood or caste" moves the *sādhus* to the periphery of society where they are free to become involved in the service of society at large. "Ironically," states K. Narayan, "the act of renunciation may in fact push an ascetic into more extensive social involvement than if he or she remained a layperson."[39] A renunciate who steps outside of society proper may even become a catalyst for social reform and a "dynamic center of religious development and change." Dumont emphasizes:

> Is it really too adventurous to say that the agent of development in Indian religion and speculation, the 'creator of values,' has been the renouncer? The Brahman, as a scholar, has mainly preserved, aggregated, and combined; he may well have created and developed special branches of knowledge. Not only the founding of sects and their maintenance, but the major ideas, the 'inventions' are due to the renouncer whose unique position gave him a sort of monopoly for putting everything in question.[40]

Even though the renouncer might be the catalyst for new ideas, conventionally, in India's religious past, a *mahātmā* or *sādhu* was identified by his renunciation of worldly ties in the pursuit of ultimate freedom. In colonial times, the world-denying philosophy so visibly represented by *sādhus* and *sannyāsins* was blamed for India's colonization. K. Narayan notes varied portrayals of *sādhus* in the colonial era "as misguided pagans [romanticized] as representative of 'the mystic mind of the East.'" She underscores John Campbell Oman's position that "it is largely due to the subtle effects of the spirit of *sadhuism* upon the character of the people of India that the country is so easily governed by a handful of foreign officials and a few thousand white soldiers." Eventually, indigenous response to foreign criticism during the colonial era led to a reinterpretation of the value of asceticism and a revolution in the role of the *sādhus*, and many late-nineteenth-century movements "ushered in the image of the socially involved renouncer."[41]

This novel tendency was justified by religious texts in which the *Kali Yuga* (the Dark Age; Gandhi used this popular Hindu term to describe the present era) is characterized by heightened suffering and a lapse into immorality.[42] Charity, compassion, and restraint of passions as extolled in the Hindu texts, therefore, must come together in a *mahātmā* of this age. The modern *mahātmā* would have to mediate between the secular and religious as well as between the public and private. Ashe says: "A belief was current that any twentieth-century Mahatma would have to identify himself with the downtrodden millions. Vivekananda had written that a Mahatma must be one whose heart bled for the poor. If it did not, he was no Mahatma."[43] Not surprisingly, in 1945, Gandhi's concern for the poor prompted Brahmachari Mahavir of the Ramakrishna Ashram, Madras, to observe that he saw "in Gandhiji a greater Vivekananda."[44]

Unlike a traditional *sannyāsin* or *sādhu*, Gandhi was not initiated into a particular religious sect. He became a *sannyāsin* and stepped outside of the world by virtue of his ascetic practices of *brahmacarya*. He then negotiated both the boundaries of a *sannyāsin* and those of a public servant. For example, he ignored caste restrictions that forbid dining with untouchables: "I regard it my sacred duty to eat only after making the pariah or the leper eat. But I am not asking you to violate any social barriers as regards eating and drinking."[45] K. Narayan points out the "opposition between renunciation and caste" and that this was not atypical in the renouncer tradition: "indigenous Brahmanical theory itself depicts renunciation as the antithesis of caste society."[46] Some scholars use Turner's theory of liminality to analyze Gandhi's actions of blending sacredness and polity.[47] Gandhi's rising beyond social confines and categories is "reminiscent of Victor Turner's conception of liminality as a state in which an individual or group leaves society to be suspended 'betwixt and between' social categories."[48] With his paradoxical philosophy and practices, Gandhi moved between the boundaries of an ascetic and a politician. Turner defines liminality: "The attributes of liminality or liminal *personae* ("threshold people") are necessarily ambiguous, since this condition and these persons elude or slip through the network of classifications that normally locate states and positions in cultural space."[49] The renouncer transcending the organizations of caste and class is free to question established norms and power structures.

K. Narayan quotes anthropologist Veena Das: "The *sannyāsī* does indeed appear to be in a permanent state of liminality, standing on the threshold between humans and deities, between caste society and the religious transcendence of society, between the living and the dead."[50] The observance of sexual purity for a prescribed period of time also marks a liminal state in the ritual performance of *yajña*, signifying the sacrificer's separation from earthly constraints in order to mediate between gods and humans. Gandhi's *sannyāsa*, virtual though it may have been (i.e., not fitting the traditional model of any religious sect), enabled him to transgress the boundaries of gender and caste and commit to trampling the system of untouchability.

Gandhi often referred to renunciates such as the Buddha, Mahavira, and Dayananda, who in their respective periods raised their voices against ailing systems and sought to change the established traditions of caste inequality, religious fanaticism, misogynist tendencies, and animal sacrifice. Gandhi was deeply impressed by the Buddha, whose renunciation allowed him to rise against the hegemonic priesthood. He is unique in interpreting the Buddha's great renunciation as an act of penance for socioreligious reform:

> Lord Buddha was moved to pity when he saw his religion reduced to such a plight. He renounced the world and started doing penance. He spent several years in devout contemplation and ultimately suggested some reform in the Hindu religion. His piety greatly affected the minds of the Brahmins, and the killing of animals for sacrifice was stopped to a great extent.[51]

However, Gandhi's liminality differs notably from that of other renunciates, including the Buddha, because Gandhi remained physically on the threshold of renunciation and active participation, and bodily and publicly demonstrated his "betwixt-and-between condition." Although he was a *brahmacārin*, he associated with women of all ages; he used the religious terminology of *rāmarājya*, *yajña*, and *tapas* only in the context of inspiring the establishment of an independent political state; he advocated the pacifist method of truth and nonviolence but used militant vocabulary; he sought to practice masculine celibacy but yearned to embody feminine virtues and vulnerability; and he established *āśramas* (religious communities) not simply to create a dwelling for renunciates but also for training men and women morally and for creating a model of a self-governing society.

Gandhi's *Āśrama*: A Liminal Space?

Traditionally, not only do ascetics embody liminality corporeally and socially, they also express it through a physical locale. Gandhi, who sought to transcend familial relationships with his *brahmacarya* vow, used a similar tactic by establishing *āśrama* communities for his activist agenda.[52] Literally, the word *āśrama*, rooted in the verb *śram* (meaning "to exert oneself"), connotes "toil," penance," and "austerity" and suggests the rigor of the ascetic life. Throughout India's religious history, and even today, many *sannyāsins* and *sādhus* renounce their homes and choose to reside on the periphery of society—in *maṭhas* or *āśramas* (hermitages) nestled away from towns, either on the banks of rivers or in the secluded surroundings of forests.[53] Gandhi's close friend C. F. Andrews wrote with regard to Gandhi's establishment of *āśramas*: "In India every great moral and spiritual leader sooner or later founds what is called an Ashram for the sake of giving a concrete expression to his own creative ideas."[54]

Āśrama life is symbolic of penance, discipline, morality, and spiritual power, and it creates wonder and inspiration in people of all classes—from kings to peasants. An *āśrama* is a concrete representation of *nivṛtti*—a life surpassing this-worldly concerns—yet it is located within the physical world. The legends in the *Mahābhārata* and the *Rāmāyaṇa* portray the *āśrama* environment as imbued with the dual elements of peace and spiritual power. The image of hermits living in *āśramas* and embodying renunciation has traditionally invoked a feeling of profound tranquillity and mysterious power in the imagination of laypeople. For instance, the poet Kālidāsa portrays the awe of the King Duḥṣanta when he sees Ṛiṣi Māricā's hermitage populated with chaste ascetics:

> In this forest of wish-fulfilling trees
> ascetics live on only the air they breathe. . . .
> They sit in trance on jeweled marble slabs
> and stay chaste among celestial nymphs,
> practicing austerities in the place
> that others seek to win by penances.[55]

Against this cultural backdrop, with his *brahmacarya* vow, Gandhi's establishment of *āśrama* communities for the purpose of political agendas was peculiar. During his stay in South Africa, he founded communities for concretely expressing his political agenda, but they were not called *āśramas*; instead, the secular words *settlement* or *farm* were used.[56] Jordens speculates: "In South Africa the founding of the Phoenix Settlement and Tolstoy Farm were not primarily inspired by religious concerns. Those communes were started basically for economic reasons."[57] Gandhi said he was hesitant to use the words "*maṭh*" or "*āśrama*" for his establishments in South Africa because the words had "Hindu connotations." Perhaps his decision was due to the fact that the community in South Africa was largely comprised of immigrants from various Indian racial and religious backgrounds. Moreover, Gandhi had not yet acquired the stature of a holy man, and this led him to take a more secular and inclusive approach to his communal living while in South Africa. He chose the inclusive and nonreligious term *phoenix* in naming his first settlement, as he was impressed by the legend of the mythical bird that "comes back to life again and again from its ashes, i.e, never dies." He related the invincible nature of the firebird to his objectives and asserted that the "aims of Phoenix will not vanish even when we are turned to dust."[58]

Nevertheless, religious disciplines were part of the daily life of the inhabitants of Tolstoy Farm, established in 1910 (after Gandhi committed himself to the vow of celibacy). Residents were expected to follow religious disciplines along with manual labor and commit to the struggle for *satyagraha*. Payne gives a snapshot of Gandhi's Tolstoy Farm where the members were "encouraged to live out their lives in purity and prayer, working cheerfully for the common good, obeying the commands of the master, never stepping out of line. . . . He seemed to be determined to make his entire captive audience of Satyagrahis into saints."[59] Even though Gandhi was setting too high an ideal, his method of *satyagraha* by definition required the participants to be pure, and he himself sought to embody the principles of truth as an example.

In 1915, on his return to India, Gandhi was no longer reluctant to call his community an *āśrama*. According to Jordens, "one of his first preoccupations was to arrange for the establishment of a commune . . . this time to be properly called an Ashram."[60] Jordens does not speculate on Gandhi's reason for this eagerness. Was the constituting of Gandhi's *mahātmāhood* a determining factor in his decision to establish an *āśrama*?[61] By the time Gandhi left South Africa, nearly a decade of *brahmacarya* practice, conjoined with the virtues of *satya*, *ahiṃsā*, and *aparigraha*, had coalesced to make him into a religious figure, a *sādhu*, a holy man—whose traditional domicile is an *āśrama*. His commitment to the ascetic vows, together with his selfless service, had already earned him the title of *mahātmā*—Great Soul.

In 1915 soon after his return to India, Gandhi made a pilgrimage to the Kumbh Mela (the most sacred and biggest religious gathering of holy men and women in India), in the holy place Hardvar, where he was reintroduced to the culture of *sādhus* and *brahmacārīns* and witnessed religious followers' response toward them. Gandhi also became "the victim of their craze for *darshan.*" He recalls, "My business was mostly to keep sitting in the tent giving *darshan* and holding religious and other discussions with numerous pilgrims." He describes the religious zest of the Indian people who sought his company: "I was followed even to the bathing *ghat* by these *darshan*-seekers."[62] Gandhi is referring to the Hindu custom of *darśan* (Hindi, *darshan*), literally "seeing," but in this context "sacred seeing or sight." *Darśan* connotes the ritual of receiving a blessing through "seeing" sacred images and pilgrimage places, or holy men and women. This ritual is universally known to the followers of the traditions of India, and during religious festivals throngs of people eagerly seek the blessings of saints and *sādhus* by coming into their presence, having their *darśan*. Due to his lifestyle of an ascetic and self-less service to India's people, religious people began to revere him, and this marked the beginning of his public status of a *sādhu*. At this time, Gandhi realized "what a deep impression my humble services in South Africa had made throughout the whole of India." Gandhi also witnessed a mix of blind faith, fanaticism, and religious hypocrisy. He commented on "the pilgrims' absentmindedness, hypocrisy and slovenliness" and on the state of *sādhus* who "have been born but to enjoy the good things of life." Gandhi concludes his reflections: the Hardvar experiences "proved for me to be of inestimable value" and helped "in no small way to decide where I was to live and what I was to do."[63] Apparently, it was this experience that led him to found his first *āśrama* community, through which he could harness the religious spirit of the Indian people for his Satyagraha movement. Gandhi founded his first *āśrama* just two months after this pilgrimage.

Historically, within India *āśramas* not only served the purpose of religious training, but of martial instruction as well. In the *Mahābhārata*, the Pāṇdavas and their cousins became residents of Guru Droṇa's *āśrama* in order to acquire the arts of weaponry, for example. After the classical period in India the *āśramas* came to be associated primarily with religious training. Gandhi's adoption of the *āśrama* model for his political activities in a unique way combines the Indian model of religious centers with the Western idea of the coffeehouse as a gathering place for intellectuals, as noted by the Rudolphs.

The Rudolphs use the theoretical framework of Jürgen Habermas to examine "why and how Gandhi reconfigured western conceptions of civil society, associational life, and the public sphere." They argue that Gandhi, for the purpose of *satyagraha*, extended the assumption of "the bourgeois public sphere to the plebeian world of non-literate villagers."[64] With regard to Gandhi's *āśrama* system they rightly conclude that "the ashram's projects were based on a more holistic vision of how to improve the human condition than that of the coffee house." Certainly Gandhi's *āśramas* system defied the normative standards governing religious communities by making the *āśrama* a training ground for nonviolent activists.

> Ashrams provided training for resisters and workshops for fashioning strategies and tactics of resistance. Volunteers observed routines and practiced discipline. . . . They were schooled to participate in risky political actions. They expected to be called upon to go on marches, attend meetings, and engage in civil disobedience by breaking unjust laws.[65]

Gandhi sought to create a public, democratic sphere that included people of all social strata, irrespective of literacy, caste, gender, or religion. This move was not entirely unique: the emergence of hosts of religious leaders from different backgrounds in the nineteenth and twentieth centuries, and the resurgence of inclusive *āśrama* communities, facilitated membership from diverse social strata. But Gandhi distinctively combined political vision with his spiritual ideals and made his communities public centers based on an egalitarian philosophy and ascetic disciplines. The Rudolphs neither discuss Gandhi's own intentions and the religiopolitical symbolism of his *āśramas*, nor do they consider the cultural meanings that provided Gandhi with authority as a leader. It would be simplistic to construe that Gandhi's intention was only to form "training centers" for those who were committed to his political agendas. Why did he choose the model of an *āśrama* in India, apparently implying a serene religious community away from political clamor? Gandhi's method combined asceticism and activism, and his version of *āśramas* community was a physical symbol of this hybrid synthesis.

Sensitive to the pulse of India's agitation under foreign oppression, Gandhi founded an *āśrama* community designed to serve the Motherland, while at the same time pursuing his personal goal of spiritual freedom. The Rudolphs trace the inception of Gandhi's idea of *āśrama* to John Ruskin's book, *Unto This Last*, and to Ruskin's notions that '"the good of the individual is contained in the good of all'; to the belief that all work is equally worthy."[66] Although the impetus for establishing communal living in South Africa may be ascribed to Ruskin's ideology, Gandhi's *āśramas* in India were based on Gandhi's objective of nourishing religious sensibility as well as engendering the spirit of service.

The *āśrama* lifestyle enabled Gandhi to create coherence between his ideal and his methods. On one hand, the *āśrama* regimen trained his followers to cultivate virtues of nonviolence, truth, and celibacy; on the other, the *āśrama*'s egalitarian principles provided a safe refuge to men and women, people of low and high caste alike. Women, in particular, felt safe in Gandhi's *āśrama*. In 1932, Gandhi wrote in his history of Satyagraha Ashram: "A woman, as soon as she enters the Ashram, breathes the air of freedom and casts out all fear from her mind. And I believe that the Ashram observance of *brahmacharya* has made a big contribution to this state of things."[67] For Gandhi, the vow of *brahmacarya* was fundamental for cultivating the attitude of freedom and equality.

At the inception of Satyagraha Ashram in 1915 in the "Draft Constitution for the Ashram," Gandhi outlined its objective: "The object of the Ashram is to learn how to serve the motherland one's whole life and to serve it."[68] The constitution devised vows, observances, and rules that precisely expressed Gandhi's blend of unconventional forms of asceticism and sociopolitical activism. The *āśrama* was to symbolize self-autonomy but at the same time operate as a community structure under the "authority of an elder." Gandhi utilized his authority as a religious leader to draft a constitution that negotiated the boundaries between the sacred and secular, the religious and political, and the individual and the community. In his research on ritual initiation rites and the role of the instructors in "connecting neophytes with one another," anthropologist Turner finds that the "authority of the elders" is essential, representing the "axiomatic values of society in which are expressed the 'common good' and the common interest."[69] On the one hand, the constitution of Satyagraha Ashram included the traditional ascetic vows of *satya, ahiṃsā, brahmacarya,* and on the other hand, it mandated nontraditional rules such as a vow against untouchability and proscription of the *varṇāśrama dharma* (traditional duties based in caste and stage of life).[70]

The establishment of Gandhi's *āśrama* community can thus be perceived as a collective statement about transcending social parameters—mediating between the sacred and the mundane. Those who belonged to the *āśrama* community, using Turner's phrase, formed a "liminal group" that transcended the socially imposed structures of caste and gender. Turner defines a liminal group as a "community or comity of comrades and not a structure of hierarchically arrayed positions. This comradeship transcends distinctions of rank, age, kinship position, and, in some kinds of cultic group, even of sex." In their shared vision, *āśrama* dwellers created *communitas* with the principle, "Each for all, and all for each," as ethnographers phrase it.[71] For Gandhi, in his straddling of the divergent values of self-denial and service, self-emancipation and political freedom, traditional rules and *unorthopractic* applications, the establishment of the *āśrama* provided a venue where commitment to renunciation and to social action could coexist.

It is apparent that Gandhi, in creating *āśramas*, was experimenting with a prototype of an ideal society based on harmony, tolerance, self-reliance, self-restraint, and interdependence. The *āśrama* lifestyle combined both the elements of political activism—including spinning *khadi* (cotton) and planning for propaganda—and the disciplines of asceticism—prayer, self-restraint, and simplicity. However, even as "ashram virtues set at an heroic high, the realities of ashram life fell generally far short of that target," according to Jordens.[72] Gandhi's biographers document that life in his *āśrama* was rife with taxing regimens, moral transgressions, personality clashes, rivalry, and tension. Gandhi admitted that his *āśrama* was "imperfect." Perhaps the *āśrama* displayed the impossibility of accomplishing the high ideals of the perfect society that Gandhi envisaged, but what stands out as a noteworthy marker of his character and intention is that his faith in his aspiration remained unshaken.[73]

The establishment of *āśramas* was a concrete step in a coherent narrative synthesizing an activism and asceticism that required mass participation. Based on the models of traditional ascetics, the physical locale enabled Gandhi to reinterpret traditional religious norms while simultaneously utilizing renunciative disciplines to strengthen his nonviolent political strategy. *Āśramas* primarily served the following purposes: (1) they constituted communal public and religious spaces where the boundaries between private and public, religious and political elements intersected; (2) they provided a nonrestrictive environment, beyond the confines of the traditional *varṇāśrama dharma*, in which the residents could nonetheless be regarded as *sannyāsins* who transcend the obligations of caste and stage of life; (3) they accorded Gandhi himself with the authority to naturalize the ascetic vows of *brahmacarya, ahiṃsā,* and so on and assign new meanings to *brahmacarya, yajña,* and *tapas*; (4) they enabled Gandhi, in creating a community of shared values and goals, to reinterpret the rigid customs of gender, caste, religion, class segregation, and hierarchy; (5) they afforded space in which to test the validity of spiritual disciplines for the modern political context; and most importantly, (6) they constituted a physical platform from which Gandhi was able to redefine the orthodox rules of *brahmacarya* so that it became an ideological weapon in his nonviolent struggle.

Private *Brahmacarya* and the Public Discourse on Sexuality: An Avenue for Social Reform

Gandhi's *āśrama* was not a typical hermitage or holy dwelling. As Ashe describes, Gandhi's *āśrama* "was not like a monastery or convent, a house of celibates of the same sex. It included both, and included married couples."[74] Moreover, according to Gandhi, the women in the *āśrama* were not "subject to any restraint which is not imposed upon men as well."[75] This unique arrangement was made possible and also motivated by Gandhi's deep conviction in the efficacy of *brahmacarya* for transcending gender constraints. In the draft of Satyagraha Ashram's constitution, Gandhi wrote: "Those who want to perform national service, or those who want to have a glimpse of the real religious life, must lead a celibate life, no matter if married or unmarried."[76] Gandhi's call to all—men or women, married or unmarried, higher or lower caste—to practice *brahmacarya* as a commitment to national service required a new interpretation of celibacy, one that included an open discourse on sexuality.

Gandhi was unusually frank and public in discussing sexual issues from the day he conceived his *brahmacarya* vow, which he never treated as a private matter. Even before discussing his decision with his wife (the person most directly affected by it), he sought the opinions of his coworkers. He documents this peculiar sequence in his *Autobiography*: "But the work set me furiously thinking in the direction of self-control, and according to my wont I discussed my thoughts with my coworkers." Gandhi recalls that he "had not shared his thoughts" with his wife "until then, but only consulted her at the time of taking the vow. She had no objection." Gandhi admits that he "had great difficulty in making the final resolve."[77]

Gandhi's admission of his hesitation shows that the vow was not an easy decision for him; it was a lifelong commitment, not a passing fad. Then he publicly announced his vow. Everyone who was interested in Gandhi's political and social work knew about his celibacy. No one, however, knows for certain why he made his personal decision to abstain from sexuality into a community matter. Was it a strategic move? Was it motivated by his aim to be a transparent servant of the community, precluded from having private concerns? It appears that Gandhi no more differentiated between private and public spheres than he did between political and spiritual ones.

Intriguingly, even to the end of his life at the age of seventy-eight, Gandhi continued publicly discoursing on the general issue of celibacy and on his sexual experiments, as well as on his accomplishments and setbacks. Traditionally, because intense renunciatory disciplines compel ascetics to seek solitude by withdrawing from day-to-day life, their inner struggles are not often known to others. The *brahmacārin* who withdraws into such seclusion remains the sole witness to the dark moments presented by deep rooted *vāsanās* (passions) and outward temptations. Ironically, despite its exaltation, *brahmacarya* remains a secret and lonely path.

Religious texts and narratives in the Indian traditions attest to the exacting nature of its practice. Gandhi often referred to the narratives, which are punctuated with the unyielding nature of Kāma, who entices great yogis into his web of delusion. Perhaps due to cultural inhibitions regarding sexual discourse, ascetic literature and the sages themselves are often silent about the particulars of the inner struggles and stresses that ascetics experience in their pursuit of *brahmacarya*. However, Kumar writes, "For this ideal, Gandhiji was ready to challenge taboos." Sexual taboos created many social problems in Indian society (from child-marriage and sexual diseases to infant mortality) and Gandhi sought to confront them through his discourse on *brahmacarya*. Unlike traditional *brahmacārins* who withdraw into silence for their inner struggle, Gandhi openly revealed the joy his observance brought and the perils he faced on the path of renunciation. Kumar documents Gandhi's 1932 confession: "I do not claim to be a perfect *brahmachari* with 'evil thoughts' having been held in a restraint, but not yet eradicated."[78] Gandhi's predecessors and the *sannyāsins* of his day who advocated the value of celibacy for India's transformation neither involved themselves in conversations on sexual issues nor exposed their inner secrets. Therefore, Gandhi's forthright confession and open public discourse do not have any Indian precedents; rather they appear to be inspired by Western examples.[79]

Gandhi certainly had to struggle to overcome his sexuality: his unguarded associations with women put him to the test each day of his life. Gandhi's open discussion of his inner struggles to remain truthful prompts Abbott to muse: "The world's most famous and flamboyant proponent of celibacy was not blessed with a propensity for it. As a youth and even an old man, he was tormented by his raging sexuality."[80] Gandhi spoke frequently of his relentless struggle with this formidable vow, which demanded control of all senses, and published letters by those who questioned his peculiar position. He admitted that when he pledged himself to a life of celibacy he did not realize the challenges that sustaining the vow would bring: "Even when I am past fifty-six years, I realize how hard a thing it is. Every day I realize more and more that it is like walking on the sword's edge, and I see every moment the necessity for eternal vigilance."[81] Notably, it was not just physical control, but Gandhi's comprehensive vow that included sense control in thought, word, and speech was likewise challenging. Gandhi also spoke widely about his experiments with fasting, with different types of food, physical labor, and prayer—claiming that they helped him sustain the vow and also recommending them to others. For example, he declared that "a married person cannot observe celibacy merely by following rules regarding diet, air and water. He must also refrain from being alone with his wife."[82]

Gandhi did not even hesitate to write about his correspondents' inner struggles. In a 1921 publication, Gandhi discusses a "pathetic letter" that he had received, in which the correspondent, despite his efforts, "suffers from discharges in sleep and often wished to commit suicide." In his extensive public response, Gandhi gave his advice and twelve essential rules that should be followed. They include everything from dietary guidelines to reading and seeking control over passions by looking "upon every woman as [one's] sister."[83] Alter notes that Gandhi used corporeal metaphors that conveyed hard work in the practice of *brahmacarya*: "A man striving for success in *brahmacharya* suffers pain as a woman does in labor."[84] Through this comparison, he intimated the creative power of suffering. At the same time, he defines male celibacy in feminine, vulnerable terms, which empowered his female followers.

Gandhi ventured to report his private dark moments, even if these came only in thoughts and dreams—in spite of the fact that his close associates advised him not to talk publicly about his private issues. In *Harijan*, Gandhi exposed his inner desire for a woman. In an unconventional move, Gandhi wrote about an incident in 1938: while hospitalized, he dreamed that he "wanted to see a woman." He called it the "darkest hour" and "the hour of my temptation."[85] Although he communicated his feelings to attendants and medical friends, they could give him no help. Parekh underscores Gandhi's reason for publicizing his dream: "He thought that since he was a public figure and his experiments had important lessons for others, he had a duty to share his experiences with them."[86] Gandhi often reflected on the pedagogic value of his experiences. The exposure of his inner battles seems to be part of his overall struggle for realizing truth in all aspects of life. Gandhi invented a new paradigm for celibacy that combined virility with vulnerability, in opposition to the sort of masculinity espoused by the contemporary militant nationalist discourse on celibacy. Alter demonstrates that the use of the term *brahmacarya* is primarily defined in masculine terms and that in the ideology of nationalism "the rhetoric of *brahmacharya* is aggressively male." Scholars note that "Gandhi's nationalist politics of nonviolence seems to cut against the grain of overt masculinity."[87] What makes Gandhi unique in the traditional discourse of ascetics and models of *brahmacarya* is the unconventional manner in which he combined the masculinity of semen control and feminine virtues like tenderheartedness.

Gandhi's guilelessness in discussing sexual issues made him susceptible to mistrust over the veracity of his accomplishments as an ascetic, evident in the response of critics and the amount of scrutiny to which his personal accounts have been subjected. B. R. Nanda enunciates that "Gandhi shared his passing thoughts even embarrassing dreams with the readers of his weekly journals, thus making himself an easy target for malicious critics."[88] However, for Gandhi, the ideal of leadership for the Satyagraha movement included both the practice of *brahmacarya* and the cultivation of transparency—both were intertwined.[89] Gandhi proclaimed: "The leader in such a movement must be a man of deeply spiritual life, preferably a *brahmachari*—whether married or unmarried. . . . All his actions must be transparent through and through." Gandhi is reported to have said that "his life was an open book and he hid nothing from the world." He stated that he revealed his mistakes that "they [who listen to him] may learn a lesson from it and never be hasty or careless in their actions."[90] Gandhi's openness about his private failings made him susceptible to criticism and created suspicion about his bold experiments.

Gandhi's persistent conversations on *brahmacarya* were not merely a public journaling of his thoughts or an obsession with celibacy as some have suggested. Rather, they served as arenas in which to discuss and resolve specific repressive social and personal customs—including child-marriage, patriarchy, and moral degradation—by advocating mechanisms of self-control. Gandhi's predecessors (such as Vivekananda) and contemporaries (such as Swami Shraddhananda) emphasized sexual discipline, semen control, and sexual purity, but did not call for comprehensive reform through conquest of the senses. For example, Swami Shraddhananda emphasized that "modern India had only one 'sacred cause—the cause of sexual purity and true national unity.' "[91] His message was encased in ancient Aryan ideology. Although Gandhi also shared these ideals, he utilized his public discussions as a platform for broader social reform: "Full development of the soul is impossible without *brahmacharya*. Without it, man may act like a well-fed but wild horse without reins, but he cannot become civilized."[92]

Gandhi's uncanny frankness enabled him to discuss the sensitive issues of sex education for boys and girls as well as to promulgate the value of *brahmacarya* for addressing social and political problems. Through his conversations, he related the pragmatic value of sexual control to the resolution of a wide range of social issues (including physical and mental health, population control, untouchability, widowhood, child-marriage, dowry, *purdha*, and male hegemony) as well as to the moral strengthening of virtues such as courage and fearlessness. Traditional ascetics and some of his *sannyāsin* contemporaries sought to deal with the issue of male physical and mental health through semen retention, but Gandhi was unique in his inclusive approach to celibacy. He recommended celibacy to women and confronted the hegemony inherent in male–female relations: "I passionately desire the utmost freedom for our women. I detest child marriages. I shudder to see a child widow, and shiver with rage when a husband just widowed contracts with brutal indifference another marriage."[93] Throughout his life, Gandhi remained deeply concerned with women's issues in India's social traditions and constructed an ideal of the feminine that was traditional in nature but progressive in purpose.

By exposing his own failings, Gandhi may have been pointing to the infirmity of all men who harshly judge women for their moral transgressions.[94] Parel ruminates: "He saw in the new celibacy that he was developing one of the powerful means of liberating men from their dominating or predatory attitude towards women, and women from accepting the submissive role assigned to them by society."[95] Toward the end of his life he summarized his philosophy in a long list, which includes this statement: "Perfect *brahamchari* means an absolutely passionless man or woman."[96] Gandhi's celibacy can be considered "new" because it did not delineate between male ascetics and forced female purity; it also exposed the hegemonic tendencies of the renouncer tradition. His writings verify that his inner struggle with sexuality paralleled his outer battle against violence, injustice, and inequity. If Gandhi was deliberately seeking to combine activism with asceticism, then it follows logically that *brahmacarya*—fundamental to that synthesis—needed to be overtly integrated into his public discourse. While Gandhi's revealing accounts of his stealthy passions opened him to criticism, paradoxically they also served to prove his genuineness as a political and religious leader. The masses, stricken over the debauchery and deceit of the foreign regime and the self-centeredness of native elites, could only but trust a man who had the courage to challenge his own inner enemies of lust and greed. The massive response to Gandhi's calls to action confirms people's trust in his veracity, his ability to relate to men and women equally, and his native ascetic approach to the Colonial regime.

Shifting the Course of Conjugal Love: Celibacy in Marriage

Gandhi's approach to conjugal love was certainly contrary to common Indian understanding. In the householder stage of life, Hindu sages license married couples to cherish and nurture familial and spousal relationships. Nehru's opinion reflects the views of many of Gandhi's followers: "I do not know why he is so obsessed by this problem of sex, important as it is. For him it is a 'soot or whitewash' question, there are no intermediate shades." Nehru himself cherished the relationship with his wife, Kamla, and did not find merit in Gandhi's views that sensual attraction, even between husband and wife, is "unnatural."[97]

Even though religious literature exalts the spiritual powers of an ascetic, the epic narratives celebrate the union between men and women. Traditional lore sets specific parameters for householders regarding the fulfillment of desires. Radhakrishnan quotes the *Mahābhārata*, "a householder who approaches his wife in the proper time is a *brahmachari*," and elaborates: "Hindu tradition affirms that a householder who controls his sex life is a brahmacāri quite as truly as one who abstains from sex altogether. To be a celibate is not to deaden the senses and deny the heart."[98] The often quoted Hindi proverb, *Ek nāri brahmacārī* (a man with one woman is *brahmacārin*), describes the norm of a householder's restraint. Conjugal love as one of the four *puruṣārthas* (human aims) sanctifies individual fulfillment and the sustenance of family and social harmony.[99]

It is noteworthy that Gandhi chose the example of the sage Vyāsa to support his view when he spoke with newly married couples: "What I read in the *Mahabharata* is daily growing upon me. Vyasa is described therein as having performed *niyoga*. He is not described as beautiful, but he was the reverse of it . . . He performed the act not for lust but for procreation. The desire for a child is perfectly natural, and once the desire is satisfied there should be no union."[100] Gandhi altogether disregarded the other multifarious episodes of love and intimacy in the grand epic.

When Gandhi committed to *brahmacarya* he was a married man with the lucrative occupation of lawyer. He was, as he himself put it, in the "prime of youth and health." Yet Gandhi not only vowed to remain celibate in marriage himself, he eventually advocated it for others—even for young married couples longing for physical intimacy. He did not view the bliss in marriage in the same way as did his ancestors, who celebrated the *saṃskāras* of marriage and progeny. On the contrary, he confessed that "true happiness came into our lives only after the vow was taken."[101] To Gandhi, physical attraction and emotional satisfaction were inferior reasons for getting married; the highest purpose was to augment the well-being of country and society. The following letter in response to one of his followers, written on his Silence Day in 1927, explains his eccentric credo on marriage and celibacy. Gandhi offers his argument in a lawyer-like mode:

> If you are content with forgoing marriage then do not marry. If not, make arrangements for getting married. You are no stranger to the difference between contentment and bliss.
>
> The idea of merging into each other if you find an ideal wife is itself a great illusion. Many have been deluded by it and it will be no wonder if you too are lost. If you will escape it till the end, that would be a matter for wonder.
>
> Having seen us all married people, if you are convinced that it is not worth while following suit—and convinced you ought to be—give up for the present the desire to taste the joy of *brahmacharya* and ponder over the joylessness of marriage, if you have observed it. Continue to think on this line—'God alone knows what bliss there is to be enjoyed in *brahmacharya*, but because there is no joy in marriage, I am not going to marry at all.'
>
> Here is an argument on a lower level:
>
> 'Indeed, under certain circumstances I may marry. But today my country is in bondage; plight of the women is miserable. As I am engaged in this work, how can I marry? I must take this vow that until we attain the swaraj of my conception, I shall not marry even if Rambha [a celestial nymph] were to solicit me.' Try to think in this way if you can. . . .

> If you can do neither try this thought. 'I do have a desire to marry and it cannot be suppressed. But I will not marry a girl of my caste as I would not marry my own sister. I will insist on breaking the barriers of caste. The girl must know Sanskrit, Marathi, Hindi and Gujarati; she should not hanker after money; if her parents are alive we must have their consent. She must have absolute love of khadi; she must appreciate and have faith in my other ideals and love the untouchables, be strong of body and prepared to live in some remote village and be willing to honour the well-known discipline of *brahmacharya* in marriage.' If you cannot do even this, know that you will not be able to observe *brahmacharya* and therefore marry at the first opportunity. If you resolve to observe the above discipline, write down the vow and proceed as before.[102]

Gandhi has been perceived by some scholars as lacking love, and this letter certainly seems stern and emotionless.[103] Gandhi contravened the purposes of marriage for the *gṛhastha* state of life as presented by the sages: "the stage of Intimacy" and "the stage of Generativity," as Erikson describes them.[104] Instead he makes marriage into a calculated, businesslike transaction with specific stipulations that nurture India's pride, economic self-reliance, and social equity. At the same time, the letter portrays Gandhi's deep conviction in the value of *brahmacarya* as part of a comprehensive plan for social reform and spiritual growth. Marriage is only advisable if it contributes to the goal of service and social reform and is imbued with the spirit of renunciation, not individual indulgence.

Gandhi's views on celibacy in marriage and his own vow of celibacy—by which he denied physical intimacy to his wife—has aroused criticism from native people as well as scholars. Some consider that it was an act of cruelty toward his wife. Kasturba Gandhi never expressed her feelings about Gandhi's vow and was always committed to him throughout all the struggles of his life. Gandhi earned her respect as a "sadhu [a holy man]." He noted her remark: "Yes, Bapu is an absolute *sadhu* where I am concerned." But Gandhi has also written that his vow of restraint, which expanded his love for humanity, also enriched his spousal relationship. Contrary to what many would suspect, *brahmacarya* did not create marital strain for him; he claimed, rather, that it actually served to inject joy and deeper meaning into his marriage and united husband and wife in the common goal of service.

> I may say that my wife and I tasted the real bliss of married life when we renounced sexual contact, and that in the heyday of youth. It was then that our companionship blossomed and both of us were enabled to render real service to India and humanity in general. . . . Indeed this self-denial was born out of our great desire for service.[105]

Gandhi's use of the pronoun "our" implies that Kasturba was a willing partner in his decision. Gandhi argued that "lustless love between husband and wife is not impossible." He also revealed that as long as he looked on his wife carnally, he and she did not have "real understanding." In a long interview by Margaret Sanger on birth control and self-control, he stated: "Our love did not reach a high plane. . . . The moment I bade good-bye to a life of carnal pleasure, our whole relationship became spiritual. Lust died and love reigned instead."[106] Gandhi is referring to the experience of pure love, which is not conditioned by sensory pleasures. He had reached this realization earlier in his life after taking the vow of celibacy, and he claimed that transcendence of sensual intimacy led to a close bond of friendship between him and his wife. By sacrificing "lust" he sought to engender that love for all of humanity.

"Gandhi," states Nanda, "agreed with the Pauline dictum that it is better to marry than to burn, but marriage was to be treated as a sacrament in which sex was the least important factor."[107] For Gandhi, marriage for sensory enjoyment was the lowest type. However, he admitted the difficult task of observing *brahmacarya* in marriage: "It is more difficult to observe unbroken *brahmacharya* in marriage than without marrying."[108] Yet at the same time he advocated celibacy for newly married couples and blessed them to "live as brother and sister" and serve the country. Apparently Gandhi even gave advice to "Vijayalakshmi Pandit [Nehru's sister, a diplomat and politician] and her husband to live like celibates at the time when he gave his blessings on the occasion of their wedding."[109] The traditional marital blessing of spousal love and progeny was ignored, and so were instinctual human desires.

Unconcerned with physical and emotional needs in his radical renunciation, Gandhi evaluated sexual relationships other than for the purpose of progeny as adulterous: "Adultery does not consist merely in sexual intercourse with another man's wife. We are taught by every religion that there can be adultery even in intercourse with one's own wife."[110] His own experience made him aware that male aggression and insensitivity could infiltrate marital sexual relations.

Wolpert regrets that "despite his saintly goodness and brilliance, Gandhi never managed to probe the dark roots of his irrational Puritanism, which haunted and obsessed him until the end of his life."[111] But Gandhi's own writings show that his decisions about his sexuality were marked with intense deliberation and very positive promises. A few scholars have undertaken the task of probing the dark roots of Gandhi's celibacy. For example, Erikson explores possible psychological reasons for Gandhi's attitude toward sexuality. But they overlook Gandhi's obvious statements as the key to understanding his desire to merge the ascetic with the political, the sacred with the secular—that required his vow of *brahmacarya*.

Although Gandhi's recommendation to practice celibacy in marriage seemed eccentric, it was propelled by his conviction in the value of *brahmacarya* for achieving three primary objectives: (1) obtaining *svarāj*; (2) empowering women who suffered from a collective inferiority complex resulting from archaic sexual conventions; and (3) strengthening his nonviolent strategy for the *svarājya* movement. Regarding the first objective, Gandhi affirmed that it was essential to conquer the passions in order to attain true *svarāj*. Therefore, he advocated celibacy not only for the young and newly married couples who took part in his movement but for individual men and women willing to commit to service. In this he deviated sharply from the norm of *brahmāṇic* celibacy, historically prescribed only for men as a religious vow.[112] Even though Gandhi underscored the power of semen control in personal empowerment, unlike traditional *brahmacārins* who only celebrate the masculine nature of celibacy, Gandhi strove to move beyond the limitations of gender.[113] Gandhi proclaimed that for both men and women "*brahmacharya* is an absolute necessity if they are to preserve the wealth of physical well-being; no one need doubt this."[114]

Second, while Gandhi believed in the traditional sanctity of the institution of marriage, he was progressive with regard to the idea of equal partnership in marriage. Ronald J. Terchek holds that for Gandhi, "marriage [was] a relationship between equals, bestowing no sexual rights or claims on men over their wives."[115] Gandhi's version of marriage was by no means normative according to Hindu customs of hierarchy. Intriguingly, Gandhi utilized *brahmacarya* as an avenue to empower women, "for it could provide a means for resisting male domination in a way that was legitimised in their culture. For men, it could provide a mark of their commitment to a non-exploitative and equal relationship with women," observes David Hardiman.[116] Impugning cultural norms that positioned women as subordinate to men, Gandhi argued for the "autonomy" of women. Gandhi did not "call on ancient texts to validate his claims for the autonomous women," as noted by Terchek; however, he seemed to derive the ability to redefine the tradition from his moral authority as a *brahmacārin*.[117] Gandhi's predecessors, including Raja Rammohan Roy (1774–1833) and Ishwar Chadra Vidyasagar (1820–91), crusaded against the evil customs of widow burning (*sati*) and polygamy, and as a counter to these customs, they introduced widow remarriage; but ascetic celibacy was not a factor in their agenda of social reforms. It is unprecedented that Gandhi presented *brahmacarya* as an essential component in addressing the issues of social restrictions on women for the purpose of empowering them internally and spiritually.

Third, Gandhi trusted in the power of *tapas* (self-suffering) for achieving success in the *svarāj* movement. By advising young people to abstain *in* marriage rather than abstain *from* marriage, Gandhi may have been looking to engender the massive inner heat of *tapas* that arises with self-restraint. Wolpert writes that Gandhi believed "the purer the suffering (*tapas*) . . . the greater the progress," and notes Gandhi's resolve "to pit the passionate powers of his sublimated suffering spirit against the world's mightiest empire."[118]

Gandhi's insistence on *brahmacarya* for married—especially newlywed—couples is ideologically contrary to his native tradition, which considers fulfilling sensual desire as one of life's essential aims. In 1937, in a private conversation with two newly married couples, Gandhi advised that "marriage for the . . . sexual appetite is no marriage. It is *Vyabhichara*—concupiscence." Then he bestowed this blessing: "The whole ceremony is performed in the presence of the sacred fire. Let the fire make ashes of all the lust in you."[119] The use of the metaphor of burning lust in the sacred fire ties in with Gandhi's belief in the power of *tapas*; however, from the traditional, cultural perspective, the blessing seems both quaint and cruel. In his youth, Gandhi himself had indulged in sexual pleasures before applying himself to an austere life. Moreover, even until his old age he lamented the fact that the observance of *brahmacarya* as he defined it—in terms of being completely unaware of one's sexual identity, male or female—was a challenge.[120]

Waging the Battle Against Kāma in the Public Arena

Gandhi's unusually close contacts with women have been a subject of much public debate and scholarly analysis. "Gandhiji had decided to wage a war against 'Kama' (the god of desire). Where others had failed he hoped to succeed. He was, however, a worthy combatant, who loved to put up a fight," states Kumar.[121] Is it original that Gandhi, the *mahātmā* who believed in the power of *brahmacarya*, decided to confront sexual temptations? Many ancient and modern ascetics—from Viśvāmitra to the Buddha and Ramakrishna Paramhansa—battled temptations. Overcoming the spell of Kāma is an essential component of Indian asceticism. However, what is unique about Gandhi's combat is that it was fought in the public arena—literally "under the open sky or in an open room . . . There was no privacy about him because other men and women also slept near him," as Bose describes it.[122]

In the 1947 article "Walls of Protection," Gandhi wrote that when he was in South Africa he read about the rules laid down in India for a *brahmacārin,* which warn against living with or looking at women. Gandhi was referring to the tradition in which ascetics cloister themselves lest temptations lure them into the bondage of Kāma. Olivelle remarks:

> In ascetic works, however, the tone is harsher and the intent is not just mistrust but total abhorrence of the female species. "A man becomes intoxicated," one ascetic text declares, "by seeing a young woman just as much as drinking liquor. Therefore, a man should avoid from afar a woman, the mere sight of whom is poison."[123]

Gandhi did not observe those restrictive rules and instead openly associated with women.[124] Far from abhorring them, he included them in his close circle of confidants. He denied outright the arguments above: "The argument, that the sight and company of women have been found to be inimical to self-restraint and are, therefore, to be avoided, is fallacious."[125]

Many Indian religious sects, especially in the Jain tradition, prohibit monks and nuns from even accidentally brushing against individuals of the opposite sex. Many *brahmacārins* stare only at the feet of women for fear that the lord of temptation may seduce them. Gandhi often referred to the prowess of Rāma's younger brother Lakṣmaṇa in the *Rāmāyaṇa,* who observed a vow of *brahmacarya* during his exile and conquered sleep by virtue of this practice. When Sītā was being abducted by the deceitful Rāvaṇa, she dropped her jewelry along the path to give clues to her destination. However, Lakṣmaṇa could only identify Sītā's ankle bracelet among the other ornaments because he had only ever beheld Sītā's feet, not her face or neck. Gandhi, in contrast, deliberately subjected himself to temptation by constantly seeking the company of women. Despite the challenges, he "routinely violated the customary brahmacharya precaution of avoiding temptation by avoiding women," reports Abbott.[126] This paradox constantly bewildered his contemporaries. Kumar writes: "For a man who abhorred bodily temptations, women constituted his entire world at one level."[127] For Gandhi, however, his associations with women were consistent with his *brahmacarya*. Women were not objects of sensual gratification, and for him, his female coworkers presented a proof of the value of *brahmacarya* in providing safety and equality for women:

> Yes, I believe in complete equality for women and, in the India I seek to build, they would have it. The reason I have so many women co-workers is, I believe, due to my adoption of celibacy and my instinctive sympathy for women.[128]

Furthermore, Gandhi held a belief that *"only by becoming a perfect Brahmachari can one truly serve the woman."*[129] Paying no heed to traditional cautionary advice and established models, Gandhi, while striving for perfect celibacy, walked happily on the razor's edge by mingling with women of all ages.

Gandhi's audacity in this arena became climactic when he tested his *brahmacarya* by sleeping with his female associates, thus making himself vulnerable to temptations—and also to public humiliation. Most biographers and Gandhi scholars grapple with possible underlying reasons for these unusual experiments. For example, Gier states, "Gandhi believed that Indian ascetics who sought refuge in forests and mountains were cowards, and he was convinced that the only way to conquer desire was to face the temptation head-on with a naked female in his bed."[130] Even though no one has accused Gandhi of breaking his vow by having sexual intercourse, he nevertheless was denounced for practicing *adharma* (unrighteous conduct) and creating an example that could weaken the foundation of "moral order."[131] His nontraditional methods—specifically his act of testing his celibacy at the age of seventy-eight with young women, including his daughter-like grandniece Manu—were the subject of intense opprobrium.

In March 1947, concerned about growing unrest among Gandhi's close followers, Swami Anand and Kedar Nath visited Bihar to express their concern about his experiments with Manu, which he called a "yajna," and to dissuade him. Gandhi was determined and replied to their accusatory remarks:

> No moral progress or reform is possible if one is not prepared to get out of the rut of orthodox tradition. By allowing ourselves to be cribbed by cast iron social conventions,

> we have lost. The orthodox conception of the ninefold wall of protection in regard to *brahmacharya* is in my opinion inadequate and defective.[132]

Parekh notes the consequence of Gandhi's aberrant form of celibacy: "Fully aware of the way Vishvāmitra, Vyāsa and other great rishis had been defeated by the sexual impulse even after hundreds of years of penance and self-mastery, many of his colleagues and friends began to suspect the worst."[133] Gandhi's efforts to acquire the supernatural power of *brahmacarya* were intended for the purpose of sustaining communal peace; but by testing his celibacy through constant experimentation with his female associates, these experiments cost him friends and unblemished fame. In spite of these setbacks, Gandhi sought to confront the alluring power of celestial nymphs such as Menakā and Rambhā by keeping the constant company of his female associates—because he believed that supernormal powers are achieved only when "our brahmacharya would remain inviolate even if Rambha came down from heaven and embraced us."[134] Gandhi's definition of *brahmacarya* was not merely sexual control but the development of a childlike purity and innocence.

To Gandhi, celibacy did not mean the gradual waning of sensory desire by avoidance of enticing situations; rather, it acquired potency only when tested by exposure. Gandhi daringly questioned the self-proclaimed *brahmacārins* who enjoyed illustrious social status but were unable to produce the effects of *brahmacarya* acclaimed by the texts and traditions. He saw *brahmacarya*, therefore, not merely as a state of sexlessness but as involving complete observance of essential virtues of truth and nonviolence. In Gandhi's opinion, if the practice of *brahmacarya* did not yield tangible results, it must be flawed. In his discussion with Swami Anand and his party, Gandhi challenged the prevailing complacency and hypocrisy surrounding the practice of *brahmacarya*:

> You have all been brought up in the orthodox tradition. According to my definition, you cannot be regarded as true *brahmacharis*. You are off and on falling ill; you suffer from all sorts of bodily ailments. I claim that I represent true *brahmacharya* better than any of you. You do not seem to regard a lapse in respect of truth, nonviolence, nonstealing, etc., to be so serious a matter. But a fancied breach in respect to *brahmacharya*, i.e., relation between man and woman, upsets you completely. I regard this conception

> of *brahmacharya* as narrow, hidebound and retrograde. To me truth, ahimsa and *brahmacharya* are all ideals of equal importance.[135]

Just as he wanted to experiment with the power of *Sat* and *ahiṁsā* in the public arena for social and political goals, so did he choose to do so with *brahmacarya*. Not only did Gandhi defy tradition by redefining women's image and publicizing his battle with sexuality, but his way of asserting purity is also unorthodox and daring. Which was more heroic—Gandhi's observation of *brahmacarya* or his subjecting himself to temptations that publicly transgressed traditional boundaries?

In a 1947 letter to Amrit Kaur Singh, Gandhi defines a true *brahmacārin* as one who is "capable of lying naked with naked women, however beautiful they may be, without being in any manner whatsoever sexually excited."[136] Edwardes charges Gandhi with egoism: "In his seventies he was . . . still trying to conquer and control his sexuality, worrying about a wet-dream he had in 1936, but caring nothing for the psychic damage he might be causing by his experiments."[137] Edwardes's opinion reflects the concern of many of Gandhi's critics and scholars. Gandhi stated he was seeking to quell the tide of violence and suffering through his *yajña* and *tapas*. But some modern scholars, steeped in the traditions of Western psychoanalysis, question Gandhi's covert intentions or, more importantly, whether he inadvertently caused psychological suffering in the young women who took part in his experiments.

Gandhi strove to realize sexual transcendence: "I deliberately want to become a eunuch mentally. If I succeed in this then I become one physically also. . . . That alone is true *brahmacharya*."[138] During the final two years of his life, Gandhi seems to have considered the issues of gender and sexuality even more profoundly. In 1945, he wrote in his "Thought of the Day" that "Woman is not helpless. She must never regard herself as weaker than man. She should not, therefore, beg for any man's mercy, nor depend on him."[139] Historically, it was during this time—when women were being violated on a massive scale, and his principle of *ahiṃsā* was being "choked"—that Gandhi ventured into "sharing his bed" with his nineteen-year-old grandniece, an act he described as a "*yajna*—a sacrifice, a penance."[140] Observers have assessed Gandhi's reasons for this behavior through a variety of lenses. Here we briefly examine Gandhi's own explanations for taking his *brahmacarya* to such extremes as involving Manu in his practice and, further, how he sought to make this consistent with his overall narrative of ascetic activism. Gandhi wrote to Krishna Kripalani, "Manu

Gandhi, my grand-daughter as we consider blood relations, shares the bed with me, strictly as my blood, not to give me animal satisfaction but as a part of what might be my last *yajna*." Gandhi invoked his favorite symbolism of *yajña* for his last—ultimate—sacrifice. During a talk with one of his female associates, Gandhi said that the nineteen-years-old Manu was a "partner" in this *yajña*, not a mere instrument for testing Gandhi's own purity.[141]

Gandhi did not consider Manu to be like his other female associates: she far surpassed the others in her purity and service.[142] Although he acknowledged that she was a "little girl," Gandhi also believed that Manu was capable of "treading the path of truth" and had spiritual strength equivalent to the young heroes Dhruva and Prahlad of Indian mythology.[143] In this context it is interesting to note that Gandhi had often said that "one true *brahmacāri*" would be sufficient to change the course of history, yet he expressed this with a significant difference to Manu Gandhi in 1947: "As against the sins of crores [millions] of men, perfect purity of even two persons will certainly have an effect. Yes, there is this that these two persons are very severely tested."[144] Did the conflagration of communal hatred that was consuming his vision of peace and of a united India motivate Gandhi to seek Manu as a partner in his *yajña*? This raises a critical point: In activating the power of perfect purity, why did Gandhi not call on any other of his acclaimed followers, such as Vinoba (later known as Acharya Vinoba Bhave [1895–1982]). He was Gandhi's greatest disciple, an Indian nationalist and a social reformer. He founded the Bhoodan and Gramdan movements), whom he had openly acknowledged as practicing "inviolate *brahmacarya*."[145] Why did he believe it necessary to involve Manu?

Was Gandhi perhaps seeking to make Manu "an ideal *brahmachāri* as well," in order to grant women the privilege of equal choice in this area of life and also to set up a model of women's inner strength?[146] The riots between Hindus and Muslims in 1946–47 anguished Gandhi and also rudely awakened him to the reality of feminine issues. He was agonized to learn that a large number of women were being abducted, molested, and even killed during the riots.[147] He saw that women were a major target of violence and were helpless when victimized. In a talk with women workers he complained:

> We hear reports, not only from Bihar or Noakhali, but from everywhere about goondas having molested or abducted women. I feel terribly upset hearing such story tales. I wonder why our women have become so timid. Their glory has been diminishing and for this you women are responsible.[148]

Brahmacarya has been generally understood as a male privilege. Indian scholar Ramchandra Gandhi states that *brahmacarya* is a "man-dominated metaphysical and moral and political thought which denies women access to a non-sexist identity."[149] Gandhi was well aware of the male dominance and misogynist tendencies of ascetic literature and realized the "imperfect nature" of the traditional norm of *brahmacarya*. In the midst of the political turmoil of 1947, Gandhi wrote in a letter that "our definition of *brahmacharya* is imperfect. I am trying to make it perfect." He noted that "except on one occasion I have not been a victim of passions" and felt that his discipline gave him authority to put forth a perfect definition.[150] What did Gandhi find inadequate about the meaning that impelled him to try to perfect it? Was it perhaps that women in the traditionally male-dominated society had been denied the privilege and power of practicing *brahmacarya* on a par with men? The complexity of these issues extends even beyond this exposition and is deserving of further analysis and discussion.

In going beyond established laws to prove that his female associates could remain innocent in his presence, Gandhi looked to the legend of Lord Kṛṣṇa and the gopis for a comparable example: "[And] when the Gopis [milkmaids] were stripped of their clothes by Krishna, the legend says, they showed no sign of embarrassment or sex-consciousness but stood before the Lord in rapt devotion."[151] Gandhi also cited the myth of Sage Śuka, who completely conquered the passions:

> When Shukadeva passed by the side of women bathing in a state of nudity, so the author of the *Bhagavata* tells us, his own mind was quite unruffled, nor were the women at all agitated or affected by a sense of shame. I do not think there is anything supernatural in this account. If in India today, there should be none who would be equally pure on a similar occasion, that does not set a limit to our striving after purity.[152]

Gandhi, immersed in his world of religious narratives, was dancing to the divine "tune," as he wrote in a 1947 letter, and appeared oblivious (consciously or unconsciously) to the fact that he was living in the twentieth century on this material earth (not in a mythical world) where the rules for a man in public life were different from those of ascetics.[153] He seemed to be responding with his *brahmacarya* ("divine conduct") for *loka-saṁgraha*, and he was not ineffectual. The Viceroy of India at the time was amazed at how Gandhi was triumphant in impeding violence "single-handedly" by entering into "some regions in flames and blood" during the Hindu-Muslim riots after India's independence.[154]

Gandhi's critics and admirers continue to argue the success and failure of his mission, as well as grapple with his unconventional behavior; however, his own resolute faith in the potency of *brahmacarya* and his persistence in its practice were relentless. Regardless of how others viewed his method, Gandhi perceived and proclaimed the coherence and consistency of his actions, which straddled his asceticism and his public life.

Just as Gandhi had redefined the principles of *yajña* and *tapas* in mobilizing his nonviolent movement, so he also reinterpreted the ascetic prohibition against touching women to avoid the "lustful" touch. "It is not," says he, "woman whose touch defiles man but he is often himself too impure to touch her."[155] In this reinterpretation, Gandhi sought to make men accountable for their own failings and, at the same time, liberate women from the charge of being temptresses. "Gandhi's controversial experiments with *brahmacharya* are an instructive example of how he put aside traditional rules and found his own way, dictated solely by his own experience, his own dispositions, and his unique way of purifying himself of sexual desire," remarks Gier.[156] Even though Gandhi was unorthodox in his experiments, he substantiated his practices within the traditional lore.

Gandhi's redefinition of orthodox rules was not merely an ideological statement; his emphatic claim that *brahmacarya* was specifically crucial to the development of women was a pragmatic step that encouraged thousands of women of all castes and status to participate in *satyagraha*. Taneja gives an account of women's politicization and their mass participation in the civil disobedience movement as well as in the "constructive programmes laid down by Gandhi like spinning and *khadi* work."[157] Nonetheless, Gandhi's position with regard to women has been considered controversial by scholars and activists alike, who argue over whether it was patriarchal or progressive. Gandhi "expected women to be pure and virtuous" and stay true to their traditional roles, as mother and mistress of the house, and, at the same time, called on them to exercise autonomy. He considered them "naturally abstemious" and "saw them as 'the mother of man' and 'too sacred for sexual love.' "[158] Such proclamations not only are inconsistent with statements about women in epic literature, but also overly simplify women's complex sexuality, which is cause for uneasiness among feminists.

However, Gandhi's strategy of *satyagraha* demanded the courage, gentleness, fearlessness, and endurance of both men and women, and his efforts to combine the strengths of each gender were novel and reflected in his ideal: on the one hand, he advocated that woman "should cast off her timidity and become brave and courageous"; on the other hand, he advised men to "cultivate the gentleness and the discrimination of woman."[159] For this ideal, Gandhi drew on various traditional Indian models found in Hindu texts and reinterpreted them for his own purposes.

An iconoclast, Gandhi not only sought to shatter the established *dharma* (religious laws) of the *āśrama* system but also to surpass conventional parameters of what is considered appropriate. Paradoxically, for Gandhi, his actions were intended to create a model confronting inhumane violence. It was the practice of *brahmacarya* that enabled Gandhi to transcend the phenomenal world of social relations, thereby fashioning a liminal character for himself and establishing his *āśramas* as liminal spaces. Because of his personal liminality he could question and redefine the traditional rules of *brahmacarya,* deconstruct its established practices, and institute a central role for *brahmacārins* in his political approach—all the while substantiating his practices within the mythical and cultural traditions. In the milieu of mythology, he intertwined *brahmacarya* and his close contact with women both to invigorate his personal strength and to energize his followers. Gandhi's interpretation of ancient narratives and his embodiment of legendary heroes synthesized a public persona capable of moving millions for action.

CHAPTER 5

Gandhi's Embodiment of Legendary Heroes and Ascetics

Toward a Coherent Narrative for Nonviolent Activism

> The story of Harishchandra may be only a parable; but every seeker will bear witness to its truth from his [own] personal experience and, therefore, that story is as precious as any historical fact.
>
> —M. K. Gandhi

> The spell of the story has always exercised a special potency in the oral-based Indian tradition and Indians have characteristically sought expression of central and collective meanings through narrative design.
>
> —Sudhir Kakar

> [T]he stories provide us with metaphors that make the arguments real to us.
>
> —Wendy Doniger O'Flaherty

Observers have responded in a multitude of ways to Gandhi's image of an ascetic: caricature, mockery, suspicion, and worship. Nevertheless, many biographical studies of Gandhi suggest that his ascetic image was an essential factor in mobilizing millions of citizens during the struggle for India's independence. Gandhi's ascetic practices, atypical in modern politics, resembled the austerities of a *tapasvin*, which in the traditional Indian context are believed to build an individual's personal power. Both during and after Gandhi's lifetime, the appraisals ascribe his authority as a leader to the "convincing power of his personality."[1] Reflecting on the "source of Gandhi's authority," contemporary British intellectual C. E. M. Joad suggested it lay "in the possession of the virtue of detachment from self." Evidently, this detachment was visible in his commitment to *brahmacarya* for public service. It is not surprising that even in Gandhi's lifetime, many of his contemporaries, scholars, followers, political leaders, and friends from different religious, social, and intellectual backgrounds expressed the common sentiment that the locus of Gandhi's spiritual authority rested in his personal detachment and moral method.[2]

The question of the root of Gandhi's "charismatic leadership" continues to be explored in academic studies. For example, the Rudolphs locate the "key to Gandhi's political potency" in his native traditional belief that "a person's capacity for self-control enhanced his capacity to control his environment."[3] The authors underscore the Hindu ethos "that a practitioner of *tapasya* ('austerities') accumulated special powers." Gandhi's belief in the ascetic power is reflected in the following words: "If my non-violence is to be contagious and infectious, I must acquire greater control over my thoughts."[4] Gandhi directly connected his personal self-control with his success in his nonviolent program.

The Rudolphs postulate a dynamic process that includes personal, religious, social, and psychological dimensions at the core of Gandhi's effectiveness as a leader. While acknowledging traditional views of Gandhi's asceticism, they bring attention to the phenomenon of "self-confidence" in the leader, which "social science calls 'charisma'" and state that "Gandhi evoked in himself and those who 'heard' him responses that transcended the routine of ordinary life, producing extraordinary events and effects on character, which, metaphorically, can be described as 'magical.'"[5] In their efforts to uncover the roots of Gandhi's charisma, they turn to a review of important events of Gandhi's past—childhood fears, his relationship with his temperamental father, and his aversion to sex for various psychological reasons. Their analysis provides some insight into psychological factors that might have underpinned Gandhi's interest in the power of asceticism.

However, there remains a need to understand what role the religious ethos that he communicated through narratives and his embodiment of the extraordinary power of *tapasya* played in Gandhi's influence on his people. What medium and method—symbols and narratives—did Gandhi use to evoke such extraordinary responses and engender trust in the masses? These questions require an analysis of Gandhi's interpretation and embodiment of ancient narratives, which intrigued him since his early childhood. It becomes apparent that the dialectic between Gandhi's creative use of the myths and people's response was a factor in mobilizing a mass movement.

Gandhi's image has also been crafted in hagiographical tones, making him into a Christ-like figure, a saint, an *avatār*, a holy man, or a *mahātmā*—a stature, scholars suggest, that played an essential role in uniting and mobilizing India's diverse population. At the same time, many studies that scrutinize Gandhi's political actions and his *brahmacarya* have deconstructed the image of Gandhi as a saint and holy man. Employing various analyses—psychoanalytical to anthropological—they seek to develop a fuller understanding of Gandhi as a man, rather than solely a religious figure.

Some critics such as Edwardes and Richard I. Cashman are suspicious of Gandhi's creation of his image as a religious figure as "myth-making." Edwardes describes Gandhi as "anti-modern," labels his spiritual stature itself as a "myth," and seeks to dismantle that specious myth through various arguments.[6] In *The Myth of the Lokamanya*, a book about Tilak (a nationalist leader who was given the honorific title of *Lokamānya*, literally meaning, "the one revered by the people or by the world"), Cashman portrays Gandhi's stature as *mahātmā* as being the construct of a "shrewd politician." In a brief remark comparing the creativity of Tilak and Gandhi with respect to their mythmaking, Cashman mentions that "there is no certain basis to the argument that Tilak was a less creative mythmaker or political tactician than Gandhi." Cashman offers the following assessment of Gandhi's success in mythmaking:

> As a shrewd politician Gandhi recognized the potential of the myth and succeeded in capturing it. But it was not Gandhi who created the myth; it was the myth and the circumstances that produced it, which established Gandhi as the *Mahatma*, the chief symbol of the nationalist movement.

Cashman does not elaborate further about *how* Gandhi "succeeded in capturing" the myth.[7] His book is a study of Tilak, but in it he makes a quick comparison between Gandhi and his fellow leader, thus leaving questions about the purpose and effectiveness of Gandhi's "myth" itself.

In his comprehensive essay "Gandhi as Mahatma," Dieter Conrad calls into question Cashman's opinion: "Whether the 'shrewd politician'

Gandhi 'capturing the myth of Mahatma' is an adequate description that answers the motivational complexities of the process is open to discussion." Conrad then presents a literal analysis of the term *mahātmā* and explains that "the designation seems traditionally to have been in use in an unspecific sense of 'holy man,' 'saint' or '*sannyasi*.'" Notably, Gandhi used these terms interchangeably for himself. Conrad also provides a probing survey of the general use of this title for various leaders in India's historical context. He provides the account of historic bestowal of the "stamp of Mahatmaship" on Gandhi by Tagore, and affirms that "the use of the epithet Mahatma has helped create a kind of mythical halo around Gandhi." Gandhi himself often expressed distaste for this stamp.[8] Even though Gandhi at times used this title for himself, he also displayed ambivalence about the unexpected privileges of being *mahātmā*. Perhaps he sometimes denied the honor on the grounds of his political motivations and, at others, embraced it on the basis of his spiritual aspiration. However, the question still remains: Was it the "mythical halo" from the title of *mahātmā* that moved the masses, as Conrad suggests? Neither Cashman nor Conrad looks beyond the conferral of the honorific title and Gandhi's skill as a political strategist to explain his power. A study of Gandhi's historical context and his own words provides additional insight.

During the Indian nationalist movement, the historic norm of attributing honorific titles to cultural heroes was extensive—and it certainly did not begin with Gandhi. Examples abound: Munshiram, an Arya Samaj leader (later known as Swami Shraddhananda), was known as Mahatmaji; Rabindranath Tagore, a poet and artist, was called *Gurudev* (divine guru); Tilak was referred to as *Lokamanya* (revered by the people); and Chitta Ranjan Das (1870–1925), the founder of the Swarajya Party, was hailed as *Deshbandhu* (comrade of the nation). These creative, idealistic men were contemporaries of Gandhi, living in the same cultural context, yet they did not capture the "mythical halo" to the extent that Gandhi did, nor did any stories about their miracles proliferate.

In spite of varying theories about when, where, and how Gandhi received this honorific epithet, and despite Gandhi's own reluctance to accept it, the title of *mahātmā* "stuck" to him.[9] It was not only Gandhi's "canonization" as a saint that differentiated him from his contemporaries but the sensation that he evoked in the religious imagination of the people, recorded by authors such as Shahid Amin, that also set him apart.[10] Numerous stories about Gandhi's divinity and miraculous powers, which were suggestive of characters from religious epics, flourished, as will be discussed later in this chapter.

Scholars and historians have considered the role of numerous historical, political, and psychological elements in Gandhi acquiring the stature of a *mahātmā* and becoming an icon who incited mass response to his call to action. These differing viewpoints have led to a multifaceted analysis of Gandhi's personality and his methods. Ironically, however, the religious narratives—out of which the concept of *mahātmā* emerges and through which Gandhi communicated his strategy—together with Gandhi's embodiment of an ascetic figure reminiscent of ancient *tapasvins*, have been overlooked. This omission in scholarly analyses may be attributed to a general ambivalence regarding the function of myth and religion in the field of secular politics. If we are to study Gandhi on his own terms for the purpose of understanding his odd synthesis, it is essential to survey selected Indian myths that he himself narrated, reinterpreted, and performed. Gandhi's own analysis of myths and the role Indian narratives play within the culture are vital to a comprehensive understanding of his emergence as *Mahātmā* and the ensuing historical events of mass mobilization.

A close analysis of Gandhi's words, including his biographical accounts of the events taking place around him, combined with other historical records, presents a complex picture of him. These descriptions suggest many ancillary factors that may have contributed to his mythical stature. Such an analysis points not to a linear process but rather to a dynamic interplay among various particulars: Gandhi's ascetic practices, specifically his vows of *brahmacarya* and poverty; his narration and reinterpretation of ancient myths to substantiate his methods of *ahiṃsā* and *satyagraha*; his reenactment of a *tapasvin* through his garb and public vows of fasting and silence; and the Indian proclivity for mythmaking. Gandhi's understanding and creative use of ancient myths emerged as a synthesizing tool that enabled him to resolve the discrepancy between his religious renunciation and political activism. His performance of the ancient narratives of *tapas* (asceticism) and self-sacrifice provided the connective tissue. Gandhi synthesized worldly and renunciatory ideologies by narrating, reinterpreting, and reenacting age-old myths. Gandhi's use of myths as a hermeneutic device for his political activism raises the following questions: Why did he communicate his twofold strategy of asceticism and political activism using religious narratives and symbols? What role did the myths he invoked play in mobilizing the masses to adopt his strategy of *satyagraha*? How was he able to reconcile the mythical world with the tangible, practical reality of twentieth-century worldly problems and predicaments?

The Indian Ethos of Religious Narratives and Gandhi's Predilection for Them

In his 1925 *Autobiography*, Gandhi reflected on his childhood experiences and the myths that influenced him. How much these reflections were filtered through the convictions he held in his 50s will always remain a mystery. Certainly he was selective in choosing events, and his recollections were not always historically accurate.[11] However, they were consistent with his goal of imparting the substance of his experiments with Truth for validating his then current convictions. It seems that by writing his *Autobiography*—a practice "peculiar to the West" (as one of his friends warned him)—Gandhi sought to make the events of his present public life coherent by illuminating carefully chosen trials of his otherwise unknown and private past. Gandhi admits in the introduction of *Autobiography*: "I should certainly like to narrate my experiments in the spiritual field which are known only to myself, and from which I have derived such power as I possess for working in the political field."[12] In his unique way, Gandhi used this Western format to show the progression of his philosophy for ascetic behavior and public actions through recounting his "experiments with Truth."

Gandhi's upbringing in a religious household and early incidents of his life provide possible reasons for his penchant for religious stories as well as for his trust in the power of moral force that later led him to embody ascetic practices. In personal reflections about his childhood, he mentions being exposed to the tradition of *kathā* (religious stories) and recalls being transfixed by the captivating power of these tales. He recounts that "a deep impression" was left on him by listening every evening to Ladha Maharaj (a *kathakar* or religious storyteller) recite the epic *Rāmāyaṇa Kathā* (Gandhi is referring to the *Ramacharitmanas* composed by Sant Tulsidās and often did not differentiate between the various versions of Lord Rama's story) to his ailing father. Ladha Maharaj was a devotee of Lord Rāma, and Gandhi remembers hearing that Maharaj cured himself of leprosy by repeating *rāmanāma* (name of Lord Rāma) and reading the *Rāmāyaṇa*. Gandhi remarks:

> This may or may not be true. We at any rate believed the story. And it is a fact that when Ladha Maharaj began his reading of the *Ramayana* his body was entirely free of leprosy. . . . He would sing . . . and explain them [the verses], losing himself in the discourse and carrying his listeners

> along with him. I must have been thirteen at that time, but I quite remember being enraptured by his reading. That laid the foundation of my deep devotion to the *Ramayana*.[13]

Although Gandhi may have been skeptical about the story itself, his belief in the magical power of *rāmanāma* and the underlying truth of the religious stories appears to have extended beyond a childhood fascination. Perhaps this childhood testimony of healing led him later to prescribe *rāmanāma* to his followers for curing the bodily ills. At the age of seventy-eight, he suffered from a persistent cough but refused the use of antibiotics; instead he trusted the power of *rāmanāma*, stating that he considered it "as the greatest of medicine. It is infallible." He recommended it to those practicing *brahmacarya*, for cleansing impurities of the mind. Gandhi emphasized to them: "There are numerous aids to *brahmacharya*. But the true and eternal one is Ramanama."[14] Gandhi also recalled that in his youth he attended a public reading of the *Bhāgavata*, the story of Lord Kṛṣṇa [commonly known as the *Bhāgavada Purāṇa*] and his various incarnations. But he was not attracted to the reading, and he describes the reader in this particular instance as "uninspiring." Later he read the text for himself in the Gujarati language "with intense interest" and discovered the devotion-engendering power of the text: "Today I see that the *Bhagavat* is a book which can evoke religious fervour."[15] Seemingly, the devotion and sincerity were central factors in the level of inspiration felt by Gandhi.

These experiences could have made Gandhi aware of the importance of the role and skill of a *kathakar* (storyteller), who could potentially ignite or discourage interest in a story. The tradition of *kathakaras* (professional religious storytellers) that Ladha Maharaj followed has been an integral part of Indian religious culture for centuries.[16] Many scholars, including van der Veer, K. Narayan, R. K. Narayan, and Hirst, analyze the formal act of narrating religious stories and the public reading of ancient epics (*kathā*) within the Indian context. For many Indians, *kathā* (the reading of religious texts) continues to hold an important place among rituals.

For the purpose of understanding Gandhi's use of religious narratives, it is essential to consider the vocabulary he utilized. The Sanskrit root verb of *kathā* is √*kath* meaning "to tell," "to narrate," "to declare." In this sense, the word *myth* is analogous to the Sanskrit word *kathā*. Mythology is also derived from the Greek root *mūthos*, meaning "story," which was always spoken. Thus, according to Hans-

Georg Gadamer, "The word *mythologein*, indeed, has to do with the act of speaking. Myth means a tale to be conveyed and to be verified by nothing else than the act of telling it."[17] Myth in this sense is not used in terms of "having no factual basis." It is important to note that the idea of "myth" is a construct embedded in the Western religious experience. Perhaps the roots of this mindset lie in the ongoing debate regarding historical versus mythical, and the literal versus metaphorical nature of the texts.

There is no Sanskrit equivalent of this notion of myth. In the Indian context, several categories such as *itihāsa* (literally, "so indeed it was," history, legend), *kāvya* (poetry), and *purāṇas* (literally "old," implying accounts of the ancients) are applied to the religious narratives, all of which are now termed myth and adopted as such by the scholarly community in general. In the context of the *Mahābhārata*, which has been woven into India's cultural psyche through oral recitation, plays, movies, and television, Ramanujan states that it "is not a text but a tradition." Many literary categories such as *itihāsa* and *kāvya* are applied to it. The *Mahābhārata*, in spite of its enormous size, is a "*structured* work." With regard to another narrative, the *Rāmāyaṇa*, one of Gandhi's favorites, Ramanujan talks about the many versions of the "telling" of the Rāma story "belonging to various narrative genres (epics, *kāvyas* or ornate poetic compositions, *purāṇas* or old mythological stories, and so forth)."[18]

Although Gandhi used the word *mythology* for the genre of religious stories in his voluminous works, he rarely referred to a religious story as a myth. When Gandhi did use the word *myth* in his extensive writings and discourses, it was to convey that something was untrue. For example, Gandhi said: "The eighteen *varnas* [castes] are mere myth; there are only four *varnas*, so divided on the basis of their occupational aptitudes."[19] Moreover, Gandhi did not rely on Western theories of myth; instead he constructed his own hermeneutic. For him, Indian religious stories were not merely imaginary tales but, rather, in the guise of stories they held moral and religious truths that shape the culture and lives of people.

In accordance with the Indian cultural tradition of storytelling, Gandhi called his *Autobiography* the *Ātma Kathā* (the story of my own self), and presented it as a truthful narration of his experiments with Truth. In the introduction Gandhi emphasized:

> The experiments narrated should be regarded as illustrations, in the light of which every one may carry on his own experiments according to his own inclinations and

> capacity. . . . I am not going either to conceal or understate any ugly things that must be told. I hope to acquaint the reader fully with all my faults and errors.[20]

Later, Gandhi promoted a similar approach toward religious stories (*kathā*). He sought to emulate what he considered to be the moral truths conveyed through the stories and, at the same time, to evaluate the faults and errors of the heroes of the narratives (e.g., Rāma's repudiation of Sītā).

Religious storytelling became an important part of his personal and political life. During his years in South Africa and later in India, Gandhi incorporated religious storytelling and listening, as well as chanting, into his *āśrama* regimen.[21] He himself routinely listened to the *Rāmāyaṇa* during his fasts and read it to his wife as part of a healing ritual when she was ill. When giving speeches, Gandhi frequently narrated or referred to ancient religious tales to substantiate his method of *satyagraha,* and often emphasized the prerequisite of an austere lifestyle reminiscent of the *tapas* of Pārvati, Prahlād, and Vasiṣṭha.

The phenomenon of India's penchant for religious narratives and how they provide insight into the culture has been discussed by many scholars. Raja Rao underscores the point: "To understand India—the Indian—one must know the *Mahabharata.*"[22] Kakar and Cashman have attempted to understand the Indian proclivity for the narrative form over other literary constructions and for preferring symbols over conceptual language. Gandhi had an intuitive insight about this and explained his idea in a 1919 letter to Esther Faering:

> You will find this law of self-denial written in every page of the *Ramayana* and the *Mahabharata*. Have you read these two books? If not, you should one of these days read them carefully and with the eye of faith. There is a great deal of fabulous matter about these two books. They are designed for the masses and the authors have deliberately chosen to write them in a manner that would make them acceptable to the people. They have hit upon the easiest method of carrying the truth to the millions, and experience of ages shows that they have been marvellously successful.[23]

For Gandhi, the endurance of ancient religious stories and their sustained influence on Indian culture served as a testimony to their appeal and effectiveness. He adopted the medium of narratives as a tried and true method for carrying the truth to the millions.

Many contemporary scholars—from social scientists and religious thinkers to psychoanalysts—have discussed of the value of stories in communication. In a psychoanalytical study of male–female relations in India, Kakar chooses several Indian tales, including Gandhi's autobiographical narrative, as a "vehicle for inquiry" because of their "unique value for the study of Indian gender relations." He gives an overview of how the "spell of the story has always exercised special potency in the oral-based Indian tradition and Indians have characteristically sought expression of central and collective meanings though narrative design." He further notes that "narrative has . . . been prominently used as a way of thinking, as a way of reasoning about complex situations, as an inquiry into the nature of reality." He suggests that to a certain extent "this preference is grounded in the universal tendency of people all over the world to understand complex matters presented as stories, whereas they might experience difficulty in the comprehension of general concepts . . . concreteness of the story, with its metaphoric richness, is perhaps a better path into the depths of emotions and imagination, into the core of man's spirit."[24]

R. K. Narayan, a novelist as well as a participant in Gandhi's *svarāj* movement, describes the multilayered purpose of such stories, contending that the preference for the symbolic over the conceptual is not merely due to the difficulty of comprehending complex matters. Indian religious epics and narratives are, in fact, repositories of ethics, philosophy, semantics, and mysticism. Narayan acknowledges their inherent complexity and points to the comprehensive role religious literature plays in the lives of the people:

> Everything is interrelated. Stories, scriptures, ethics, philosophy, grammar, astrology, astronomy, semantics, mysticism, and moral codes—each forms part and parcel of a total life and is indispensable for the attainment of a four-square understanding of existence. Literature is not a branch of study to be placed in a separate compartment, for the edification only of scholars, but a comprehensive medium of expression to benefit the literate and the illiterate alike.[25]

Apart from theoretical reasons, on the social and ritualistic level Gandhi was aware that the activities of listening to religious discourses and reading (*svādhyāya*, literally "self-study") sacred literature (*kathā*) were religious acts that both inspired people and created a common shared experience. Gandhi repeatedly encouraged his people to read and listen to the ancient tales. For example, on April 29, 1936, the day of Lord Rāma's birth, instead of giving his daily discourse on the *Gītā*, Gandhi devoted the day to the reading of the *Rāmāyaṇa*:

> Today is Ramanavami Day. On this day we have a reading from the *Ramayana* for two hours and, in the morning, there is a discourse on the incarnation of Rama. People fast, or take only one meal or eat only fruit. We shall put into practice what we have learnt from the *Gita* by celebrating the Ramanavami today in this manner.[26]

Gandhi's call to "put into practice" represents a norm in the tradition of *kathakaras*. In an ethnographic study of Indian *sādhus* and storytellers, K. Narayan underscores the deeply embedded tradition of storytelling in India. While deliberating on the value of religious story-telling, she notes that the purpose of *kathā* and drama is "indigenously recognized as a means of implanting values and attitudes."[27] Customarily, *kathā* is orally delivered in *āśramas*, temples, and other community settings. In the process of narration, the stories are expanded and new stories are added to existing ones. The convention of religious storytelling, which has been vibrant in India since the time of the epics, is an integral part of Indian communities to this day. Hirst notes that thousands throng around modern *mahātmās* and *kathakaras* such as Morari Bapu (b. 1946-), who recites and reinterprets ancient epics and myths so that they are relevant to current political events.[28] Devout followers also seek *darśan* of holy men and women. The dialectic of "hearing" religious stories and "witnessing" the presence of a holy being creates emotional response to the narrative, through which the storytellers, as Gandhi himself recalled in his *Autobiography*, seek to strengthen belief in moral power and promote both personal and social transformation.

Mapping the Religious Narratives: Impetus for Gandhi's Ascetic Activism

During India's freedom struggle, the dissemination of religious literature and the public performance of religious myths played important roles in the construction of a national identity and provided a springboard for social change. Y. B. Damle, for example, reports that in the Maharashtra state the classic themes of Kṛṣṇa and Kaṃsa were utilized to "pinpoint the misdeeds of the British rulers." Consequently, "many storytellers were arrested."[29] Folk performances of epic tales, such as the theatrical performance of *Rāma Līlā* (the acts of Lord Rāma) and dramatic performances of *Purāṇic* themes, proved especially effective in giving the myths a living reality.[30] Doniger O'Flaherty states: "Of all literary forms, drama best reproduces the effects of myths. . . . The voices and bodies of the actors serve to bring the mythical and supernatural alive for us on an anthropomorphic level, to make them physically real."[31] Not surprisingly, the medium of drama in the form of folklore performances to retell the story continues to be an important part of India's religious culture.

In his *Autobiography*, Gandhi recounts the effect that the performance of ancient stories had on his young mind. He recalls two stories that he says left "an indelible impression" on him and "captured his heart" in his childhood. The first was a play derived from the *Rāmāyaṇa* and titled *Śrvaṇa Pitṛbhakti Nātaka* (about the young man Śravaṇa Kumar's devotion to his parents), which Gandhi had read in a picture book. The second of these influential stories was a play about Hariścandra (from the *Mahābhārata*) that young Gandhi saw performed by a traveling drama company.[32] Even though Gandhi repeatedly commented on various religious narratives and asserted that such stories played a vital role in the development of his strategy of service, renunciation, and *satyagraha*, these stories have escaped the close attention of most scholars.[33] Even those who do refer to these narratives as influences present an understanding that differs from Gandhi's own self-reported perceptions.

While engaged in a comprehensive study of the religious elements in Gandhi's life and works, Jordens notes that the two plays, *Śrvaṇa Pitṛbhakti Nātaka* and *Hariścandra*, "strongly reinforced in Gandhi's young mind the high ideal of service." Jordens simplistically perceives the two plays as having one lesson: "heroic parental devotion to the point of suffering all and sacrificing one's life,"[34] even though *Hariścandra* is a story about suffering for the sake of Truth, not about suffering to serve one's parents (which is the theme of *Śrvaṇa Pitṛbhakti Nātaka*). The Rudolphs refer only to the legend of Hariścandra, not that of Śravaṇa, when they explain Gandhi's idealistic statement: "All happiness and pleasure should be sacrificed in devoted service to my parents."[35] Although the two plays do portray the ideal of service and the virtue of self-sacrifice, they actually have distinctly different plots. Gandhi reported that he used them as models for "service," "self-sacrifice," and "fearlessness."[36]

Śrvaṇa Pitṛbhakti is the story of young Śravaṇa's devotion to his blind and feeble elderly parents. When the parents express their desire to go on a pilgrimage, there is no vehicle available to transport them.

To remedy the situation, young Śravaṇa devises seats for them that are suspended from a pole that he carries across his shoulders. Bearing their heavy weight, he undertakes the arduous journey to fulfill their desires. The story takes a climactic turn when, in the course of their pilgrimage, Śravaṇa goes to fetch some water to quench his parents' thirst and is accidentally pierced by an arrow from the bow of King Daśratha. In the twilight of the day King Daśratha, who was out hunting, had mistaken Śravaṇa—who had long, matted hair and was wearing attire made out of deer skin—for his prey. The King quickly realizes his grave mistake, but it is too late. Fatally wounded and in extreme pain, young Śravaṇa is only concerned for his parents' future now that they have no one left to care for them. In the *Rāmāyaṇa*, the sage Vālmīki narrates Śravaṇa's last lament:

> I do not so much lament my end of life,
> as I lament it on account of my mother and father.
> The old couple, ever sustained by me,
> to what will they betake themselves when my body returns
>   to the five elements?[37]

Śravaṇa pleads with the king to go to his parents and console them. However, the parents are devastated on hearing the news of their son's death. In their unbearable grief they make a funeral pyre and give up their lives by setting themselves on fire.[38]

Gandhi writes that Śravaṇa's story had a profound impact on his young, idealistic mind. "'Here is an example for you to copy,' I said to myself," recalls Gandhi.[39] Years later, in 1928, he wrote in an article: "I worshipped my father and my devotion to my parents equalled [*sic*] that of Shravana."[40] One can therefore imagine Gandhi's pain at discovering that his father had taken his last breath while Gandhi himself was occupied in fulfilling his sexual desire. Some psychoanalysts have concluded that this event explains his aversion toward sex. In any case, making this figure of an ancient legend his model, Gandhi inadvertently set himself up for additional "guilt" when his father died. His inclination to emulate Śravaṇa provides insight into his use of religious stories as a hermeneutic in constructing his own narrative of selfless service. Gandhi often referred to the tale of Śravaṇa for cultivating the qualities of sacrifice, service, and strength that he himself sought to harness for the service of his greater parent, Bhārat Mātā (Mother India).[41]

> The Mother who gave us birth was bound to die some day; not so the Universal Mother who bears and sustains

> us. She must die some day, but when she passed away she would take all her children also along with her. She therefore demands a life-long dedication.[42]

The symbolism of India as Mother had been utilized by many contemporary leaders, but Gandhi, who expressed his lifelong devotion to his own mother and who sought to embody sacrifice and maternal qualities, invoked the emotions through this imagery to call for complete dedication to India's cause.

The second play that Gandhi said deeply inspired him was an enactment of the tale of Mahārajā Hariścandra—a story from the *Mahābhārata*—which he saw performed by a traveling company. Hindu children often hear stories of the *Mahābhārata* from their parents or read them in school books, but Gandhi expressed particular fascination with this story, saying that he watched the play many times and yet never became "tired of seeing it."[43] A synopsis of the story provides insight into Gandhi's deep interest.

King Hariścandra of Ayodhyā is renowned for his virtues of charity, sacrifice, and truth. Even gods and sages marvel at his commitment to truth and keeping his word at any cost. The Sage Viśvāmitra, intent on testing the will of the King, appears before the King and asks him for a gift. The generous King gladly agrees to give the Sage anything he desires. The Sage asks the King for everything he possesses: "Your kingdom with the entire contents of treasury, ornaments and dress on you, and your wife, and son. Now you may leave the capital at once." Committed to honoring his word, the King exits the city empty-handed and in rags, accompanied by his wife Tārāmati and his young son Rohitaśva—leaving behind his kingdom, entourage, and possessions. However, the Sage is not yet finished testing him. He tells the King that his gift is worth nothing "unless it is properly presented. A gift must be accompanied with *dakṣiṇā* [a gift or monetary offering; it is given to a *Brahmin* at the completion of the religious rite. The King made a religious act of charity and therefore he should give an additional offering] to make it complete." The King agrees and asks for some time in which to raise the funds to pay his due. The Sage grants him exactly thirty days.

The time to pay his debt approaches swiftly, but the homeless King is unable to find a way to gather money. Helpless, but determined to keep his promise, he has no choice left but to sell his wife and son, and finally himself, into servitude. Queen Tārāmati, together with the young prince, is sold as a maid and compelled to do lowly household tasks. The King himself is purchased to labor "as an untouchable menial among fetid corpses in a cremation ground."[44] The King thus pays what he owes to the Sage; however, his ordeal is far from over. "Harischandra is an Indian Job," says Ashe, and just like Job's testing in the Old Testament story, his trial continues.[45]

Hariścandra's son, while gathering wood in the forest for a sacrifice, gets bitten by a poisonous snake and dies. Lamenting the loss of her most precious possession, Tārāmati takes her son to the cremation grounds, where, unbeknownst to her, Hariścandra works. Seeing her in a nearly mad condition, carrying a young boy in her arms, a patrolman suspects her to be a witch and orders her beheaded by Hariścandra, the keeper of the cremation ground. Hariścandra at this point does not have a clue that the lady is his wife and the boy his own beloved son. Tārāmati asks him to let her cremate her son before he beheads her. Hariścandra, torn by compassion for the helpless woman yet bound by his duty, asks her to pay the required tax to cremate her son. The woman pleads: "Alas, I possess neither money nor any valuables." Just then, in the light of the burning pyres, Hariścandra's eyes fall on her wedding necklace. He recognizes that she is none other than his wife. Now they both lament the loss of their only son and decide to throw themselves onto the pyre with him as "there was no meaning in existence any more [*sic*]." This moment marks the climax of Hariścandra's resolve: "Hardly had they set their foot in the fire when the gods in heaven realized that the limits had been reached in the trial of this hardy soul."

The Sage Viṣvāmitra appears on the scene and declares, "No other creature could have borne trials as you have." The sage returns his kingdom, kingship, and his beloved son and announces Hariścandra as victorious: "I accept my defeat gladly. . . . I am surrendering all the merit and powers of my spiritual life to you, with all my heart."[46]

Intriguingly, Gandhi was deeply impressed by the "truthful" nature of King Hariścandra and recalls reenacting Hariścandra's character after watching the play. Was it the theatrical presentation of the character's limitless sacrifice that invoked the *anubhava* (experience) of *adhbuta rasa* (emotion of wonder) in the young Gandhi's heart? Gandhi describes the emotional impact that this myth had on him:

> This play—*Harishchandra*—captured my heart. I could never be tired of seeing it. But how often should I be permitted to go? It haunted me and I must have acted *Harishchandra* to myself times without number. 'Why should not all be truthful like Harishchandra?' was the question I asked myself day and night. To follow truth and to go through

> all the ordeals Harishchandra went through was the one ideal it inspired in me. I literally believed in the story of Harishchandra. The thought of it all often made me weep.[47]

Even though the story can be morally repellent to a modern Western audience, for Indians, this tale presents an example of truth and integrity. Indian myths are thought to convey ideals generally beyond the reach of common people. Gandhi's deep emotion might have been a short-lived experience for other spectators, yet it stayed with him throughout his life. For Gandhi, Mahārājā Hariścandra represented an archetypical character of endurance who forsakes all for the sake of commitment to Truth. Gandhi described him as a *satyagrahi*. The story of Hariścandra may be a "myth," yet it conveyed a deep meaning to Gandhi's young mind.

Childhood is normally a time of fun and carefree life; so what was really pulling the young mind of Gandhi to the trying messages of these stories? Why did Gandhi, even in childhood, seek to emulate these characters from ancient stories, which he admitted were not even historical and belonged to a world so different from his own? Gandhi seems to have ensnared himself in an idealistic world, which would eventually lead him to sacrifice even the customary rights to his wife and children. These two myths illustrate suffering and giving up all for the sake of commitment, determination, and dedication; they assert the power of the soul over the strength of the body. Gandhi traced back his use of these myths to early indigenous influences in explaining his attraction to the virtues of Truth and self-sacrifice—which formed the basis of *satyagraha*. He recalls some of his Western influences but does not narrate them in such an emotional tenor. Might this tone and selection of certain events for his *Autobiography* be a result of his love of the Indian ethos? Historically, he had already gained the status of a religious figure and was writing for his Indian audience. Perhaps he was choosing familiar religious stories, hoping they too could be awakened to truth by their power.

Nevertheless, some scholars, such as the Rudolphs, set aside Gandhi's own accounts—perhaps because his response to these myths in his youth seems idiosyncratic. The Rudolphs construe Gandhi's image of his father as "demanding" and argue that "the story of Maharaja Harishchandra, a well-known classic tale acted by a passing traveling troupe, 'haunted' Gandhi as a boy [and] may tell something about Gandhi's feeling for the relationship between father and son." They suggest that Gandhi's affinity for this story—which relates the "degradation" of the King by the "severe older man who imposes painful demands"—may be reflective of Gandhi's own relationship with his father. They compare the "relentless demands of a saintly Brahman" in the story of *Hariścandra* with Gandhi's father who, according to them, was "demanding" and "probably inspired fear and anger." According to the Rudolphs, Gandhi's affinity for the character of Hariścandra offered clues to his relationship with his father and to Gandhi's actions of "secret rebellion," in which he "led a double life. In one, he experimented with everything that was forbidden in the other."[48] Looking at Gandhi's own accounts, he pointed out some of the flaws in his father's behavior, but he always spoke of his service to his parents in a very positive light: "While my parents were alive, I conducted myself regarding Shravana as an ideal. I believe that whatever I have achieved is due to my devotion to my parents and the fruit of their blessings."[49] Hindu tradition prescribes service and dedication to parents as a son's primary moral responsibility (*dharma*), and Gandhi apparently was seeking to follow his duty.

A survey of Gandhi's works and his childhood influences suggests that the model of *tapas*—which yields miraculous powers—was for Gandhi the source of inspiration and his inclination for service. The Rudolphs glance at this idea: "Self-suffering in the name of honouring duty and of pursuing truth, which Gandhi identified with each other, has its reward. The gods themselves come to his [Hariścandra's] side, rewarding his self-control, fortitude, and respect for truth with heaven itself." The Rudolphs agree that the tale of "endless misery and suffering [is] unlikely to speak to the mind and heart of a Western youth."[50] Ashe posits that Gandhi in his youth was not even aware of the "crux" of the story, that is "how far can you force the consequences on the others—above all, those who depend on you?" Ashe's position is that Gandhi was so "enraptured" by the charm of "the ideal of Absolute Truth," that he "embraced the ideal in earnest."[51] Gandhi's own writings reveal that he was fully aware of the crux of the story as an adult and, after deep deliberation, still chose to embrace the ideal of truth (in the form of *brahmacarya*) in earnest.

Ashe compares Gandhi's immediate attraction to the ideal of Truth to "the mad logic of a fairy-tale."[52] Gandhi's life does not have a "fairy tale" ending like that in Hariścandra's tale. In spite of Gandhi having endured severe testing for the sake of Truth—dedicating his wealth, his sexual impulses, and even his duty as a husband and as a father—ultimately his wife Kasturba remained poor (without even propitious ornaments for a married Hindu woman), and his estranged son Harilal sank into the depths of depression. The "mad logic" was Gandhi's apparently irrational expectation of the power of *brahmacarya*, of the force by which he sought to change the course of history. The purpose of Gandhi's sacrifice was not obedience to a revered sage or the hope of ultimately regaining his sacrificed possessions and relationships; rather, his sacrifices were sealed by his vow of *brahmacarya* for attaining "salvation through the service and salvation of the nation and humanity."[53]

Gandhi himself indicates that in these stories he found the model for his personal and political strategy of self-sacrifice: he frequently referred to them to substantiate his method. During his discourses, Gandhi listed Hariścandra among various other historical figures, as models of those who were ready to give up life for the sake of Truth:

> Harishchandra was a satyagrahi, Prahlad was a satyagrahi, Mirabai was a satyagrahi. Daniel, Socrates and those Arabs who hurled themselves on the fire of the French artillery were all satyagrahis. We see from these examples that a satyagrahi does not fear for his body, he does not give up what he thinks is Truth.[54]

Interestingly, these examples suggest that Gandhi is describing a universal, noble, human quality. He would reject the claim of the Rudolphs and of Ashe that his concept of self-suffering would have no appeal to Westerners. Gandhi was inspired by these narratives to suffer for the sake of truth and service. Yet, at the same time, he was aware of the nonhistorical nature of the characters:

> My commonsense tells me today that Harishchandra could not have been a historical character. Still both Harishchandra and Shravana are living realities for me, and I am sure I should be moved as before if I were to read those plays again today.[55]

Gandhi believed in these characters from the ancient epics as "living realities," not as historical fact. It is apparent that Gandhi freely utilized the narratives as a strategy in communicating his personal asceticism and political project. However, precisely because he was presenting these characters as models for his ascetic activism, he was often faced with questions of how to interpret the myths. Gandhi had to confront the practical question of whether the characters were historical or fictional realities in using them to validate his method.

In his writings, Gandhi does not mention any scholarly theories on reconciling the mythical and the factual. He resolved the question of literal or fictional in sacred literature by utilizing his own interpretive strategies, which he claimed bore approximate likeness to native hermeneutics. He created a new category for religious narratives: they were neither works of fiction, nor were they historical.

Gandhi's Theoretical Framework for Interpreting Religious Narratives

Gandhi encountered the stories of powerful legendary heroes in his childhood and began to utilize them to communicate his political methods. He soon realized a need to present a theory of his interpretations. In his works, Gandhi never revealed awareness of contemporary Western theoretical discussions about mythology, such as the writings of thinkers like James George Frazer (1854–1941), Sigmund Freud (1856–1939), or Carl Jung (1875–1961); neither does he refer to any native discourse about understanding myths. Nevertheless, when he became aware of the need to explain his creative usage of the myths, he sought to describe the complex, dynamic spectrum of myth, which includes historical as well as fictional elements. Gandhi never saw the mythic as fiction; rather, he saw the narrative structure of myth-telling as a literary device to make Truth accessible to the masses. Gandhi was so unwavering about the use of truthful means that he openly expressed his revulsion for works of pure fiction. Green records an anecdote told by Mulk Raj Anand, "an Indian-writer-in-English," who undertook to write a novel titled, *Untouchable*. In his interaction with the author, Gandhi emphasized the need to speak directly, instead of telling tales, when reform was called for:

> In 1929, in order to prepare himself to write his novel *Untouchable*, he [Mulk Raj Anand] went to Sabarmati to get Gandhi's advice. He was no Gandhian, so he declared himself immediately an atheist and a socialist, and refused to use Gandhi's term for the Untouchables, Harijans, on the grounds that Indian society did not grant them that status. Gandhi listened to his project, and said, "It is important to write about this question. But why not write a straightforward book attacking caste? The straight book is truthful and you can reform people by saying things frankly."[56]

For this, Gandhi has been criticized as having a lack of interest in art of any description. However, Gandhi was always looking for a practical plan and, he said, he could not spare the time for fiction. For Gandhi, the ancient Indian narratives were a direct source of "strength" that enabled his following the path of Truth. In a 1931 letter Gandhi writes:

> We have with us those three shields to protect us, the *Anasaktiyoga* [the *Gītā*], the *Bhajanavali* [his collection of prayers] and the *Ramayana*. I believe, and I want you all to believe, that the constant reading of these with faith will be a greater source of strength than letters from me or than living with me.[57]

To illustrate this claim he compared the *Rāmāyaṇa* with *rotli* (bread), which sustains the life of a poor person; and he equated Bāṇabhatta's *Kādambari* (the famous romantic fiction of the seventh century) with a relish of almonds and pistachio that only the affluent could afford.

> I want, not Banabhatta's *Kadambari*, but Tulsidas's *Ramayana*. I have my doubts whether *Kadambari* will be with us for ever, but Tulsidas's work will certainly endure. Let us at present get just *rotli*, ghee and milk from our literature. Later on we shall add almonds, pistachio nuts, etc., and produce something like *Kadambari*.[58]

In this remark, Gandhi presents two key points about the difference between religious literature and fiction. First, the perennial nature of sacred tales demonstrates that they have enduring values. Second, the religious narratives provide nourishing energy from which people are able to derive sustenance throughout the generations. Although Gandhi may not have been familiar with scholarly theorization regarding myth, he was certainly knowledgeable about the religious experience that a community shares collectively through its myths. He created a new category for religious stories, which he called "history of the human soul." He circumvented the controversy of mythical *versus* factual by establishing this category as arising out of the native context. Gandhi's views on the *Mahābhārata* are representative of his perspective on such a history of souls. He states: "*Mahabharata* is neither fiction nor history commonly so called. It is the history of the human soul in which God as Krishna is the chief actor." However, Gandhi was aware that the *Mahābhārata* also contained fiction. Therefore, rather than likening it to a "treasure chest," he compared it to a "mine which needs to be explored, which needs to be dug deep and from which diamonds have to be extracted after removing much foreign matter."[59]

Even though Gandhi acknowledged that Indian myths are not simply historical, he treated them as having a living reality that fiction was incapable of bringing forth. The legendary heroes draw on spiritual strength to resolve dilemmas and can serve as examples in the present context. Gandhi's personal experience of the transformative value of myth gave rise to his own theory of the efficacy of myth as a vehicle to convey ideals of character and exalted action.

> Fiction means an imagined story. It is beyond doubt that the *Ramayana* and the *Mahabharata* have less of history and more of imagination. They are both sacred books; tens of millions of people look upon them as more than history, and rightly. Maybe there was no brother of Rama exactly like Bharata, but there have been such Bharatas at any rate in India and that is why Tulsidas could conceive one.[60]

For his call to sacrifice in the form of service, Gandhi offered ancient models, seemingly referring to what is now known as the "archetypal" nature of mythical characters and to the religious experience myth invokes. Many scholars of the history of religion and mythology, such as Zimmer, Eliade, and Joseph Campbell, have reflected on the nature of religious experience that myth generates.[61] According to Gandhi, many people seek to emulate mythical characters and consult the myths for answers to life's dilemmas, just as he did. Along this line, Herbert Mason expressed the essence of myth as follows: "The myth that heralds a call to the heart to be faithful is rooted in the deepest and highest possible knowledge: of *ma'rifa* or *gnosis;* not of mere facts, but of transcendent truth."[62] In his reinterpretation of ancient narratives, Gandhi appears to "dig deep" and extract "diamonds" of "transcendent" Truth (*Sat*) by contrasting fiction with myth.

In short, Gandhi's theoretical analysis of myth freed him to choose stories that suited his purpose. He was not confined to the literal reading of texts, nor compelled to treat all myths equally. Rather, in his search for Truth, Gandhi was selective: he chose myths that enhanced his message and inspired his people, and rejected those that did not. Gandhi's life of renunciation inclined him to focus on stories that validated the theme of sacrifice and service and allowed him to disregard the genre of myths filled with orgies and sensual love. Unconcerned with scholarly methodology, Gandhi furthermore reinterpreted certain texts to suit his method of nonviolence. For example, he was cognizant that the popular epic narratives of war did not support his strategy of responding to political strife with practices of renunciation and nonviolence. The most apparently war-affirming treatise, the *Gītā*, which Gandhi called his "spiritual reference book," posed a specific dilemma.[63] Gandhi, therefore, rendered his own exegesis of the text to make it coherent with his nonviolent strategy, as discussed in chapter 2.

Gandhi's religious vow of *brahmacarya* and his commitment to God and, thereby, to the service of humanity evidently gave him sufficient stature as a religious figure that he could render his interpretation, even though he lacked the credentials of a religious scholar. In 1926, during his regular prayer meetings in the Satyagraha Ashram, embodying the role of a *mahātmā* and a *kathakar*, Gandhi was able to deliver an interpretation of the *Gītā*, in which he emphasized the ideology of nonviolence.[64] Even though Gandhi never claimed to be a *mahātmā* or a religious leader, his actions drew from the traditions of the *sādhu* imparting teaching through oral discourses.

Reinterpretation of the Violent Epics for Nonviolent Strategy

Many Hindu nationalist contemporaries of Gandhi were revolutionaries who looked to the war motif in the myths—such as the battles between *devas* (gods) and *asuras* (demons) in the Vedic and Purāṇic literature, and the epic wars of the *Rāmāyaṇa* and the *Mahābhārata*—to legitimize confronting a "Satanic Government, a *Ravanarajya* possessed by a Satanic spirit," as Gandhi himself termed it. The *Bhagavad-Gītā*, specifically, provided a paradigm for militant action rather than for nonviolence or renunciation. Gandhi acknowledged: "The grim fact is that the terrorists have in absolute honesty, earnestness and with cogency used the *Gītā*, which some of them know by heart, in defence of their doctrine and policy."[65] In an earlier chapter, we discussed how Gandhi utilized the teaching of the *Gītā* to validate his strategy, which combined *pravṛtti* and *nivṛtti*, and espoused the lesson of *karma sannyāsa* (renunciation in action). Inspired by the Sermon on the Mount, the writings of Tolstoy, and the Indian models of self-sacrifice, Gandhi developed his method of nonviolent resistance and interpreted the war context of the *Gītā* allegorically. At this juncture, we will focus on the way Gandhi presented his unconventional interpretation to his followers by enacting the role of a *kathakar.*

Gandhi had discussions with many revolutionaries such as Shyamji Krishnavarma and Vinayak Damodar Savarkar, who interpreted Kṛṣṇa's call to fight as a literal justification of their violent strategy.[66] Even Sri Aurobindo, who understood the significance of passive resistance in his early years, warned of the limits of nonviolence and passive resistance:

> Every great *yajña* has its Rakshasas who strive to baffle the sacrifice . . . Passive resistance is an attempt to meet such disturbers by peaceful and self-contained *brahmatejas,* but even the greatest Rishis of old could not, when the Rakshasas were fierce and determined, keep up the sacrifice without calling in the bow of the Kshatriya.[67]

Such critique of Gandhi's method of passive resistance was not limited to Sri Aurobindo; many revolutionaries defended their militant orientation toward the British regime by citing the same texts, especially the *Gītā,* as Gandhi did to support his nonviolent methods. Gandhi initially alluded to random verses from the *Gītā* to support *ahiṃsā.* He also substantiated his view by referring to the examples of *bhaktas* (devotees) like Narsinh Mehta who were "nurtured" by the *Gītā.* According to Gandhi, Narsinh Mehta, the first poet of Gujarat, "conquered his enemies only by love." Gandhi stated, "that encouragement from [*sic*] violence can be deduced from the *Bhagavad Gita* demonstrates the deadliness of *Kaliyuga.*" Then Swami Anand, one of his prominent followers, asked Gandhi to translate the entire text with a commentary, so that his followers could appreciate Gandhi's "meaning of the message of the *Gita.*" Gandhi recalls the concern Swami Anand expressed to him: "I do not think it is just on your part to deduce *ahimsa* [nonviolence] from stray verses."[68] Heeding his advice, Gandhi proceeded to present the purport of the *Gītā,* showing that his strategy of *ahiṃsā* was consistent with traditional lore. Just as the militant factions had used the *Gītā* to justify their violent actions, Gandhi sought to interpret the ancient myths and texts as justification for *ahiṃsā.* He focused on the *Gītā,* which was often quoted to counteract and discount his strategy of renunciatory nonviolence, and responded to some of his revolutionary-minded predecessors and contemporaries as follows:

> They [some Hindu friends] say that in the *Bhagavad Gita* Sri Krishna has encouraged Arjuna to slay his relations and they therefore argue that there is warrant in that work for violence and that there is no satyagraha in it. Now the *Bhagavad Gita* is not a historical work. . . . The poet has seized the occasion of the war between the Pandavas and the Kauravas on the field of Kurukshetra for drawing attention to the war going on in our bodies between the forces of Good (Pandavas) and the forces of Evil (Kaurvas). . . . To confuse the description of this universally acknowledged spiritual war with a momentary world strife is to call holy unholy.[69]

Gandhi had already prepared a *padārthakośa* (concordance) of the *Gītā* during his stay in the Yeravada Jail (1922–23); he proceeded to translate the entire text, using his own commentary to interpret the war allegorically. Gandhi was extremely active during the year 1925, but was disturbed by emerging factions based on religious orientation and found that "political . . . India was 'disrupted and demoralized.'" In 1926, in a highly politically and religiously charged period, he withdrew from political activity and ceased traveling, taking "a vow of a year's 'political silence.'"[70] Gandhi vowed "not to stir out of the ashram, [and] certainly not out of Ahmedabad."[71] This decision was perceived as strange even by some of his friends, given the urgency of securing *svarāj* for India. Was Gandhi's "political silence" solely motivated by his desire to recharge his spiritual energies or was the hiatus also needed to produce a commentary on the *Gītā* in order to convince the religious factions? In his article, "Action in Inaction," Gandhi himself presents his "inaction" as "really concentrated action."[72] Gandhi is referring to the *Gītā*'s teaching of renunciation in action (IV: 18): "Who sees inaction in action and action in inaction, he is enlightened among men. He is a *yogi*. He has done all he need do."[73] Through this statement the text expresses the importance of disinterested attitude in the midst of action. But, in this instance, Gandhi physically removes himself from political activities and terms it "concentrated action." During this one year's retreat from public life, in the manner of a *kathakar*, Gandhi delivered his version of the *Gītā* to his followers at Satyagraha Ashram over a span of nine months, from February 24 to November 27, 1926.[74]

In his interpretation, Gandhi looked under the veil of Kṛṣṇa's endorsement of war for hidden spiritual meanings: "The battle described here is a struggle between *dharma* [duty, right conduct] and *adharma* [its opposite] . . . this work was written to explain man's duty in this inner strife."[75] Gandhi "mythicized" the *Gītā* as a "Kamadhenu [wish-fulfilling cow]" and considered it "a spiritual dictionary,"[76] and he utilized concepts such as renunciation in action and the ideal of *sthitaprajña* for his political strategy of *ahiṃsā* and his personal *tyāga* (renunciation).

Traditionally, a radical interpretation such as this presupposes that the interpreter is not merely a scholar, but a sage—a *pandit, sādhu,* or *mahātmā*—whose primary concern is the spiritually edifying message of the text. Although Gandhi undoubtedly took scholastic license through his study and analytical methods, it was his austere conduct and his stature as a *mahātmā* that gave him the spiritual authority that made such a radical reinterpretation plausible. Gandhi's writings reveal that he had read all the major classical and contemporary commentaries.[77] "Gandhi was not a scholar, certainly not a Sanskrit scholar, and did not pretend to be one, but his views on the *Gita* greatly influenced others," states Bolle.[78] Parel attributes Gandhi's "credibility" as an interpreter of the *Gītā* to Gandhi's own concordance and his study of various translations and commentaries on the work over the years.[79] Gandhi's views on this text were also influential because he delivered a consistent reinterpretation, locating his ideas in the Hindu tradition.

It is commonly understood that myths and symbols convey hidden messages that need to be decoded. Pietro Della Valle (a seventeenth-century traveler), coming across seemingly bizarre Indian fables and images, remarked: "But I doubt not that, under the veil of these Fables, their ancient Sages have hid from the vulgar many messages, either of Natural or Moral Philosophy, and perhaps also of History."[80] Gandhi often referred to the established precedent in the Indian traditions for such reinterpretation of religious texts and concepts. The texts are perceived as having multiple layers of meaning, and various literary devices have been employed to decipher their underlying messages. Numerous expositions of the *Gītā* have been composed by scholars and sages in order to discover the underlying truth of the teaching.

Jordens surmises that "Gandhi rejected the claim that the task of the interpreter was limited to discovering the exact meaning of the text," but he taught that "one should not stick to its letter, but try to understand its spirit, its meaning in the total context."[81] In his search for new and relevant meaning in the context of the *Gītā*, Gandhi asserted that he was not inventing a new method, but rather mirroring the hermeneutics of the *Gītā* (and Indian tradition) itself:

> It [the Gita] has given a new meaning to karma, sannyasa, *yajna*, etc. It has breathed new life into Hinduism. . . . What I have done is perfectly historical. I have followed in the footsteps of our forefathers. At one time they sacrificed animals to propitiate angry gods. Their descendants, but our less remote ancestors, read a different meaning into the word 'sacrifice' and they taught that sacrifice was meant to be of our baser self, to please not angry gods but the one living God within.[82]

Just as the *Gītā* had redefined the ancient concepts of sacrifice and developed its inner meaning, so too Gandhi considered himself to be following its precedent in unfolding the esoteric meaning inherent in the *Mahābhārata, Rāmāyaṇa,* and the *Purāṇas* and in applying it to the political situation of his day. No matter how unconventional, elucidation of such texts by a *mahātmā* did indeed capture the religious imagination of a populace that was only too well aware of the daily inner struggle between duty and unrighteous conduct. It also provided a consistent narrative for Gandhi's strategy of activist renunciation.

It appears that Gandhi's intent in his commentary was neither to strive for philosophical consistency nor to attest to literary scholarship but rather to validate his ascetic practices and his method of *ahiṃsā* in order to pursue his political goals. For instance, although the word *aparigraha* (nonpossession) occurs only once in the *Bhagavad-Gītā,* Gandhi made it a focus of his meditation. In 1903, he pondered: "I turned to this dictionary of conduct [the Gita] for a ready solution of all my troubles and trials. Words like aparigraha (non-possession) . . . gripped me. . . . How was one to divest oneself of all possessions? Was not the body itself possession enough? Were not wife and children possessions?"[83] These thoughts seem to presage Gandhi's life of intense renunciation. Soon after the discovery of this idea, he discontinued his insurance and within a couple of years (1906) took his vow of *brahmacarya.* Thinking of a wife and children as "possessions" may be a shocking idea in modern humanistic society, but in the world of myths and legends such as Hariścandra's it is a common concept.[84] Moreover, it is possible to propose that after being "gripped" by the concept of *aparigraha*, Gandhi reflected on his own past behavior as a "jealous" husband who had habitually treated his wife Kasturba as a possession. He sought to divest himself of this habit and "free" Kasturba, moving from one attitude to another—from jealous possessiveness to objective dispassion. Gandhi apparently took the idea of *aparigraha* to previously unknown extremes.

The war theme of the *Bhagavad-Gītā*, on the one hand, provided a backdrop for his nonviolent strife, which he termed as "*Satyagraha Yuddha*," on the other hand, the text validated his form of *tapas* (*brahmacarya*, silence, Truth) for *pravṛtti*.[85] Furthermore, in his discourses, Gandhi carefully incorporated indigenous myths of *tapas*, in which the active power of asceticism is depicted. He not only sought to present the coherence of his strategy through myths, he also deliberately narrated selected myths to frame his personal asceticism and political goals. A brief survey of prominent myths that Gandhi selected will reveal their strategic value in arousing mass mobilization of his people.

Narratives of *Tapas* for the Modern Arena of *Pravṛtti*

We have discussed earlier that Gandhi's life of suffering and sacrifice caused his early Christian followers to perceive him as a Christ-like figure. Wolpert subsequently theorizes that his *tapas* resembled the Christian notion of *passion*. Even though Gandhi drew on Jesus's model of "suffering," he claimed he developed his framework of self-suffering and sacrifice primarily in the traditional context of *tapas*. While transforming his practices of *nivṛtti* for the arena of *pravṛtti*, Gandhi did not focus on the traditional discourse of the renouncer; rather he reverted to the concept of *tapas* ubiquitous within Hindu mythology.

In the framework of Indian asceticism, austerities are undertaken not simply for religious goals; they are intentionally practiced in order to acquire supernatural powers (*siddhis*), as well as for the purposes of penance and purification. Gandhi spells this out in his discourses and writings and frames his own actions as *tapas*. In 1924, he writes for *Navajivan* under the title "Importance of '*Tapas*' ":

> There are instances of *tapas* [penance] at every step in Hindu mythology. Parvati desired to win Shankara and she took to *tapas*. Siva did something wrong and so he undertook *tapas*. Vishwamitra was the very incarnation of *tapas*. When Rama went into exile, Bharata plunged into yoga discipline, practised austere *tapas* and wore out his body. . . . I have not the strength today to narrate the story of my *tapas* but I state this much that I cannot possibly live without *tapas*.[86]

The tradition of the practice of austerity that Gandhi is referring to is depicted in Indian religious literature as having been observed by ascetics, kings, *devas* (gods), and *asuras* (demons) alike for religious and mundane purposes. Gandhi attributed the inspiration for his austere actions to the myths and expressed deep faith in the wish-fulfilling power that results from *tapasya* or voluntary suffering: "I have always believed that, if our capacity for *tapascharya* or voluntary suffering is real enough, we are bound to reap the fruit."[87] His personal *tapas* (self-suffering in the form of austerity) undertaken for self-discipline and purification, and his call for collective *tapas* (self-suffering in the form of nonviolent resistance and noncooperation) adopted for fighting an empire and the social evil of untouchability, were unprecedented applications even in the Indian context. Gandhi himself admitted that "the weapon was a new one."[88] He obviously believed that the principle of *tapas* could be transferred to all spheres of attainment—from the spiritual to the political. Even though Gandhi's homology of *tapas* and voluntary suffering for political goals was a unique application, it served to create a coherent strategy that justified the sacrificial nature of his actions of protest and noncooperation. The technique he proposed might have been a "new one," but by drawing on Indian mythology he showed that the principles on which it was based were ancient.

Gandhi's choice of selected passages from the *Rāmāyaṇa*, the *Mahābhārata*, and the *Purāṇas* supported his ascetic practices and legitimated the method of nonviolent resistance for his political agenda. These popularly known myths also illustrated the potency of ascetic practices. In particular, the vow of *brahmacarya*, initially undertaken by Gandhi for its practical value, became a form of *tapas* imbued with actual power. In his discussion on *brahmacarya*, Gandhi recounted the tales of Lakṣmaṇa, the younger brother of Lord Rāma, and of Indrajīt, a valiant son of the demon King Rāvaṇa, both legendary characters of the *Rāmāyaṇa* who acquired supernormal powers by means of *brahmacarya*. Lakṣmaṇa, while accompanying Rāma and Sītā to the forest during their exile, left his wife behind in Ayodhya and observed an unbroken vow of *brahmacarya* for fourteen years. According to Gandhi, Lakṣmaṇa conquered sleep by virtue of celibacy. The demon Indrajīt also observed ascetic practices, including celibacy, for many years, and obtained magical powers and celestial weaponry as a result. He became so powerful that he even defeated Indra, the King of gods. Thus, he became known as Indrajīt (conqueror of Indra). Gandhi points out, however, that since Indrajīt was on the side of *asat* (untruth; evil represented by Rāvaṇa), he ultimately met his defeat at the hands of Lakṣmaṇa.[89]

> Lakshman and Indrajit were both celebates [*sic*] (*brahmacharis*) and had conquered sleep and were therefore equally valorous. But the valour of the former was divine, while that of the latter ungodly. This means that the vow of *brahmacharya* and other vows are holy and bring happiness only when they are taken as a spiritual discipline.[90]

Referring to the examples of Lakṣmaṇa's and Indrajīt's supernormal powers, Gandhi asserted that his own *brahmacarya* vow was part of a larger "spiritual discipline" and was motivated by the immediate goals of securing India's freedom and removing untouchability. Unlike many ascetics and kings who had undertaken *brahmacarya* as a temporary measure only for gaining *siddhis*, Gandhi's vow was permanently sealed by his commitment to public service. Gandhi's belief in *brahmacarya* was unequivocal. He believed that a single satyagrahi would be sufficient to achieve the goal of *svarājya*, and by his vow of *brahmacarya* he sought to be that one. He sometimes lamented that if he had attained a complete self-control, the effect of his thoughts and speech would have been much greater.

Gandhi's vow can perhaps best be compared to that of Bhīṣma in the *Mahābhārata*, who took the solemn oath of *brahmacarya* so that he would not have progeny of his own and could thus fulfill his father's desire. Similarly, Gandhi's vow of *brahmacarya* prevented him from having additional children and enabled him to detach himself from the duties of a husband and a father in order to fully dedicate himself to public service. In his commitment to pragmatic purposes, Gandhi, like Bhīṣma, realized the miraculous powers accrued through *brahmacarya*.

The *Mahābhārata* chronicles the toils and turbulence that the Bhārata race had to endure as a consequence of Bhīṣma's vow and the temptations that he had to confront. Bhīṣma, even so, remained firm in his vow; nothing could cause him to break it. His valor was feared even by the celestials. Gandhi similarly struggled with the consequences that his family had to face due to his vow. He sacrificed the needs of his wife and children, forcing them into a life of poverty. Eventually Gandhi gained the title "Father of the Nation," but his own sons never received the love of a normal father. He wrote in a letter to his son, Ramdas Gandhi: "You will have to struggle. Manliness consists in struggling. . . . You should be very vigilant so that you may not have involuntary emission during sleep . . . we should recall to mind perfect *brahmacharis* like Bhishma."[91] Gandhi set high moral standards for young men and women, not by giving them living examples but by looking at mythical models.

The myths of *tapascarya* are drawn across the canvas of Gandhi's lectures, letters, and news articles. Gandhi integrated most of the awe-inspiring symbols such as *Kāmadhenu* (the wish-fulfilling divine cow), *Kalpataru* (the wish-granting tree), and *Rāmarājya* with exalted models of austerity, sacrifice, and commitment. Gandhi invoked these symbols and models to bear on modern issues of cow protection, absolute commitment to Truth and nonviolence, and willingness to sacrifice. The large and complex narrative of King Dilip and his service to the divine cow Surbhi, retold by Gandhi and published in the *Young India* in 1928, is typical of his ability to integrate myths emphasizing the power of *satya* and *tapascarya* with mundane social and political matters. This narrative, although published under the title of "Cow-Protection True and False," reaches far beyond the matter of Hindu belief in the sacredness of the cow and commitment to cow-protection (see appendix 2).[92]

The narratives about voluntarily suffering, sacrifice, and trial that Gandhi referred to—such as those of Hariścandra-Tārāmati, Prahlād, Nala-Damyantī, Mira Bai, Pārvati, Rāma and Sītā, Hanuman, and Lakṣmaṇa—all end in triumph. And, since these narratives about *tapas* do not have tragic endings, they provided hope for Gandhi's followers who were called to go to jail and to bear flogging without retaliation. R. K. Narayan says of Indian stories:

> In every story, since goodness triumphs in the end, there is no tragedy in the Greek sense; the curtain never comes down *finally* on corpses strewn about the stage. The sufferings of the meek and the saintly are temporary, even as the triumph of the demon is; everyone knows this."[93]

It is within this cultural context that Gandhi developed his own concept of suffering that empowers and triumphs.

Analyzing Gandhi's use of myth reveals the value of these stories in communicating the role of renunciation as a political act, as well as in awakening the masses to their inherent spiritual power. It can be concluded that myths served three purposes for Gandhi: first, they illustrated the supernatural power of *tapascarya* (austerities, specifically *brahmacarya*) that he sought to apply to all endeavors; second, they demonstrated the proactive nature of ascetic practices while at the same time epitomizing the unyielding power of *vrata*; and third, they enabled the masses to see the homology between *tapas* and his method of ascetic activism—which fired their religious imagination and, in turn, conferred authority on Gandhi. The moral authority earlier conferred on Gandhi by a small group of intellectuals, which shall be discussed later in this chapter, combined with Gandhi's own initiatives taken during the 1920s, established his authority as a leader in the minds of the people.

Gandhi drew his principles of renunciation from the yogic and ascetic traditions of India and, to some extent, from Western religious traditions, and took his style of delivery from his native lore. However, he even went a step further. Not only did he narrate myths in order to validate his method of ascetic activism and inspire his followers, he also sought to personally and publicly embody sacrifice and thereby present a model of personal *svarāj* and triumph.

Gandhi's Re-enactment of Legendary Characters: Mediating Between Secular Politics and Sacred Renunciation

In the *Myth of Lokamanya*, Cashman states that India has "freely assimilated and synthesized a wide variety of myths." While glossing the "myth" of the *mahātmā* as one of "the most powerful" of many political myths, he offers insight into the complexity that underlies Gandhi's character:

> In modern India the myth of the *Mahatma* (great soul) was one of the most powerful political myths. It was established to describe the career of India's foremost leader, Mohandas Karamchand Gandhi. . . . The *Mahatma* concept underlined Gandhi's efforts to combine religion and politics, to bring morality into the sphere of politics. It also suggested his concern for non-violence, which was necessary to establish truly moral means to reach a spiritual end. Asceticism was another ingredient of the myth; in order to arrive at the most truthful positions Gandhi abstained from certain foods, liquor, and sexual activity.[94]

Cashman is correct in his observation that the "myth" of the *mahātmā* was powerful in the nationalist movement of India, but it is not clear what he intends by the statement, "the *Mahatma* concept underlined Gandhi's efforts to combine religion and politics." The author seems to perceive "the *mahatma* concept" as a construct that Gandhi deliberately sought to achieve. However, a study of Gandhi's life, writing, and biographical records reveals that his *mahātmāhood*—not merely the honorific title, but his actual stature as a *mahātmā*—evolved organically as a result of his open practice of austerities, his performance as an ascetic, his devotion to public service, and partly as a result of the tendency of religious-minded people, especially in his native culture, to mythologize public personas. Cashman views asceticism as the essential "ingredient" in the myth of the *mahātmā*, but this "ingredient" was the core of Gandhi's role as a religious figure, as well as a testimony of his selfless commitment to his people.

It has been argued that even before Gandhi emerged as a political leader, his sanctification had occurred; interestingly, it was initiated by his close Christian friends in South Africa. Mark Juergensmeyer reflects, "The canonization of Gandhi by those who admired him occurred rather early in his public life." Henry S. L. Polak, an early follower of Gandhi, recalls that when he first met Gandhi in South Africa, "he felt that he was 'in the presence of a moral giant, whose pellucid soul is a clear, still lake, in which one sees Truth clearly mirrored.' "[95] A survey of early literature about Gandhi reveals that these authors had one thing in common: they were inspired by Gandhi's asceticism and his ideology of self-sacrifice that was so clearly visible in his simplicity, loving presence, detached demeanor, and his religious fervor.[96]

Gandhi's decision to choose the life of an ascetic, his personal proclivity for austere living, his emotional relationship with specific stories, and his intuitive grasp of the Indian mindset that exalts the legends of *tapasvins* and renunciation must all have been significant in his metamorphosis from Mohandas to *mahātmā*. Sobo and Bell, in their discussion of celibacy from a cross-cultural perspective, note that "individuals or groups who refrain from sexual activity are, in addition to creating themselves after a specific fashion, communicating something about themselves in relation to others and so about their own standing in society."[97] Certainly many followers belonging to many religious traditions who participated in Gandhi's movement perceived his abstinence from sex and wealth, and his constant effort to subdue the passions, as signs of his stature as a holy man.

It must be noted that Gandhi's embrace of religious symbolism was not a novel idea. Gandhi's predecessors, including Vivekananda and Tilak, used religious metaphors for political actions and sought to embody them. However, the Rudolphs show that Gandhi's unconventional use of symbols was more inclusive than his contemporaries': "Unlike his predecessors Gandhi leavened traditional symbolism with reformist ideas, tried to find symbols and issues that would avoid Hindu-Muslim confrontations, and pursued a nonviolent strategy."[98] Not only did Gandhi seek to find unbiased and universal symbols, he also used his body to communicate his method of *satyagraha* and his conviction in the power of *tapas* for securing *svarāj*.

Gandhi's ascetic practices and their public display have been perceived both as the facade of an astute politician and the religious apparatus of a holy man. But for Gandhi himself they were required vehicles in achieving *pūrṇa svarājya*. In 1931, during an interview with journalists, Gandhi defined *pūrṇa svarāj* in religious terms as a "sacred word, a Vedic word, meaning self-rule and self-restraint."[99]

According to Gandhi, the renunciatory practices of celibacy, fasting, silence, poverty, and ascetic garb were essential to his philosophy. Gandhi asserted that "the adoption of the loin-cloth was for me a sheer necessity." However, this clothing (or a lack of) also carried symbolic value. For example, Gandhi's decision to wear only a loincloth was solely based on his desire to identify with the millions of destitute "compulsory naked men, save of their langoti four inches wide." He was also aware that the loincloth "spells simplicity."[100] But the loincloth also came to be seen as the religious representation of a *sannyāsin* and symbolic of his sacrifice. Gandhi presented both his ascetic garb as well as his boycott of British goods and Western trousers as being politically symbolic of *swadeshi* (literally "of one's own country" and "self-reliance") and necessary for attaining *svarāj*, thereby integrating political actions with renunciatory vows.[101] It is apparent that Gandhi, aware of the language of symbols, at times utilized his image of a *sādhu* (who is not bound by the constraints of social parameters) to justify his acts of "begging" for the Swaraj Fund and of freely mixing with women and *Harijans* (untouchables, literally "the people of god").[102] He asserted: "As far as I am concerned I am a fakir, who has given up the world, a sannyasi who is not bound by social customs. . . . I do like renouncing the world and its ways. I also like *brahmacharya*."[103] However, on other occasions Gandhi denied his status as an ascetic, presenting himself as a pragmatic thinker and his continence as a necessary condition to the call for public service. For Gandhi, this apparent dichotomy did not reflect conflicting ideologies but rather complementary aspects of his program that combined asceticism with activism.

Furthermore, Gandhi himself positioned his actions, which became a public spectacle and focus of debate, in the context of the myths, and portrayed himself as emulating legendary characters. For instance, in a rare letter to his son Ramdas, Gandhi writes:

> I was pained to see your condition yesterday, your broken health and your mental suffering. I had no remedy for either. . . . I felt as Harishchandra had done. He had become ready to sell his only son for the sake of dharma. I have been doing very much the same thing.[104]

In these words, Gandhi refers to himself as being bound to the commitment of service like Hariścandra, who sold his wife and son for the sake of a commitment to truth. Gandhi is admitting here to enacting in real life the role of Hariścandra, whose steadfast conduct had fascinated him as a child, explaining that he could not assist his son because he was bound by his *dharma* for humanity.

In another instance, Gandhi compared his self-control with Lakṣmaṇa, the younger brother of Rāma in the *Rāmāyaṇa*: "A man of self-restraint like Lakshman had seen only Sita's toes, for he used to salute her feet. Hence, when sisters come to bless me, I never feel embarrassed in their presence because of my loin-cloth."[105] Even in reflective accounts such as these, Gandhi seems to be associating the mythical with his own actions.

Gandhi sought to practice self-rule and self-restraint in his personal life and in the public sphere.

> The human race is essentially idolatrous. Since that is so, I want to say that man requires a visible, tangible manifestation of the thing he believes in and, as a corollary, is looking for miracles to happen . . . that will prove the power of truth.[106]

Perhaps Gandhi was supplying "tangible" proof of his *tapas* and self-rule through his embodied practices. Gandhi's public pronouncement of the *brahmacarya* vow; his poor and austere lifestyle as a *brahmacārin*; his wearing of a loincloth suggestive of an ascetic; his observance of silence each Monday; his daily routine of prayer in an *āśrama* setting; his presiding over prayer meetings; his travels in third-class railway compartments; his preference for staying in *harijan* (untouchable) colonies; his public fasts; and his pattern of freely mingling with men and women alike—all could be construed simply as the veneer of a shrewd politician; however, they could also be seen as the embodiment of a self-sacrificing *tapasvin*—a paragon of *svarāj*, that is, "self-rule and self restraint"—as Gandhi defined it.

Gandhi not only fought the inner war with his passions in public, providing tangible proof of his serious struggle to his followers, he also sought to wage a political war nonviolently in order to present a tangible and visible public display of the inner power of truth. Gandhi invoked ritual symbolism to interpret his political actions. Even though Jordens describes Gandhi as "disenchanted with ritualism and myth"[107] because he did not follow specific Hindu rituals, nonetheless, Gandhi's language is imbued with rituals and myths. For example, he often gave a ritualized interpretation to his activities of nonviolent activism and insisted that the fight for the goal of *pūrṇa svarājya* required the spiritual weapon of *satyagraha*.

Historically, one of the most documented examples of Gandhi's visible public display of the "power of truth" was the Dandi Salt March (from March 12 to April 6, 1930)—led by Gandhi and select followers to defy the salt tax. Among the populace, the increased taxes on the essential commodity of salt by the British authorities were extremely unpopular because they affected every individual; the poor people, in particular, felt this burden. Gandhi intuited that an action of civil disobedience in defiance of the salt tax had the potential for a mass participation. A well-orchestrated march to the sea for deliberate violation of salt laws imbued salt with symbolic meaning of the extent of the colonial oppression, but also held a concrete promise of awakening the common masses to the British inequities. Dalton notes, "He wanted a group of followers scrupulously disciplined in his mode of nonviolent conduct and unequivocally committed to *ahimsa* as a creed," because he believed the success of the March depended on the dedication and integrity of the participants.[108] By uniting his followers for a just cause, the protest—which was political in nature—could have been undertaken simply as a political act to defy an unjust law. But Gandhi ritualized the event, presenting it to its participants as a "sacred pilgrimage," "a life-and-death struggle, a holy war," and comparing it to "an all-embracing sacrifice in which," he said, "we wish to offer ourselves as oblation."[109] Gandhi, already claiming himself to be the "director" and "expert in making," assumed leadership in this *satyagraha* enterprise. He carefully selected seventy-eight *satyagrahis* from his own *āśrama* to lead the march. He stated that "Satyagraha is a purely spiritual weapon," and emphasized the importance of a qualified leader. He believed that "everyone cannot use surgical instruments" but "many may use them if there is an expert behind them directing their use."[110]

The launch of the march was imbued with ritual symbolism. On the morning of March 12, 1930, thousands of people gathered at the Sabarmati Ashram. Before Gandhi and his followers set out for the march, a prayer meeting was held, replete with prayers and chanting of *bhajans*. During the prayer meeting, Gandhi invoked the imagery of *raṇa yajña* (war sacrifice) reminiscent of the motif of the *Mahābhārata* war:

> God willing, we shall set out exactly at 6.30. Those joining the march should all be on the spot at 6.20. If our first step is pure, all our subsequent tests will be good and pure. . . .
>
> This fight is no public show; it is the final struggle—a life-and-death struggle. If there are disturbances, we may even have to die at the hands of our own people. Even in that case, we shall have made our full contribution to the satyagraha struggle. . . . If we do not have the strength for this, we should not join the struggle. For my part I have taken no pledge not to return here, but I do ask you to return here only as dead men or as winners of swaraj. . . . The marchers have vowed to follow life-long poverty and to observe *brahmacharya* for life. They leave here with the determination to observe *brahmacharya* and will remain faithful to that determination. The man who always follows the truth and always proclaims what he does is a brave man.[111]

Dalton, in *Gandhi's Power*, gives an eloquent and detailed description of the *Salt Satyagraha*, and records the ritualistic commencement of the march. When Gandhi's prayer meeting discourse ended, his wife Kasturba applied a "benedictory *tilak* to his forehead and garlanded him, not with flowers but with *khadi*, and handed to him the walking stick that became his trademark on the march." In the course of his thorough analysis, Dalton does not mention Gandhi's astounding proclamation that the marchers chosen to lead the march had vowed "to follow *brahmacharya* for life." While he does point out that Gandhi expressed concern "with preserving the 'purity' of the march near its end and wanted everyone 'to turn the searchlight inward' and examine 'lapses' that had occurred," he does not engage with Gandhi's own definitions of inner and outer purity, which he had always interlinked with *brahmacarya*.[112]

Did this unique selection criterion represent Gandhi's eccentric bias toward *brahmacārins* because he himself was one? Would the success of the march depend on the sexual life of its leaders? The correlation between the success of a political protest and the protestors' sexual lives does not seem obvious. However, it appears that Gandhi believed that success of this march depended on the leaders' purity. Even at the end of the march on April 6, Gandhi invoked the symbolism of "purity." "This religious war of civil disobedience should be started only after purifying ourselves by bathing in the salt water."[113] This indicates that, for Gandhi, *brahmacarya, ahiṃsā, satya,* and *svarāj* were inseparable.

It is evident from Gandhi's writings that he was not merely looking for political "independence" but was bent on achieving the goal of *pūrṇa svāraj.* According to Gandhi, self-restraint and self-rule were analogous, and the Salt March was an experiment to prove "the power of truth." For Gandhi, this protest—which could have been led simply as a political protest—was a "battle sacrifice" (*raṇa yajña*) for confronting injustice (*adharma*), and he was ready to offer himself as an "oblation."

Even though Gandhi presented his actions as a pragmatic necessity, it would be naive to assume that he was not careful in choosing symbols and expressions evocative of specific myths. Gandhi was aware of the emotional impact of the legends, rituals, and symbols that he himself had encountered in his childhood. It would appear that Gandhi was testing and seeking to manifest the power of truth promised by *tapas,* self-suffering. "This was a saint at war, with penance as his weapon, and however somber and sincere their meaning, these words [Gandhi's speech before the march] were also theatrical in the extreme," Dalton suggests.[114] The emotional force of his actions and words was due to his analogizing his political action with religious narratives.

Dalton's account of the thoughts of Mahadev Desai, one of Gandhi's closest associates, at the launch of the march is revealing:

> I beheld in Gandhiji an ideal Vaishnav, Lord Rama on this way to conquer Sri Lanka. But more than this I am reminded of Lord Buddha's great March to attain divine wisdom. Buddha embarked on his march bidding farewell to the world, cutting through the darkness, inspired by the mission of relieving the grief-stricken and downtrodden.[115]

It is difficult to determine whether or not these reminiscences reflected the exact experience of the participants at that time, or if they were memories filtered through Gandhi's now mythicized figure and his accomplishments. However, such reflections marked the process that transformed him into an honorific figure. This reference to Gandhi as being like Lord Rāma and the Buddha provides an insight into the minds of his followers, who were prepared to die for his call to sacrifice. Although the Buddha was not a political activist of any sort, he did actively challenge the hegemony of the *brahmins* and raised his voice against the corruption in the caste system. Desai compares the Buddha's and Gandhi's "farewell to the world" as an act to leave their personal comforts and pleasures in order to "relieve" the pain of the "downtrodden."

Gandhi frequently emphasized that he truly believed in the power of renunciation and its instrumentality in accomplishing both mundane and spiritual goals; he sought to experiment with it in all walks of life. He trusted the power of ascetic practices and believed that if he could somehow acquire the power of a true *brahmacārin*, he would be able to change the course of India's destiny. The embrace by the masses of Gandhi as a *mahātmā* organically arose out of his strategy of ascetic activism. Gandhi carefully selected and embodied the symbols of self-sacrifice, service, and self-rule. The communication of his strategy of nonviolence through emulation of the myths of *tapasvins* incited the religious imagination and created a mythical halo around him.

Stories About Gandhi's Miracles: Idolizing the Power of Truth

The strong impression made by specific religious narratives on Gandhi's mind during his youth suggests that he was aware of the reaction that the tales of heroes of the ancient legends and the living ascetics were capable of producing in people's minds. Was it, then, Gandhi's living out of the myths in the public arena that created the myths around him?

Many biographers and historians have commented on the "theatrical" nature of Gandhi's personal and political actions. For example, Percival Spear suggests:

> He [Gandhi] dramatized his ideas by a constant stream of articles, speeches, and declarations, and above all by his own example. Gandhi, in the peasant's loin-cloth and shawl, sitting at the spinning wheel, writing notes on his weekly day of silence, sitting lost in contemplation or lying exhausted during a fast, were all ways of getting his image across to a largely illiterate population.

Spear goes on to say that Gandhi could not only "dramatize" himself but that he could also "dramatize an issue with an unerring instinct."[116]

It becomes clear after looking at Gandhi's life and works that the construction of his own image was part of the moral ethos he sought to live in his daily life, but he indeed had the ability to create an extraordinary public display of otherwise ordinary events. For example, a broad positive public response to Gandhi's fasts, which were carefully staged, has been recorded by historians. The custom of abstaining from food has been an essential part of the austere vows in Hindu tradition. Renunciates and laymen and women observe fasts for long and short periods of time for various reasons from purifying the self to obtaining worldly goals, including wealth and a good spouse. However, Gandhi resorted to fasting for attaining specific political objectives, such as confronting the custom of untouchablity and halting the tide of communal violence.

Gandhi's fasting has been viewed by some as an act of political blackmail, having "coercive effect." But he differentiated them from hunger strikes by labeling them as "spiritual fasts." He explained them as the act of "*tapas*," a religious technique of "penance and purification," and "great weapon in the armoury of satyagraha."[117] However, he avowed to fasting not for personal purification, but rather to awaken the moral consciousness of his people. The experience of the effect of his fast has been recorded: "Restaurants and amusement centers did little business; some of them were voluntarily closed by the proprietors. . . . The nerve of feeling had been restored; the pain began to be felt. . . . Gandhiji knew when to start the redemptive process."[118] Although this recollection may not represent a literal account, it certainly provides insight into its effect. The imagery of fasting invoked a palpable response among all walks of Indian people, and even British authorities. Gandhi's ascetic fasts were oriented toward the concrete actions of social and political reform and were made effective by his embodiment of an ascetic and a narrative that combined the religious symbolism of rituals with his political goals. The Indian Annual Register for 1943 reports Gandhi's breaking of the twenty-one-day fast at Aga Khan Palace prison:

> The inmates . . . sang . . . '*Vaishnava jana to*' and two stanzas from . . . *Gitanjali*. "Lead Kindly Light" and the Koran were also recited. After prayers, those present observed a five minutes' silence. With folded hands Mahatma Gandhi was seen to close his eyes and to be in meditation. Prayers over, Kasturba . . . handed him a glass containing six ounces of orange juice. He is reported to have taken twenty minutes to sip the juice.[119]

Such imagery was evocative of the ancient sages who sacrificed themselves in order to keep their vows. Generally, Gandhi's fasts were effective in moving the hearts of the masses, in spite of critical assessments by some. People felt that Gandhi was "dying for their own crimes" and also resorted to fasting in expressing solidarity with him, as evidenced by many reports.[120] The responses were overwhelming. Paine notes the effects of one of Gandhi's last fasts: "The Viceroy, Lord Mountbatten, observed that Gandhi singlehandedly quelled riots when Mountbatten's own soldiers, though mounting into the thousands, were helpless to affect anything."[121]

In his depiction of the Salt Satyagraha, Dalton also underscores the dramatic nature of Gandhi's words and use of symbols. Gandhi's public display of his private ascetic practices, his ability to involve mass media, and his "masterful awareness and use of symbols"[122] must certainly have appeared as "performance" with theatrical overtones. Indeed, Gandhi himself once told a missionary friend, "You must watch my life—how I live, eat, sit, talk, behave in general. The sum total of all those in me is my religion."[123] He echoes the *Bhagavad-Gita*'s (II) description of *sthitaprajña* (the man of wisdom), whose wisdom is mirrored in his actions.

But can mere performance move millions? Dalton provides a glimpse into the minds of Gandhi's followers, who were transformed by his strict discipline and conduct, which was practical in nature, but also fired the religious imagination. He offers a snapshot of the diversity of people—high castes, *Harijans*, Hindus, Muslims, Christians, men, women, and children of all ages—who grew united in their "adherence to Gandhian nonviolence and personal devotion to its prophet."[124] Dalton's historical assessment, however, does not consider Gandhi's own words about asceticism and the religious context in which Gandhi's symbolism is situated.

It can be argued that the way in which Gandhi's self-dramatization was perceived within the Indian context of his time was another crucial factor in his political tactics. Notwithstanding the fact that Gandhi's practices have been construed as "dramatization," "theatrical," or even "shrewd," his actions invoked, in the minds of the masses, memories of the *tapasvins*—who, by their penance, were able to perform miracles. Gandhi's contemporary, novelist Raja Rao, writes about the impact of Gandhi's teachings on nonviolent resistance and captures how Indians perceived Gandhi's actions against the backdrop of the myth of Bhīṣma:

> The people in India always live a *Mahabharata* war. Indians are perhaps the world's most complex people, with layer behind layer of argument and explanation, for, every virtue

> or vice seen from one point of view there's always one seen from another. . . . Remember Bhishma on the field of battle, on his bed of arrows, speaking of the greatness of Truth. . . .
>
> Such, too, Mohandas Karamchand Gandhi, who, on his field of battle, lying on his bed of arrows while his adversaries and kinsmen brought him lime and water to drink, talked of love, and was finally killed by an un-understanding man.

Rao concludes that Gandhi and Bhīṣma—the great *brahamcārin*—"both fought on the side of Truth," and explains that the "revolutionary" cry "*Gandhi Mahatma ki jai*" meant "victory to the Truth."[125]

India has a long-standing tradition of intertwining mythology and iconography, and during the independence movement this vehicle was used to disseminate political ideas and agendas. In her book, *Performative Politics and the Cultures of Hinduism*, Raminder Kaur provides an account of how political ideologies are expressed and disseminated through the visual and performative festivals in India. For example, in the popular Ganpati celebrations in Maharashtra, many leaders, including Gandhi and Subash Chandra Bose, were depicted as Lord Ganeśa. In Indian society, religious festivals and visual presentations became a medium to convey the political ideas to the masses through their familiar stories and symbols.[126] Throughout the 1930s and 1940s, the myth of Gandhi as a holy man and miracle-working icon proliferated. Biographer Ved Mehta recounts:

> Despite his constant disavowals, people began worshipping Gandhi as a god, as a divine manifestation, like Krishna or Buddha, and claiming that his touch or his mere presence had cured them of disease or spared them death. They tried to get close to him and touch his feet. . . . Inspired by his presence, people promised to dedicate themselves to the Constructive Programme.[127]

Gandhi's immediate contact mesmerized many and motivated them to contribute to his program, even though this effect was not always long-lasting.

The lore of the divinity of Gandhi, *Mahātmā,* circulated in the form of both lithographs and legends. A 1930 poster reinterpreted the myth of Lord Śiva's protection of the Sage Mārkaṇdeya from Yama: Lord Śiva was replaced by Gandhi (not wielding weapons but holding his nonviolent tool, the spinning wheel, a visual pun on Śiva's circle of flames, and waving a newspaper, his ultimate weapon of propaganda to mobilize the masses, invoking the image of Śiva's trident), Sage Mārkaṇḍeya was replaced by Mother India, and Yama by an officer of the British Raj. "The new interpretation is of a divinely invested Gandhi—the protector, rising to the defence of Mother India who is under the power of what is portrayed as the 'demonic' and 'destructive' force of the Raj" (fig. 1). There were many such posters in which Gandhi was portrayed as an *avatār* and savior of Mother India. In one of the lithographs, Gandhi is portrayed as being held in the embrace of Goddess Mother India, and both appear under the protection of Lord Krishna (fig. 2).[128] This image invokes the classic iconography of mother and child found in multiple religious cultures. These illustrations are testament to the ways that Gandhi's divinity was being infused in the consciousness of the common people (*sadharn janata*), becoming an underlying facilitator of the phenomenon of mass mobilization. This too can be construed as a tactic of a "shrewd politician," as noted by van der Veer: "Gandhi was certainly a shrewd politician. He projected a saintly image on the scene of nationalist politics, and, when he toured through the country, people made great efforts to gain his *darshan*."[129] It must be noted that historical records reveal that his saintly image was the result of his ascetic lifestyle, which gave him the persona of *mahātmā*; it certainly invoked a religious response in the masses. The image of the *mahātmā* emerged gradually out of his consistent commitment to public service and personal detachment, until Indian masses immersed in the tradition of Hindu saints recognized him as such.

Amin's seminal article "Gandhi as Mahatma" is an account of how Gandhi's charisma "registered in peasant consciousness." He gives a historical analysis of Gandhi's visit, at the height of the noncooperation movement in 1921, to the district of Gorakhpur in the then eastern United Provinces. He states that "Gandhi, the person, was in this particular locality for less than a day, but the 'Mahatma' as an 'idea' was thought out and reworked in popular imagination in subsequent months." Amin, by quoting newspaper reports, affords a glimpse of the feeling of "devotion" people held toward Gandhi, which was expressed by their relentless demand to experience his *darśan* at all hours of the day and their willingness to give him offerings such as are given at the feet of the statues of gods and holy men and women. During this visit Gandhi, addressed many large crowds who responded by "rending the sky with cries of '*jai*' and demanding *darshan*." Amin quotes a 1921 Tendulkar's account of "the Mahatma's 'tour of mass conversions to the new creed.'"

Figure 1 (left): "Bharatuddhar" (Gandhi, the Protector of India). Prabhu Dayal, c. 1930. A mythological depiction of Gandhi as Lord Śiva, saving Mother India from the depredations of colonial rule. Reproduced by permission of the British Library.

Figure 1 (right): 1935. The mythological template for the previous image. An image from the 1935 film re-creating a scene from Hindu mythology in which the powerful god Śiva comes to protect the pious sage Mārkaṇḍeya from the lord of death, Yama. Courtesy of Amrit and Rabindra Kaur Singh.

> In a Bihar village when Gandhi and his party were stranded in the train, an old woman came seeking out Gandhi. 'Sire, I am now one hundred and four,' she said, 'and my sight has grown dim. I have visited various holy places. . . . Just as we had Rama and Krishna as *avatars*, so also Mahatma Gandhi has appeared as an *avatar*, I hear. Until I have seen him death will not appear.' . . . This simple faith moved India's millions who greeted him.[130]

This account exemplifies how the religious imagination of the people was constantly enlivened by new myths. Yearning for Gandhi's *darśan*

Figure 2. *"Bharat Mata,"* or *"Mother India."* Post-1948? Gandhi in the lap of Mother India. This image imbued with Gandhian symbolism, depicts Gandhi, who was committed to defending India's cause, being nurtured by Goddess Mother India. Lord Viṣṇu at the top of the image represents the sustaining force being activated through Gandhi. Courtesy of Amrit and Rabindra Kaur Singh.

among India's masses grew over time, resulting in unmanageable crowds. In 1946, the *Harijan* reports "six lakhs [six hundred thousand] had gathered at the prayer meeting at Madura. . . . They had sat on the roadside without food and shelter just to have a *darshan*."[131] Such massive responses to Gandhi's presence have also been recorded in photos.

Myths about Gandhi's divinity were not confined to individuals but became part of the mass consciousness. The local press played an important role in provoking the mass response by disseminating stories about "Gandhi's occult power." For example, an issue of *Swadesh* (1921) announced his arrival in the district under the heading: "Gandhi in dream: Englishmen run away naked [*swapn mein Mahatma Gandhi: Angrez nange bhage*]." The story reported the dream of a man who saw Gandhi's victory being achieved through the assertion of the superior power of moral methods, as well as the subsequent plight of the British and the berating of their power.[132] Countless awe-inspiring rumors circulated. Lal also elaborates:

> One set of rumours and stories referred to the power of the Mahatma; another enumerated the consequences of opposing him, or a particular aspect of his creed; and yet another referred to the boons conferred on those who paid heed to Gandhi's teachings. . . . A man who abused Gandhi found his eyelids stuck. . . . One pundit who was told to give up eating fish is reported to have said in anger, 'I shall eat fish, let's see what the Mahatmaji can do.' When he sat down to eat, it is said, the fish was found to be crawling with worms.[133]

In many of the stories, according to Amin, "the Mahatma's image takes form within the pre-existing patterns of popular belief, and ritual actions corresponding to these." The stories reveal that men and women performed ritualistic actions such as Gandhi *manauti* (taking a vow on his name), *varat* and *arādhanā* (fasting and worshiping in his name), and offering cooked food to his image so that he would fulfill their specific wishes. Uncannily, their wishes were fulfilled, so said the reports.[134]

Newspapers circulated the stories of Gandhi's miracles. At the same time, myths were also used in pro-British accounts to cast suspicion on Gandhi's message. In 1921, the *Pioneer* featured an editorial reporting four miracles attributed to Gandhi and then rendered the assessment that they only reflected the "unhealthy nervous excitement" of Indian villagers.

> In the 'Swadesh,' a paper published in Gorkakhpur, four miracles were quoted last month as being popularly attributed to Mr. Gandhi. Smoke was seen coming from wells and, when water was drunk, it had the fragrance of keora . . . an aloe-like plant which is used in the manufacture of perfume; a copy of the Holy Quran was found in a room which had not been opened for a year; an Ahir who refused alms to a Sadhu begging in Mahatma Gandhi's name, had his gur and two buffalos destroyed by fire, and a skeptical Brahmin, who defied Mr Gandhi's authority, went mad and was cured three days afterwards by the invocation of the saintly name! *All these events admit of an obvious explanation, but they are symptoms of an unhealthy nervous excitement such as often passed through the peasant classes of Europe in the Middle Ages, and to which the Indian villager is particularly prone. . . . In all these instances we see the mythopoeic imagination of the childlike peasant at work.*[135]

Even though the editorial dismissed the miraculous stories as "the mythopoeic imagination of the childlike peasant," the paper went on to publish additional stories in which Gandhi's teachings were embedded. Despite their editorial skepticism, these stories further fueled the peoples' religious imagination.

Gandhi's biographers and the historians of the nationalist movement, especially those who focused on the marginalized classes' interactions with Gandhi, have established that the religious fervor was not limited to the peasantry of Gorakhpur, but extended from Brahmins to Adivasis (aborigines), and from eastern to western states. Tendulkar notes: "Prostitutes of Barisal, the Marwari merchants of Calcutta, Oriya coolies, railway strikers, Santals eager to present khadi *chaddars*, all claimed his attention."[136] Gandhi sought to reach out to and assimilate all these groups in his nationalist movement. These groups, such as *Dalits* and *Adivasis*, were particularly encouraged by Gandhi and his followers to purify themselves by giving up liquor and meat, to take up the practice of spinning *khadi*, and to live a clean and simple life.[137]

Hardiman writes about the influence of Gandhian ideology on the Adivasis of South Gujarat: "Gandhi was projected by the Adivasis as a divine being who was somehow working to ameliorate their condition. Vows were taken on his name, and miracles were expected from him."[138] In another study, "Origins and Transformations of the Devi," Hardiman recounts the regeneration of a goddess cult during the nationalist movement. He describes the advent of a "new goddess" among Adivasis, who lived on the eastern border of the Surat district of the Bombay presidency. On 9 November 1922, about two thousand *advasis* congregated to listen to the "teachings of [a] new goddess of great power known as Salabai." The eyewitness reports of this event found their way into the records of Bombay government.

> In December, some new commands of the Devi began to be heard. Salabai [a new goddess of great power] was telling the adivasis to take vows in Gandhi's name, to wear khadi cloth, and to attend nationalist schools. Rumors were heard that spiders were writing Gandhi's name in cobwebs. It was said that Gandhi had fled from jail and could be seen sitting in a well side by side with Salabai, spinning his *charkha* (spinning wheel).

In another village, the movement to follow Gandhi was even more impassioned. The local newspaper reported that Adivasis were bathing twice a day, women were wearing *khadi,* and some had vowed to abstain from liquor. People participating in a procession expressed the deification of Gandhi by shouting, "Gandhiji ki jai!" and "Devi-Mata ki jai!"[139]

Widespread sentiment for the mythical persona of Gandhi was also reflected in literary writings of the time. Many short stories and novels, such as K. S. Venkataramani's *Desabhakthan Kandan* (published as a book in 1931) and Rao's *Kanthapura* (published in 1938) portray the impact of Gandhi's nonviolent movement on Indian villages. The religious imagination of Indians toward Gandhi is illustrated in *Kanthapura*—which reflects much more than the literary device of its author. The story in the novel is a snapshot of the oral tradition that was developing around the figure of Gandhi. Rao narrates the "myth of Mahatma Gandhi" as an incarnation of Śiva born on Indian soil to free his daughter India from the clutches of slavery. Rao puts Gandhi's birth story in the mouth of a Harikatha-man (religious storyteller) at a village *bhajan* (religious gathering):

> [T]here was born in a family in Gujerat a son such as the world has never beheld! As soon as he came forth, the four wide walls began to shine like the kingdom of

> the sun, and hardly was he in the cradle than he began to lisp the language of wisdom. You remember how Krishna, when he was but a babe of four, had begun to fight against demons. . . . So too our Mohandas began to fight against the enemies of the country . . . his voice was so pure, his forehead so brilliant with wisdom, that men followed him, more and more men followed him as they did Krishna the flute-player; and so he goes from village to village to slay the serpent of the foreign rule. Fight, says he, but harm no soul. . . . Don't be attached to riches, says he, for riches create passions, and passions create attachment, and attachment hides the face of truth.[140]

Kanthapura does not present historical details but is precise in portraying the complex feelings of the people in relation to Gandhi and his method of noncooperation. Prema Nandakumar, an author and translator, explains that India has necessarily depended heavily on its literature for constructing its history. "In more senses than one, this so-called record in 'Kanthapura' happens to be a true history of the times," says Nandakumar. It provides, in her words, the "raw material" from which history emerges.[141]

Gandhi utilized myths of *tapasvins* as models to substantiate his message and in the process—despite his personal contempt for being regarded as an icon—became a legendary figure in a mythmaking culture.[142] This became a key factor in advancing his message. Although many of his contemporaries attempted to dismiss myths about Gandhi as the "imagination of peasants," the myth of the *mahātmā* was instrumental in conveying his teachings. Lal reflects:

> It was, however, far more than the 'mythopoeic imagination of the childlike peasant at work' in the circulation of rumours. Gandhi's teachings—among others, the stress on Muslim-Hindu unity; the injunction to give up bad habits, such as gambling, drinking, and whoring; the renunciation of violence; and the daily practice of spinning or weaving—were doubtless distilled in these rumours, but an entire moral and political economy was also transacted in their exchange.[143]

In traditional texts, intense renunciation and the acquiring of inner power converge in paradoxical agreement. Deeply influenced by religious stories, Gandhi drew on their heroes as models of actions, creating his own narrative that he then used as a pedagogical tool. The legendary characters were, for him, a "living reality," and he sought to emulate them in his daily life. Against the backdrop of a country steeped in myths and faith in divine *avatārs*, Gandhi came to be perceived as a legendary character himself. As a character of legends, he imparted his method of nonviolence and soul power for the cause of *svarājya*. The matrix of myths, and his embodiment of a *brahmacārin*, allowed Gandhi to create his own epic tale in which he could reinterpret the ascetic disciplines and concepts, including *yajña, tapas, satkyariyā, rāmarājya,* and *sannyāsa*, rendering them consistent to his *satyagraha* movement for acquiring *svarājya*. The interaction among Gandhi's personal asceticism, his hermeneutic of myths, his embodiment of sacrifice and power, his authority as *Mahātmā* to interpret *nivṛtti* for the purpose of *pravṛtti*, and the Indian proclivity for mythmaking characterized his unconventional synthesis of asceticism and activism.

Conclusion

Gandhi's Dynamic Synthesis of Renunciation and Social Action

> At the time of writing I never think of what I have said before. My aim is not to be consistent with my previous statements on a given question, but to be consistent with truth as it may present itself to me at a given moment. The result has been that I have grown from truth to truth.
>
> —M. K. Gandhi

> Foolish consistency is the hobgoblin of little minds, adored by little statesmen and philosophers and divines. With consistency a great soul has simply nothing to do.
>
> —Ralph Waldo Emerson

> In formal logic a contradiction is the signal of a defeat; but in the evolution of real knowledge it marks the first step in progress towards victory.
>
> —Alfred North Whitehead

The comprehensive value of *brahmacarya* for Gandhi in the political arena was a surprise both to those within and those outside his cultural context. This book is an attempt to clarify some of the ways in which Gandhi's applications of *brahmacarya* were too radical to be called traditional and, ironically, were too traditional for radicals, prompting Lal's comment that "to a very large extent, his [Gandhi's] views on sexuality and brahmacharya have been an embarrassment to his admirers, while provoking outrage among his detractors."[1] This research has reexamined the foundations of Gandhi's integration of asceticism with activism in order to understand anew the way he interwove apparently world-denying ascetic disciplines with modern secular ideologies of political independence, democracy, and gender and caste equality. With a synthesis such as this—combining the distinct categories of *pravṛtti* and *nivṛtti*—it is impossible to create a philosophy with smooth edges.[2] There are bound to emerge inconsistencies as well as contradictions. Nevertheless, Gandhi's *brahmacarya* emerges as a connecting thread, which runs through his religious, social, and political ventures.

Using Gandhi's own words, I have explored the dynamic behaviors, complex communications, and traditional religious and cultural resources (literature and myths) that relate his ascetic disciplines to his modern-day political activism. Avoiding any particular interpretive lens has allowed an analysis of Gandhi's ascetic activism that focuses attention on *what Gandhi himself said that he was doing*. This is not to devalue previous scholarship that uses various angles to understand Gandhi, but there has been a need to retrieve the underlying principles of Gandhi's religio-philosophical foundations that he himself considered to be essential.

The sheer volume and diversity of Gandhi's writings has created what appears to be a "politico-religious mishmash"[3] and "unsystematized and often inconsistent jungle."[4] However, it affords a view of both the scope and integration of overarching concepts in Gandhi's thinking, and their development over time. This hermeneutic validates Gandhi's own claim that "there is a consistency running through" his "seeming inconsistencies."[5] It is apparent in his dynamic use of myths, folklore, religious symbols and vocabulary, and reinterpretation of religious texts and rules for personal and political aspirations. Gandhi's engaged renunciation occurs within his traditional Indian framework, which presented him with the paradigms of *pravṛtti* and *nivṛtti*, which he saw as complementary, not contradictory. He selectively extrapolated modes of practice such as *tapas*, *yajña*, and ascetic disciplines to integrate them into a strategy for his nonviolent struggle through the method of *satyagraha*, which by definition comprises opposing ideologies. Although his consistency may not be readily visible because of his constant experimentation, Gandhi's commentary nonetheless reveals the coherence of his actions with his goals.

Gandhi himself did not see his thought processes as a theoretical pursuit, but always in the context of his actions. Just because Gandhi "never used the word 'dialectic' to define it does not mean that his method was undialectical," argues Richard Lannoy. At the same time, notwithstanding an apparent "dialectic of creative conflict," Gandhi's innovative synthesis, expressed through a wide variety of traditional myths, symbols, and embodied performance, was not bereft of logical coherence.[6] Gandhi claimed that he was simply extrapolating a tested technology from ancient tradition (asceticism) and applying it to modern goals. He often emphasized the importance of letting go of any profitless theoretical arguments when studying religious texts. Gandhi's approach to a philosophy of ascetic activism was not that of a theorist or scholar; rather, as he himself claimed, it was that of an artist. Even though Gandhi has been charged with indifference to art and aesthetics, he used the creative power of self-control depicted in myths and symbols in multiple ways—using his body, explaining himself through his commentary comprising thousands of written pages. Gandhi had an intuitive understanding of the communicative power of symbols and must have been influenced by the Tolstoyan definition of art as the transmission of emotion.[7]

This analysis seeks to make original contributions regarding Gandhi's synthesis and his applications of *nivṛtti* to the field of *pravṛtti*, in three areas specifically. First, Gandhi's synthesis of *pravṛtti* and *nivṛtti* was not a static political strategy; rather it was an organically evolving and dynamic program based on the ascetic disciplines of *sat, ahiṃsā, brahmacarya, aparigraha, mauna*, and fasting. In other words, he reinterpreted and used the disciplines of *nivṛtti* as instruments for the *telos* of *pravṛtti* (which for Gandhi meant social action for gaining India's political freedom). Moreover, in order to make his method consistent with this goal, Gandhi defined and described India's independent state in terms of the ideal of *rāmarājya* or *svarājya*, and political actions as *tapas* and *yajña*. Second, Gandhi took the unprecedented step of extending the scope of the practice of *nivṛtti*, traditionally the domain of the individual, to the masses, demanding that his fellow citizens—irrespective of caste, gender, and personal disposition—follow the same ascetic disciplines that he himself practiced. Third, Gandhi was original in creating a coherent narrative with which to communicate his strategy, most significantly in making *brahmacarya* central to his synthesis. His vow of *brahmacarya* presented proof of his complete dedication to service and the cause of India as an independent state. His status and moral standing as a *brahmacārin* allowed him to interweave selected traditional myths, folklore, and symbols to communicate the supernatural powers of *brahmacarya*, as well as to advocate his strategy—both of which aimed at inspiring mass mobilization.

Indeed, Gandhi's ascetic disciplines can be seen as expressions of his dedication to his religion. As Lipner puts it, "Gandhi's regimen of ascetic discipline, his subjugation of the body by recourse to dietary restrictions and other bodily practices, so often the cause of derision and criticism, was not undertaken for aesthetic or ethical reasons; it was an expression of religious belief."[8] Nevertheless, Gandhi's regimen of austerity was inextricably connected to his personal ethics, which he extended to his social and political ethos. Gandhi may not have been concerned about aesthetics in our sense of the term, but he carefully chose symbols for greatest effect in making himself the embodiment of his vision and practice. Gandhi's asceticism in the context of personal religious belief, his *brahmacarya,* has been, and still is, generally considered irrelevant to his political method. Gandhi scholars have, of course, analyzed his celibacy, or more specifically sexuality, using limited perspectives. Among scholars there exists a common suspicion about the relationship between Gandhi's unconventional practice of *brahmacarya* and his activism—a suspicion not limited to Western scholars but held even by his contemporaries in India, where the categories of *pravṛtti* and *nivṛtti* are typically considered in opposition.

Within Indian culture, Gandhi's adaptation of religious rhetoric and ascetic disciplines for the purpose of achieving public goals was not a novel idea. Many of Gandhi's predecessors and contemporaries had applied themselves to religious disciplines and invoked myths to inspire India's people for social action. In spite of the classic dichotomy between *pravṛtti* and *nivṛtti,* the permeability of their boundaries is evident in the traditional myths of religious literature, in which numerous *tapasvins,* priests, and kings observe intense austere disciplines—including vows of fasting, *brahmacarya,* and silence—to accrue celestial powers for material goals. Gandhi used such mythical examples to substantiate his actions. The more these components of renunciation are explored, the more difficult it becomes to confine them within closed categories. Gandhi's construction of an entire political strategy based on the ascetic principles was unprecedented. His unique application of religious renunciation for political purposes was neither entirely consistent with his native Indian paradigms nor with secular principles. His synthesis presents a paradigm shift within his own long-standing cultural tradition.

This study has attempted to analyze the role that Gandhi's austere practices, specifically his *brahmacarya,* played in his nonviolent activism. Through careful analysis of Gandhi's writings, I have focused attention on his own representation of *brahmacarya*. It has become evident that his vast and versatile rhetoric, used to appropriate, interpret, and substantiate the elements of *brahmacarya,* as well as his embodied representation of his brand of celibacy, constituted the core of his synthesis of asceticism and activism.

Brahmacarya: Its Ethical and Functional Value in Nonviolent Activism

How was Gandhi able to create a political instrument out of his apparently "world-denying" ascetic practices? In Gandhi's political strategy, the functional role of *brahmacarya* (in the sense of the private virtue of sexual restraint) continues to be a subject of public debate. For example, even in a recent study of Gandhi's celibacy and sexuality in the context of the *puruṣārthas* (the four aims of life), Parel assesses celibacy as "one of the eleven virtues recognized by Gandhi's moral philosophy." He argues that even though *brahmacarya* is one of the major virtues in Gandhi's "moral lexicon," it "does not play a foundational role in his ethics as do the virtues of truth and non-violence."[9] Parel's comment reflects a general consensus, in academic as well as activist circles, which deems celibacy to be simply a virtue or private pursuit, and Gandhi's *brahmacarya* to be a private ascetic discipline, a troubling obsession, or an expression of religious belief. However, for Gandhi, *brahmacarya* held an essential place in his activism. Eleven "observances" comprised his political strategy and personal ethics for the service of the country, and observance of truth and nonviolence was "impossible without the observance of celibacy."[10] Gier makes a connection between virtue and "self-mastery, freedom, and virility."[11] For Gandhi the private virtues of self-mastery were directly related to his vision of personal and political freedom (*svarāj*). However, even within the Indian religious context, where the power of renunciation is accepted, Gandhi's call on common people to renounce basic private pleasures for secular political goals did not fit traditional religio-cultural models in which renunciation is largely an individual pursuit. In the modern Western sociopolitical context, fulfillment of individual desires such as those related to sex and food is a sign of freedom, virility, and mental soundness; renunciation and sacrifice of sensual pleasures are accorded little or no value, especially in resolving political conflicts and involvement in social action. Therefore, the relevance of *brahmacarya* as a practice for activists addressing modern problems has not been taken seriously. As difficult as this practice is to understand, the role that Gandhi's ascetic practice of *brahmacarya* played in his nonviolent activism should not be ignored.

Specifically, *brahmacarya* was integrated with his activist strategy in the following ways. First, as discussed in chapter four, *brahmacarya* for Gandhi was never a private practice of a personal spiritual discipline. From the inception of his vow, he placed his *brahmacarya* in the context of public service, and directly related it to the origins of *satyagraha*. Moreover, he saw it is as an ethical necessity for a leader of a nonviolent movement to demand sacrifice from the movement's participants. Second, Gandhi located *brahmacarya* within the larger framework of his renunciatory practices—all of which he vociferously advocated as essential to *satyagraha*. As detailed in chapter 3, he scrupulously connected the pursuit of *sat* and *ahiṃsā* with *brahmacarya* and described the five *yamas* as interconnected. This integration subsequently led to his vision of *rāmarājya* or *pūrṇa svarājya*—a concept consistent with spiritual freedom, and far more comprehensive than the common concept of political freedom. Third, Gandhi explained the instrumental value of *brahmacarya* in terms of *tapas* and *satkriyā*—the moral force or power of truth acquired through austerities—as well as in terms of its strategic significance to *satyagraha*, which mandated noncooperation, self-restraint, and self-sacrifice.[12] Fourth, against the backdrop of Indian religious myths, *brahmacarya* facilitated Gandhi's dynamic embodiment of autonomy and sacrifice, and created his authority as a *mahātmā* and charismatic leader, which became a factor in mobilizing the masses. As a *brahmacārin*, Gandhi used symbols and myths that invoked the imagery of traditional ascetics in the Indian mind and lent coherence to his narrative.

Gandhi's Embodied Performance of Ascetic Activism

The potency of Gandhi's reworking of tradition leads us to review the role of ascetic disciplines in Gandhi's public image as "naked fakir" and "a poor mendicant"—an image that symbolized to the masses his synthesis of asceticism and activism.[13] Many scholars have written about Gandhi's genius in the use of symbols. Gandhi himself agreed that "idol-worship is part of human nature. We hanker after symbolism."[14] His public display of his ascetic lifestyle—his fasting, dietary experimentation, wearing of a loincloth, *āśrama* residence—as well as his open discussion of celibacy, were imbued with symbolic meanings intelligible within his culture. Gandhi's choice of metaphors was neither the contrived effort of a politician nor the prescribed hallmark of an ascetic. For example, with regard to his much talked about decision to wear a loincloth (*langoti*)—generally considered "a central symbol of ascetic identity," Gandhi emphasized that "my loin cloth is an organic evolution in my life. It came naturally, without effort, without premeditation." During his visit to England he admitted that his "loin-cloth [was] criticized, [and] made fun of" and "some seem to resent my wearing it." He explained that through this attire he sought to identify with the millions of naked Indians and, therefore, it was the dress of his convictions.[15]

Many of Gandhi's contemporaries and predecessors dedicated themselves to the uplifting of the poor, but others did not display their dedication through the body the way Gandhi did. Intriguingly, asceticism in Gandhi's view did not represent *nivṛtti* (in the conventional sense of withdrawal or turning inward); rather, he called it "the greatest art," and emphasized that "outward action is a symbol of inner action."[16] Gandhi embodied symbols that communicated his political strategy—a strategy based on simplicity, self-sacrifice, and self-reliance—as well as his private conviction that service requires renunciation of private pleasures. Asceticism became the medium of his communication, as conveyed by E. M. Forster in his well-known tribute to Gandhi: "He is with the great artists, though art was not his medium."[17]

Traditional Narratives of *Tapasvins*: The Precedents for Ascetic Activism

Most scholars have overlooked Gandhi's prolific use of ancient narratives of *tapasvins* to substantiate the role of his personal austere disciplines in relation to his political methods of *sat* and *ahiṃsā*. The traditional myths provided a backdrop against which Gandhi displays the inherent power of *tapas* for *svarāj*. Through the symbolic power of his bodily ascetic practice, specifically *brahmacarya*, Gandhi mediated between the mythical and the real world. In his practice of *brahmacarya*, Gandhi himself became a metaphor of renunciation and self-suffering reminiscent of ancient *tapasvins* of the epics and the *Purāṇas*. Using traditional stories and legends, Gandhi asserted the supremacy of soul-force over brute-force and substantiated his political method of *satyagraha*.

While claiming that his vow of *brahmacarya* was for practical purposes, Gandhi embraced the broad spectrum of psychosomatic and ascetic powers associated with the practice of *brahmacarya*. However, given the inclusive nature of his political strategy, he was selective in his choice of stories and creative in reinterpreting them.[18] Gandhi not only narrated traditional stories and referred to legendary characters, he also portrayed his own actions and controversial unorthodox practices of *brahmacarya* in the milieu of myths. In serious interviews about the validity of his method of *ahiṃsā*, he would interject obscure religious stories to connect the ascetic disciplines with mundane political ends.[19] Gandhi associated *brahmacarya* with mythical heroes and, at the same time, claimed its necessity for selfless and resolute service to India. The public response was immense.

The preceding analysis reveals that, seen through the Indian philosophical framework of the binary ideologies of *pravṛtti* and *nivṛtti* and in the modern secular context, Gandhi's *brahmacarya* may appear enigmatic—merely part of his personal "religious belief" or simply one of his "fads," or perhaps it was even "a Faustian bargain, bartering libido in exchange for social charisma."[20] Nonetheless, according to Gandhi, it was from the start an integral part of his sociopolitical program and eventually became the core of his ascetic activism.

Gandhi's application of the personal ascetic disciplines such as *ahiṃsā*, *sat*, *brahmacarya*, and *tapas* are vehicles for modern political and social issues; at the same time, his reinterpretation of the sociopolitical actions of noncooperation, protest, passive resistance, and self-reliance as ascetic disciplines is both original and paradoxical. Gandhi's use of *brahmacarya* for the purpose of sociopolitical activism is counterintuitive, and forms paradoxes in which religious parameters are reconfigured, social boundaries transgressed, and laws reinterpreted. Although the paradoxes invoke questions about Gandhi's synthesis, they also contribute to an evolution of the ideologies of asceticism and politics. Through his paradoxical synthesis, Gandhi sought not only to revolutionize religious paradigms but also to reform political principles and methods.

Gandhi's actual living out of his strategies produced paradoxes (in the sense of outcomes that were "unexpected" or "contrary to received opinion") that are not only inescapable but are also illustrative of his methods and objectives. The present analysis can therefore serve as a starting point for future research that analyzes such paradoxes and the revolutionary possibilities they present—in Gandhi's context in particular and in activist movements in general.

In his extensive study, philosopher R. M. Sainsbury underscores this point: "Historically, they [paradoxes] are associated with crises in thought and with revolutionary advances."[21] Gandhi's relentless negotiation between the religious and the secular, the saintly and the political, the mythical and the factual, between virility and femininity, love and detachment, and between his practice of *brahmacarya* and his simultaneous effort to empower women—all generated ambiguity and great anxiety.[22] This ambiguity has been described by Victor Turner as liminality—the betwixt-and-between condition—in the context of ritual process and performance. Gandhi's overstepping of the prescribed boundaries of public and private, religious and secular, raises questions. His self-control created awe in native Indians as well as fear in his British counterparts. This led British Professor Gilbert Murray, who met Gandhi in England, to warn against this "dangerous" enemy, Gandhi—who was a threat because he defied the normal human ambitions and cared "nothing for sensual pleasure, nothing for riches, nothing for comfort or praise or promotion."[23] By applying ritual theory, a critical study of Gandhi's ritualization of political actions and its utility in mass mobilization may lead to a deeper understanding of the role of ritual in secular public space. Perhaps ritual theory itself could be reworked in light of Gandhi's innovative performance and commentary. Gandhi's defiance of the standard boundaries between private and public could lead to an examination of the possibly arbitrary nature of these constraints in the field of social action.

Traditional descriptions of the ideologies of *pravṛtti* and *nivṛtti* have led some scholars to doubt the outcome of combining religious disciplines with mundane political actions. However, in addition to future theoretical and critical studies of Gandhi's philosophy, this research also opens up revolutionary possibilities inherent in his synthesis for addressing modern conflicts. In spite of rapid globalization—or perhaps because of it—interest in Gandhi's nonviolent methods continues to grow. Terrorism and war have ignited a debate about nonviolent approaches among individuals and groups seeking alternative methods for confronting aggression. Lipner underscores Gandhi's relevance to such discussions and emphasizes that "Gandhi helped us see . . . the various modes and agencies of violence in our lives, and its scope and moral complexity."[24] This understanding invites us to experiment with new methods consistent with our own cultural context and current challenges. It is clear that Gandhi's unique approach was a result of the dynamic interplay of his own convictions, his moral attitude, his enactment and narration of relevant myths, and Indian cultural understanding of *brahmacarya*'s inherent power. This particular combination will not apply in every modern context, but it suggests a fresh paradigmatic approach to contemporary conflicts.

Appendix 1

The following is a paraphrase of the story from the Mahābhārata *in which Śakuntalā narrates to King Duḥṣanta the story of her birth, which resulted from the celestial nymph Menakā's seduction of the renowned hermit Viśvāmitra. This classic tale underscores the yogic powers accrued through* brahmacarya *and also the challenges of controlling sensual desires. All the quoted material is from Van Buitenen's the* Mahābhārata *(Volume 1), unless marked otherwise.*

Sage Viśvāmitra performed great austerities so that "he bitterly mortified Indra, lord of the hosts of Gods. Fearful lest the ascetic, whose puissance had been set ablaze by his austerities, would topple him from his throne, the Sacker of Cities therefore spoke to Menakā. 'Menakā, you are distinguished in the divine talents of the Apsarās. Take my welfare to heart, I do ask you, listen. That great ascetic Viśvāmitra, who possesses the splendor of the sun, has been performing awesome austerities that make my mind tremble . . . and lest he topple me from my throne, go to him and seduce him. Obstruct his asceticism, do me the ultimate favor! Seduce him with your beauty, youth, sweetness, fondling, smiles, and flatteries, my buxom girl, and turn him away from his austerities.' "

Considering the difficult task at hand, Menakā expresses her own fear: "Should I not fear him of whose heat, austerity, and fury you yourself stand in fear?" Viśvāmitra was by birth a *kṣatriya*, but later became a Brahmin due to the force of his austerities. His prowess was legendary: he had been known for creating "an unfordable river of plentiful waters" and even creating a new galaxy. "A man of such austerity, blazing like a fire, master of his senses—how could a young woman like me ever touch him?" pleads Menakā. However, the fair-skinned Menakā, bound to fulfill the order of the King of the gods, descends from celestial regions to the *āśrama* of the sage. To protect herself from the wrath of the ascetic, she begs assistance of the Wind-god to blow open her skirt, and the "callipygous nymph" approaches the sage's hermitage.

> Then, while she, after saluting him,
> Was sporting in the sage's presence.
> Away the Wind-god carried
> Her garment, white as moonlight.[1]

Thus, the ever-moving wind blew her skirt and exposed her to the sage. The seer saw young and beautiful Menakā nude and became overwhelmed with her celestial beauty. "And remarking the virtue of her beauty the bull among brahmins fell victim to love [*kāmavaśa*] and lusted to lie with her. He asked her, and she was blamelessly willing. The pair of them whiled away a very long time in the woods, making love . . . and it seemed only a day." Thus, out of that bond of love the daughter Śakuntalā was born to the hermit and the Apsarā, Menakā.[2]

Appendix 2

The following is an extract of the mythical legend that Gandhi published in Young India *(1928) in order to address the contemporaneous and polarizing issue of "cow-protection." Gandhi creatively integrates his concrete applications of truth and nonviolence for the service of the masses with this mythical story.*

The story [in Kālidāsa's Raguvaṁsa] runs that King Dilip of the famous Raghu line, finding himself in his declining years without issue, went to seek the advice of sage Vasiṣtha his preceptor, and was told that the attainment of his desire was prevented by a curse pronounced upon him by Surabhi, the Divine Cow, on account of an unintended insult that he had once offered to her, and that the only way to remedy it was to propitiate her by personally serving her and by protecting her against all harm in her roamings in the forest. So dismissing all his servants, the King entered upon his penance . . . "offering her palatable mouthfuls of grass, rubbing her body, keeping off the gnats, following her as her shadow, halting where she halted, sitting down where she lay down, moving forth when she moved." . . .

Such was the power of the King's penance and so all-conquering his love that even wild Nature felt its spell. "When he entered the forest as its protector, forest conflagrations would become extinguished even without any shower of rain . . . the stronger animals no longer oppressed the weaker ones."

Thus, it went on for "thrice seven" days, at the end of which, wishing to test the devotion of her protector, the cow entered a cave in the Himalayas . . . and was suddenly seized upon by a lion unnoticed by the King, who was lost in contemplating the beauty and grandeur of the surrounding mountain scenery. Startled from his reverie by the plaintive lowing of the cow, the King, ashamed of his absent-mindedness, fitted an arrow to his bow to shoot at the lion, but to his utter amazement and dismay feel [felt] himself hold [held] as if by a spell and all his strength paralysed. . . . The lion . . . told him that all his prowess was vain, since he was not an ordinary lion but Kumbhodara the servant of God Śiva and was protected by the blessing of that God in consequence of which no arms could prevail against him. . . . "I know I am helpless," replied the King . . . but one thing still remains to me. I offer my body to thee as ransom for the cow and I beseech thee to appease thy hunger on my flesh and let the cow go."

The lion tries to move him from his resolve by a variety of arguments. "If compassion is your motive," he expostulates, "then your decision is wrong, since by your death you will save only one cow, whereas if you live you will as their father ever protect your people against all troubles." . . . The King . . . once more presses his request. "So be it," replies the lion at last and the King laying down his arms throws himself before the wild beast "like a lump of flesh," so that it might make a meal of him. . . . But . . . instead of the dreadful leap of the lion which he was expecting, flowers begin to shower from the heavens and he hears a gentle voice speak, "Rise up, my son." He gets up and finds the cow standing before him like his own mother, with milk overflowing from her udders and "nowhere the lion!" . . .

And since the King has discharged his trust so nobly she grants him his wish. "Do not think I can produce milk alone," she says to him, "if pleased I can grant any wish."

Dilip is here depicted as love incarnate. Faced with the dilemma whether to lay down his life to save the cow or to gain the merit of giving crores [millions] of cows in charity he unhesitatingly chooses the former and finds that he has thereby propitiated an angel unawares. His relentless pursuit of truth leads him to the discovery of the true way of cow-protection—the way of *ahiṃsā*, of perfect love and there through everything else is added unto him. . . .[3] The cow whose service and protection is enjoined by Hinduism as a sacred duty is not cow, the animal merely, but cow that in our sacred lore appears as the personification of the "agony of the Earth," and that pleads for redress before the Great White Throne whenever the Earth grows weary under its load of iniquity. Its service includes the service of the entire afflicted humanity, of all those "who toil and suffer and are weary and need rest," the service of Daridranarayana . . .

Notes

Introduction

1. Regarding the prevalent problem of "sensuality—adultery," Gandhi states: "Ordinarily, people fight [*sic*] shy of discussing this question. We, too, feel some hesitation. However, we think it our duty to place our views before the readers." Mohandas K. Gandhi, "India's Plight," in *Indian Opinion* (December 28, 1907), in *The Collected Works of Mahatma Gandhi,* 98 vols. [electronic book, CD-ROM] (Delhi: Publication Division Ministry of Information and Broadcasting, Government of India, 2001), 8: 33. Hereafter, the *Collected Works* is referred to as *CWMG*. Note: The volume numbers in the CD-ROM may not always correspond with the volume numbers in the printed collection. The total number of volumes also differs in the electronic and hardback editions of the *CWMG* (published by Publications Division, Ministry of Information and Broadcasting, Government of India: 1960–94).Therefore, to make Gandhi's work more accessible to the reader, the original publication title and date are provided. Note also: Due to a controversy, the Government of India has decided to withdraw the revised edition of the *CWMG* and CD-ROM until a further review.

2. Here I do not mean "this-worldly" in terms of what Oliver Freiberger describes as the Weberian "distinction between 'other-worldly' asceticism (the practice of monastics and renunciants) and 'this-worldly' asceticism (the practice rooted in the vocational ethic of Protestantism)," which is also identified by Weber as "the basis of capitalism." I rather mean by "this-worldly," the religious vows and practices oriented toward achieving specific goals, including miraculous power for affecting the environment, prosperity, and progeny. Oliver Freiberger, "Introduction: The Criticism of Asceticism in Comparative Perspective," in *Asceticism and Its Critics* (New York: Oxford University Press, 2006), 3.

3. Arti Dhand, *Woman as Fire, Woman as Sage: Sexual Ideology in the* Mahābhārata (Albany, NY: State University of New York Press, 2008), 65.

4. Qtd. in "Notes on Tilak's Letter," in *Young India* (Jan. 28, 1920), *CWMG*, 19: 331 n. 1; ibid., 331.

5. "Talk with Bhai Paramand," in *Harijan* (Jan. 20, 1940), *CWMG*, 77: 212.

6. Lubin elaborates on the broad spectrum of ascetic practices as utilized by householders. Timothy Lubin, "The Householder Ascetic and the Uses of Self-Discipline," in *Asceticism and Power in South and Southeast Asia,* ed. Peter Flügel and Gustaaf Houtman, Royal Asiatic Society (London: Routledge, forthcoming).

7. Richard Lannoy, *The Speaking Tree: A Study of Indian Culture and Society* (New York: Oxford University Press, 1971), 377.

8. Joan V. Bondurant, *Conquest of Violence: The Gandhian Philosophy of Conflict,* new rev. ed. (Princeton, NJ: Princeton University Press, 1988), vi, vii.

9. "My Friend, the Revolutionary," in *Young India* (Apr. 9, 1925), *CWMG,* 31: 142. Gandhi responds to a correspondent who defends India's revolutionary movement.

10. "My Inconsistencies," in *Young India* (Feb. 13, 1930), *CWMG,* 48: 314.

11. A. K. Ramanujan, "Is There an Indian Way of Thinking?" in *The Collected Essays of A. K. Ramanujan,* ed. Vinay Dharwadker (New Delhi: Oxford University Press, 1999), 41, 40, 42.

12. Girja Kumar, *Brahmacharya: Gandhi and His Women Associates* (New Delhi: Vitasta Publishing, 2006), 28.

13. See Edwardes, Erickson, Parekh, Alter, and Rudolph and Rudolph, for examples.

14. Bhikhu Parekh, *Colonialism, Tradition, and Reform: An Analysis of Gandhi's Political Discourse,* rev. ed. (Thousand Oaks, CA: Sage Publications, 1999), 205.

15. David Cortright, *Gandhi and Beyond: Nonviolence for an Age of Terrorism* (Boulder, CO: Paradigm Publishers, 2006), 9.

16. Winston Churchill (1930), qtd. in Larry Collins and Dominique Lapierre, *Freedom at Midnight* (New York: Simon and Schuster, 1976), 70.

17. Nicholas F. Gier, *The Virtue of Nonviolence: From Gautama to Gandhi* (Albany NY: State University of New York Press, 2004), 171.

18. Pat Caplan, "Celibacy as a Solution? Mahatma Gandhi and *Brahmacharya,*" in *The Cultural Construction of Sexuality,* ed. Pat Caplan (New York: Tavistock Publication, 1987), 271; Joseph Alter summarizes opinions of various Gandhi scholars regarding his celibacy. Qtd. in Joseph S. Alter, *Gandhi's Body: Sex, Diet, and the Politics of Nationalism* (Philadelphia: University of Pennsylvania Press, 2000), 5.

19. See for a broad survey of literature in Gandhi studies: Veena Howard, "Gandhi, The Mahatma: evolving Narratives and Native Discourse in Gandhi Studies," *Religion Compass* 1, no. 3 (Apr. 2007): 380–97.

20. G. Kumar, *Brahmacharya,* 25, 13, viii.

21. Nirmal Kumar Bose, *My Days with Gandhi* (New Delhi: Orient Longman Limited, 1999), 165–166. Ved Mehta also elaborates on this. Ved Mehta, *Mahatma Gandhi and His Apostles* (New York: Penguin Books, 1976), 190–196.

22. Erik H. Erikson, *Gandhi's Truth: On the Origins of Militant Nonviolence* (New York: W. W. Norton & Co., 1969), 97, 65.

23. Sudhir Kakar, *Intimate Relations: Exploring Indian Sexuality* (Chicago: University of Chicago Press, 1989), 1, 128.

24. Susanne Hoeber Rudolph and Lloyd I. Rudolph, *Gandhi: The Traditional Roots of His Charisma* (Chicago: The University of Chicago Press, 1983), 5, 95, 94.

25. Alter, *Gandhi's Body*, x, 138.

26. Jad Adams, *Gandhi: Naked Ambition* (London: Quercus, 2010), 91, 92.

27. Joseph Lelyveld, *Great Soul: Mahatma Gandhi and His Struggle with India* (New York: Alfred A. Knopf, 2011), 88, 306. 307.

28. Vinay Lal, "Nakedness, Nonviolence, and Brahmacharya: Gandhi's Celibate Sexuality," *Journal of the History of Sexuality* 9, no. 1–2 (Jan.–Apr. 2000), 105, 119, 133.

29. Gier tests "Douglas R. Brooks' Ten 'Principal Generic Features of Hindu Tantricism' Against Gandhi's Spiritual Practices." Nicholas F. Gier, "Was Gandhi a Tantric?" *Gandhi Marg* 29, no. 1 (Apr.–June 2007), 29, 33.

30. "The Doctrine of the Sword," in *Young India* (Aug. 11, 1920), *CWMG*, 21: 134.

Chapter 1

1. Etymologically, the word *nivṛtti* consists of √vṛtti, meaning "fluctuation or movement" plus the prefix *ni*, meaning "cessation of activity"; in *pravṛtti*, the prefix *pra* added to √vṛtti implies "outward movement"; *mārga*, meaning "path."

2. Mahadevbhaini Diary (July 21, 1932), *CWMG*, 56: 226.

3. Ibid., 227.

4. Kripalani underscores a common critical sentiment about Gandhi's synthesizing the material and spiritual in his personal political philosophy. J. B. Kripalani, *Gandhi: His Life and Thought* (Delhi: Publications Division, Government of India, reprinted 2005), 324–325.

5. June O'Connor, *The Quest for Political and Spiritual Liberation: A Study in the Thought of Sri Aurobindo Ghose* (Rutherford, NJ: Associated University Presses, 1977), 62.

6. T. S. Rukmani, *Saṁnyāsin in the Hindu Tradition: Changing Perspectives* (New Delhi: D. K. Printworld (P) Ltd., 2011), 23.

7. In his comprehensive study of the virtue of nonviolence and postmodern interpretation of Gandhi, Gier considers Gandhi's approach contrary to Indian ascetic traditions: "Gandhi's this-worldly asceticism and political activism stands in stark contrast to this yogic tradition." Gier, *The Virtue of Nonviolence*, 19, 58, 59.

8. "To the Learned Narasinharao," in *Navajivan* (Dec. 29, 1920), *CWMG*, 22: 159.

9. Louis Dumont, *Religion/Politics and History in India: Collected Papers in Indian Sociology* (Paris and Hague: Mouton Publishers, 1970), 45, 43.

10. Patrick Olivelle, "Deconstruction of the Body in Indian Asceticism," in *Asceticism*, ed. Vincent L. Wimbush and Richard Valantasis (New York: Oxford University Press, 2002), 188.

11. Bailey maps out the historical development of these ideologies in Indian thought—including in the heterodox philosophies of Jainism and Buddhism, and provides literal definitions as well as the end goals of these ideologies. Bailey's analysis suggests cognation of *vṛtti* with the Latin *vertere*, meaning "to turn," and he also sees a semantic relationship with the English words, *extrovert*, meaning "turning outwards," which he equates to *pravṛtti*, and *introvert*, meaning "turning inward," which he equates to *nivṛtti*. Greg Bailey, *Materials for the Study of Ancient Indian Ideologies: Pravṛtti and Nivṛtti* (Torino, Italy: Indologica Taurinensia, 1985), 17, 18.

12. *Nivṛtti* "centres on renunciation of the social world and advocates the adoption of an ascetic life-style"; *pravṛtti* "centres on the figure of the householder" who "participates actively in the world and embodies in his life-style all that evaluates the world and society in a positive manner." Ibid., 10, 17.

13. Dhand, 33, 38–40.

14. Śaṃkarācārya in his commentary on the *Bhagavad-Gītā* cites various passages from the *Upaniṣads* highlighting the value of renunciation for the seeker for ultimate freedom. For example: "[R]enunciation of all action is enjoined on the seeker of moksha, as the following passages from the *sruti* show: . . . 'Renunciation alone excelled' (Taittriya-Up. 4–78, 79)." *The Bhagavad Gita with the Commentary of Sri Sankaracharya*, Samata ed., trans. Alladi Mahadeva Sastry (Madras, India: Samata Books, 1977), 86.

15. *Srīmad Bhagavad Gītā Bhāṣya of Sri Saṁkarācārya*, trans. Dr. A. G. Krishna Warrier (Madras, India: Sri Ramakrishna Math, 2005), 96.

16. *Mahābhārata*, Vol. 6, trans. M. N. Dutt (Delhi: Parimal Publications, 1994), (Shanti Parva CCXLI: 7), 365.

17. Patrick Olivelle, *The Āśrama System: The History of Hermeneutics of a Religious Institution* (New York: Oxford University Press, 1993), 65.

18. *The Dhammapada*, trans. and ed. S. Radhakrishnan (New Delhi: Oxford University Press, 1950), chapter VII: 2, 89.

19. "The End of the Struggle," in *Indian Opinion* (July 8, 1914), *CWMG*, 14: 205.

20. M. G. Bhagat, *Ancient Indian Asceticism* (New Delhi: Munshiram Manoharlal Publishers, 1976), 14.

21. *Tapaścāsmi tapasviṣu* (I am the austerity in ascetics)—and later enumerates the austerities of body, speech, and mind. *The Bhagavad Gita with the Commentary of Sri Sankaracharya* (VII: 9 and XVII: 14–16), 211, 433–435.

22. S. Radhakrishnan, trans. and ed., *The Principal Upaniṣads* (Atlantic Highlands, NJ: Humanities Press, 1992), 109.

23. Richard L. Park, *India's Political System* (Englewood Cliffs, NJ: Prentice-Hall, 1967), 8.

24. Norman D. Palmer, *The Indian Political System* (Houghton Mifflin Company: Boston, 1961), 26.

25. Qtd. in Ramachandra Guha, *India After Gandhi: The History of the World's Largest Democracy* (New York: HarperCollins Publishers, 2007), 4.

26. Mohandas K. Gandhi, *Hind Swaraj or Indian Home Rule* (Ahmedabad, India: Navajivan Publishing House, 2009), 92. Gandhi records "Testimonies by Eminent Men" (for other documents, see pp. 92–96).

27. Robert D. Baird provides an account of religious movements such as Arya Samaj and Brahmo Samaj and religious thinkers including Vivekananda, Swami Dayanand Sarasvati (both of them were *saṁnyāsins*), Rabindra Nath Tagore, and Sri Aurobindo who led the way to revitalize Hindu tradition and put forth their constructive social, religious, and political vision for India. Robert D. Baird, "'Secular State' and the Indian Constitution," in *Religion in Modern India*, ed. Robert D. Baird (New Delhi: Monohar Publications, 1981), 394.

28. J. T. F. Jordens, "Gandhi's Religion and the Hindu Heritage," in *Gandhi India and the World: An International Symposium*, ed. Sibnarayan Ray (Philadelphia: Temple University Press, 1970), 53.

29. Alter, *Gandhi's Body*, 51.

30. *Navajivan* (Jan. 27, 1921), *CWMG*, 22: 233.

31. Bhagat, 14.

32. J. A. B. van Buitenen, trans., *The Mahābhārata: The Book of the Beginning*, vol. 1, paperback ed. (Chicago: University of Chicago Press, 1980), 436 n. 1.1.

33. Ibid., 333. See the entire story of "Vasiṣṭha," pp. 329–342.

34. R. K. Narayan, *Gods, Demons, and Others* (Chicago: The University of Chicago Press, 1993), 83. See the story "Viswamitra," pp. 64–84.

35. "Letter to Nagjibhai" (Apr. 8, 1926), *CWMG*, 35: 41.

36. *The Bhagavad Gita with the Commentary of Sri Sankaraçharya* (XVII 14–19) 433–436.

37. Rukmani, *Saṁnyāsin*, 20, 22.

38. Shyamji Krishnavarma was a renowned scholar and nationalist. He was also a political activist who propounded political, religious, and social reform. He demanded "complete *swaraj*." Gandhi praised: "He dresses simply and lives like an ascetic. His mission is service to his country." "The Deputation's Voyage—V," in *Indian Opinion* (Dec. 1, 1906), *CWMG*, 5: 490. Gopal K. Gokhale, a prominent Indian leader and politician, was considered by Gandhi his "political guru." "Speech at Reception in Hyderabad, Sind" in *Hindu* (Feb. 29, 1926), *CWMG*, 15: 191.

39. Bal Gangadhar Tilak gave the famous dictum: "Swaraj [Self-rule] is my birthright and I shall have it." "Triumph of Civil Disobedience," in Young India (Aug. 12, 1926), CWMG, 36: 191. Gandhi writes: "There can be no swaraj without swadeshi. 'Swaraj is my birthright' is the first part of the Tilak-Gita; the second part runs: 'Swadeshi is the duty born with me.'" "Fitness to Pay Homage," in *Navajivan* (Aug. 7, 1921), *CWMG*, 24: 49.

40. B. R. Nanda, *In Search of Gandhi: Essays and Reflections* (New Delhi: Oxford University Press, 2002), 25.

41. "Discussion with Workers in Poona," in *Navajivan* (Sept. 14, 1924), *CWMG*, 29: 96; "Interview to Yuga Dharma," in *The Hindu* (Feb. 18, 1924),

27: 6; "Opening Speech at Kathiawar Political Conference, Bhavanagar," in *Navajivan* Supplement (Jan. 18, 1925), 30: 71.

42. Gandhi wrote about some of the critics who criticized him to be a "shrewd fellow," "coward," and "cunning." "Doctrine of the Sword" in *Navajivan* (Aug. 15, 1920), *CWMG*, 21: 157.

43. Mohandas K. Gandhi, *All Men Are Brothers: Autobiographical Reflections*, comp. and ed. Krishna Kriplani (New York: Continuum Publishing Co., 1990), 77, 89.

44. Peter Phillimore, "Private Lives and Public Identities: An Example of Female Celibacy in Northwest India," in *Celibacy, Culture, and Society: An Anthropology of Sexual Abstinence*, ed. Elisa J. Sobo and Sandra Bell (Madison, WI: University of Wisconsin Press, 2001), 29.

45. In 1936, Gandhi published the letter by a young man in its entirety in the *Harijan*. "Heading for Promiscuity," in *Harijan* (Oct. 3, 1936), *CWMG*, 69: 422–423.

46. Gandhi writes for the *Young India* in August, 4, 1927. Gandhi, *All Men Are Brothers*, 54.

47. "Gujarat's Duty," in *Navajivan* (July 11, 1920), *CWMG*, 21: 28.

48. "Speech at Public Meeting, Vadtal," in *Navajivan* (Jan. 27, 1921), *CWMG*, 22: 239. *Yamas* and *Niyamas* include ethical principles such as non-harming, truthfulness, purification of the body and mind, and have been traditionally prescribed as prerequisites for the practice of yoga.

49. "Speech at Meeting of Sadhus, Vadtal," in *Navajivan* (Jan. 23, 1921), *CWMG*, 22: 240.

50. It is important to note that most of the physical intimidation perpetrated by the British was actually performed by Indians; the British themselves were rarely physically involved. Thus, Gandhi's use of religious language and mythic paradigms, while ostensibly directed toward British rulers, may have indirectly targeted the Indians who enforced their regime. For example, from the 1921 Records of Intelligence Branch, I.G.P. Calcutta report: "He [Mr. Gandhi] asked police not to do any zoolum [oppression] over the ryots [sic] who were their own countrymen. He wanted to tell the police and the army to do their job but not to interfere with the work which they were doing for the country." "Speech at Belur Math" (Jan. 30, 1921), *CWMG*, 22: 292.

51. Gandhi, *An Autobiography: The Story of My Experiments with Truth*, trans. Mahadev Desai (Boston: Beacon Press, 1957), 325, 326.

Chapter 2

1. Alter states that "almost all studies interpret Gandhian thought in terms of fairly standard Hindu concepts such as *shakti* (power) . . . *moksha* (final liberation), and *sannyas* (world renunciation)." He interestingly compares the wrestler's intense exercising with Gandhi's practices of fasting and walking: "one might even contrast, in terms of radical binary opposition, fasting and dietetic simplicity with exaggerated consumption, walking

and spinning with the seemingly endless repetition of *dands* [push-ups] and *bethaks* [squats]." Alter, *Gandhi's Body*, Introduction, x; 138.

2. Wolpert, 3, 4.

3. Alter suggests that the Rudolphs place "too much importance on the psychology of desire and power in Hinduism." Alter, *Gandhi's Body*, 5.

4. S. Radhakrishnan, *Indian Philosophy*, 2nd centenary ed., Vol. 2 (Delhi: Oxford University Press, 1989), 659.

5. "Letter to D." (Mar. 13, 1929), *CWMG*, 45: 226.

6. Raghavan N. Iyer, *The Moral and Political Thought of Mahatma Gandhi* (New York: Concord Grove Press, 1983), 10–11.

7. Julius Lipner, *Hindus: Their Religious Beliefs and Practices* (New York: Routledge, 1994), 122.

8. "Speech at Gandhi Seva Sangh Meeting—III" (Mar. 3, 1936), *CWMG*, 68: 260.

9. *Harijan* (Mar. 3, 1946), *CWMG*, 90: 1.

10. Karl Potter succinctly identifies the ultimate goal of classical Hinduism. Karl H. Potter, *Presuppositions of India's Philosophies* (Delhi: Motilal Banarsidass Publishers, 1991), 3, see for full discussion, 3–15,

11. Ibid., 36–37, 38.

12. "Letter to Lord Samuel" (May 15, 1943), *CWMG*, 83: 302.

13. "Answers to Questions" (ca. Dec. 1947), *CWMG*, 98: 344–345. Gandhi provides answers to a list of questions posted by Maganbhai Shankerbhai Patel.

14. "Who Is a 'Sanatani' Hindu?" in *Navajivan* (Feb. 6, 1921), *CWMG*, 22: 313; "Letter to Mathuradas Trikumji" (Nov. 1, 1921), *CWMG*, 25: 38.

15. "Answers to Questions," *CWMG*, 98: 344.

16. Mohandas K. Gandhi, *The Bhagavad Gita: According to Gandhi*, ed. John Strohmeier (Berkeley, CA: Berkeley Hills Books, 2000), 114.

17. Anthony J. Parel, *Gandhi's Philosophy and the Quest for Harmony* (New York: Cambridge University Press, 2006), 196.

18. "Letter to Shankaran" (Apr. 28, 1927), *CWMG*, 38: 327.

19. Qtd. in S. Radhakrishnan, *Eastern Religions and Western Thought* (New Delhi: Oxford University Press, 1993), 381.

20. Parel, 180.

21. Gandhi, *Autobiography*, 67, 265.

22. Gandhi states: "Renouncing through knowledge the worldly life—this is the attainment of *moksha*." "Problems of Non-violence," in *Navajivan* (Aug. 9, 1925), *CWMG*, 32: 274.

23. Georg Feuerstein, *The Yoga Tradition: Its History, Literature, Philosophy and Practice*, Unabridged, new format ed. (Prescott, AZ: Hohm Press, 1998), 49, 50. Emphasis in the original.

24. Satyagraha Leaflet No. 18: "True Meaning of 'Bhagavad Gita's' Teachings" (May 8, 1919), *CWMG*, 18: 25.

25. "Letter to Santoji Maharaj" (July 2, 1927), *CWMG*, 39: 146. Gandhi's writings also reveal that he had read the commentaries by Ramanuja, Madhav, and Vallabha. Gandhi wrote: "I have read Lokamanya Tilak's and

Shankaracharya's commentaries and tried to understand them as well as I could." "My Jail Experiences—XI," in *Young India* (Sept. 4, 1924), 39: 142. In his "Jail Experiences—XI," Gandhi writes down a long list of books, which include various translations by renowned scholars.

26. Arvind Sharma, *The Hindu Gītā: Ancient and Classical Interpretations of the Bhagavadgītā* (London: Duckworth, 1986), Introduction, xvi.

27. Śaṃkarācārya explains that Arjuna's grief arose due to his ignorance of his true nature and was "caused by his attachment for, and the sense of separation from, dominion, the elders, sons, friends, well-wishers . . . near and remote relations,—all this arising from his notion that 'I am theirs and they are mine.' It was when discrimination was overpowered by grief and delusion that Arjuna . . . abstained from fighting and proposed to lead a mendicant's life, which was the duty of a different caste." *The Bhagavad Gita with the Commentary of Sri Sankaracharya,* 22. Rāmānuja was also surprised by the despondent character of Arjuna, who "felt weak, overcome as he was by his love and extreme compassion for his relatives. He was also filled with fear, not knowing what was righteous and what unrighteous." *Śrī Rāmānuja Gītā Bhāṣya,* trans. Svāmī Ādidevānanda (Mlyapore, Madras, India: Sri Ramakrishna Math, 1992), 55.

28. Bankim Chandra Chatterji was a Bengali poet, essayist, and journalist. He is most famously known for his composition of the song "Vande Matram," which inspired the freedom fighters of India (and was later declared as the National song of India). His many prominent works include *The Śrimadbhagavadgītā,* a commentary on the *Gītā*—published in the Bengali journal *Pracāra,* later (his unfinished work) appeared in book form (1902). Tilak authored *Srimad Bhagavadgītā-Rahasya or Karma-Yoga-Sastra.* Vinoba Bhave's commentary on the *Bhagavad-Gītā* is published as *Talks on the Gita.* Aurobindo Ghose wrote his commentary called *Essays on the Bhagavad-Gītā.* For a list of prominent modern interpretations of the *Bhagavadgītā,* see Robert N. Minor, ed., *Modern Indian Interpreters of the Bhagavadgita* (Albany, NY: State University of New York Press, 1986).

29. Bal Gangadhar Tilak, *Srimad Bhagavadgītā-Rahasya or Karma-Yoga-Sastra,* trans. Bh Alchandra Sitaram Sukthankar (India: Kesari Press, 2000), 35. Tilak cites references from the *Bhagavad-Gītā* (Gī. 2. 18; 2.37; 3. 30; 8.7; 11.34), 1207.

30. Sri Aurobindo Ghose, *Essays on the Gita* (Pondicherry, India: Sri Aurobindo Ashram Trust, 1966), 58.

31. Qtd. in Michel Danino, "Śrī Aurobindo and the *Gītā,*" in *Holy War: Violence and the Bhagavad Gita,* ed. Steven J. Rosen (Virginia: Deepak Heritage, 2002), 45.

32. Ghose, 38.

33. J. T. F. Jordens, "Gandhi and the *Bhagavadgita,*" in *Modern Indian Interpreters of the Bhagavadgita,* ed. Robert N. Minor (Albany, NY: State University of New York Press, 1986), 88, 89. It must be noted that Gandhi does not mention his second encounter with the Theosophists in his *Autobiography.* See James D. Hunt, *Gandhi in London* (New Delhi: Promilla & Co.,

Publishers, 1978), 34. Hunt provides an account of Gandhi's encounters with the Theosophists.

34. Jordens, "Gandhi and the *Bhagavadgita,*" 88. Jordens notes that in 1929, during his stay in Yeravada Jail, Gandhi wrote a Gujarati translation of the *Gita.* In 1930 and 1932, "while in the same jail . . . Gandhi sent weekly letters about the Gita to be read out at Ashram prayer meetings." "Altogether, Gandhi wrote 360 pages about his favourite scripture, more than he wrote on any other topic." Ibid., 88.

35. "Letter to Parasram Mehrotra" (June 23, 1932), *CWMG,* 56: 43.

36. J. T. F. Jordens, *Gandhi's Religion: A Homespun Shawl* (New York: Palgrave, 1998), 135.

37. "Speech at Satyagraha Ashram, Ahmedabad," in *The Hindu* (Feb. 2, 1922), *CWMG,* 26: 29, 30; "Discussion with B. G. Kher and others" in *Harijan* (Aug. 25, 1940), 79: 127.

38. "I felt that it was not a historical work, but that, under the guise of physical warfare, it described the duel that perpetually went on in the hearts of mankind, and that physical warfare was brought in merely to make the description of the internal duel more alluring." Gandhi, *Bhagavad Gita,* 16.

39. Kees W. Bolle, "Gandhi's Interpretation of the Bhagavad Gita," in *Gandhi's Significance for Today,* ed. John Hick and Lamont C. Hempel (Houndmills, Basingstoke, and Hampshire, UK: Macmillan Press, 1989), 139.

40. Ibid., 137, 138.

41. "The object of Gita," says Gandhi, "appears to me to be that of showing the most excellent way to attain self-realization." He further states, "Salvation of the Gita is perfect peace." Gandhi, *Bhagavad Gita,* 17–18, 19.

42. Gandhi was reading all these books in his second year in England. He was approximately twenty years old. Gandhi, *Autobiography,* 68–69.

43. Hunt, *Gandhi in London,* 34, see for full discussion pp. 20–36, 100–101.

44. "Preface to Leo Tolstoy's 'Letter to a Hindoo'" in *Indian Opinion* (Dec. 25, 1909), *CWMG*: 10: 240. Gandhi summarizes some important points of Tolstoy's philosophy. He writes that Tolstoy believes that men should not accumulate wealth, no one should take part in fighting, and we should always do good to those who do evil to us. "Count Tolstoy" in *Indian Opinion* (Sept. 2, 1905), 4: 400.

45. "In India, we would have described him [Tolstoy] as a *maharshi* [great seer] or fakir." *Indian Opinion* (Nov. 26, 1910), *CWMG,* 11: 176.

46. Gandhi, *Bhagavad Gita,* 83.

47. "A Revolutionary's Defence," in *Young India* (Feb. 12, 1925), *CWMG,* 30: 248. (Gandhi published the "unchanged full text of the letter" by a critic who disagreed with Gandhi's methods of nonviolence and noncooperation.); 30: 243–249.

48. Mohandas K. Gandhi, *The Bhagavad-Gita: According to Gandhi,* ed. John Strohmeier (Berkeley: Berkeley Hill Books, 2000), 108.

49. Margaret Chatterjee, *Gandhi's Religious Thought* (Notre Dame, IN: University of Notre Dame Press, 1983), 174, 175.

50. Gandhi, *The Bhagavad-Gita,* 91.

51. Raghavan N. Iyer, ed. *The Essential Writings of Mahatma Gandhi* (Delhi: Oxford University Press, 1991), 311.

52. Jordens, *Gandhi's Religion,* 37.

53. James D. Hunt, *Gandhi and the Nonconformists* (New Delhi: Promilla & Co., Publishers, 1986), 51, 53.

54. Gandhi, *Autobiography,* 319.

55. "Satyagraha—Not Passive Resistance" (ca. Sept. 2, 1917), *CWMG,* 16: 9, 10.

56. Bondurant, *Conquest of Violence,* 109.

57. Iyer, *Moral and Political Thought,* 151.

58. "Letter to Purushottam Gandhi" (Apr 18, 1932), *CWMG,* 55: 256. "A Thought for the Day" (Nov. 20, 1944), 85: 255. "At the request of Anand T. Hingorani Gandhiji on November 20, 1944, started the practice of writing 'a thought' for each day and continued it for about two years." Ibid., n. 1.

59. Iyer, *Moral and Political Thought,* 150.

60. Gandhi, *Autobiography,* 34.

61. "Speech on 'Ashram Vows' at Y.M.C.A., Madras," in *The Indian Review* (Feb. 16, 1916) *CWMG,* 15: 167.

62. Bhikhu Parekh, *Gandhi's Political Philosophy: A Critical Examination* (Delhi: Ajanta Publications, 1989), 156.

63. "Interview with Louis Fischer" (June 1942), *CWMG,* 82: 417.

64. Qtd. in Iyer, *Essential Writings of Gandhi,* 225.

65. Iyer, *Moral and Political Thought,* 175.

66. "Talk with Congress Workers" (Apr. 17, 1947), *CWMG,* 94: 322.

67. The word *saccakiriyā* appears in Pali literature. In Sanskrit it is *satyakriyā*. W. Norman Brown, "The Metaphysics of the Truth Act (**Satyakriyā*)," in *Mélanges d'Indianisme a la mémoire de Louis Renou,* ed. Louis Renou (Paris: Boccard, 1968), 171.

68. Eugene Watson Burlingame, "The Act of Truth (Saccakiriya): A Hindu Spell and Its Employment as a Psychic Motif in Hindu Fiction," *The Journal of the Royal Asiatic Society* (July 1917), 436. Burlingame describes an Act of Truth (*satyakriyā*) as a magic spell—a favorite theme of Hindu storyteller. He highlights the manner in which the Act of Truth was performed and defines *satyakriyā* as "a formal declaration of fact, accompanied by a command or resolution or a prayer that the purpose of the agent shall be accomplished." Ibid., 429.

69. Heinrich Zimmer, *Philosophies of India,* ed. Joseph Campbell (Princeton, NJ: Princeton University Press, 1974), 166.

70. W. Norman Brown, "Duty as Truth in Ancient India," *Proceedings of American Philosophy Society* 116, no. 3 (June 1972), 252, 255.

71. Ibid., 260.

72. In this article, Brown cites legends from Hindu, Buddhist, and Jain literature in which characters perform the Truth Act by virtue of their commitment to their duty. The story of the prostitute Bindumati illustrates that the power of Act of Truth can be acquired by anyone who is committed to a specific virtue or commitment (*dharma*).

73. Zimmer, 160.

74. W. Brown, "Duty as Truth," 252, 259.

75. "Speech at Bombay," in the *Bombay Chronicle* (Oct. 22, 1925), *CWMG*, 33: 127.

76. Gandhi, *Autobiography*, 112.

77. "Speech on 'Ashram Vows' at Y.M.C.A., Madras" in *The Indian Review* (Feb. 16, 1916), *CWMG*, 15: 167. "Prahlad was a devotee of God persecuted by his unbelieving father, the demon-king, Hiranyakashipu. Gandhiji often spoke of him as an ideal satyagrahi." Ibid., n. 1.

78. "The Doctrine of the Sword," in *Young India* (Aug. 11, 1920), *CWMG*, 21: 135.

79. W. Brown, "Duty as Truth," 267. George Thompson also sees the connection between *satyāgraha* and *satyakriyā* as "immediately apparent and unobjectionable." George Thompson, "On Truth-Acts in Vedic," *Indo-Iranian Journal* 41 (1998), 129.

80. "My Followers," in *Navajivan* (Apr. 20, 1924), *CWMG*, 27: 276.

81. W. Brown, "Duty as Truth," 259; Thompson, 125.

82. "Discussion with B. G. Kher and Others," in *Harijan* (Aug. 25, 1940), *CWMG*, 79: 124. Gandhi clarifies his views on *ahiṃsā* in an interview with B. G. Kher (a former Prime Minister of Bombay), who visited Gandhi with a party from Poona. Ibid., 121–129.

83. Qtd. in Thompson, 140.

84. "My Followers," in *Navajivan* (Apr. 20, 1924), *CWMG*, 27: 276.

85. "What Is Truth?" in *Navajivan* (Nov. 20, 1921), *CWMG*, 25: 138.

86. Gandhi used examples from Hindu mythology. Kāmadhenu is a divine cow who could give her owner whatever he or she desired. The Philosopher's Stone is known as *Pāras*. When iron objects come into contact with *Pāras* they turn into gold. Mohandas K. Gandhi, *Non-Violent Resistance (Satyagraha)* (New York: Dover Publications, 2001), 39.

87. "Who Is a Satyagrahi?" in *Indian Opinion* (Nov. 5, 1910), *CWMG*, 11: 151.

88. Gandhi, *Autobiography*, 504.

89. Gandhi, *Bhagavad Gita*, 82.

90. "Speech at Workers' School, Bogra," in *Young India* (June 4, 1925), *CWMG*, 31: 381.

91. Denis Dalton, *Gandhi's Power: Nonviolence in Action* (New Delhi: Oxford University Press, 2004), 46.

92. Gandhi published Lala Lajpat Rai's (1865–1928) critique of *ahiṃsā* and his response in *Modern Review* (Oct. 1916), *CWMG*, 15: 251; "Is This Humanity-I," in *Young India* (Oct, 21, 1926), 36: 391.

93. Dalton, 46.

94. Bondurant, *Conquest of Violence*, 111.

95. *Hiṁs* is desiderative form of √*han*, literally meaning desiring to kill. Sir Monier Monier-Williams, *A Sanskrit-English Dictionary*, new ed. (Delhi: Motilal Banarsidass Publishers, 1990), 1297.

96. Zimmer, 171.

97. "Statement to the Press," in the *Bombay Chronicle* (Sept. 18, 1934), *CWMG*: 65: 8.

98. Parekh, *Colonialism, Tradition, and Reform*, 127.

99. "Is This Humanity-I," in *Young India* (Oct. 21, 1926), *CWMG*, 36: 391.

100. "Speech at Morvi," in *Navajivan* (Jan. 29, 1928), 41: 143; "Ahimsa v. Compassion," 45: 285.

101. Gandhi, *All Men Are Brothers*, 81.

102. Parekh, *Colonialism, Tradition, and Reform*, 121.

103. "Speech at Gurukul Anniversary" (Mar. 20, 1916), *CWMG*, 15: 205.

104. "On Ahimsa: Reply to Lala Lajpat Rai," in *Modern Review* (Oct. 1916), *CWMG*, 15: 252.

105. Patañjali, the author of the *Yoga Sūtrā* (II: 30–32) enumerates eight limbs (constituents) of yoga. The first two of these limbs are ethical precepts: *yamas* (codes of self-regulation) and *niyamas* (observances). *Yamas*: *ahiṃsā* (nonviolence), *satya* (truth), *asteya* (nontheft), *brahmacarya* (divine conduct, celibacy), and *aparigraha* (nonpossessiveness). *Niyamas*: *śauca* (purity), *santośa* (contentment), *svādhyāya* (self-study), *tapas* (austerity), and *Iśvara-praṇidhāna* (surrender to God). *Yoga Sūtras of Patañjali with the Exposition of Vyāsa*, vol. II, trans. Swāmī Veda Bhāratī (Delhi: Motilal Banarsidass Publishers, 2004), 473–504.

106. Parel, 121.

107. "Discourse on the 'Gita' (5)," *CWMG*, 46: 192.

108. *The Yoga Sutras of Patanjali*, trans. Sri Swami Satchidananda (Yogaville, VA: Integral Yoga Publications, 1990), 130.

109. *The Yoga-System of Patañjali: Or the Ancient Hindu Doctrine of Concentration of Mind*, trans. James Haughton Woods (Delhi: Motilal Banarsidass, 1988), 186.

110. Gandhi, *Autobiography*, 27, 28.

111. "A satyagrahi therefore expects to conquer his opponents or his so-called enemies not by violent force but by force of love, by process of conversion." "Speech at Nagercoil," in *Young India* (Oct. 20, 1927), *CWMG*, 40: 223.

112. Qtd. in Bradley S. Clough, "Gandhi, Nonviolence and the Bhagavad-gītā," in *Holy War: Violence and the Bhagavad Gita*, ed. Steven J. Rosen (Virginia: Deepak Heritage, 2002), 67.

113. "Speech at Gandhi Seva Sangh Meeting" (Mar. 28, 1938), *CWMG*, 73: 66.

114. "What Is Truth?" in *Navajivan* (Nov. 20, 1921), *CWMG*, 25: 138.

115. Parel, 63.

116. Monier-Williams, 1276.

117. Dalton, 3.

118. Ibid., 4, 6.

119. "Interview to Journalists," in *Young India* (Mar. 19, 1931), *CWMG*: 51: 220.

120. For Gandhi *svarāj* was "disciplined rule from within" not "license to do as you like" as the definition of independence may suggest. Qtd. in Iyer, *The Moral and Political Thought*, 349.

121. "Notes" in *Young India* (Dec. 8, 1920), *CWMG*, 22: 63; "Appeal to People of Rajkot," in *Harijan* (Mar. 18, 1939), 75: 178–179.

122. Peter van der Veer, *Religious Nationalism: Hindus and Muslims in India* (Los Angeles: University of California Press, 1994), 174.

123. *Pyarelal, Mahatma Gandhi: The Last Phase,* Vol., Book 2 (Ahmedabad: Navajivan Publishing House, 1997), 189–190.

124. "Two Posers," in *The Hindu* (June 12, 1945), *CWMG,* 87: 104.

125. "Speech to Christians, Kolhapur," in *Young India* (Mar. 31 1927), *CWMG,* 38: 236.

126. Chatterjee, 17.

127. Qtd. in Gene Sharp, *Gandhi as a Political Strategist: With Essays on Ethics and Politics* (Boston: Porter Sargent Publishers, 1979), 289.

128. "Speech at Delhi," in *The Hindustan Times* (Feb. 2, 1931), *CWMG,* 51: 164; "Rajkot," in *Harijan* (Jan. 7, 1939), 74: 391.

129. "Academic v. Practical," in *Young India* (Oct. 6, 1929), *CWMG,* 47: 202; "Speech at Prayer Meeting," in *Harijan* (June 2, 1946), 91: 21.

130. "Independence," in *Harijan* (July 28, 1946), *CWMG,* 91: 326; "Speech at Prayer Meeting" in *Harijan* (Mar. 23, 1947), 94: 46.

131. "Speech at Women's Conference, Sojitra" (Jan. 16, 1925), *CWMG,* 30: 107.

132. Qtd. in van der Veer, 173.

133. "Speech at Women's Meeting, Mymensingh," in *Amrita Bazar Patrika* (May 22, 1925), *CWMG,* 31: 364.

134. "To Women" in *Navajivan* (Nov. 28, 1920), *CWMG,* 22: 25; "Speech at Women's Conference, Sojitra" (Jan. 16, 1925), 30: 108.

135. Jacqueline Suthren Hirst, *Sita's Story,* Series ed. Julius Lipner (Calgary, Alberta, Canada: Bayeux Arts Incorporated, 1997), 34; qtd. in 51.

136. "My Notes," *Navajivan* (Aug. 17, 1924), *CWMG,* 29: 7.

137. See for further discussion on this topic: Veena Howard, "Gandhi's Reconstruction of the Feminine: Toward an Indigenous Hermeneutics," in *Woman and Goddess in Hinduism: Reinterpretations and Re-envisionings,* ed. Tracy Pintchman and Rita D. Shrerma (New York: Palgrave Macmillan, 2011).

138. Anup Taneja, *Gandhi, Women, and the National Movement, 1920–47* (New Delhi: Har-Anand Publications, 2005), 52–53.

139. "Benevolent Parsis," in *Navajivan* (Sep. 17, 1921), *CWMG,* 24: 201.

140. Dalton, 33. Scholars such as Spear, Dalton, W. Brown, and Parekh also note Gandhi's use of Hindu symbols.

141. Parekh, *Gandhi's Political Philosophy,* 107.

142. "Speech on 'Gita,' Madras," in *The Hindu* (Sept. 4, 1927), *CWMG,* 40: 21.

143. Gandhi, *Bhagavad Gita,* 63.

144. Ananda Coomaraswamy, "*Ātmayajña*: Self-sacrifice," in *Coomaraswamy: Selected Papers: Metaphysics,* ed. Roger Lipsy (Princeton NJ: Princeton University Press, 1977), 107.

145. M. Hiriyanna, *Outlines of Indian Philosophy* (Delhi: Motilal Banarsidass Publishers, 2005), 35.

146. A. L. Basham, *The Wonder That Was India* (New Delhi: Rupa & Co., 1967), 239.

147. W. Brown, "Duty as Truth," 264.

148. "Some Questions on Religious Issues," in *Navajivan* (Mar. 28, 1926), *CWMG*, 34: 469; "Discourses on the 'Gita' (77)" (June 9, 1926), 37: 196.

149. "Discourses on the 'Gita' (86)" (June 20, 1926), *CWMG*, 37: 204.

150. "[T]he word 'Yajña' does not mean only 'the Jyotiṣṭoma and other Yajñas prescribed by the Śrutis' or, 'sacrificing something or other into the Fire (*agni*) . . . The word 'Yajña' embraces all Action, which was enjoined by Brahmadeva on all created beings . . . in order to achieve the smooth running of the Cosmos, that is to say, for *lokasaṁgraha* (universal welfare)." Tilak, 915.

151. Gandhi, *The Bhagavad-Gita*, 23.

152. "Letter to Narandas Gandhi" (Dec. 18–23, 1930), *CWMG*, 50: 429–430; "Duty as Self-Sacrifice," in Navajivan (June 20, 1920), 20: 404.

153. Gandhi stated during his daily discourses on the *Bhagavad-Gītā* to his *ashram* mates. "Discourses on the 'Gita' (76)" (June 9, 1926), *CWMG*, 37: 196.

154. "My Notes," in *Navajivan* (Sept. 19, 1926), *CWMG*, 36: 332.

155. Parekh, *Gandhi's Political Philosophy*, 107.

156. Tilak elaborates: "[A]s the Bhāgavata religion considered the slaughter of animals included in the Yajñas as objectionable . . . Yajñas by sacrifice of wealth took the place of the sacrifice of animals; and ultimately, the opinion that the Yajña by means of prayer (*japayajña*), or by means of knowledge (*Jñāna-Yajña*) was the most superior Yajña, came into vogue." Tilak, 919.

157. W. Brown, "Duty as Truth," 262.

158. Mircea Eliade, *Yoga: Immortality and Freedom* (Princeton, NJ: Princeton University Press, 1969), 111. For an example of ritual transubstantiation see: The *Śvetśvatara Upaniṣad* (I. 14) symbolizes meditation as *yajña:*

> By making one's own body the lower friction-stick
> And the syllable *Om* the upper friction-stick,
> By practising the friction of meditation (*dhyāna*)
> One may see the God (*deva*) who is hidden, as it were.

Robert Ernest Hume, trans., *The Thirteen Principal Upanishads* (Delhi: Oxford University Press, 1931), 396.

159. T. S. Rukmani, "Tagore and Gandhi," in *Indian Critiques of Gandhi*, ed. Harold Coward (Albany, NY: State University of New York Press, 2003), 116, 115.

160. Yogesh Chadha, *Gandhi: A Life* (New York: John Wiley & Sons, 1997), 217.

161. "Letter to Naranndas Gandhi" (June 22–26, 1932), *CWMG*, 56: 58. Gandhi quotes a *mantra* from the *Ṛg Veda* (X: 130. 1) that states: "Hundred and one artists are working at the sacrifice which through the myriad threads overspreads the earth. Here are the elderly guardians. They watch the processes saying, 'Weave on here, do this right there.'" "The Wheel of Life and the Vedas," in *Young India* (June 2, 1927), 38: 485.

162. Gandhi, *Bhagavad Gita*, 217.

163. "Speech at Nadiad," in the *Bombay Chronicle* (June 12, 1918), *CWMG*, 17: 60.

164. Qtd. in Parekh, *Gandhi's Political Philosophy*, 99–100.

165. Qtd. in Danielle Feller, *The Sanskrit Epics' Representation of Vedic Myths* (India: Motilal Banarsidass, 2004), 268.

166. "Princely States," in *Hindi Navajivan* (Nov. 28, 1929), *CWMG*, 48: 36.

167. "Need for Firmness and Courage," in *Navajivan* (Oct. 3, 1920), *CWMG*, 21: 327.

168. Coomaraswamy, 132.

169. "The Forthcoming Conference," in *Navajivan* (May 11, 1924), *CWMG*, 27: 383; "Speech on Non-Co-Operation, Madras," in *The Hindu* (Aug. 13, 1920), 21: 156.

170. Radhakrishnan, *Eastern Religions Western Thought*, 329.

171. "The Wheel of Life and the Vedas," in *Young India* (June 2, 1927), *CWMG*, 38: 485–487. He quotes various *mantras* for spinners and weavers in the *Ṛg Veda* and cites the *Ṛg Veda* (X: 53. 6 and X: 130. 1). Most devout Hindus were familiar with the Vedic *mantras* through home or community rituals. Prominent hymns call for a collective performance of sacrifice. See, for example: "Meet together, talk together, let your minds apprehend alike: in like manner as the ancient gods concurring accepted their portion of the sacrifice . . . Common (worshippers) be our intention; common be (the wishes of) your hearts; common be your thoughts, so there may be thorough union among you." *Ṛg-Veda-Saṁhitā*, vol. 6, trans. and ed. H. H. Wilson and W. F. Webster (Delhi: Nag Publishers, 1990), (X: 12. 40. 2, 4), 519–520.

172. "Letter to Narahari D. Parikh" (Nov. 2, 1945), *CWMG*, 88: 271.

173. McWhorter describes ritual as "a highly versatile tool for imposing hierarchy and order . . . for producing docile and useful types of human selves." Ladelle McWhorter, "Rites of Passing: Foucault, Power, and Same-Sex Commitment Ceremonies," in *Thinking Through Rituals: Philosophical Perspectives*, ed. Kevin Schillbrack (New York: Routledge, 2004), 82.

174. "Speech at Dandi," in *Navajivan* (Apr. 13, 1930), *CWMG*, 49: 16, 17, 18.

175. Dalton, 115.

176. T. C. Kline III, "Moral Cultivation Through Ritual Participation: Xunzi's Philosophy of Ritual," in *Thinking Through Rituals: Philosophical Perspectives*, ed. Kevin Schillbrack (New York: Routledge, 2004), 199.

177. Scalmer presents a study of "the diffusion of Gandhian Satyagraha (or nonviolent direct action) from India to Britain." He draws on Turner's theory to "develop a deeper understanding of the forces that shape 'translation' and 'reinvention' in other contexts." He concludes by saying that "when Turner meets Gandhi, the intellectual sparks fly," affirming that Turner's theoretical ideas are relevant in understanding the "reinvention" of Gandhi's methods. Sean Scalmer, "Turner Meets Gandhi: Pilgrimage, Ritual, and the Diffusion of Nonviolent Direct Action," in *Victor Turner and Contemporary Cultural Change, ed.* Graham St. John (New York: Berghahn Books, 2007), 243, 244, 253.

178. Qtd. in Dalton, 192.

179. "Discussion with Hyderabad Aryasamaj Leaders," in *Harijan* (May 27, 1939), *CWMG*, 75: 191, 190.

180. Victor Turner, *The Ritual Process: Structure and Anti-Structure* (New York: Aldine De Gruyter, 1995), 108.

181. Rudolph and Rudolph, *Traditional Roots of Charisma*, 56.

182. Qtd. in Kevin Schillbrack, "Ritual Metaphysics," in *Thinking Through Rituals: Philosophical Perspectives*, ed. Kevin Schillbrack (New York and London: Routledge, 2004), 129–130.

183. See Abbott's discussion on Gandhi in Elizabeth Abbott, *A History of Celibacy: From Athena to Elizabeth I, Leonardo da Vinci, Florence Nightingale, Gandhi and Cher* (New York: Scribner, 2000).

Chapter 3

1. Judith M. Brown, *Gandhi: Prisoner of Hope* (New Haven and London: Yale University Press, 1989), 86.

2. "Heading for Promiscuity," in *Harijan* (Oct. 3, 1936), *CWMG*, 69: 421.

3. Jawaharlal Nehru, *An Autobiography* (New Delhi: Jawaharlal Nehru Memorial Fund, 1980), 513, 512.

4. "N.K. Bose's Letter to Kedar Nath and Others" (Mar. 16, 1947), *CWMG*, 94: 423.

5. Many scholars have drawn parallels between Gandhi's ideas on chastity and Victorian celibacy. According to Pat Caplan, "Chastity for both men and women was a key ideal in the Victorian value system. As Basch points out: 'The Protestant middle classic ethic required the man to repress his instincts and manifestations of pleasure and eroticism; he was thereby wasting his precious energy required for work and production.'" Caplan, "Celibacy as a Solution?" 287.

6. Gandhi, *Autobiography*, 21.

7. Qtd. in Lannoy, 388.

8. "My Jail Experiences—XI, What I Read [-I]," *CWMG*, 29: 87.

9. Gandhi, *Autobiography*, 89.

10. "My Jail Experiences—XI, What I Read [-I]," *CWMG*, 29: 87.

11. Vivekananda describes the physical, mental, and spiritual power of chastity: "Continence gives wonderful control over mankind. The spiritual leaders of men have been very continent, and this is what gave them the power." Qtd. in Jordens, *Gandhi's Religion*, 26.

12. "Heading for Promiscuity," in *Harijan* (Oct. 3, 1936), *CWMG*, 69: 422; The list of books that Gandhi presents is very long—around two hundred. The booklist is broad in topics and includes religious and nonreligious texts such as: the *Mahābhārata*, Tulsidas's *Rāmāyaṇa*, the *Upaniṣads*, Patañjali's *Yogadarśana*, *Bible View of the World Martyrs*, the *Crusades*, *Manu Smṛti*, the *Koran*, Cunningham's *Sikhs*, Hassan's *Saints of Islam*, the *Bhagavad-Gītā*, and

various commentaries by Śaṃkarācārya, Tilak, and Aurobindo, Vivekananda's *Rājayoga*, Shaw's *Man and Superman*, *Dialogues of Plato*, Carus's *Gospel of Buddha*, James's *Varieties of Religious Experience*, and Woodroffe's *Shakta and Shakti*. "My Jail Experiences—XI, What I Read [-I]," 29: 88–91.

13. Parekh, *Colonialism, Tradition, and Reform*, 85.

14. Gandhi, *Autobiography*, 209.

15. "Speech on 'The Secret of Satyagraha in South Africa" (July 27, 1916), *CWMG*, 15: 242.

16. "Letter to Narandas Gandhi" (Aug. 3–5, 1930), *CWMG*, 49: 422.

17. *Brahmacarya* holds a high status among other restraints because, as declared in the *Mahābhārata*: "Brahmacharya is highly difficult to practice." *Mahābhārata*, vol. 6 (CCXIV: 11), 318.

18. "How Did I Begin It?" in *Harijan* (June 8, 1947), *CWMG*, 95: 189.

19. During his didactic sermon Bhīṣma emphasizes the value of *brhamacarya* for attaining *mokṣa*. *Mahābhārata*, vol. 6 (CCXIV: 7), 318.

20. Gavin Flood, *An Introduction to Hinduism* (Cambridge: Cambridge University Press, 1996), 63.

21. Phillimore, 29.

22. Geoffrey Ashe, *Gandhi* (New York: Stein and Day, 1968), 94.

23. "Letter Manjulabehn Mehta" (Feb. 6, 1941), *CWMG*, 80: 54; "Speech at Gujarati Political Conference-I" (Nov. 3, 1917), 16: 119. In his long speech, Gandhi outlined in a great detail the meanings and results of *svarāj* regarding India's future as an independent state.

24. Parekh, *Colonialism, Tradition, and Reform*, 205.

25. "What Is Truth?" in *Navajivan* (Nov. 20, 1921), *CWMG*, 25: 136.

26. Ibid., 138.

27. Gandhi's interruption while cataloging his daily readings in his diary seems to represent his sudden grasp of meaning in midst of his self-study. "Jail Diary, 1922" (Wednesday, June 14), *CWMG*, 26: 412–413; "Speech at Gandhi Seva Sangh Meeting-VI" (Mar. 6, 1936), 68: 283.

28. J. Brown, 86.

29. "Fragment of Letter" (Mar. 22, 1914), *CWMG*, 14: 132.

30. Zimmer, 66.

31. Ramchandra Gandhi, "Brahmacarya," in *Way of Life King, Householder, Renouncer*, ed. Tirloki Nath Madan (Delhi: Motilal Banarsidass Publishers, 1988), 220.

32. During his discussion of *dhyāna yoga* (VI: 14), Krishna declares that the *yogi* pursues the path to self-realization by being *brahmacāri-vrate sthitaḥ*—established in the *brahmacārin* vow of celibacy. Śaṃkarācārya, in his commentary on the *Bhagavad-Gītā* praises *brahmcāri-vrata* as "the vows of godly life"—consistent with the literal meaning of the word. *The Bhagavad Gita with the Commentary of Sri Sankaracharya*, 191.

33. Mohandas K. Gandhi, *To Students*, ed. Bharatan Kumarappa (Ahmedabad, India: Navajivan Publishing House, 1953), 91.

34. "Speech at Samaldas College, Bhavnagar," in *Young India* (Jan. 29, 1925), *CWMG*, 30: 79–80.

35. Walter O. Kaelber, "The *Brahmacārin*: Homology and Continuity in Brāhmaṇic Traditions," *History of Religions* 21, no. 1 (Aug. 1981), 80. Emphasis in original.

36. Under the *Āśrama* System of Hinduism, the human life is divided into four stages (*āśramas*): The student (*brahmacharya*); the householder (*gṛhastha*), hermit (*vānaprastha*), and recluse (*sannyāsa*).

37. The *Chāndogya Upaniṣad* (8.5.1) compares the life of chastity of a student with *yajña*. Hume, *The Thirteen Principal Upanishads*, 266.

38. "Speech at Samaldas College, Bhavnagar," in *Young India* (Jan. 29, 1925), *CWMG*, 30: 79. Brackets in the original.

39. "Oriental Ideal of Truth," in *Indian Opinion* (Apr. 1, 1905), *CWMG*, 4: 228. Gandhi referred to the *Muṇḍaka Upaniṣad* (3.1.6) to argue against Lord Curzon's claim that "the highest ideal of truth is to a large extent a Western conception." The *Muṇḍaka Upaniṣad* (3.1.5) mentions *brahmacarya*, among other disciplines required for self-realization. "The Soul (Ātman) is obtainable by truth, by austerity (*tapas*), by proper knowledge (*jñāna*), by the student's life of chastity (*brahmacarya*) constantly [practised]." Hume, *The Thirteen Principal Upanishads*, 374.

40. "Letter to Labhubehn A. Sheth" (Dec. 16, 1934), *CWMG*, 66: 3.

41. *Chāndogya Upaniṣad* (8.7–13). Hume, *The Thirteen Principal Upanishads*, 268–273. Also *Brihadārṇyaka Upaniṣad*: (The Threefold offspring of Prajāpati—god, men, and devils (*asura*)—dwelt with Prajāpati as students of sacred knowledge (*brahmacharya*), (5.2.1), 150.

42. "Understanding as Distinct from Literacy," in *Navajivan* (Oct. 30, 1921), *CWMG*, 25: 28.

43. Radhakrishnan, *Source Book in Indian Philosophy*, 178; see pp. 177–179 for further elaboration on the rules for a *brahmacārin* (student).

44. Zimmer, 155–156.

45. The missionaries had discovered these facts. Bruce Tiebout McCully, *English Education and the Origins of Indian Nationalism* (New York: Columbia University Press, 1940), 186, 185.

46. The list of the influential figures educated in England include Dr. Bhima Rao Ambedkar (1891–1956), an Indian nationalist and Dalit political leader, and Muhammad Ali Jinnah (1876–1948), a leader of the Indian Muslim League and the founding father of Pakistan. Gandhi had close relations with each of these leaders.

47. McCully, 214.

48. Gandhi, *Autobiography*, 35–36.

49. Ibid., 39, 40.

50. Gandhi, *To Students*, 213.

51. Nehru, 73.

52. "Speech at Students' Meeting, Hyderabad," in *Young India* (Feb.28, 1929), *CWMG*, 45: 76.

53. "Swamiji as I Knew Him," in *Young India* (Jan. 6, 1927), *CWMG*, 38: 14; "Speech to Mysore Students, Banglore," in *The Hindu* (July 13, 1927), 39: 209.

54. "An Ideal Students' Hostel," in *Navajivan* (Mar. 3, 1929), *CWMG*, 45: 158.

55. Gandhi spoke at many colleges and student conferences. He received letters from students asking guidance and direction. One of the letters that Gandhi publishes shows "a student's perplexity": "Two things completely possess me: my nationalism and my overbearing passions . . . I want to be the first servant of my country and at the same time enjoy the physical pleasures of the world." The student ends the letter asking Gandhi's guidance.

56. Gandhi, *To Students*, 46.

57. Phillimore, 29.

58. "Speech in Reply to Seva Mandal Address, Bhadran," in *Navajivan* (Mar. 1, 1925), *CWMG*, 30: 253.

59. "What people call 'silent asceticism' (*mauna*) is really the chaste life of a student of sacred knowledge [*brahmacarya*], for only in finding the Soul through the chaste life of a student of sacred knowledge [*brahmacharyeṇa*] does one [really] think (*manute*)." *Chāndogya Upaniṣad* (8.5.2). Hume, *The Thirteen Principal Upanishads*, 266. Brackets in the original.

60. Zimmer, 144–145. Namuci, a word commonly interpreted as "he who does not (*na*) let go (*muc*)."

61. Vardhamāna (the twenty-fourth Tīrthāṇkara) came to be known as Mahavīra, the "Great Hero," because he conquered his passions by means of severe asceticism. Mahavira advocates five vows—noninjury (*ahiṃsā*), truth (*satya*), nonstealing (*asteya*), celibacy (*brahmacarya*), and nonpossession/nonattachment (*aparigraha*)—to exhaust the past *karmas* and stop the cycle of making negative *karmas*, which continue to bind the soul. The Jain text *Tattvārthādhigama Sūtra* prescribes five meditations for the vows against unchastity: "renunciation of hearing stories inciting attachment for women, renunciation of seeing their beautiful bodies, renunciation of remembrance of past enjoyment of women, renunciation of aphrodisiacs, and renunciation of beautifying one's own body." Radhakrishnan, *Source Book in Indian Philosophy*, 258.

62. R. Gandhi, 213–214.

63. Gandhi, *Autobiography*, 206.

64. Zimmer, 199–200.

65. Sikhism describes the five cardinal vices: *kam* (lust), *krodh* (anger), *lobh* (greed), *moh* (delusion or worldly attachment), and *ahankar* (pride or ego).

66. Gandhi, *To Students*, 47.

67. "Is There Satan in Hinduism?" in *Young India* (Sept. 17, 1925), *CWMG*, 32: 420.

68. "Discourses on the 'Gita' (59)" (May 2, 1926), *CWMG*, 37: 165.

69. "Ashram Bhajanavali" (Aug. 6, 1930), *CWMG*, 50: 350.

70. Gandhi was certainly familiar with early Buddhist legends that narrate the Buddha's encounters with Kāma. Kāma—the Tempter—appeared before the Buddha with the "bait" of the delights of the world and the "hook" of suffering and death to interrupt his realization of freedom.

71. In the original Gujarati version, Gandhi uses the Sanskrit word *viṣaya* for "carnal desire," implying all sensory enjoyments, which include sexual enjoyments. Gandhi, *Autobiography*, 31.

72. Kakar, *Intimate Relations*, 89.

73. Qtd. in Mehta, 196.

74. R. Gandhi, 215.

75. Mohandas K. Gandhi, *Vows and Observances*, ed. John Strohmeier (Berkeley, CA: Berkeley Hills Books, 1999), 50.

76. "Sex Education," in *Harijan* (Nov. 11, 1936), *CWMG*, 70: 102.

77. Martin B. Green, *The Challenge of the Mahatmas* (New York: Basic Books, 1978), 20.

78. "Discourses on the 'Gita' (60)" (May 4, 1926), *CWMG*, 37: 165. (Kumbhakarna is brother of *Rāvaṇa* in the *Ramāyaṇa* who was powerful, but slept for days at a stretch.)

79. In a letter to Gandhi one correspondent asked about the weapons used by Rāma to recover Sītā. According to Gandhi, "the weapons that Rama used were purely spiritual." "To Correspondents," in *Young India* (Dec. 1, 1991), *CWMG*, 25: 182.

80. Nehru, 512.

81. *A Sanskrit English Dictionary* offers various usages of the root word *tap*. For example, "to give out heat," "to be hot," "shine (as the sun)," to torment one's self," undergo self-mortification," etc. The noun *tapa* has also several connotations, such as "consuming by heat," "causing pain or trouble," "religious austerity." Monier-Williams, 436.

82. Walter O. Kaelber, "Tapas and Purification in Early Hinduism," *Numen* 26, no. 2 (Dec. 1979), 193.

83. Eliade, *Yoga*, 106.

84. "Letter to Maurice Frydman" (July 10, 1939), *CWMG*, 76: 105.

85. Eliade, *Yoga*, 50.

86. "A Key to Health," in *Gujarati* (Oct. 11, 1942), *CWMG*, 83: 244.

87. "Speech on Non-co-operation, Calcutta," in *Young India* (Dec. 22, 1920), *CWMG*, 22: 89.

88. Iyer, *Moral and Political Thought*, 235.

89. "Duty of Self-Sacrifice," in *Navajivan* (June 20, 1920), *CWMG*, 20: 404.

90. The Ṛg Veda's Hymn to Creation (X: 129) states: "That One (Ekam) was born by the power of tapas, power of heat." Eliade explains: "Prajāpati creates the world by 'heating' himself to an extreme degree through asceticism—that is, he creates it by a sort of magical sweating. Eliade, *Yoga*, 106.

91. "I call [the Empire which rules us today] *Ravanarajya*." "Speech at Meeting in Nasik," in *Navajivan* (Nov. 10, 1920), 21: 449; "Speech on Non-co-operation, Allahabad," in the *Bombay Chronicle* (Dec. 1, 1920), *CWMG*, 22: 29.

92. "Speech at London School of Economics" (Nov. 10, 1931), *CWMG*, 54: 142.

93. "On the basis of several Ṛg Vedic passages Blair has suggested that 'the heat of the sacrificer himself was projected by magic off into space to

strike down the enemy wherever he might be.'" Kaelber, "Tapas and Purification," 194. The power of tapas is directed primarily against the rākṣasas, a group of demons or evil spirits: "Pluck up the Rakshasas, INDRA, by the root; cut asunder the middle . . ." *Ṛg-Veda-Saṁhitā* (III: 3. 17), vol. 3, 56.

94. Basham, *The Wonder That Was India*, 123.

95. "Speech on Indian Civilization" (Mar. 30, 1918), *CWMG*, 16: 377.

96. "Letter to Satavalekar" (Apr. 14, 1927), *CWMG*, 38: 285.

97. Qtd. in Jordens, *Gandhi's Religion*, 216. There is ample literature on Gandhi's public fasts undertaken for specific goals.

98. Kaelber, "Tapas and Purification," 201.

99. "Letter to Narandas Gandhi" (Oct. 9–14, 1930), *CWMG*, 50: 135.

100. Gandhi, *Autobiography*, 4.

101. Timothy Lubin, "Vratá Divine and Human in the Early Veda," *Journal of the American Oriental Society* 121, no. 4 (Oct.–Dec. 2001), 565, 579.

102. Lanman quotes the *Mahābhārata*: "By resolute will a man should control the organ of generation and the belly *(Dhṛtyā çiçṣnodaraṁ rakshet).*" Charles Rockwell Lanman, "Hindu Ascetics and Their Powers," *Transactions and Proceedings of the American Philological Association* 46 (1917), 138.

103. Jordens, *Gandhi's Religion*, 217.

104. Wolpert, 5.

105. Gandhi, *To Students*, 87.

106. "Notes," in *Young India* (Aug. 14, 1924), *CWMG*, 28: 487.

107. "What Should We Do?" in *Navajivan* (Sept. 13, 1925), *CWMG*, 32: 398.

108. "Speech at Gujarati Political Conference-I" (Nov. 3, 1917), 16: 116.

109. "Letter to Mahadev Desai" (Nov. 7, 1921), *CWMG*, 25: 62.

110. Nanda, *In Search of Gandhi*, 11.

111. Iyer, *Moral and Political Thought*, 75.

112. Joseph S. Alter, "Celibacy, Sexuality, and the Transformation of Gender into Nationalism in North India," *The Journal of Asian Studies* 53, no. 1 (Feb. 1994), 52.

113. Jeffery Paine, *Father India: How Encounters with an Ancient Culture Transformed the Modern West* (New York: HarperCollins Publishers 1998), 242.

114. *General Knowledge About Health [-XVII]*, "An Intimate Chapter," in *Indian Opinion* (Apr. 26, 1913), *CWMG*, 13: 98.

115. Swāmi Hariharānanda Āraṇa, *Yoga Philosophy of Patañjali*, 3rd ed., trans. P. N. Mukerji (Calcutta, India: University of Calcutta, 1981), 222.

116. Feuerstein, 67. Monier-Williams translates *ojas* as bodily strength, vigor, energy, ability, power. Monier-Williams, 235.

117. Qtd. in Gregory P. Fields, *Religious Therapeutics: Body and Health in Yoga, Āyurveda, and Tantra* (Albany, NY: State University of New York, 2001), 57.

118. Swami Vivekananda, *The Complete Works of Swami Vivekananda*, vol. 1, Mayavati Memorial, ed. (Calcutta, India: Advaita Ashrama, 1989), 169–170.

119. "Letter to Premabehn Kantak" (May 21, 1936), *CWMG*, 69: 24; "Physical Training and Ahimsa," in *Harijan* (Oct. 13, 1940), 79: 273–274;

"Speech at Women's Meeting, Madras," in *The Hindu* (Jan. 31, 1946), 89: 321.

120. Radhakrishnan, in Introduction to *The Principal Upaniṣads,* 110.

121. "An Intimate Chapter," in *Indian Opinion* (Apr. 24, 1913), *CWMG,* 13: 92.

122. Gandhi, *Autobiography,* 64.

123. "A Key to Health" (Dec. 11, 1942), *CWMG,* 83: 246.

124. Rudolph and Rudolph, *Traditional Roots of Gandhi's Charisma,* 67–68.

125. Meena Khandelwal, "Sexual Fluids, Emotions, Morality: Notes on the Gendering of Brahamacharya," in *Celibacy, Culture, and Society: An Anthropology of Sexual Abstinence,* ed. Elisa J. Sobo and Sandra Bell (Madison, WI: University of Wisconsin Press, 2001), 169, 167, 169.

126. "Questions on Education—IV," in *Navajivan* (June 24, 1928), *CWMG,* 42: 168.

127. Qtd. in Green, 38.

128. "Truth v. 'Brahmacharya,'" in *Young India* (Feb. 25, 1926), *CWMG,* 34: 293.

129. "Ethics of Destruction," in *Young India* (Sept. 1, 1921), *CWMG,* 24: 162.

130. Kakar, *Intimate Relations,* 96.

131. "Religious Authority for Non-Co-Operation," in *Young India* (Aug. 25, 1920), *CWMG,* 21: 201.

132. "Letter to 'Indian Opinion,'" in *Indian Opinion* (Jan. 7, 1914), *CWMG,* 14: 28.

133. Kaelber cites Eliade, "how two rather different *conceptual* systems, namely, Vedic sacrifice on the one hand and asceticism (i.e., *tapas*) on the other, were assimilated to each other." Qtd. in Kaelber, *The Brahmacārin,* 77.

134. Abbott, 225–226.

135. Parekh, *Colonialism, Tradition, and Reform,* 201.

136. *Mahābhārata,* Vol. 6 (*Śanti Parva,* CCXIV: 10), 318.

137. "In Confidence," in *Young India* (Oct. 13, 1920), *CWMG,* 21: 356.

138. "By the tapas (austerity) of brahmacarya, a king defends his kingdom;
A teacher by *brahmacarya* seeks a *brahmacārin* [a student].
observing the discipline of *brahmacarya,* a girl wins a youthful husband. . . .
By the *tapas* of *brahmacarya,* the gods drove away death;
Indra (the king of the gods) by *brahmacarya* brought heaven for the gods."

This entire section of the *Atharva Veda* is devoted to the praise of *Brahmacarya.* (Translation with my alterations.) *Atharva-Veda Saṁhitā,* trans. Satya Prakash Sarasvati. Delhi: Veda Pratishthana, 1992), 82.

139. "In Confidence," in *Young India* (Oct. 13, 1920), *CWMG,* 21: 357.

140. Paine, 242, 241.

141. Brackets in Lal. Qtd. in Lal, "Nakedness, Nonviolence, and Brahmacharya," 123.

142. Gandhi's constant company with female associates, his personal care from them, and his later life experiments of sleeping naked with women.

143. Johann Jakob Meyer, *Sexual Life in Ancient India: A Study in the Comparative History of Indian Culture* (Delhi: Motilal Banarsidass Publishers, 1971), 260.

144. In a Jain story, Subhadra is a celibate woman who keeps her sexual purity even in marriage. She is able to perform a miracle on the basis of her purity. Anne Vallely, *Guardians of the Transcendent: An Ethnography of a Jain Ascetic Community* (Buffalo: University of Toronto Press, 2002), 230–231.

145. Robert Payne, *The Life and Death of Mahatma Gandhi* (New York: E. P. Dutton & Co., 1969), 466.

146. Gier, *The Virtue of Nonviolence*, 11.

Chapter 4

1. Nehru, 512, 513.

2. Ashe, 183, 368.

3. "Letter to Amrit Kaur" (Mar. 18 1947), *CWMG*, 94: 137.

4. Gier, *The Virtue of Nonviolence*, 171, 129.

5. Sardar Patel spoke openly about Gandhi's practice of sleeping with women as an indulgence in *adharma*. Kumar, 336.

6. Gandhi admits that he gave up milk and other animal products for different reasons. "Walls of Protection," in *Harijan* (June 15, 1947), *CWMG*, 95: 230.

7. Gandhi, *Autobiography*, 208, 206. See for a full discussion pp. 204–211.

8. Jordens, *Gandhi's Religion*, 24.

9. Jordens, *Gandhi's Religion*, 24.

10. Gandhi, *Autobiography*, 314. "The Medical Officer in charge welcomed us. . . . he was at his wit's end. He hailed our arrival," Gandhi recalled.

11. "Satyagraha in South Africa" (Nov. 1923–Dec. 1924), *CWMG*, 34: 83. Gandhi wrote the assessment of the *satyagraha* campaign in South Africa during the voyage to London. Ibid., n. 1.

12. Gandhi, *Autobiography*, 316.

13. "Mr. Hills regarded these methods as cutting at the root of morals," recalled Gandhi. Gandhi, *Autobiography*, 59; 316.

14. "The Doctrine of the Sword," in *Young India* (Aug. 11, 1920), *CWMG*, 21: 134.

15. "The Meaning of the Moplah Rising," in *Young India* (Oct. 20, 1921), *CWMG*, 24: 448.

16. "Message to Countrymen," in *The Hindu* (Apr. 10, 1919), *CWMG*, 17: 408; 409.

17. Gandhi, *Autobiography*, 317, 207.

18. "He was not at that time aware of its mystic power, nor of its central function in the birth of spiritual man." Jordens, *Gandhi's Religion*, 24. Lannoy argues that Gandhi "was religious, but he certainly was no mystic." Lannoy, 389.

19. Gandhi, *Autobiography*, 315.

20. Parekh, *Gandhi's Political Philosophy*, 5.

21. R. Gandhi, 221.

22. Gandhi, *Autobiography*, 158, 159, 316.

23. "Discourses on the 'Gita,' (89) and (91)" (June 24 and 26, 1926), *CWMG*, 37: 208, 210; "Letter to Ashram Women" (Jan. 17, 1927), 38: 76–77.

24. "Prayer Speech at Ashram," in *Navajivan* (Apr 8, 1928), *CWMG*, 41: 357.

25. Parel, 148.

26. Gandhi, *Autobiography*, 317.

27. Ashe, 94.

28. Parekh, *Colonialism, Tradition, and Reform*, 204. These various leaders include Swami Dayananda (1824–83) of the Arya Samaj Movement, Vivekananda (1863–1902) of the Vedanta Society, and Swami Sivananda (1887–1963).

29. Sudhir Kakar, *The Essential Writings of Sudhir Kakar* (New Delhi: Oxford University Press, 2001), 104.

30. Elisa J. Sobo and Sandra Bell, "Celibacy in Cross-Cultural Perspective: An Overview," in *Celibacy, Culture, and Society: An Anthropology of Sexual Abstinence*, ed. Elisa J. Sobo and Sandra Bell (Madison, WI: University of Wisconsin Press, 2001), 7.

31. Nehru, 513.

32. *Saṃnyāsa Upaniṣads: Hindu Scriptures on Asceticism and Renunciation*, ed. Patrick Olivelle (New York: Oxford University Press, 1992), 42–43.

33. "Forward to Volume of Gokhale's Speeches" (before Feb. 19, 1918), *CWMG*, 16: 269.

34. Jonathan Schell, *Unconquerable World* (New York: Henry Holt and Company, 2003), 114–115.

35. Abbott, 16, 22.

36. Gandhi, *Autobiography*, 209.

37. In the *Chāndogya Upaniṣad* (8. 5. 2-3), the vow of *brahmacarya* is identified with various disciplines, including *mauna* (silence) and *anāśakāyna* (a course of fasting). *The Principal Upaniṣads*, 498–499. In the *Praśna Upaniṣad*, Sage Pippalāda also declares: ". . . They indeed possess that Brahma-world, who possess austerity (*tapas*) and chastity (*brahmacarya*), In whom the truth [*satya*] is established." *Praśna Upaniṣad* (1.15). Hume, *The Thirteen Principal Upanishads*, 380.

38. "Notes," in *Young India* (May 21, 1925), *CWMG*, 31: 376, 377.

39. Kirin Narayan, *Storytellers, Saints, and Scoundrels: Folk Narrative in Hindu Religious Teaching* (Philadelphia: University of Pennsylvania Press, 1989), 64, 79.

40. Dumont, 46.

41. Qtd. in K. Narayan, 70, 71, 72.

42. In *Kali Yuga* (the Dark Age)—when *dharma* (Truth, ethical laws) was rapidly degenerating due to foreign invasions and religious corruption, a *mahātmā* came to be defined as one who fulfills the prophecy of ancient

scriptures—the restoration of *dharma*. The Hindu scriptures laud the virtues of compassion and restraint of the passions in *Kali Yuga*: "'In the *Krita Yuga*,' says Vrihaspati, 'the prevailing virtue is declared to be religious austerity; in the *Trita*, divine knowledge; in the *Divapara*, sacrifices; and in the *Kali Yuga*, charity, compassion, and restraint of passions."' John Campbell Oman, *The Mystics, Ascetics and Saints of India: A Study of Sadhuism, with an Account of the Yogis, Sanyasis, Bairagis, and Other Strange Hindu Sectarians* (London: T. F. Unwin, 1903), 141.

43. Ashe, 144.

44. "Telegram to Mridula Sarabhai" (May 7, 1945), *CWMG*, 86: 320 n. 1. "Vivekananda used to say fifty years ago, 'India required great Vivekanandas to serve the poor and the downtrodden and bring about their liberation, both political and spiritual.'"

45. "Opening Speech at Kathiawar Political Conference, Bhavnagar," in *Navajivan* Supplement (Jan. 18, 1925), *CWMG*, 30: 72.

46. K. Narayan, 75.

47. In her article, "Feminine Behavior and Radical Action," Phyllis Mack draws on Turner's theory to explain the religious behavior of three radical religious movements: Franciscans, the early Quakers, and the followers of Gandhi. Phyllis Mack, "Feminine Behavior and Radical Action: Franciscans, Quakers, and the Followers of Gandhi," *Signs: Journal of Women in Culture and Society* 11, no. 3 (1986): 457–477.

48. K. Narayan, 75.

49. Turner, *Ritual Process*, 95.

50. Qtd. in K. Narayan, 75.

51. "Lectures on Religion," in *Indian Opinion* (Apr. 15, 1905), *CWMG*, 4: 244.

52. Sabarmati Ashram on the banks of Sabarmati River (1917), and then Wardha Ashram (1934) in a village setting. Sabarmati Ashram is famous as Satyagraha Ashram and Wardha Ashram is also known as Sevagram Ashram.

53. Evidently, the tradition of ascetics residing in *āśramas* had become fully established by the time of the *Upaniṣads*. *Śri Jābāldarśnopaniṣad*, 5.4 recommends that an ascetic create a dwelling in a calm and secluded place: "In front of a mountain, on the banks of a river, / in the root of a bilva tree, or in a forest, / in such a pleasant and pure place having created a dwelling [a seeker] remains still." (My own translation.) *Satsang Yoga*, ed. Mahrishi Parmhansji Maharaj (Bihar: Akhil Bhartiya Santmat Satsang Prakashan, 1985), 57.

54. Qtd. in Gandhi, *Vows and Observances*, 11.

55. "Śakuntalā and the Ring of Recollection," in *Theater of Memory: The Plays of Kālidāsa*, trans. and ed. Barbara Stoler Miller (New York: Columbia University Press, 1984), 166.

56. In South Africa, for the purpose of fighting for the rights of the Indian community, Gandhi established two communities, Phoenix Settlement near Durban in 1904 and Tolstoy Farm near Johannesburg in 1910. The Phoenix Settlement "sought to put into practice the essential teachings of

Ruskin and Tolstoy to assist in the removal of the grievances of Indians in South Africa." "Address to Ashram Inmates" (Feb. 17, 1919), *CWMG*, 17: 286 n. 1.

57. Jordens, *Gandhi's Religion*, 161.

58. "Letter to Maganlal Gandhi" (Nov. 24, 1909), *CWMG*, 10: 316. Many words, such as *maṭha* and *āśrama*, are Sanskrit words that have been adopted in the other Indian languages. They are usually used for the dwellings of ascetics, *sādhus*, and *mahātmās*.

59. Payne, 231.

60. Jordens, *Gandhi's Religion*, 161.

61. Ashe traces the history of the honorific title of *mahātmā*: "At least one admirer saluted him in this way while he was still in South Africa. But Tagore launched the cultus. He was already referring to 'Mahatma Gandhi' in correspondence that February [1914], and he spoke in a poem of 'the Great Soul in beggar's garb,' an allusion to the simplicity of dress which Gandhi was beginning to practise." Ashe, 144.

62. Gandhi, *Autobiography*, 389.

63. Gandhi, *Autobiography*, 389, 394.

64. "Habermas bases his early conceptualization of civil society and the public sphere on an examination of political life in 18th-century England, France, and Germany. He finds a public sphere embedded in the activities of coffee houses, literary and cultural societies, political clubs, and literary journals and journals of opinion." Susanne Hoeber Rudolph and Lloyd I. Rudolph, *Postmodern Gandhi and Other Essays* (Chicago: University of Chicago Press, 2006), 145, 149.

65. In this vein, the Rudolphs compare Gandhi's *āśramas* with the Habermasian "bourgeois public sphere" concerned with "politics, law, and institutional change." They also draw similarities and point out differences between the Western model of Habermas's "public spheres" and Gandhi's *āśrama* communities. According to them, the coffeehouse and *āśramas* both lend themselves to "civic virtue and realizing the public good." Ibid., 162, 159.

66. Ibid., 162.

67. Gandhi, *Vows and Observances*, 114.

68. "Draft Constitution for the Ashram" (before May 20, 1915), *CWMG*, 14: 453.

69. Victor Turner, *The Forest of Symbols: Aspects of Ndembu Ritual* (Ithaca: Cornell University Press, 1967), 100.

70. Gandhi announced that "the Ashram does not follow the *varnashram* dharma." "Draft Constitution for the Ashram" (before May 20, 1915), *CWMG*, 14: 456.

71. Turner concludes that much of the behavior in seclusion situations that has been recorded by ethnographers "falls under the principle: 'Each for all, and all for each.'" Turner, *The Forest*, 100–101.

72. Jordens, *Gandhi's Religion*, 164.

73. "My Shame and Sorrow," in the *Bombay Chronicle* (Apr. 8, 1929), *CWMG*, 45: 308.

74. Ashe, 180.

75. Gandhi, *Vows and Observances*, 114.

76. Ibid., 40.

77. Gandhi, *Autobiography*, 206, 208.

78. Kumar, 13. Qtd. in 15.

79. "Discussion with Swami Anand and Kedar Nath" (Mar. 15–16, 1947), *CWMG*, 94: 119. Gandhi states that he had been in closest touch with the West in South Africa. He also had known the writings on "sex by eminent writers like Havelock Ellis and Bertrand Russell and their theories." Also see, Pyarelal, *Last Phase*, Vol. IX, Book 2, 226–229.

80. Abbott, 220.

81. Gandhi, *Autobiography*, 209.

82. *General Knowledge About Health* [-XVII], "An Intimate Chapter," in *Indian Opinion* (Apr. 26, 1913), *CWMG*, 13: 99.

83. "How Celibacy Can Be Observed," in *Navajivan* (Nov. 10, 1921), *CWMG*, 25: 79.

84. Qtd. in Alter, *Gandhi's Body*, 27.

85. Qtd. in Payne, 465.

86. Parekh, *Colonialism, Tradition, and Reform*, 209.

87. Alter, "Celibacy, Sexuality, and Nationalism in North India," 61, 62 (Alter quotes Ashis Nandy).

88. B. R. Nanda, *Gandhi and His Critics* (New Delhi: Oxford University Press, 1985), 17.

89. "Discussion with Swami Anand and Kedar Nath" (Mar. 15–16, 1947), *CWMG*, 94: 119. Some critics pointed to Gandhi's "secrecy" in his "experiment in *brahmacarya*, involving Manu Gandhi." But Gandhi insisted that "no secrecy was intended. Everything was fortuitous."

90. "Discussion with Hyderabad Aryasamaj Leaders," in *Harijan* (May, 27, 1939), *CWMG*, 75: 190; "Speech at Prayer Meeting" in *Hindustan Times* (Oct. 13, 1946), 92: 319.

91. Parekh, *Colonialism, Tradition, and Reform*, 204–205. Swami Shraddhananda, also known as Mahatma Munshiram (1856–1926), was a contemporary of Gandhi and the nationalist leader of the Arya Samaj who took an active part in public activities.

92. "Questions on Education—IV," in *Navajivan* (June 24, 1928), *CWMG*, 42: 169.

93. Qtd. in Ronald J. Terchek, *Gandhi: Struggling for Autonomy* (New Delhi: Vistaar Publications, 2000), 66.

94. For a detail discussion on this topic, see Howard, "Gandhi's Reconstruction of the Feminine: Toward an Indigenous Hermeneutics."

95. Parel, 143.

96. "Notes for Surendranath," *CWMG*, 98: 421.

97. Nehru, 513.

98. *The Bhagavadgītā*, trans. S. Radhakrishnan (Delhi: Oxford University Press, 1989), 197–198. *Bhāryaṁ gacchan brahmachāri ṛtau bhavati vai dvijāḥ*, ibid., 198 n. 1.

99. For the holistic fulfillment of an individual and sustenance of society, Hindu dharma laws lay out a scheme with four ends: *Dharma* (righteousness, morality), *artha* (wealth), *Kāma* (pleasure and love), and *mokśa* (Absolute Freedom).

100. "Advice to Newly Married Couples," in *Harijan* (Apr. 24, 1937), *CWMG*, 71: 159.

101. Ibid., 160.

102. "Letter to Gopalrao" (July 11, 1927), *CWMG*, 39: 202–203. Gandhi's response to a letter from Gopalrao, who expressed his interest "to enjoy the full bliss of *brahmacarya* immediately." Only excerpts are quoted of this long letter.

103. Michael Edwardes writes: "As George Orwell suggested in his 1949 essay, the Mahatma lacked love, ordinary human love." Michael Edwardes, *The Myth of the Mahatma: Gandhi, the British and the Raj* (London: Constable, 1986), 259.

104. Erikson, 180.

105. "Letter to Mridula Sarabhai" (Mar. 30, 1933), *CWMG*, 60: 212; "Self-Restraint in Marriage," in *Harijan* (July 7, 1946), 91: 217–218.

106. "On Brahmacharya," in *Young India* (Apr. 29, 1926), *CWMG*, 35: 18; "Interview to Margret Sanger," in *Harijan* (Jan. 25, 1936), 68: 193.

107. Nanda, *Gandhi: A Biography*, 85.

108. "Letter to Jamnadas Gandhi" (July 19, 13), *CWMG*, 13: 216.

109. Taneja, 68.

110. "India's Plight," in *Indian Opinion* (Dec. 28, 1907), *CWMG*, 8: 33.

111. Wolpert, 75.

112. Khandelwal writes: "Brahmanic Hinduism has considered lifelong celibacy to be a male pursuit and chastity to be its proper female counterpart." Khandelwal, 159.

113. "My ideal is this. A man should remain man and yet should become woman; similarly a woman should remain woman and yet become man." Qtd. in Terchek, 66–67.

114. "An Intimate Chapter," in *Indian Opinion* (Apr. 26, 1913), *CWMG*, 13: 93.

115. Terchek, 66.

116. David Hardiman, *Gandhi in His Time and Ours: The Global Legacy of His Ideas* (New York: Columbia University Press, 2003), 110.

117. Terchek, 67.

118. Wolpert, 5.

119. "Advice to Newly Married Couples," in *Harijan* (Apr. 24, 1937), *CWMG*, 71: 157.

120. Gandhi states with regard to one who observes *brahmacarya*: "He should be a man who has made himself a eunuch. If the person is a woman, she should not be conscious at all of being a woman." "Discourses on the 'Gita' (39)" (Apr. 9, 1926), *CWMG*, 37: 130.

121. Kumar, 11–12.

122. Bose, 176.

123. Patrick Olivelle, "Deconstruction of the Body in Indian Asceticism," 196.

124. "Walls of Protection," *CWMG*, 95: 230. Gandhi says he never observed prohibitive rules.

125. Mohandas K. Gandhi, *The Law of Continence: Brahmacarya*, ed. Anand T. Hingorani (Bombay: Bharatiya Vidya Bhavan, 1964), 64.

126. Abbott, 223.

127. Kumar, 4.

128. "Myself, My Spinning-Wheel and Women," in *Daily Herald* (Sept. 28, 1931), *CWMG*, 53: 426.

129. Qtd. in Pushpa Joshi, comp., *Gandhi on Women: Collection of Mahatma Gandhi's Writings and Speeches on Women* (New Delhi: Navajivan Publishing House, 1988), 379.

130. Gier, "Was Gandhi a Tantric?" 22.

131. "Discussion with Swami Anand and Kedar Nath" (Mar. 15–16, 1947), *CWMG*, 94: 119.

132. Ibid.

133. Parekh, *Colonialism, Tradition, and Reform*, 213.

134. "Letter to Surendra" (Apr. 4, 1932), *CWMG*, 55: 196.

135. "Discussion with Swami Anand and Kedar Nath" (Mar. 15–16, 1947), *CWMG*, 94: 120–121.

136. "Letter to Amrit Kaur" (Mar. 18, 1947), *CWMG*, 94: 137.

137. Edwardes, 259.

138. "Letter to Krishnachandra" (Mar. 1, 1945), *CWMG*, 85: 448.

139. "A Thought for the Day" (Sept., 10, 1945), in Joshi, 332.

140. "Discussion with A. V. Thakkar," *CWMG*, 94: 36. Gandhi describes his present practice of sleeping with Manu.

141. "Talk with Ashadevi Aryanayakum" (May 2, 1947), *CWMG*, 95: 12.

142. Gandhi wrote that "in matter of service Manu, considering her age, surpasses all the others." "Letter to Jaisukhlal Gandhi" (Jan. 2, 1948), *CWMG*, 98: 157.

143. Gandhi said during his talk with Manu Gandhi: "In the matter of devotion or purity, or in treading the path of truth years hardly count; what is needed is spiritual strength. Wasn't Prahlad very young? Had little Dhruva attained a mature age? But they had the strength to tread the path of truth." "Talk with Manu Gandhi" (June 1, 1947), *CWMG*, 95: 183. In the aforementioned myths, the young children Prahlad and Dhruva display inner spiritual strength and even gods are fearful of the spiritual powers they acquired by their asceticism.

144. "Talk with Manu Gandhi" (June 26, 1947), *CWMG*, 95: 336.

145. "Letter to Gopalrao" (July 11, 1927), *CWMG*, 39: 203. Gandhi speaks of Vinoba, Surendranath, and others who, he believed, observed "inviolate *brahmacharya*" and were in a better position to describe the bliss of *brahmacharya*.

146. Gier, *The Virtue of Nonviolence*, 170.

147. Gandhi said in a speech at a prayer meeting: "Some say that 12,000 women had been abducted by Hindus and Sikhs and twice that number had been abducted by Muslims in Pakistan." Joshi, 365.

148. "Talk with Women Workers" (Apr. 17, 1947), *CWMG*, 94: 320.

149. R. Gandhi, 210.

150. "A Letter" (Mar. 17, 1947), *CWMG*, 94: 131.

151. Pyarelal, *The Last Phase*, Vol. IX, Book 2, 224. Note: There are many oral and written versions of this story from the *Bhāgavata Pūraṇa.*

152. "Satyagraha in South Africa" (Nov. 1923–Dec. 1924), *CWMG*, 34: 12–13. Gandhi wrote this while imprisoned in the Yeravda Central Jail.

153. "Fragment of a Letter" (Nov. 24, 1947), *CWMG*, 97: 381. "All of us are . . . playthings in the hands of Rama. We have to dance to His tune," wrote Gandhi. Ibid.

154. Paine, 242.

155. Gandhi, *The Law of Continence*, 79.

156. Gier, *The Virtue of Nonviolence*, 108.

157. Taneja, 53.

158. Qtd. in Hardiman, *Gandhi in His Time*, 103.

159. Qtd. in Terchek, 67.

Chapter 5

1. Albert Einstein offered this glowing appraisal to Gandhi on his seventy-fifth birthday. Qtd. in Haridas T. Muzumdar, *Mahatma Gandhi: Peaceful Revolutionary* (New York: Charles Scribner's Sons, 1952), 96.

2. Qtd. in S. Radhakrishnan, *Mahatma Gandhi: Essays and Reflections on His Life and Work*, Thirteenth Jaico Impression (Mumbai, Delhi: Jaico Publishing House, 2005), 150. *Mahatma Gandhi: Essays and Reflections on his Life and Work* is an extensive volume, which presents a wide array of reflections on Gandhi's life and work from a variety of prominent individuals including Mazumdar, Polak, Fischer, and Tendulkar.

3. Rudolph and Rudolph, *Traditional Roots of Gandhi's Charisma*, vii, viii.

4. Ibid., 42, qtd in 44.

5. Rudolph and Rudolph, *Traditional Roots of Gandhi's Charisma*, 45, 46.

6. In the *Myth of the Mahatma*, Edwardes offers a sharp critique of the "imagined myth" of Gandhi calling him "anti-modern" and laments the fact that "the imagined myths triumphs over the real." Edwardes, 260.

7. Richard I. Cashman, *The Myth of the Lokamanya: Tilak and Mass Politics in Maharashtra* (Berkeley, CA: University of California Press, 1975), 220.

8. Dieter Conrad, "Gandhi as Mahatma: Political Semantics in an Age of Cultural Ambiguity," in *Charisma and Canon: Essays on the Religious History of the Indian Subcontinent*, ed. Vasudha Dalmia, Angelika Malinar, and Martin Christof (New Delhi: Oxford University Press, 2001), 224, 227, 225, 233.

9. Ashe, 144.

10. Shahid Amin, "Gandhi as Mahatma," in *Subaltern Studies III: Writings on South Asian History and Society*, ed. Ranajit Guha (Delhi: Oxford University Press, 1984).

11. Some discrepancies about accuracy of dates have been noted in Gandhi's *Autobiography*. Hunt, *Gandhi and Nonconformists*, 47 n. 3. Also, Hunt, *Gandhi in London*, 8 n. 10.

12. Gandhi, *Autobiography*, Introduction, xxvi, xxv.

13. Ibid., 32.

14. "Speech at Prayer Meeting," *CWMG*, 97: 103; "Who and Where Is God?" in *Harijan* (June 22, 1947), 95: 275.

15. Gandhi, *Autobiography*, 33.

16. *Kathakar* is a Hindi word. The Sanskrit word is *kathaka. Itihāsas* and *Purāṇas* are composed in the literary form of storytelling.

17. Hans-Georg Gadamer, "Religious and Poetical Speaking," in *Myth, Symbol, and Reality*, ed. Alan M. Olson (Notre Dame, IN, and London: University of Notre Dame Press, 1980), 92.

18. Dharwadker, 162, 133.

19. "Speech at Morvi," in *Navajivan* (Jan. 29, 1928), *CWMG*, 41: 140.

20. Gandhi, *Autobiography*, Introduction, xxix.

21. "Letter to Harilal Gandhi" (Jan. 26, 1913), *CWMG*, 12: 392. "At 5.30 the boys have dinner. After *katha kirtan* from 7 to 7.30, the boys go to sleep."

22. Raja Rao, *The Great Indian Way: A Life of Mahatma Gandhi* (Delhi: Vision Books, 1998), 217.

23. "Letter to Eshter Faering" (Jan. 25, 1919), *CWMG*, 17: 264.

24. Kakar, *Intimate Relations*, 1, 2.

25. R. K. Narayan, 4.

26. "Discourses on the 'Gita' (49)" (Apr. 21, 1926), *CWMG*, 37: 149.

27. K. Narayan, 225.

28. "A skilful story-teller adds explanations, additional stories, modern examples and jokes to keep both young and old entertained. One of the most famous Gujarati narrators is Morari Bapu." Hirst, 26. Morari Bapu is a contemporary storyteller internationally famous for his *kathās* of the *Rāmcaritmānas* of Tulsidas. Pandurang Shastri Athavale (1920–2003) founded the Swadhyay movement to promote the study of the texts such as the *Bhagavad-Gītā* to carry activities of social good.

29. Qtd. in K. Narayan, 225.

30. Krishna Kripalani elaborates on the Indian renaissance of the nineteenth to twentieth centuries that was inspired by Western models. In this period various literary forms such as novel, drama, essay, poetry, and modern drama performances flourished. Krishna Kripalani, "Modern Literature," in *A Cultural History of India*, ed. A. L. Basham (New Delhi: Oxford University Press, 1975), 410–411.

31. Wendy Doniger O'Flaherty, *Other Peoples' Myths: The Cave of Echoes* (New York: Macmillan Publishing Company, 1988), 121.

32. Gandhi, *Autobiography*, 7.

33. Gandhi gives the example of Hariścandra, who for the sake of truth "allowed himself to be sold to a low-caste man; he gave up his throne and suffered separation from his wife and son." "Divine Law," in *Indian Opinion* (July 27, 1907), *CWMG*, 7: 89.

34. Jordens, *Gandhi's Religion*, 7.

35. Rudolph and Rudolph, *Postmodern Gandhi*, 214.

36. "Harishchandra was a satyagrahi . . . a satyagrahi does not fear for his body, he does not give up what he thinks is Truth." "Satyagraha—Not Passive Resistance" (ca. Sept. 2, 1917), *CWMG*, 16:12. In another instance Gandhi asserted that with Shravṇa was his ideal of service. "Injustice to Kathiawaris," in *Navajivan* (June 6, 1924), 28: 78.

37. My translation from Sanskrit. *Rāmāyaṇa of Vālmīkī*, vol. 1, trans. and ed. M. N. Dutt and Ravi Prakash Arya, 1st ed. (Delhi: Parimal Publications, 1998), (Ayodhyā-Kāṇḍa, section 63: 30–32), 167.

38. A paraphrase of the story (Ayodhyā-Kāṇḍa, sections 63–64). *Rāmāyaṇa of Vālmīkī*, 165–174.

39. Gandhi, *Autobiography*, 7.

40. "Injustice to Kathiawaris," in *Navajivan* (June 1, 1924), *CWMG*, 28: 78.

41. Gandhi said that "his whole life and work was dedicated entirely to the feet of Sri Krishna and Bharat Mata." "Speech at Prabartak Ashram, Chandernagore," in *Amrita Bazar Patrika* (May 8, 1925), *CWMG*, 31: 279.

42. "Speech at Bharat Mata Mandir, Banaras," in *Harijan* (Oct. 31, 1936), *CWMG*, 70: 8.

43. Gandhi, *Autobiography*, 7.

44. Rudolph and Rudolph, *Postmodern Gandhi*, 215.

45. Ashe, 6.

46. A paraphrase of "Harishchandra." Qtd. in R. K. Narayan, 217–228. All quoted references are taken from this exposition.

47. Gandhi, *Autobiography*, 7.

48. Rudolph and Rudolph, *Postmodern Gandhi*, 214–215.

49. "Obedience to Parents," in *Harijanbandhu* (Apr. 9, 1933), *CWMG*, 60: 317.

50. Rudolph and Rudolph, *Postmodern Gandhi*, 215, 214.

51. Ashe, 7.

52. Ibid.

53. Gandhi emphasized that he was "strictly a mumukshu or *mokshartht*"—one seeking "salvation." "Speech at Prabartak Ashram, Chandernagore," in *Amrita Bazar Patrika* (May 8, 1925), *CWMG*, 31: 279.

54. "Satyagraha—Not Passive Resistance" (ca. Sept. 2, 1917), *CWMG*, 16: 12.

55. Gandhi, *Autobiography*, 7–8.

56. Green, 188.

57. "Letter to Narandas Gandhi" (before May 28, 1931), *CWMG*, 52: 184.

58. "Speech at Gujarati Sahitya Parishad," in *Navajivan* (Apr. 4, 1920), *CWMG*, 20: 197.

59. "On the Verge of It," in *Young India* (May 21, 1925), *CWMG*, 31: 373.

60. "Letter to Jamnadas Gandhi" (Mar. 28, 1915), *CWMG*, 14: 393.

61. Eliade notes: "The 'religiousness' of this experience is due to the fact that one re-enacts fabulous, exalting significant events, one again witnesses the creative deeds of the Supernaturals." Mircea Eliade, *Myth and Reality*, trans. Willard R. Trask (New York: Harper Torchbooks, 1963), 19.

62. Herbert Mason, "Myth as an 'Ambush of Reality,'" in *Myth, Symbol, and Reality*, ed. Alan M. Olson (Notre Dame. IN, and London: University of Notre Dame Press, 1980), 18.

63. Gandhi, *Bhagavad Gita*, 15.

64. "Discourses on the 'Gita' (1)" (Feb. 24, 1926), *CWMG*, 37: 75 n. 1. The talks were given at the Satyagraha Ashram, Ahmedabad, during morning prayers over a period of nine months from February 24 to November 27, 1926. They were edited by Narahari Parikh and published in book form in 1955 under the title *Gandhijinu Gitashikshan*.

65. "Speech at Mehmedabad," in *Navajivan* (Nov. 7, 1920), *CWMG*, 21: 419; "The Law of Our Being," in *Harijan* (Sept. 26, 1936), 69: 399.

66. "Discourses on the 'Gita' (8)" (Mar. 4, 1926), *CWMG*, 37: 82. Gandhi mentions his enccounters with revolutionaries who disagreed with his interpretation of the *Gītā*.

67. Qtd. in Danino, 50.

68. "Sayagraha Leaflet No. 18" (May 18, 1919), *CWMG*, 18: 26; Gandhi, *Bhagavad-Gita*, 14.

69. "Sayagraha Leaflet No. 18" (May 18, 1919), *CWMG*, 18: 25–26. Gandhi explains the "True Meaning of Bhagvad Gita's Teachings.

70. Fischer, *The Life of Mahatma Gandhi*, 235, 234.

71. "Indulgence or Self-Denial," in *Young India* (Jan. 7, 1926), *CWMG*, 33: 376–377.

72. Gandhi addressed the criticism of his friends who were concerned by his choice of inaction. "Action in Inaction," in *Young India* (Sept. 9, 1926), *CWMG*, 36: 270.

73. Gandhi, *The Bhagavad Gita*, 88.

74. Gandhi delivered his discourses in Gujarati. The unabridged version of his talks can be found in the section, "Discourses on the 'Gita'" (Feb. 24–Nov. 27, 1926), *CWMG*, 37: 75–354.

75. Gandhi, *Bhagavad Gita*, 27.

76. "The more I study the *Gita*, the more I am made aware of its uniqueness. . . . It is indeed a Kamadhenu," says Gandhi. "Preface to 'Gitapadarthakosha'" (Sept. 24, 1936), *CWMG*, 69: 390.

77. Parel, 182.

78. Bolle, 138.

79. Parel, 182.

80. Qtd. in Paul B. Courtright, *Ganeśa: Lord of Obstacles, Lord of Beginnings* (New York: Oxford University Press, 1985), 3.

81. Qtd. in Jordens, *Gandhi's Religion*, 138.

82. "Teaching of Hinduism," in *Harijan* (Oct. 3, 1936), *CWMG*, 69: 420.

83. Gandhi, *Autobiography*, 265.

84. "One does not have to be a militant feminist to realize that we could not write anymore like that about our wives and children as possessions." Bolle, 141.

85. The Navajivan Publishing House published a booklet with the title "*Satyagraha Yuddha*." "Satyagraha Yuddha," in *Hindi Navajivan* (Apr. 17, 1930), *CWMG*, 49: 121.

86. "Importance of 'Tapas,'" in *Navajivan* (Oct. 12, 1924), *CWMG*, 29: 238–239.

87. "Speech to Ahmedabad Mill-Hands" (Mar. 15, 1918), *CWMG*, 16: 335.

88. Chatterjee, 83.

89. Although the claim of Indrajīt's celibacy cannot be supported by the *Rāmāyaṇa*, there exists a vast oral tradition of *Rāmāyaṇa* stories. Perhaps Gandhi bases his story on those traditions. *Rāmāyaṇa* gives a general account of the austerities performed by Indrajīt.

90. "Letter to Maganlal Gandhi" (Dec. 28, 1908), *CWMG*, 9: 222.

91. "Letter to Ramdas Gandhi" (June 4, 1927), *CWMG*, 39: 3.

92. "Appendices, Appendix I," in *Young India* (Sept. 20, 1928), *CWMG*, 43: 521–522.

93. R. K. Narayan, 5.

94. Cashman, 1, 2.

95. Qtd. in Mark Juergensmeyer, "Saint Gandhi," in *Saints and Virtues*, ed. John Stratton Hawley (Berkeley, CA: University of California Press, 1987), 189, 187. In his critical appraisal of "Saint Gandhi," the author traces the genesis of Gandhi's emergence as a "saint."

96. See early accounts by Rev. Joseph Doke, Romain Rolland, John Haynes Holmes, and Haridas T Muzumdar.

97. Sobo and Bell, 7–8.

98. Rudolph and Rudolph, *Traditional Roots of Charisma*, 39.

99. "Interview to Journalists," in *Young India* (Mar. 19, 1931), *CWMG*, 51: 220.

100. "My Loin-Cloth," in *Young India* (Apr. 30, 1931), *CWMG*, 52: 8.

101. The newspaper reported Gandhi's speech: "He then explained why he adopted the present change in his dress and took only to the loin-cloth. He wanted to set an example, when so many of his own countrymen and women were going naked." "Speech on Swadeshi, Surat," in the *Bombay Chronicle* (Oct. 22, 1921), *CWMG*, 24: 405.

102. Gandhi responded to a critic who raised the issue of indecency in his scanty dress by saying that "crores of people in India do not get even a loin-cloth to wear." He further stated that "the sadhus wear only a *langoti* [a piece of cloth that is worn like a brief]." "My Loin-cloth," in *Navajivan* (July 27, 1924), *CWMG*, 28: 370.

103. "Opening Speech at Kathiawar Political Conference, Bhavnagar," in *Navajivan* Supplement (Jan. 18, 1925), *CWMG*, 30: 71.

104. "Letter to Ramdas Gandhi" (Feb. 25, 1933), *CWMG*, 59: 389.

105. "My Loin-cloth," in *Navajivan* (July 27, 1924), *CWMG*, 28: 371.

106. "Speech at Meeting, Paris" (Dec. 5, 1931), *CWMG*, 54: 258.

107. Jordens, "Gandhi and the Bagavadgita," 108.

108. Dalton, 103.

109. "Talk to Volunteers," in *Young India* (Mar. 17, 1930), *CWMG*, 48: 450; "Speech at Prayer Meeting, Sabarmati Ashram" (Mar. 12, 1930), 417.

110. "Statement to the Press" (Apr. 2, 1934), *CWMG*, 63: 348.

111. "Speech at Prayer Meeting, Sabarmati Ashram" (Mar. 12, 1930), *CWMG*, 48: 416–417.

112. Dalton, 109, 110.

113. Qtd. in Dalton, 115.

114. Ibid., 108.

115. Ibid., 109.

116. Percival Spear, *History of India: Volume Two* (New Delhi: Penguin Books, 1978), 199.

117. "Was It Coercive?" in *Harijan* (Sept. 9, 1933), *CWMG*, 61: 377, 378.

118. Qtd. in Dipesh Chakrabarty, *Provincializing Europe: Postcolonial Thought and Historical Difference* (Princeton, NJ: Princeton University Press, 2000), 39.

119. "Talk Before Breaking the 21-Day Fast" (Mar. 3, 1943), *CWMG*, 83: 295 n. 1 (ellipses in the original).

120. Qtd. in Chakrabarty, 38.

121. Paine, 242.

122. Dalton, 108.

123. Pyarelal, Gandhi's personal secretary, records an incident. Pyarelal, *The Last Phase*, V ol. IX, Book 1, 329.

124. Dalton, 104.

125. Rao, *Great Indian Way*, 219–220, 220.

126. See for illustration Raminder Kaur, *Performative Politics and the Culture of Hinduism: Public Use of Religion in Western India* (London: Anthem Press, 2005), 68.

127. Mehta, 159.

128. Amrit Kaur Singh and Rabindra Kaur Singh, *Images of Freedom* (New Delhi: Indialog Publications, 2003), Plate 19, 52–53, Plate 24, 64–55.

129. Van der Veer, 96.

130. Amin, 2, 3–4.

131. "Talk with V. S. Srinivasa Sastri," in *Harijan* (Apr. 28, 1946), *CWMG*, 89: 354.

132. Amin, 25–26.

133. Vinay Lal, *The History of History: Politics and Scholarship in Modern India* (New Delhi: Oxford University Press, 2003), 211–212.

134. Amin, 44.

135. Ibid., 4–5. Italics in the original.

136. Ibid., 4.

137. It must be noted that many *Dalits* and *Harijans* were uneasy about Gandhi's use of Hindu references that proclaimed their marginality.

138. Hardiman, *Gandhi in His Time*, 142.

139. David Hardiman, "Origins and Transformations of the Devi," in *A Subaltern Studies Reader, 1986–1995*, ed. Ranajit Guha (Minneapolis, MN: University of Minnesota Press, 1997), 100, 101, 131.

140. Raja Rao, *Kanthapura*, 8th printing (New York: New Directions, 1963), 11–12.

141. "Tracing History Accurately, the Literary Way," *The Hindu*, May 9, 2003, Accessed on January 20, 2012. http://www.hindu.com/thehindu/fr/2003/05/09/stories/2003050901130500.htm.

142. "Do not ask for my darshan or want to touch my feet. I am not God; I am a human being. I am an old man and my capacity to stand the strain is limited. If I am to appear before you again and again my strength will be exhausted. And I will not be able to do work." "Speech After Prayer Meeting," in *Amrita Bazar Partika* (Dec. 3, 1945), *CWMG*, 88: 413.

143. Lal, *The History of History*, 211.

Conclusion

1. Lal, "Nakedness, Nonviolence, and Brahmacharya," 120.

2. For example, thinkers such as George Orwell note that Gandhi's ascetic practices in public life caused anguish to his family, friends, and followers. "The essence of being human is that one does not seek perfection . . . that one does not push asceticism to the point where it makes friendly intercourse impossible." George Orwell, *A Collection of Essays* (San Diego: A Harvest Book, Harcourt, 1981), 176.

3. Paine, 240.

4. Bondurant, *Conquest of Violence*, vi.

5. "My Inconsistencies," in *Young India* (Feb. 13, 1930), *CWMG*, 48: 314.

6. Lannoy, 377; qtd. in ibid., 376.

7. Gandhi "had a deep and sustained interest" in Tolstoy's significant work *What Is Art?* (1898), and had this text translated into Gujarati. For Tolstoy, "art is the expression, through appropriate symbols, of deeply experienced feelings that the artist has undergone, expression that can evoke similar feelings in those who come into contact with the art." Parel, 160.

8. Julius Lipner, "Conclusion: A Debate for Our Times," in *Indian Critiques of Gandhi*, ed. Harold Coward (Albany, NY: State University of New York Press, 2003), 251.

9. Parel, 137.

10. Gandhi, *Vows and Observances*, 30.

11. Gier gives an original insight into the word virtue. He states: "There was a strong connection between self-mastery, freedom, and virility. (The Latin *virtus* stems from *vir*, meaning "manhood," so that Roman virtue meant "excellence of manly qualities.") Gier, *The Virtue of Nonviolence*, 119.

12. For example, noncooperation with the senses (asceticism) was a part of the political activities of noncooperation and passive resistance, which required self-control. Gandhi published a letter by Tagore who stated: "The idea of non-co-operation is political asceticism." *Young India* (July 21, 1921), *CWMG*, 23: 485.

13. "Replies to Customs Inspector," in *The Daily Mail* (Sept. 12, 1931), *CWMG*, 53: 339.

14. "Hinduism," in *Young India* (Oct. 6, 1921), *CWMG*, 24: 374.

15. K. Narayan, 119; "A Countryman's Advice," in *Young India* (July 9, 1931), *CWMG*, 53: 36; "Myself, My Spinning-Wheel and Women," in *The Daily Herald* (Sept. 28, 1931), 53: 425.

16. "Interview to Dilip Kumar Roy," in the *Bombay Chronicle* (Feb. 5, 1924), *CWMG*, 27: 5; "Discourses on the 'Gita' (5)," 37: 215.

17. E. M. Forster, "Mahatma Gandhi," in *Mahatma Gandhi: Essays and Reflections on His Life and Work*, ed. S. Radhakrishnan, Thirteenth Jaico Impression (Mumbai, Delhi: Jaico Publishing House, 2005), 389.

18. O'Flaherty sees storytelling itself as art: "Storytelling is one of the few truly universal human bonds. . . . Putting together words to reproduce events that engage the emotions of the listener is surely a form of art that ranks among the great human experiences." O'Flaherty, 1.

19. For example, in 1948 B. G. Kher, a former prime minister of Bombay, and others visited Gandhi to clarify their doubts about his method of *ahiṃsā*. During the long interview, Gandhi told Kher of the success of the Salt March, which brought a "magical awakening"; thousands participated in his movement as a result of it. According to Gandhi, initially his close followers, including Motilal Nehru, expressed doubt about the idea. To substantiate the power of truth over the power of arms, Gandhi referred to an episode from Tulsidas's *Ramayana*, when Vibhishina wondered how Rama would be able to conquer an enemy such as Ravana when he had no equipment of a warrior, such as chariot, armor, and shoes. This passage gives a long list of virtues—strength, determination, compassion, forgiveness, equanimity, mental quietude, contentment, pure and unwavering mind, and so on—which constitute the apparatus (e.g., chariot, shield, sheaf of arrows, and armor) of *Rama*. Gandhi concluded: "That is the equipment that can lead us to victory." Mahadev Desai provided the verses from the Ramayana for the benefit of the reader. "Discussion with B. G. Kher and Others," in *Harijan* (Aug. 25, 1940), *CWMG*, 79: 125.

20. Paine, 241.

21. R. M. Sainsbury, *Paradoxes*, 2nd ed. (Cambridge: Cambridge University Press, 1995), 1.

22. As Alter points out, "Gandhi came to embody, therefore, a kind of androgynous, charismatic vitality. Far from being clearly defined and revolutionary . . . Gandhi's androgyny provoked high anxiety. There were many who regarded him as dangerously effeminate and ambiguously enigmatic." Alter, *Gandhi's Body*, 139.

23. Qtd. in Nanda, *In Search of Gandhi*, 36–37.
24. Lipner, "Conclusion," 240.

Appendices

1. *Abhivādya tataḥ sā taṁ*
prākrīḍad rsi-saṃnidhāu
apovāha ca vāso 'syā Mārutaḥ,
śaśi -saṁnibham.

In Lanman, "Hindu Ascetics and Their Powers," 139. Note: Some of the diacritical marks have been changed to the modern standards and the translation has been adjusted according to Sanskrit transcription.

2. A paraphrase of the episode, in which Śakuntalā tells King Duḥṣunta the story of her birth. Van Buitenen, *The Mahābhārata*, vol. 1, 161–163.

3. "Cow-Protection True and False," in *Young India* (Sept. 20, 1928), *CWMG*, 43: 521–523. An exact copy of the original.

Glossary

abhaya	a state without fear
āgraha	force
ahiṃsā	nonviolence
anāśakāyna	fasting as penance
anāsakti	nonattachment
aparigraha	nonpossession, freedom from possessiveness
arādhanā	ritual worship of god
asahyoga	noncooperation
asat	untruth
āśrama/ashram	hermitage, religious communes
asteya	nonstealing
asuras	demons
asvādavrata	control of palate
avatār	incarnation of some divine form
bandhana	bondage
brahmacārin/brahmachari	one who takes a vow of celibacy
brahmacaryāśrama	first stage of the student in Hindu *varṇāśrama-dharma*
brahmacarya/brahmacharya	literally "divine conduct," which includes control of all sense organs and desires; commonly translated as celibacy or continence

charkha	spinning wheel, made famous by Gandhi
dāna	charity
dānavas	demons
darśan/darshan	literally to "observe," generally is used in the context of being in the presence of a holy person, the image of a deity, or a holy object
devas	gods
dharma	duty, religion, ethics
dharmarājya	kingdom of righteousness
gṛhastha	householder
Harijan	"people of god"; a term coined by Gandhi for untouchables, also the name of one of Gandhi's weekly newspaper
hiṃsā	violence
jagat	the physical world
japayajña	sacrifice by means of prayer
kāma	sexual desire, pleasure, also personified as a tempter
karma sannyāsa	renunciation in action
karma yoga	the path of action, one of the three ways of obtaining *mokṣa*
kathā	religious stories, myth
kathakar	religious storyteller
khadi	hand-spun cloth
lokasaṃgraha	the welfare of the world
mahātmā/mahatma	great soul, an honorific title of a holy person
maitri	friendship
manauti	taking a vow on a holy person or deity's name for the purpose of fulfillment of a desire

mauna	silence
mokṣa	spiritual freedom, liberation
munis	renunciates
naishṭhika brahmacarya	lifelong celibacy
nivṛtti	renunciation; withdrawal
nivṛtti mārga	the path of renunciation and withdrawal that prescribes the ascetic disciplines; the path of renunciation for the purpose of attaining liberation or Truth
niyamas	literally, holding back and the rules of controlling
ojas	bodily strength, vigor, energy, power
pahalwans	Indian wrestlers who often practice strict disciplines, including celibacy
pravṛtti	engagement in action
pravṛtti mārga	the path of worldly engagement as in householder state of life
pūrṇa svarājya/purna swaraj	complete independence or self-rule, full national independence
rāja dharma	the duties of a king or ruler
rāmarājya/ramaraj	Gandhi called it *ramraj*, the kingdom of Lord Rāma, kingdom of God, the reign of Rāma, the ideal state, the golden age
raṇa yajña	war sacrifice
saccakriyā (Pāli)/ *satyakriyā/satkriyā* (Sanskrit)	Act of Truth
sādhu	a holy man
śakti	power
saṃsāra	the temporal cycle of birth, death, and rebirth
sannyāsa	world renunciation, life of renunciation

sannyāsin	one who practices *sannyāsa*
sarvabhūtahite ratāḥ	who delights in the welfare of all beings
śāstra	scripture
sat	Truth, ultimate reality
satyagraha	soul-force or love-force, Truth-force, firm adherence to truth (combination of two words *sat* and *āgraha*)
satyagrahi	one who practices *satyagraha*
siddhi	supernatural power, yogic power
sthitaprajña	a man with perfect control; person of stable wisdom
svādhyāya,	self-study
swadeshi	of one's own country, home-grown goods, economic self-reliance
svarāj/swaraj	self-rule, national independence
svarāj yajña	sacrifice for self-rule
tapas/tapasya	literally heat; physical and mental austerities
tapasvin	ascetic
tejas	splendor, brilliance; often related to yogic powers
tīrthaṅkara	prominent Jain teacher, literally a "crossing-builder"
tyāga	renunciation
vairāgya	nonattachment
vānaprastha	the forest-dweller stage (third stage in *varṇāśrama-dharma*)
varṇa	"caste" in traditional Hindu social structure
varṇāśrama-dharma	ethics or duties based on *varṇa* and *āśrama*
vicāra	the passions that disturb the soul

viṣaya	perceptible by the senses; used by Gandhi in the sense of sensual pleasures
vīrya	semen
vrata	commitment, vow, discipline, pledge
yajña	traditional ritual sacrifice; Gandhi extended the meaning of ritual sacrifice to his political actions
yama-niyamas	restraints and observances traditionally undertaken for spiritual evolution

Bibliography

Sources in Hindi and Gujarati

Gandhi, Mohandas K. *Anaskti Yoga* (*The Yoga of Non-Attachment: The* Bhagavad-Gita *with a Translation*). New Delhi: Sasta Sahitrya Mandal Prakashan, 2002.

———. *Atmakatha* (Autobiography—Gujarati). Ahmedabad: Navbhavan Prakshan Mandir, 1927.

———. *Atmakatha* (Autobiography—Hindi). Delhi: Sasta Sahitya Mandal Prakashan, 2005.

———. *Gita Mata* (Mother Gita). New Delhi: Saṛsta Sahitrya Mandal Prakashan, 1995.

Satsang Yoga: Four Parts. Ed. Mahrishi Parmhansji Maharaj. Bihar: Akhil Bhartiya Santmat Satsang Prakashan, 1985.

Sources in English

Abbott, Elizabeth. *A History of Celibacy: From Athena to Elizabeth I, Leonardo da Vinci, Florence Nightingale, Gandhi and Cher*. New York: Scribner, 2000.

Adams, Jad. *Gandhi: Naked Ambition*. London: Quercus, 2010.

Alter, Joseph S. "Celibacy, Sexuality, and the Transformation of Gender into Nationalism in North India." *The Journal of Asian Studies* 53, no. 1 (Feb. 1994): 45–66.

———. *Gandhi's Body: Sex, Diet, and the Politics of Nationalism*. Philadelphia: University of Pennsylvania Press, 2000.

Amin, Shahid. "Gandhi as Mahatma." In *Subaltern Studies III: Writings on South Asian History and Society*. Ed. Ranajit Guha. Delhi: Oxford University Press, 1984. 1–61.

Ashe, Geoffrey. *Gandhi*. New York: Stein and Day, 1968.

Atharva-Veda Saṃhitā—Atharvaveda Saṃhitā. Trans. Satya Prakash Sarasvati. New Delhi: Veda Pratishthana, 1992.

Bailey, Greg. *Materials for the Study of Ancient Indian Ideologies: Pravṛtti and Nivṛtti*. Torino, Italy: Indologica Taurinensia, 1985.

Baird, Robert D. "'Secular State' and the Indian Constitution." In *Religion in Modern India*. Ed. Robert D. Baird. New Delhi: Monohar Publications, 1981.

Basham, A. L., ed. *A Cultural History of India*. New Delhi: Oxford University Press, 1975.

———. *The Wonder That Was India*. New Delhi: Rupa & Co., 1967.

Bhagat, M. G. *Ancient Indian Asceticism*. New Delhi: Munshiram Manoharlal Publishers, 1976.

The Bhagavadgītā. Trans. S. Radhakrishnan. Delhi: Oxford University Press, 1989.

The Bhagavad Gita with the Commentary of Sri Sankaracharya, Samata ed. Trans. Alladi Mahadeva Sastry. Madras, India: Samata Books, 1977.

Bhave, Acharya Vinoba. *Talks on the Gita*. London: G. Allen & Unwin, 1960.

Bolle, Kees W. "Gandhi's Interpretation of the Bhagavad Gita." In *Gandhi's Significance for Today*. Ed. John Hick and Lamont C. Hempel. Houndmills, Basingstoke, and Hampshire, UK: The Macmillan Press, 1989. 137–151.

Bondurant, Joan V. *Conquest of Violence: The Gandhian Philosophy of Conflict*, new rev. ed. Princeton NJ: Princeton University Press, 1988.

Bose, Nirmal Kumar. *My Days with Gandhi*, Reprint. New Delhi: Orient Longman Limited, 1999.

Bronkhorst, Johannes. *The Two Sources of Indian Asceticism*. Bern: Peter Lang, 1993.

Brown, Judith M. *Gandhi: Prisoner of Hope*. New Haven and London: Yale University Press, 1989.

Brown, W. Norman. "Duty as Truth in Ancient India." *Proceedings of the American Philosophy Society* 116, no. 3 (June 1972): 252–268.

———. "The Metaphysics of the Truth Act (*Satyakriyā)." In *Mélanges d'Indianisme a la mémoire de Louis Renou*. Ed. Louis Renou. Paris: Boccard, 1968. 171–177.

Burlingame, Eugene Watson. "The Act of Truth (Saccakiriya): A Hindu Spell and Its Employment as a Psychic Motif in Hindu Fiction." *The Journal of the Royal Asiatic Society* (July 1917): 429–457.

Caplan, Pat. "Celibacy as a Solution? Mahatma Gandhi and *Brahmacharya*." In *The Cultural Construction of Sexuality*. Ed. Pat Caplan. New York: Tavistock Publication, 1987. 271–295.

Cashman, Richard I. *The Myth of the Lokamanya: Tilak and Mass Politics in Maharashtra*. Berkeley and Los Angeles: University of California Press, 1975.

Chadha, Yogesh. *Gandhi: A Life*. New York: John Wiley & Sons, 1997.

Chakrabarty, Dipesh. *Provincializing Europe: Postcolonial Thought and Historical Difference*, new edition. Princeton, NJ: Princeton University Press, 2007.

Chatterjee, Margaret. *Gandhi's Religious Thought*. Notre Dame, IN: University of Notre Dame Press, 1983.

Clough, Bradley S. "Gandhi, Nonviolence, and the *Bhagavad-ītā*." In *Holy War: Violence and the* Bhagavad-gītā. Ed. Steven J. Rosen. Virginia: Deepak Heritage, 2002. 59–80.

Collins, Larry and Dominique Lappierre. *Freedom at Midnight*. New York: Simon and Schuster, 1976.

Conrad, Dieter. "Gandhi as Mahatma: Political Semantics in an Age of Cultural Ambiguity." In *Charisma and Canon: Essays on the Religious History of the Indian Subcontinent*. Ed. Vasudha Dalmia, Angelika Malinar and Martin Christof. New Delhi: Oxford University Press, 2001. 223–249.

Coomaraswamy, Ananda. "*Ātmayajña*: Self-sacrifice." In *Coomaraswamy: Selected Papers: Metaphysics*. Ed. Roger Lipsy. Princeton, NJ: Princeton University Press, 1977.

Cortright, David. *Gandhi and Beyond: Nonviolence for an Age of Terrorism*. Boulder, CO: Paradigm Publishers, 2006.

Courtright Paul B. *Ganeśa: Lord of Obstacles, Lord of Beginnings*. New York: Oxford University Press, 1985.

Dalmia, Vasudha, Angelika Malinar and Martin Christof, eds. *Charisma and Canon: Essays on the Religious History of the Indian Subcontinent*. New Delhi: Oxford University Press, 2001. This text is cross-referenced by others.

Dalton, Denis. *Gandhi's Power: Nonviolence in Action*. New Delhi: Oxford University Press, 2004.

Danino, Michel. "Śrī Aurobindo and the *Gītā*." In *Holy War: Violence and the* Bhagavad-gītā. Ed. Steven J. Rosen. Virginia: Deepak Heritage, 2002. 43–58.

The Dhammapada. Tran. and ed. S. Radhakrishnan. New Delhi: Oxford University Press, 1950.

Dhand, Arti. *Woman as Fire, Woman as Sage: Sexual Ideology in the* Mahābhārata. Albany, NY: State University of New York Press, 2008.

Dharwadker, Vinay, ed. *The Collected Essays of A. K. Ramanujan*. New Delhi: Oxford University Press, 1999.

Doke, Joseph John. *M.K. Gandhi: An Indian Patriot in South Africa*. Madras: The London Indian Chronicle, 1909.

Dumont, Louis. *Religion/Politics and History in India: Collected Papers in Indian Sociology*. Paris and Hague: Mouton Publishers, 1970.

Edwardes, Michael. *The Myth of the Mahatma: Gandhi, the British and the Raj*. London: Constable, 1986.

Eliade, Mircea. *Myth and Reality*. Trans. Willard R. Trask. New York: Harper Torchbooks, 1963.

———. *Yoga: Immortality and Freedom*. Princeton, NJ: Princeton University Press, 1969.

Erikson, Erik H. *Gandhi's Truth: On the Origins of Militant Nonviolence*. New York: W. W. Norton & Co., 1969.

Feller, Danielle. *The Sanskrit Epics' Representation of Vedic Myths*. India: Motilal Banarsidass, 2004.

Feuerstein, Georg. *The Yoga Tradition: Its History, Literature, Philosophy and Practice*, unabridged, new format ed. Prescott, AZ: Hohm Press, 1998.

Fields, Gregory P. *Religious Therapeutics: Body and Health in Yoga, Āyurveda, and Tantra*. Albany, NY: State University of New York, 2001.

Flood, Gavin. *An Introduction to Hinduism*. Cambridge: Cambridge University Press, 1996.

Forster, E. M. "Mahatma Gandhi." In *Mahatma Gandhi: Essays and Reflections on his Life and Work*. Ed. Sarvepalli Radhakrishnan, Thirteenth Jaico Impression. Mumbai, Delhi: Jaico Publishing House, 2005. 387–389.

Freiberger, Oliver. *Asceticism and Its Critics*. New York: Oxford University Press, 2006.

Gadamer, Hans-Georg. "Religious and Poetical Speaking." In *Myth, Symbol, and Reality*. Ed. Alan M. Olson. Notre Dame, IN: University of Notre Dame Press, 1980. 86–98.

Gandhi, Mohandas K. *All Men Are Brothers: Autobiographical Reflections*. Comp. and ed. Krishna Kriplani. New York: Continuum Publishing Co., 1990.

———. *An Autobiography: The Story of My Experiments with Truth*. Trans. Mahadev Desai. Boston: Beacon Press, 1957.

———. *The Bhagavad Gita: According to Gandhi*. Ed. John Strohmeier. Berkeley: Berkeley Hills Books, 2000.

———. *The Collected Works of Mahatma Gandhi*. 98 vols. [electronic book]. Delhi: Publication Division Ministry of Information and Broadcasting, Government of India, 2001.

———. *Hind Swaraj or Indian Home Rule*. Ahmedabad, India: Navajivan Publishing House, 2009.

———. *The Law of Continence: Brahmacharya*. Ed. Anand T. Hingorani. Bombay: Bharatiya Vidya Bhavan, 1964.

———. *Non-Violent Resistance (Satyagraha)*. New York: Dover Publications, 2001.

———. *To Students*. Ed. Bharatan Kumarappa. Ahmedabad, India: Navajivan Publishing House, 1953.

———. *Vows and Observances*. Ed. John Strohmeier. Berkeley, CA: Berkeley Hills Books, 1999.

Gandhi, Ramchandra. "*Brahmacarya*." In *Way of Life King, Householder, Renouncer*. Ed. Tirloki Nath Madan. Delhi: Motilal Banarsidass Publishers, 1988. 205–221.

Ghose, Sri Aurobindo. *Essays on the Gita*. Pondicherry, India: Sri Aurobindo Ashram Trust, 1966.

Ghurye, G. S. *Indian Sadhus*. Bombay: The Popular Book Depot, 1953.

Gier, Nicholas F. *The Virtue of Nonviolence: From Gautama to Gandhi*. Albany, NY: State University of New York Press, 2004.

———. "Was Gandhi a Tantric?" In *Gandhi Marg* 29, no. 1 (Apr.–June 2007): 21–36.

Green, Martin B. *The Challenge of the Mahatmas*. New York: Basic Books, 1978.

Guha, Ranajit, ed. *A Subaltern Studies Reader, 1986–1995*. Minneapolis, MN: University of Minnesota Press, 1997.

———. ed. *Subaltern Studies III: Writings on South Asian History and Society*. Delhi: Oxford University Press, 1984.

Guha, Ramachandra. *India After Gandhi: The History of the World's Largest Democracy*. New York: HarperCollins Publishers, 2007.

Hardiman, David. *Gandhi in His Time and Ours: The Global Legacy of His Ideas*. New York: Columbia University Press, 2003.

———. "Origins and Transformation of the Devi." In *A Subaltern Studies Reader, 1986–1995*. Ed. Ranajit Guha. Minneapolis, MN: University of Minnesota Press, 1992. 100–139.

Hiriyanna, M. *Outlines of Indian Philosophy*. Delhi: Motilal Banarsidass Publishers, 2005.

Hirst, Jacqueline Suthren. *Sita's Story*. Series ed. Julius Lipner. Calgary, Alberta, Canada: Bayeux Arts, 1997.

Howard, Veena. "Gandhi, The Mahatma: Evolving Narratives and Native Discourse in Gandhi Studies." *Religion Compass* 1, no. 3 (Apr. 2007): 380–397.

———. "Gandhi's Reconstruction of the Feminine: Toward an Indigenous Hermeneutics." In *Woman and Goddess in Hinduism: Reinterpretations and Re-envisionings*. Ed. Tracy Pintchman and Rita D. Sherma. New York: Palgrave Macmillan, 2011. 197–217.

Hume, Robert Ernest, trans. *The Thirteen Principal Upanishads*. Delhi: Oxford University Press, 1931.

Hunt, James D. *Gandhi and the Nonconformists: Encounters in South Africa*. New Delhi: Promilla, 1986.

———. *Gandhi in London*. New Delhi: Promilla, 1978.

Iyer, Raghavan N., ed. *The Essential Writings of Mahatma Gandhi*. Delhi: Oxford University Press, 1991.

———. *The Moral and Political Thought of Mahatma Gandhi*. New York: Concord Grove Press, 1983.

Jordens, J. T. F. *Gandhi's Religion: A Homespun Shawl*. New York: Palgrave, 1998.

———. "Gandhi and the *Bhagavadgita*." In *Modern Indian Interpreters of the Bhagavadgita*. Ed. Robert N. Minor. Albany, NY: State University of New York Press, 1986.

———. "Gandhi's Religion and the Hindu Heritage." In *Gandhi India and the World: An International Symposium*. Ed. Sibnarayan Ray. Philadelphia: Temple University Press, 1970. 39–56.

Joshi, Pushpa, comp. *Gandhi on Women: Collection of Mahatma Gandhi's Writings and Speeches on Women*. New Delhi: Navajivan Publishing House, 1988.

Juergensmeyer, Mark. "Saint Gandhi." In *Saints and Virtues*. Ed. John Stratton Hawley. Berkeley: University of California Press, 1987. 187–203.

Kaelber, Walter O. "The Brahmacārin: Homology and Continuity in Brāhmaṇic Religion." In *History of Religions* 21, no. 1 (Aug. 1981): 77–99.

———. "Tapas and Purification in Early Hinduism." *Numen* 26, no. 2 (Dec. 1979): 192–214.

Kakar, Sudhir. *The Essential Writings of Sudhir Kakar*. New Delhi: Oxford University Press, 2001.

———. *Intimate Relations: Exploring Indian Sexuality*. Chicago: University of Chicago Press, 1989.

Kaur, Raminder. *Performative Politics and the Cultures of Hinduism: Public Use of Religion in Western India*. London: Anthem Press, 2005.

Kaur Singh, Amrit and Rabindra. *Images of Freedom*. New Delhi: Indialog Publications, 2003.

Khandelwal, Meena. "Sexual Fluids, Emotions, Morality: Notes on the Gendering of Brahamacharya." In *Celibacy, Culture, and Society: An Anthropology of Sexual Abstinence*. Ed. Elisa J. Sobo and Sandra Bell. Madison, WI: University of Wisconsin Press, 2001. 157–179.

Kline III, T. C. "Moral Cultivation Through Ritual Participation: Xunzi's Philosophy of Ritual." In *Thinking Through Rituals: Philosophical Perspectives*. Ed. Kevin Schillbrack. New York and London: Routledge, 2004. 188–206.

Kripalani, J. B. *Gandhi: His Life and Thought*. Delhi: Publications Division, Government of India, reprinted 2005.

Kripalani, Krishna. "Modern Literature." In *A Cultural History of India*. Ed. A. L Basham. New Delhi: Oxford University Press, 1975. 406–422.

Kumar, Girja. *Brahmacharya: Gandhi and His Women Associates*. New Delhi: Vitasta Publishing, 2006.

Lal, Vinay. *The History of History: Politics and Scholarship in Modern India*. New Delhi: Oxford University Press, 2003.

———. "Nakedness, Nonviolence, and Brahmacharya: Gandhi's experiments in Celibate Sexuality." *Journal of the History of Sexuality* 9, nos. 1–2 (Jan.–Apr. 2000): 105–136.

Lanman, Charles Rockwell. "Hindu Ascetics and Their Powers." *Transactions and Proceedings of the American Philological Association* 46 (1917): 133–151.

Lannoy, Richard. *The Speaking Tree: A Study of Indian Culture and Society*. New York: Oxford University Press, 1971.

Lelyveld, Joseph. *Great Soul: Mahatma Gandhi and His Struggle with India*. New York: Alfred A. Knopf, 2011.

Lipner, Julius. "Conclusion: A Debate for Our Times." In *Indian Critiques of Gandhi*. Ed. Harold Coward. Albany, NY: State University of New York Press, 2003. 239–258.

———. *Hindus: Their Religious Beliefs and Practices*. New York: Routledge, 1994.

Lubin, Timothy. "The Householder Ascetic and the Uses of Self-Discipline." In *Asceticism and Power in South and Southeast Asia*. Ed. Peter Flügel and Gustaaf Houtman. Royal Asiatic Society Books. London: Routledge, forthcoming.

———. "*Vratá* Divine and Human in the Early Veda." *Journal of the American Oriental Society* 121, no. 4 (Oct.–Dec. 2001): 565–579.

Mack, Phyllis. "Feminine Behavior and Radical Action: Franciscans, Quakers, and the Followers of Gandhi." *Signs: Journal of Women in Culture and Society* 11, no. 3 (1986): 457–477.

Madan, Triloki Nath, ed. *Way of Life: King, Householder, Renouncer: Essays in Honour of Louis Dumont*. Delhi: Motilal Banarsidass Publishers, 1988.

Mahābhārata. Vol. 6. Trans. M. N. Dutt. Delhi: Parimal Publications, 1994.

Mason, Herbert. "Myth as an 'Ambush of Reality.'" In *Myth, Symbol, and Reality*. Ed. Alan M. Olson. Notre Dame, IN, and London: University of Notre Dame Press, 1980. 15–19.

McCully, Bruce Tiebout. *English Education and the Origins of Indian Nationalism*. New York: Columbia University Press, 1940.

McWhorter, Ladelle. "Rites of Passing: Foucault, Power, and Same-Sex Commitment Ceremonies." In *Thinking Through Rituals: Philosophical Perspectives*. Ed. Kevin Schillbrack. New York and London: Routledge, 2004. 71–90.

Mehta, Ved. *Mahatma Gandhi and His Apostles*. New York: Penguin Books, 1976.

Meyer, Johann Jakob. *Sexual Life in Ancient India: A Study in the Comparative History of Indian Culture*. Delhi: Motilal Banarsidass Publishers, 1971.

Minor, Robert N., ed. *Modern Indian Interpreters of the Bhagavadgita*. Albany, NY: State University of New York Press, 1986.

Monier-Williams, Sir Monier. *A Sanskrit-English Dictionary*, new ed. Delhi: Motilal Banarsidass Publishers, 1990.

Muzumdar, Haridas T. *Gandhi the Apostle: His Trail and His Message*, 1st ed. Chicago: Universal Publishing Co., 1923.

———. *Mahatma Gandhi: Peaceful Revolutionary*. New York: Charles Scribner's Sons, 1952.

Nanda, B. R. *Gandhi and His Critics*. New Delhi: Oxford University Press, 1985.

———. *In Search of Gandhi: Essays and Reflections*. New Delhi: Oxford University Press, 2002.

Narayan, Kirin. *Storytellers, Saints, and Scoundrels: Folk Narrative in Hindu Religious Teaching*. Philadelphia: University of Pennsylvania Press, 1989.

Narayan, R. K. *Gods, Demons, and Others*. Chicago: The University of Chicago Press, 1993.

Nehru, Jawaharlal. *An Autobiography*. New Delhi: Jawaharlal Nehru Memorial Fund, 1980.

O'Connor, June. *The Quest for Political and Spiritual Liberation: A Study in the Thought of Sri Aurobindo Ghose*. Rutherford: NJ: Fairleigh Dickinson University Press, 1977.

O'Flaherty, Wendy Doniger. *Other Peoples' Myths: The Cave of Echoes*. New York: Macmillan Publishing Company, 1988.

Olivelle, Patrick. *The Āśrama System: The History of Hermeneutics of a Religious Institution*. New York: Oxford University Press, 1993.

———. "Deconstruction of the Body in Indian Asceticism." In *Asceticism*. Ed. Vincent L. Wimbush and Richard Valantasis, New York: Oxford University Press, 2002. 188–210.

Olson, Alan. M., ed. *Myth, Symbol, and Reality*. Notre Dame, IN: University of Notre Dame Press, 1980.

Oman, John Campbell. *The Mystics, Ascetics, and Saints of India: A Study of Sadhuism, with an Account of the Yogis, Sanyasis, Bairagis, and Other Strange Hindu Sectarians*. London: T. F. Unwin, 1903.

Orwell, George. *A Collection of Essays*. San Diego: A Harvest Book, Harcourt, 1981.

Paine, Jeffery. *Father India: How Encounters with an Ancient Culture Transformed the Modern West*. New York: HarperCollins Publishers, 1998.

Palmer, Norman D. *The Indian Political System*. Houghton Mifflin Company: Boston, 1961.

Parekh, Bhikhu. *Colonialism, Tradition, and Reform: An Analysis of Gandhi's Political*, rev. ed. Thousand Oaks, CA: Sage Publications, 1999.

———. *Gandhi's Political Philosophy: A Critical Examination*. Delhi: Ajanta Publications, 1989.

Parel, Anthony J. *Gandhi's Philosophy and the Quest for Harmony*. New York: Cambridge University Press, 2006.

Park, Richard L. *India's Political System*. Englewood Cliffs, NJ: Prentice-Hall, 1967.

Payne, Robert. *The Life and Death of Mahatma Gandhi*. New York: E. P. Dutton & Co., 1969.

Phillimore, Peter. "Private Lives and Public Identities: An Example of Female Celibacy in Northwest India." In *Celibacy, Culture, and Society: An Anthropology of Sexual Abstinence*. Ed. Elisa J. Sobo and Sandra Bell. Madison, WI: University of Wisconsin Press, 2001. 29–46.

Pinney, Christopher. *'Photos of the Gods': The Printed Image and Political Struggle in India*. London: Reaktion Books, 2004.

Polak, Henry Salomon Leon, Henry Noel Brailsford, and Lord Pethick-Lawrence. *Mahatma Gandhi*. London: Odhams Press, 1949.

Potter, Karl H. *Presuppositions of India's Philosophies*. Delhi: Motilal Banarsidass Publishers, 1991.

Pyarelal. *Mahatma Gandhi: The Last Phase*. Vol. IX. Books 1 and 2. 2nd reprint. Ahmedabad: Navajivan Publishing House, 1997.

Radhakrishnan, S. *Eastern Religions and Western Thought*. New Delhi: Oxford University Press, 1993.

———. *Indian Philosophy*, 2nd centenary ed. Vol. 2. Delhi: Oxford University Press, 1989.

———. ed. *Mahatma Gandhi: Essays and Reflections on His Life and Work*, Thirteenth Jaico Impression. Mumbai, Delhi: Jaico Publishing House, 2005.

———. ed. and trans. *The Principal Upaniṣads*. Atlantic Highlands, NJ: Humanities Press, 1992.

Ramanujan, A. K. "Is There an Indian Way of Thinking?" *The Collected Essays of A. K. Ramanujan*. Ed. Vinay Dharwadker. New Delhi: Oxford University Press, 1999.

Rāmāyaṇa of Vālmīki, 1st ed. Vol. 1. Trans. and ed. M. N. Dutt and Ravi Prakash Arya. Delhi: Parimal Publications, 1998.

Rao, Raja. *Kanthapura*. Eighth printing. New York: New Directions, 1963.

———. *The Great Indian Way: A Life of Mahatma Gandhi*. Delhi: Vision Books, 1998.

Ṛg-Veda-Saṁhitā. Trans. and ed. H. H. Wilson and W. F. Webster. Delhi: Nag Publishers, 1990.

Rolland, Romain. *Mahatma Gandhi: The Man Who Become One with the Universal Being*. India: Srishti Publishers, 2000.

Rudolph, Susanne Hoeber and Lloyd I. Rudolph. *Gandhi: The Traditional Roots of His Charisma*. Chicago: The University of Chicago Press, 1983.

———. *Postmodern Gandhi and Other Essays*. Chicago: University of Chicago Press, 2006.

Rukmani, T. S. *Saṁnyāsin in the Hindu Tradition: Changing Perspectives*. New Delhi: D.K. Printworld (P) Ltd., 2011.

———. "Tagore and Gandhi." In *Indian Critiques of Gandhi*. Ed. Harold Coward. Albany, NY: State University of New York Press, 2003. 107–128.

Sainsbury, R. M. *Paradoxes*, 2nd ed. Cambridge: Cambridge University Press, 1995.

"Śakuntalā and the Ring of Recollection." In *Theater of Memory: The Plays of Kālidāsa*. Trans. and ed. Barbara Stoler Miller. New York: Columbia University Press, 1984. 85–176.

Saṃnyāsa Upaniṣads: Hindu Scriptures on Asceticism and Renunciation. Trans. Patrick Olivelle. New York: Oxford University Press, 1992.

Scalmer, Sean. "Turner Meets Gandhi: Pilgrimage, Ritual, and the Diffusion of Nonviolent Direct Action." In *Victor Turner and Contemporary Cultural Change*. Ed. Graham St. John. New York: Berghahn Books, 2007. 242–251.

Schell, Jonathan. *The Unconquerable World: Power, Nonviolence, and the Will of the People*. New York: Henry Holt and Company, 2003.

Schillbrack, Kevin. "Ritual Metaphysics." In *Thinking Through Rituals: Philosophical Perspectives*. Ed. Kevin Schillbrack. New York and London: Routledge, 2004. 128–147.

Sharma, Arvind. *The Hindu Gītā: Ancient and Classical Interpretations of the Bhagavadgītā*. London: Duckworth, 1986.

Sharp, Gene. *Gandhi as a Political Strategist: With Essays on Ethics and Politics*. Boston: Porter Sargent Publishers, 1979.

Sobo, Elisa J. and Sandra Bell. "Celibacy in Cross-Cultural Perspective: An Overview." In *Celibacy, Culture, and Society: An Anthropology of Sexual Abstinence*. Ed. Elisa J. Sobo and Sandra Bell. Madison, WI: University of Wisconsin Press, 2001. 3–26.

Srīmad Bhagavad Gītā Bhāṣya of Sri Saṁkarācārya. Trans. Dr. A. G. Krishna Warrior. Madras, India: Sri Ramakrishna Math, 2005.

Spear, Percival. *History of India: Volume Two*. New Delhi: Penguin Books, 1978.

Śrī Rāmānuja Gītā Bhāṣya. Trans. Svāmī Ādidevānanda. Mlyapore, Madras, India: Sri Ramakrishna Math, 1992.

Swāmi Hariharānanda Āraṇa. *Yoga Philosophy of Patañjali*, 3rd ed. Trans. P. N. Mukerji. Calcutta, India: University of Calcutta, 1981.

Swami Vivekananda. *The Complete Works of Swami Vivekananda*. Vol. 1. Mayavati Merhorial ed. Calcutta, India: Advaita Ashrama, 1989.

Taneja, Anup. *Gandhi, Women, and the National Movement, 1920–47*. New Delhi: Har-Anand Publications, 2005.

Tendulkar, Dinanath Gopal. *Mahatma: Life of Mohandas Karamchand Gandhi*. 8 vols. New ed. New Delhi: Publication Division Government of India, 1963.

Terchek, Ronald, J. *Gandhi: Struggling for Autonomy*. New Delhi: Vistaar Publications, 2000.

Thompson, George. "On Truth-Acts in Vedic." *Indo-Iranian Journal* 41 (1998): 125–153.

Tilak, Bal Gangadhar. *Srimad Bhagavadgītā-Rahasya or Karma-Yoga-Sastra*. Trans. Bh Alchandra Sitaram Sukthankar. India: Kesari Press, 2000.

"Tracing History Accurately, the Literary Way." *The Hindu*. May 9, 2003. Accessed on Jan 20, 2012. http://www.hindu.com/thehindu/fr/2003/05/09/stories/2003050901130500.htm.

Turner, Victor. *The Forest of Symbols: Aspects of Ndembu Ritual*. Ithaca: Cornell University Press, 1967.

———. *The Ritual Process: Structure and Anti-Structure*. New York: Aldine De Gruyter, 1995.

Vallely, Anne. *Guardians of the Transcendent: An Ethnography of a Jain Ascetic Community*. Buffalo: University of Toronto Press, 2002.

Van Buitenen, J. A. B., trans. *The Mahābhārata: I. The Book of the Beginning*, paperback ed. Chicago: University of Chicago Press, 1980.

Van der Veer, Peter. *Religious Nationalism: Hindus and Muslims in India*. Los Angeles: University of California Press, 1994.

Wimbush, Vincent L. and Richard Valantasis, eds. *Asceticism*. New York: Oxford University Press, 2002.

Wolpert, Stanley. *Gandhi's Passion: The Life and Legacy of Mahatma Gandhi*. New York: Oxford University Press, 2001.

Yoga: Discipline of Freedom the Yoga Sutra Attributed to Patanjali. Trans. Barbara Stoler Miller. New York: Bantam Books, 1998.

The Yoga Sutras of Patanjali. Trans. Sri Swami Satchidananda. Yogaville, VA: Integral Yoga Publications, 1990.

Yoga Sūtras of Patañjali with the Exposition of Vyāsa. Trans. Swami Veda Bharati. Delhi: Motilal Banarsidass Publishers, 2004.

The Yoga-System of Patanjali: Or the Ancient Hindu Doctrine of Concentration of Mind. Trans. James Haughton Woods. Delhi: Motilal Banarsidass, 1988.

Zimmer, Heinrich. *Philosophies of India*. Ed. Joseph Campbell. Princeton, NJ: Princeton University Press, 1974.

Index

Note: Page numbers in *italics* indicate illustrations.

Abbott, Elizabeth, 79, 118–119, 133, 144, 155
abhayadānam (gift of protection), 60
activism. *See* ascetic activism
Adams, Jad, 15
adharma (immorality, injustice), 75, 124, 155, 187, 199, 249n4
adultery, 91, 151, 227n1
Advaita Vedānta, 25, 31, 43
Agni (god of fire), 105, 107
ahiṃsā (nonviolence), xi, 8, 12, 17, 26, 38, 44, 108, 220; absolute, 52, 57; asceticism and, 6, 54, 157; *brahmacarya* and, 24, 92, 142; civil disobedience and, 35, 197; *dharma* and, 58–59; in *Gita,* 45, 49; in Hinduism, 60–61; in Jainism, 59; *maitri* and, 60; power of *sat* through, 57–62; as *pravṛtti,* 62; as *sat,* 57–62; in *Yoga Sūtra,* 61
Alter, Joseph S., 14, 30, 38, 228n18; on celibacy, 112; on Gandhi's practices, 119, 232n1
Ambedkar, Bhima Rao, 244n46
Amin, Shahid, 166, 204, 207
Anand, Swami, 155–157
anāśakāyna. See fasting
anāsakti (nonattachment), 46; definition of, 45; in *Gītā,* 42, 45
Andrews, C. F., 111, 137
aparigraha (nonpossession), 17, 26, 45
Aristotle, 8, 28
Arnold, Edwin, 45, 47
artha (public affairs, worldly motives), 28, 254n99
Arya Samaj movement, 119, 166, 250n28, 253n91
asahyoga. See noncooperation
asat (untruth), 91–92, 190
ascetic activism, 2–3, 21–24, 200, 214, 218–219; in *Bhagavad-Gītā,* 41; *brahmacarya* and, 125, 193; legends of, 18, 173–181, 193; paradoxical, 9–10; precedents for, 219–221; principles of, 16, 49, 90, 92, 109, 117; *tapas* for, 192–193
asceticism, 2–6, 30, 34; activism and, 21–24; Jain, 83–85, 99, 100; liminality of, 132–137; origins of, 27; silent, 99, 245n59; "this-worldly," 32; Weber on, 227n2
Ashe, Geoffrey, 89, 124, 130, 135, 143, 177–180
āśramas, 25–26, 76–80, 93–95; for activist training, 131, 136–143; Gandhi on, 98, 141, 161, 196, 252n70; life stages and, 244n36; in *Upanisads,* 251n53; women in, 124, 141
asteya (nonstealing), 26, 156, 238n105, 245n61
asvādavrata (control of palate), 108

Atharva Veda, 120, 248n138
Athavale, Pandurang Shastri, 257n28
Attenborough, Richard, 2
Augustine of Hippo, Saint, xv
Aurobindo, Sri, 23, 63; on *Gītā*, 42–44, 234n28; on passive resistance, 185; Western education of, 95–96

Bailey, Greg, 24–26, 230n11
Baird, Robert D., 29, 231n27
Bapu, Morari, 257n28
Basham, A. L., 70
Bell, Sandra, 131, 194
Bhagat, M. G., 27
Bhagavad-Gītā, 5, 17, 76, 202; Gandhi on, 22, 40–49, 50, 99, 101, 129; *Rāmāyaṇa* and, 173; Śaṃkarācārya on, 230n14; *tapas* in, 31; *yajña* in, 571
Bhāgavata Purāṇa, 16, 159, 169, 256n151
Bhai, Raychand, 129, 130
Bhatt, Shamal, 50
Bhave, Acharya Vinoba, 42, 158
Bhīṣma, 26, 45, 54, 119, 191, 203
Bhoodan movement, 158
birth control, 121, 126, 127, 151
Bolle, Kees W., 46, 187
Bondurant, Joan V., 6–7, 50–51, 58
Bose, Nirmal Kumar, 13, 84, 102, 154
Bose, Subash Chandra, 203
brahmacārin (a celibate), 18, 93–95, 139, 146, 157, 195–197
brahmacarya/*brahmacharya* (self-restraint), xi–xvii, 79–80, 217–218; *ahiṃsā* and, 24, 92, 142; *Atharva Veda* on, 248n138; conjugal love and, 148–153; definitions of, xvi, 87–90; elements of, 24, 133; Gandhi on, 35–36, 78, 81, 87–88, 108, 156–157, 254n120; in *Gītā*, 45; hermeneutics of, 10–12, 16, 22; Kumar on, 13; as life stage, 244n36; *mokṣa* and, 40, 88; power of, 4–7, 112–119; *sannyāsa* and, 94, 132; *satyagraha* and, 6, 24, 87, 90, 98, 114, 131, 160–161, 213–221; *siddhi* and, 119–122; among students, 92–99; *tapas* and, 90, 105–112, 190; traditional views of, 81–82, 123, 159, 213–214; unorthodox views of, 123–136, 148–161, 213–214; as *vrata*, 26; *yajña* and, 76, 79. *See also* celibacy
Brahman (Ultimate Reality), 51, 88, 91
bravery, Gandhi on, 127, 147, 155, 198
Bronkhorst, Johannes, 24–27
Brown, Judith M., 81, 91
Brown, W. Norman, 52, 53, 55, 56, 70, 72
Buddha, 26, 47, 129, 199–200; *brahmacarya* in, 47; Gandhi on, 23–24, 48, 136; *nirvāṇa* of, 99; as path philosopher, 39–40; temptations of, 154
Buddhism, 49, 53, 101, 107, 230n11
Burlingame, Eugene Watson, 52, 53, 92, 236n68
Burns, James, 78

Canning, Lord, 95
Caplan, Pat, 12, 242n5
Carak Saṁhitā, 113
Cashman, Richard I., 165–166, 171, 193–194
caste system. See *varṇa*
celibacy, xv–xvii, 1, 11–16, 143–144, 194–195, 217; Phillimore on, 33, 89, 99; Shivananda on, 112; of students, 82–83, 92–99; Victorian views of, 83, 242n5; virility/vulnerability of, 91, 146, 152, 254n113. **See also** *brahmacarya;* marriage
Chadha, Yogesh, 73
charkha (spinning wheel), 76, *205, 206,* 209. See also *khadi*
Chatterjee, Bankim Chandra, 43, 97, 234n28

Chatterjee, Margaret, 48
Christianity, 38, 46–47, 50, 56, 71, 165, 202; *agape* in, 78; asceticism of, 83; on marriage, 151; *passion* in, 38, 110, 189; sexuality and, 101
civil disobedience, 74, 96, 140, 160. *See also* Salt March
civil rights movement (U.S.), 12, 78
communitas, 76–80, 103, 142. See also *āśramas*
Conrad, Dieter, 165–166
consistency, Gandhi on, 7–8, 46, 213
Coomaraswamy, Ananda, 75
Cortright, David, 11
courage, Gandhi on, 127, 147, 155, 198
cow-protection, in Hinduism, 103, 163, 177–178, 180, 192, 196, 225–226
Curzon, Lord, 244n39

Dalton, Dennis, 58, 63; on Salt March, 77, 197–199, 202
Damle, Y. B., 173–174
dāna (charity), 53, 67, 73–74
Daniels, Pamela, 131
darśan/darshan (ritual blessing, sacred audience), 139, 173, 204–207
Das, Chitta Ranjan, 166
Das, Veena, 136
Dayananda, Swami, 43, 70, 136, 250n28
Desai, Mahadev, 111, 199
Dhand, Arti, 4, 25
dharma (religious duties), xviii, 25, 27, 161; *ahiṃsā* and, 58–59; in *Gītā*, 49; goals of, 254n99; politics and, 28–29, 97; *pravṛtti* and, 25, 27; restoration of, 251n42; truth and, 90
dharma yuddha (ethical struggle), 43
dharmarājya (kingdom of truth), 35, 64, 118
Dumont, Louis, 21, 24, 32, 132, 134
Dvaita Vedānta (dualist philosophy), 43
Dvivedi, M. N., 86

education, 9, 18, 29, 92–99; missionary, 244n45; reform of, 32; sex, 101, 147
Education Act (1902), 50
Edwardes, Michael, 157, 165, 254n103
Einstein, Albert, 256n1
Eliade, Mircea, 73, 105, 240n158, 246n90, 259n61
Ellis, Havelock, 253n79
Emerson, Ralph Waldo, 213
Erikson, Erik H., 13, 102, 124, 150, 152

Faering, Esther, 171
fasting, 10, 50, 145, 196, 200–203, 207, 215, 250n37; political uses of, 35, 45, 77, 84, 202; *as tapas*, 26–27, 31, 76, 108–109, 133, 201. See also *vratas*
Feuerstein, Georg, 42, 113
Fisher, Louis, 51
Flood, Gavin, 88
Forster, E. M., 219
Foucault, Michel, 77
Francis of Assisi, Saint, 60, 251n47
Freiberger, Oliver, 227n2

Gadamer, Hans-Georg, 169–170
Gandhi, Kasturba (wife), 71, 96, 143, 145, 150–151, 198
Gandhi, Manu (grandniece), 15, 155–158, 253n89, 255nn142–143
Gandhi, Mohandas K., 2–6, 13–16; on adultery, 151, 227n1; as Buddha, 23–24; on consistency, 7–8, 46, 213; deification of, 76, 200–211, 205, 206, 262n142; in England, 96–97; as "Father of the Nation," 9, 191; female relationships of, 11–14, 124–125, 136, 144–145, 153–155; film about,

Gandhi, Mohandas K. *(continued)* 2; on marriage, 148–153; on novels, 181–182; as paradoxical figure, 9–10, 24–29, 154–155, 220; parents of, 84, 102, 109; as path philosopher, 38–41; on scriptural interpreters, 37; on sex education, 101, 147; in South Africa, 47, 50, 54, 86, 126–128, 137–138, 154; Western influences of, 47, 86–87, 96–98, 168, 242n12, 253n79
Gandhi, Ramchandra (scholar), 92, 100, 102, 128
Gandhi, Ramdas (son), 191, 195–196
gender. *See* women
Ghose, Aurobindo. *See* Aurobindo, Sri
Ghurye, G. S., 27
Gier, Nicholas F., 12, 16, 23, 121, 124, 155, 217, 229n7
Gokhale, Gopal K., 32
Gramdan movement, 158
Green, Martin B., 103–104
gṛhasthas (householders), 5, 24, 26, 30, 32, 85, 89, 94; in *āśrama* system, 244n36; conjugal love and, 148–153; religious duties of, 87; *sannyāsa* and, 132. See also *varṇa*
Growse, F. S., 67

Habermas, Jürgen, 139–140, 252nn64–65
Hardiman, David, 208–209
harijans (untouchables), 17, 103, 135, 181, 195, 196, 261n137. See also *varṇa*
Hariścandra (King), 61, 71, 163, 174–180, 188, 192, 196, 258n33, 258n36
Hinduism, 42; asceticism in, 24, 83–85; cow-protection in, 103, 163, 177–178, 180, 192, 196, 225–226; Gandhi's philosophy and, 37–38, 64, 68–69; Islam and, 64; politics and, 30; sexuality and, 101
Hirst, Jacqueline Suthern, 67, 169
homosexuality, 15
householders. See *gṛhasthas*
Hunt, James D., 50

Indian ethos, religious narratives and, 168–184
Indra (Vedic deity), 94, 121
Indrajīt (son of Demon Rāvaṇa), 190–191, 260n89
Islam, 17, 33, 61, 64–65, 202; Hindi-Muslim riots and, 158, 160, 195, 256n147
itihasa (legend), 170
Iyer, Raghavan, 38–39, 50; on power of truth, 52; on *tapas*, 106

Jainism, 49, 59, 230n11; asceticism in, 83–85, 99, 100; celibacy in, 154; war and, 107
japayajña (sacrifice by means of prayer), 72
Jesus Christ, 56, 71, 110, 165, 189; Sermon on the Mount of, 47, 50. *See also* Christianity
Jinnah, Muhammad Ali, 244n46
Jñana-yajña (sacrifice by means of knowledge), 72
Joad, C. E. M., 164
Jordens, J. T. F., 30, 45–46, 119, 235n35; on *āśramas*, 138, 142; on *brahmacarya*, 128
Juergensmeyer, Mark, 194, 260n95

Kaelber, Walter, 93, 108
Kakar, Sudhir, 13–14, 102, 117; on narrative, 171, 172; on Vivekananda, 131
Kali Yuga (Dark Age), 135, 250n42
Kālidāsa (poet), 41, 137
Kallenbach, Hermann, 15
kāma (desire), 99–104, 117–118, 144; *dharma* and, 254n99; Gandhi's views of, 101–102, 153–161
karma sannyāsa (renunciation in action), 25, 46, 49
karma yoga (path of action), 25, 42, 43, 234n28
karmakānda (ceremonial acts), 72

kathā (religious narratives), xvii, 4, 45, 190, 210–211, 223–226; ascetic activism and, 173–181; etymology of, 169; Indian ethos of, 168–173; nonviolent reinterpretation of, 184–189
kathakara (religious storyteller), 45, 168–69, 173, 184–86, 257n16
Kaur, Amrit, 124
Kaur, Raminder, 203
kāvya (poetry), 170
khadi (hand-spun cloth), 73, 76, 103, 150, 160, 198, 208
Khandelwal, Meena, 116, 254n112
Kher, G. G., 263n19
King, Martin Luther, Jr., 12, 78
Kingsley, Ben, 2
Kipling, Rudyard, 28
Kline, T. C., III, 77
Kripalani, Krishna, 157–158, 257n30
Krishnavarma, Shyamji, 32, 231n38
Kumar, Girja, 11, 13, 124, 144, 155
Kumarappa, J. C., 111
Kumbh Mela, 139
Kumbhakarṇa (brother of demon Rāvaṇa), 104

Lakṣmaṇa (brother of Lord Rāma), 190–192, 196
Lal, Vinay, 15–16, 123, 207, 210, 213
Lanman, Charles Rockwell, 109, 247n102
Lannoy, Richard, 214, 249n18
Lelyveld, Joseph, 15
Lipner, Julius, 39, 215–216, 221
loincloth, Gandhi's adoption of, 132, 195–196, 200, 218–219, 260nn101–102
Lubin, Timothy, 5, 109, 228n6

Mack, Phyllis, 251n47
Madhavācārya (philosopher), 42, 43
Mahābhārata, 4, 8, 10, 48, 120; asceticism in, 31, 88; *āśramas* in, 137, 139; *brahmacarya* in, 123, 243n17; on conjugal love, 102–103, 148–149; cultural influence of, 170, 171; Dhand on, 25; duty in, 53–55; *nivṛtti* in, 26; political uses of, 29, 190, 198
Maharaj, Ladha, 168–169
mahātmā (great soul), xii, xviii, 2, 9, 131, 135, 218; *āśramas* of, 138; Gandhi's sanctification as, 165–167, 193–194, 200, 204–207; in *Kali Yuga,* 250n42; Tagore on, 252n61
Mahavir, Brahmachari, 135
Mahavira, Lord, 26, 100, 136, 245n61
maitri (compassion), 60
mantras, 72, 240n161, 241n171
Manu Smṛti, 94
Mārkaṇḍeya (sage), 203–204, *205*
marriage, 78, 143, 148–153; children and, 91, 100, 126, 144, 147; polygamous, 153. *See also* celibacy
mauna (silence), 26, 133, 215, 250n37
McWhorter, Ladelle, 77, 241n173
Mehta, Ved, 203
Meyer, Johann Jacob, 121
mokṣa (spiritual liberation), 22–25, 37–41, 90; *brahmacarya* and, 40, 88; celibacy for, 117; *dharma* and, 254n99; in *Gita,* 49; *tapas* and, 106; *yajña* and, 74; *Yoga Sūtra* and, 60–61
Moore, Arthur, 116–117
Mountbatten, Lord, 202
Munshiram, Mahatma, 43, 146–147, 166, 253n91
Murray, Gilbert, v, 221
mythology, xvii–xviii, 37, 189, 208–211, 223–226; coherence of, 8; political uses of, 192–193, 202–203; storytelling and, 3–4, 169–170

Nanda, B. R., 146, 151
Naoroji, Dadabhai, 63
Narasinharao, Shri, 23–24
Narayan, Kirin, 134–136, 169, 173
Narayan, R. K., 169, 172, 192
Nath, Kedar, 155–156
Nehru, Jawaharlal, 12, 96; on Gandhi's asceticism, 83, 104, 123–124, 132, 148; Western education of, 95–96

Nehru, Motilal, 263n19
nirvāṇa, 26, 37, 99
nirvikara (passionless) state, v, 5
nishkriya pratirodha. *See* passive resistance
niṣkāma karma (desire-less action), 44
nivṛtti (withdrawal from worldly involvement), 1–7, 11, 16, 22; *ahiṃsā* and, 62; *āśramas* for, 137; *brahmacarya* and, 17, 82, 90, 99–104, 131; components of, 17, 37; etymology of, 229n1; Gandhi on, 103; in Gita, 42, 46; in *Mahābhārata*, 26; *pravṛtti* and, 7, 17–18, 21, 25–36, 80, 189, 214–216, 221; "technology" of, 33; *yajña* and, 76. See also *sannyāsa*
nivṛtti mārga (path of renunciation), 22
noncooperation, xii, 24, 32, 36, 204, 220; asceticism and, 71, 190, 263n12; *brahmacarya* and, 92, 118; Rao on, 210; *satyagraha* and, 218
nonviolence. See *ahiṃsā*

O'Connor, June, 23
O'Flaherty, Wendy Doniger, 263n18
ojas (vitality), 113–114, 118
Olivelle, Patrick, 26, 154
Oman, John Campbell, 134–135
Orwell, George, 254n103, 262n2

pahalwans (wrestlers), 14, 38, 119, 232n1
Paine, Jeffery, 112, 120
Pakistan, 158, 160, 195, 244n46, 256n46
Pal, Bipin Chandra, 63
Pandit, Vijayalakshmi, 151
Paramhansa, Ramakrishna, 154
Parekh, Bhikhu, 11, 12, 50, 60, 69, 145; on Gandhi's celibacy, 87–90, 119, 156; on *satyagraha*, 51; on *yajña*, 72; on Zulu rebellion, 128
Parel, Anthony, 40–41, 60–61, 130, 147, 217
Park, Richard L., 28
passion, Christian view of, 38, 110, 189
passive resistance, xvii, 12, 21, 118, 220, 263n12; Aurobindo on, 185; sources of, 49–51, 96
Patañjali, v, 60–61, 86, 112–113, 130, 238n105
Patel, Sardar, 249n5
path philosophy, 38–41
Paul, Apostle, 151
Payne, Robert, 121, 138
Phillimore, Peter, 33, 89, 99
Phoenix Settlement (South Africa), 138, 251n56
Platonism, 51, 56, 71, 120, 180
Poddar, Hanumanprasad, 22
Polak, Henry S. L., 194
Potter, Karl H., 39–40, 233n10
pravṛtti (worldly engagement), xvi, 1, 3, 7, 37, 42; *ahiṃsā* as, 62; *brahmacarya* and, 82; etymology of, 229n1; Gandhi on, 22; in *Gītā*, 42, 46; *nivṛtti* and, 7, 17–18, 21, 25–36, 80, 189, 214–216, 221; *tapas* for, 189–193; *telos* of, 33
pravṛtti mārga (path of worldly engagement), 22
psychoanalytic studies, 172; of Gandhi, 13–14, 38, 102, 103, 152
Purāṇa(s), 102–103, 170, 190, 219; *Bhāgvata*, 16, 159, 169, 256n151
puritanism, 83, 121, 124, 152
pūrṇa svarājya (complete independence), 62, 63, 65–66. See also *svarāj*
Pyarelal (writer), 97, 124

Quakers, 251n47

Radhakrishnan, S., 38, 75, 114; on conjugal love, 148; on *tapas*, 27
Rai, Lala Lajpat, 58
rāja dharma (political laws), 87
Rāmānuja (philosopher), 39–40, 43
Ramanujan, A. J., 8, 170

rāmarājya (Lord Rama's kingdom), 8, 35, 104; *svarāj* and, 62–68, 104; women and, 66–67
Rāmāyaṇa (epic), 4, 5, 63, 88, 104, 120, 263n19; asceticism in, 31, 102–103, 154; *āśramas* in, 137; *Gītā* and, 173; medical powers of, 168–169; politics and, 29, 190
Ramcaritmanas (Tulsidas), 64, 66–67, 168
Ramtirtha, Swami, 32
Rao, Raja, 171, 202–203, 209–210
Ravanarajya, 107
Raychandbhai (poet), 85
religious narratives. See *kathā*
Ṛg Veda, 63, 73–74, 76, 240n161; *mantras* in, 241n171; *tapas* in, 107; on world's creation, 246n90
Roy, Raja Rammohan, 32, 153
Rudolph, Lloyd, 14, 79, 102, 139–140, 164, 194–195
Rudolph, Susanne Hoeber, 14, 38, 79, 102, 139–140, 164, 194–195
Rukmani, T. S., 23, 31–33, 37
Ruskin, John, 140–141, 252n56
Russell, Bertrand, 253n79

Sabarmati Ashram, 181, 197–198, 251n52
sādhus, 5, 30, 85, 131–139, 173, 195, 260n102
Salt March, 56, 77, 120, 197–199, 202, 263n19
Śaṃkarācārya, Śri, 21, 26; on *Gītā,* 42, 230n14, 234n27; philosophy of, 39–40, 43
saṃsāra, 100, 132
Sanger, Margaret, 151
Sankara (philosopher), 31–32
sannyāsa (stage of renunciation), xvi, 87, 144; *brahmacarya* and, 94, 132; Gandhi on, 99, 104, 133–134; in *Gita,* 49; ideal of, 131; *karma,* 46; as life stage, 132, 244n36; liminality of, 136; *mahātmā* and, 166. See also *nivrtti*
Saraswati, Dayananda, 32
śāstra (scripture), 73–74, 125
sat (truth), 8, 38; *brahmacarya* as, 90–92; power of, 57–62; qualities of, 911
Satsang Yoga, 251n53
satya (truth), 17, 26, 35, 50–51; definition of, 90; *dharma* and, 51; etymology of, 51; *tapascarya* and, 192
satyagraha (Truth-force), xi, xiv–xvii, 11, 36, 110; *ahiṃsā* and, 58; *brahmacarya* and, 6, 24, 87, 90, 98, 114, 131, 160–161, 213–221; definitions of, 54; fasting and, 201; *Gita* and, 45, 49; *kathā* and, 171; power of, 38, 49–57, 78; *rāmarājya* and, 66–67; Salt March and, 197; *sannyāsa* and, 104; *svarājya* and, 32, 56–57, 197, 211; *tapas* and, 49, 57, 192–193, 195
Satyagraha Ashram, 141–143, 251n52
satyakriyā (Truth Act), 52–57, 92, 236nn68–69, 237n79
Savarkar, Vinayak Damodar, 32, 95–96
Scalmer, Sean, 241n177
Schell, Jonathan, 132–133
Sen, Keshub Chandra, 43
Sermon on the Mount, 47, 50. *See also* Christianity
sex education, 101, 147
Sharma, Arvind, 43
Sharp, Gene, 65
Shivananda, Swami, 112
Shraddhananda, Swami, 43, 146–147, 166, 253n91
siddhi (supernatural powers), 59; *brahmacarya* and, 119–122; *tapas* for, 189
Sikhism, 101, 245n65, 256n147
Singh, Amrit Kaur, 157
Sītā (wife of Lord Rama), 67–68, 104, 114, 171, 192, 196, 246n79
Śiva (deity), 101–102, 189, 226; Gandhi as, 203–204, 205, 209

Sivananda, Swami, 250n28
Sobo, Elisa J., 131, 194
Socrates, 56, 71, 180
South Africa, Gandhi in, 47, 50, 54, 86, 126–128, 137–141, 154
Spear, Percival, 200
spinning cloth. See *khadi*
Śravaṇa Kumar (ideal son), 174–175, 179, 180
Sri Rāmānuja Gītā Bhāṣya, 81
sthitaprajña (person with perfect control), 46
Suffragette movement, 50
Sullivan, B., 74
svadharma (individual moral duty), 44, 51
svādhyāya (self-study), 172–173, 239n105
svarāj (self-rule/home rule), xvii, 5, 23, 32, 41, 193, 217; Gandhi's manifesto on, 97; *pūrṇa*, 195, 196, 199; *rāmarājya* and, 62–68, 104; *sannyāsa* and, 134; *swadeshi* with, 231n39; *tapas* and, 49, 77, 153, 195
svarāj-yajña (ritual sacrifice for self-rule), 69–70, 75
svarājya (sovereignty), 28–29, 35, 63; *brahmacarya* and, 88, 152; *satyagraha* and, 32, 56–57, 197, 211
swadeshi (self-reliance), 36, 231n39
Swadhyay movement, 257n28
Swarajya Party, 166
symbolism, Gandhi's use of, 77–79, 171, 194–199, 218

Tagore, Rabindranath, 73; on Gandhi as *mahātmā*, 166, 252n61; as *Gurudev*, 166; on noncooperation, 263n12; Western education of, 95–96
Taneja, Anup, 68
Tantricism, 16
tapas/tapasya (austerities), xvi–xviii, 3, 8, 17, 37, 118, 164; *brahmacarya* and, 90, 105–112, 190; etymology of, 105, 246n81; fasting as, 26, 27, 31, 76, 108–109, 133, 201; Gandhi on, 189–190; in *Mahābhārata*, 31; *mokṣa* and, 106; for *pravṛtti*, 189–193; Radhakrishnan on, 27; *satyagraha* and, 49, 57, 192–193, 195; *svarāj* and, 49, 77, 153, 195; *yajña* and, 68–76, 105, 106, 142
tapascarya, 72, 74, 108, 110–111, 190, 192
tapasvins, 107–108, 112, 118, 167, 219–221; legends of, 194, 196, 200, 202, 210, 216; power of, 163–164
Tattvarthadhigama, 245n61
tejas (splendor), 113, 114
Tendulkar, Dinanath Gopal, 61, 204–208
Terchek, Ronald J., 152
Theosophy, 45, 234n33
Thompson, George, 237n79
Tilak, Bal Gangadhar, 5, 23, 32; on Gandhi's asceticism, 83; on Gita, 42–44, 47–48, 234n28; as *Lokamanya*, 165, 166; on *svarāj*, 63; on Western culture, 97; on *yajñas*, 240n156
Tolstoy, Leo, 47, 48, 50, 235n44, 262n7
Tolstoy Farm (South Africa), 138, 251n56
truth. See *sat*
Truth Act. See *satyakriyā/saccakriyā*
Tulsi Das (poet), 64, 66–67
Turner, Victor, 76–79, 135, 141–142, 221, 241n177, 252n71

untouchables. See *harijans*
Upaniṣad(s), 26, 69, 129; *āśramas* in, 251n53; *Chāndogya*, 94, 99, 245n59, 250n37; *Muṇḍaka*, 94, 244n39; *Praśna*, 250n37; *Śvetṣvatara*, 240n158
utopianism, 66–67

Vallabha (philosopher), 42
van Buitenen, J. A. B., 31
van der Veer, Peter, 64, 169, 204

vānaprastha (forest-dweller), 94, 244n36
Vardhamāna. *See* Mahāvīra, Lord
varṇa (caste), 25–29, 93–98, 141–142, 170, 202; *brahmacarya* and, 93–94, 98, 143, 214–215; Buddha on, 200; challenges to, 6, 33, 35, 61, 71, 77–79, 134–136, 150; by occupation, 170; Turner on, 141–142
Vedanta Society, 250n28
Venkataramani, K. S., 209
Vidyasagar, Ishwar Chadra, 153
Virocana (demon), 94
viṣaya (carnal desire), 103, 246n71. See also *kāma*
Viśiṣtadvaita philosophy, 43
Viśvāmitra (sage), 31, 102, 121, 154, 176–177, 223
Vivekananda, Swami, xv, 17, 32, 70, 130–131; on chastity, 113–114, 146, 242n11; on liberation, 251n44; on *mahatma,* 135; Vedanta Society of, 250n28; on *Yoga Sutra,* 86, 130
vratas (ascetic vows), xvii–xviii, 3, 26–27, 85, 106, 109, 112, 192

Weber, Max, 227n2
Whitehead, Alfred North, 213
Wolpert, Stanley, 38, 110, 151–153, 189
women, 172; in *āśramas,* 141; *brahmacarya* and, 81, 98; chastity and, 98, 99, 116, 152; "feminine" virtues of, 68, 146, 147; *rāmarājya* and, 66–67; rights of, 50, 152–153, 155, 157–160; widowed, 99, 147, 153
wrestlers *(pahalwans),* 14, 38, 119, 232n1

yajña (sacrifice), xvi, 6, 8, 94, 108, 118; of animals, 240n156; celibacy as, 157–158; *communitas* and, 76–80; in *Gita,* 49; *kāma* and, 117–118; meditation as, 136, 240n158; *raṇa,* 198, 199; "spinning," 73, 76, 142; *tapas* and, 68–76, 105, 106, 142
yama-niyamas (restraints and religious observances), 35, 37, 49, 62, 64
yamas (restraints for self-control), 59, 101, 112–113
Yoga Sūtra (Patañjali), v, 60–61, 112–113, 238n105; commentaries on, 86, 130

Zimmer, Heinrich, 50, 52–54; on *ahiṃsā,* 58–59; on *brahmacarya,* 95; on *mokṣa,* 99–100; on *satyakriyā,* 92
Zulu Rebellion, 126–128

71994734R00187

Made in the USA
Middletown, DE
02 May 2018